Quantitatives Controlling

Edited by
C. Homburg, Köln, Germany

The series serves as a panel for outstanding research in the field of accounting. The underlying concept of accounting goes beyond the scope of traditional corporate accounting including, for instance, aspects of behavior control. The series focuses on quantitative analyses of current topics in management and financial accounting and considers both analytical and empirical research designs.

Edited by
Carsten Homburg
Universität zu Köln

More information about this series at http://www.springer.com/series/12419

Philipp Plank

Price and Product-Mix Decisions Under Different Cost Systems

With a foreword by Prof. Dr. Carsten Homburg

Springer Gabler

Philipp Plank
Köln, Germany

Dissertation Universität zu Köln, 2016

Quantitatives Controlling
ISBN 978-3-658-19320-1 ISBN 978-3-658-19321-8 (eBook)
DOI 10.1007/978-3-658-19321-8

Library of Congress Control Number: 2017952697

Springer Gabler

Printed on acid-free paper

This Springer Gabler imprint is published by Springer Nature
The registered company is Springer Fachmedien Wiesbaden GmbH
The registered company address is: Abraham-Lincoln-Str. 46, 65189 Wiesbaden, Germany

Foreword

This dissertation addresses the product-mix and pricing decision problem, based upon full cost information. The focus lies on the performance of cost-based decisions compared to a first-best-model, optimally solving the underlying problem and serving as a benchmark. Essentially, by using a simulation approach, it is examined if cost-systems that are more precise lead to better decisions. It can be shown that those systems usually outperform simple cost systems. This effect is even more pronounced in growing markets. In addition, in this context the influence of cost-stickiness is analyzed. By using a cost-driver controlling especially for cost-stickiness significantly better results are achieved.

The author introduces a price- and capacity planning model, that can be specified either as a one- or a multi-period model considering either hard or soft capacity constraints. This model is used as the first-best solution to benchmark simplified solutions.

Different cost-models allocate heuristically costs to products. In the simulation, varying environmental situations can be applied. This accounts for e.g. different market situations or diversified against specialized company types. The performance of such cost-systems is measured upon its deviation to the benchmark model. The author separates the resulting error in four components: a volume error, representing the portion of the total error, which can be attributed to identical portfolio strategies while considering different production volume of each product and an error resulting from different portfolio strategies. The latter error is either based upon product-cost underestimation (Keep Error) or overestimation (Drop Error). The residual error describes the error from false capacity allocation. The error separation is innovative and interesting, since it further enables the identification of root-causes for profit errors.

Moreover, the problem of cost-stickiness in this context is examined. For this purpose initially the benchmark-model is extended. The extension enables different valuations of costs for invest- and divestments. Following the cost-stickiness paradigm, costs for disinvestments out value investment costs. A cost stickiness driver extends the standard cost-systems from chapter 3. Both are compared against the extended benchmark model. Thus it can be shown that the extended systems are able to close the profit gap even further.

This dissertation is characterized by its successful extension of existing literature towards the influence of cost-system design on pricing- and product-mix decisions. In addition it examines the influence of (external) factors – i.e. market parameters or company types on the above stated decision-quality. Hereby, this dissertation raises new research questions, to be practically validated by further empirical studies (field studies, questioners, etc.).

Prof. Dr. Carsten Homburg

Acknowledgment

This dissertation essentially came into being during my employment as a research assistant at the department of Business Administration and Management Accounting between 2009 and 2014.

While the nature of a dissertation of course is at its heart an individual task and in the end conducted mainly for and solely by oneself, its creation – from my experience – strongly depends on the fruitful environment it grows upon and the continuous support it relies on.

Such an environment I was happy and fortunate to find in so many different ways. Being most probably the starting point of each such a work and the very essential corner stone of the vivid and sometimes fragile fundament of a dissertation is its academic father. Therefore many thanks to Prof. Dr. Carsten Homburg for giving me this phone call while being in the tram in Berlin and never giving up on me, even extending his support while I was already in a new employment. Prof. Dr. Kuntz and Prof. Dr. Overesch I thank for a favorable second assessment and leading an overall gratifying oral exam.

A fruitful environment was also the department. In this garden I was invited to play already as a student counting in total 10 years of service. In those years I most probably troubled, enervated and entertained the ever changing lot of like-minded fellow campaigners (you are all in my heart but too many to name!). In all this change, there was one constant, always being there for us and especially for me. While I guess it was good that SAP was only introduced late in her time at the university, I sincerely can say, that this work would have not found its happy end without her – thanks Elli.

What would be PhD time without ...

- a solid room mate. We shared it all – well almost. Thanks Chris.
- a co-author to share the joy of publication with. Thanks Julia.
- a research best man. Thanks Lars.
- a practical research project. Thanks for countless headaches BILANZ.

Where I got the creeps when asked “handed in yet?”, I can only assume how annoying my constant chatter on my thesis could have been. Therefore, a special *thank you* to my friends – who are astonishingly all still with me.

PhD comics says: both, marriage and the PhD culminate in a ceremony where you walk down an aisle dressed in a gown. One is true, the other still to come. Thanks Mikki for sticking to me all the way through the end game of the PhD!

Last but definitely not least there is my family. Having already gone all the way with me through the up and downs of my studies, India and China, I can hardly express how grateful I am. Thanks Charly, Jochen, Margarethe and especially Gisela and Werner.

Philipp Plank

Table of contents

Abbreviations

ABC	Activity based costing
ACP	Activity cost pool
Adj.	Adjusted
ANOVA	Analysis of variance
AR	Autoregressive
AVG	Average method
BHL	Balakrishnan, Hansen and Labro (2011)
BM	Benchmark model
BP	Big Pool
CE	Capacity error
cont'd	continued
COR	Correlation of resource
Correl.	Correlation
cs	cost-stickiness
DE	Drop error
DENS	Density of the consumption matrix
DOE	Design of experiments
EUCD	Euclidean distance
ext	extended
H1,...,HN	Hypothesis 1 to n
HPC	High Performance Computing
IMF	International Monetary Fund
INT1	Intermediate method 1
INT2	Intermediate method 2
KE	Keep error
misc	miscellaneous
NAG	The Numerical Algorithms Group Ltd
NM	Noisy Model
num	Heuristics on stage 2
Num	Number, Number
obs.	Observations
OLS	Ordinary Least Squares
PC	Product costs
PQE	Production quantity errors
PRN	Pseudo random number-generator
RCV	Resource costs variance
Size_M	size misc
std.	standard
TRC	Total resource costs
TVC	Total variable costs
UK	United Kingdom
VCV	Variable costs variance
vs	versus

Symbols

Latin Symbols

$A, (A_{it})$	Market size (per product i and period t)
ABC_i	Activity-based costs of product i
ad_{ki}	Activity driver of ACP_k and product i
ACP_k^{total}	Total portfolio level activity costs of activity cost pool k
ACP_k^{pl}	Total product level activity costs of activity cost pool k
BM^{ext}	The extended benchmark model
b_i	Price elasticity of product i
$c, (c_j)$	Resource costs (of resource j)
c_j^{bias}	Biased resource costs of resource j
c_j^{BM}	BM resource costs of resource j
c_j^+	Resource costs for additional resources
c_j^-	Resource costs for divested resources
CV	Coefficient of variance
CR_S	Cost system refinement in simulation run s

Latin Symbols (cont'd)

ΔC	Cost error
D_i	Demand in period i
FC_i	Full cost of product i
ΔFC_i	Delta of full cost of product i between benchmark and noisy model
FC_i^{BM}	Full cost of product i in the benchmark model
FC_i^{NM}	Full cost of product i in the noisy model
h_{cs}	Heterogeneity driver
i, I	Index of products, total products
j, J	Index of resource, total resources
k	Index of activity cost pool
$L, (L_j)$	Long-term capacity (for resource j)
$L, (L^{BM})$	Total long-term capacity (benchmark model)
${L_k}^{NM}$	Pseudo long-term capacity for resource j for ACP_k in the noisy model
L^{NM}	Total pseudo long-term capacity in the noisy model

Latin Symbols (cont'd)

$m, (m_{ij})$	Resource consumption matrix (for product i and resource j)
m_{ij}^{bias}	Biased resource consumption matrix for product i and resource j
m_{ij}^{BM}	BM resource consumption matrix for product i and resource j
NM^{std}	The standard noisy model
NM^{ext}	The extended noisy model
P_i	Generic term for prices of product i independent of the model
P_{it}	Generic term for prices of product i in period t independent of the model
P_{it}^{BM}	Price for product i in period t of the benchmark model
$P_{it}^{BM^{ext}}$	Price for product i in period t of the extended benchmark model (chapter 4)
P_{it}^{NM}	Price for product i in period t of the noisy model
$P^{NM^{std}}$	Price for product i in period t of the standard noisy model (chapter 4)
$P^{NM^{ext}}$	Price for product i in period t of the extended noisy model (chapter 4)
PC_i^{BM}	Benchmark model product cost of product i

Latin Symbols (cont'd)

PC_i^{bias}/PC_i^{NM}	Biased / Noisy model product cost of product i
ΔPC_i	Delta between unbiased (BM) and biased (NM) product costs of product i
$\overline{PCE_s}$	Mean product cost error
$Profit^{BM}$	Profit benchmark model
$Profit_{product}^{BM}$	Profit out of product related decisions (benchmark model)
$Profit_{capacity}^{BM}$	Profit out of capacity related decisions (benchmark model)
$PF^{BM^{ext}}$	Profit extended benchmark model (chapter 4)
$Profit^{NM}$	Profit noisy model
PF^{eff}	Profit efficiency
$PF^{NM^{std}}$	Profit standard noisy model (chapter 4)
$PF^{NM^{ext}}$	Profit extended noisy model (chapter 4)
$\Delta PF_i^{NM^{std}}$; $Profit\ Error^{NM^{std}}$	Profit error between extended benchmark and standard noisy model (chapter 4)
$\Delta PF_i^{NM^{ext}}$; $Profit\ Error^{NM^{ext}}$	Profit error between extended benchmark and extended noisy model (chapter 4)
$\Delta Profit$	Profit error between benchmark and noisy model

Latin Symbols (cont'd)

$\Delta Profit_{product}$	Profit error out of product related decisions
$\Delta Profit_{capacity}$	Profit error out of capacity related decisions
$\Delta Profit_{PQE}$	Production quantity error
$\Delta Profit_{DE}$	Drop error
$\Delta Profit_{KE}$.	Keep error
$\Delta Profit_{CE}$.	Capacity Error
Q_i	Quantity of product i
q_{it}	Quantity of product i in period t
$R, (R_{jt})$	Short-term capacity (of resource j in period t)
R^{BM}	Short-term capacity of the BM
R_{jt}^{+}	Short-term capacity investment in period t for resource j
R_{jt}^{-}	Short-term capacity divested in period t for resource j
R^2	Coefficient of determination
rd_{jk}	Resource driver for resource j and ACP_k

Latin Symbols (cont'd)

RS	Resources supplied
RU	Resources used
s	standard deviation
t,T	Period t, total Period T
TC^{BM}	Total costs BM
TC^{NM}	Total costs NM
$v, (v_i)$	Variable cost (of product i)
$Var\_PF^{NM^{std}}$	Variance of Profits standard NM
$Var\_PF^{NM^{sext}}$	Variance of Profits extended NM
$+, -, \circ$	In DOE method, indicator for factor levels

Greek Symbols

α	Intercept
β	Regression coefficients
ε_t	Residual error
ε_{it}	Demand uncertainty
λ_i^{NM}	Noisy model portfolio
$N(0,1)$	Normal distribution, with mean 0 and variance 1.
μ	Mean of the simulation results
μ_i	Markup of product i (in the context of chapter 2.4.3)
π_{cs}	Cost driver rate
ϕ_j	Premium price for one on capacity unit j
ϕ_j^+	Premium price for investing in additional capacity of j
ϕ_j^-	Premium price for disinvesting capacity of j

Tables

Figures

1. Introduction

Taking the right pricing and product-mix decision is vital for the success of a firm. Various surveys indicate that these decisions are based upon product costs relying on full-costs and simple cost allocation schemes (e.g. Drury and Tayles (1994); Shim and Sudit (1995); Altomonte, Barattieri and Basu (2015)). Cooper and Kaplan (1988) are often quoted in the same breath, highlighting the possible inadequacy of these methods: Allocating overhead, even using the most sophisticated method, remains to be heuristic.

> *"We need research that further examines the implication of errors in the design of cost pools and the selection of allocation bases [...] on the use of full costing in capacity-planning and product-pricing decisions. For example, a simulation that assesses how full-cost-based rules perform relative to other planning and pricing rules as the degree of error in the cost system increases, may offer new insights."*
>
> (Balakrishnan and Sivaramakrishnan (2002), p. 28)

This citation reads not only as an introduction to this thesis, but is the benchmark it should be measured upon. The basic idea is to facilitate simulations and evaluate the influence of cost system design on product & portfolio decisions.

1.1 On the adequacy of full-costing for decision making

If there exists one consensus in the debate on the adequacy or inadequacy of full costing for decision-making, it is his inexistence.[1] The discussion dates back to the thirties of the last century: Robinson (1933) laying a fundament for the marginal theory, opposed by Hall and Hitch (1939). Hall and Hitch introduced the 'full cost' policy and found that: *"A large proportion of businesses make no attempt to equate marginal revenue and marginal cost*

[1] See Lucas (1999), p. 35.

in the sense in which economists have asserted that this is typical behaviour".[2]

Since then, economic and managerial theory has faced this 'reality gap'.[3] Seventy years later a comprehensive study on the discussion has been done by Lucas (2003). He states: *"Indeed both literatures appear to neglect the possible insights provided by the other"*. He addresses this issue and discusses several research possibilities. Specifically he points out that a sound understanding of the nature of cost information is necessary to close the gap. He also emphasizes that the activity based costing (ABC) framework could be the key to this understanding if it complies with certain assumptions and captures the true incremental or avoidable costs of a product.[4]

While various full-cost models exist (e.g. Banker and Hughes (1994); Christensen and Demski (1997); Banker, Hwang and Mishra (2002)), Balakrishnan and Sivaramakrishnan (2002) try to establish a model syllabus by summarizing and comparing the before mentioned literature. In doing so they suggest - as Lucas (2003) did - that one key is the understanding of cost systems.

1.2 From cost system design to pricing and portfolio decisions

The basic fundament for the underlying approach has most probably been led by Hwang, Evans and Hegde (1993). They analyze cost systems in a pricing context, particularly the loss related to product cost distortions. Based on the results of this study, it becomes evident to consider a broader range and more complex costing system.

The most recent and comparative study is Anand, Balakrishnan and Labro (2013). The focus of this study is on the "tidiness" of a cost system. Tidiness

---

2 Hall and Hitch (1939), p. 32.

3 See Scapens (1994), p. 301.

4 See Lucas (2003), pp. 211, 215.

is defined as the difference between total resource costs and total production costs. In a *tidy system,* both costs are equal. The idea is, that at first planning forecasted resource costs are not meeting realized product costs at the end of the period. Different costing systems are now investigated regarding their capability to adjust the forecast to meet production costs at the end of the period. The speed of convergence between both values, within a given time horizon, is the performance measure for a given costing system.

Both beforehand cited models use a two-stage allocation process comparable to the ABC approach. Anand, Balakrishnan and Labro (2013) never mention ABC explicitly but implement the ABC cost allocation process developed in an earlier publication of Balakrishnan, Hansen and Labro (2011).[5]

Taking up Lucas' (2003) discussion, the applicability of ABC in planning has to be reviewed. Schneeweiss (1998) documents that ABC is not generally usable as a planning tool, but highlights that by using ABC management is able to implement enhanced quantitative planning tools. In contrast, Dearman and Shields (2001) stress that cost-based judgment is improved by ABC. Also Kennedy and Affleck-Graves (2001) find that UK firms generate higher firm values by using ABC systems compared to traditional cost systems. Ittner, Lanen and Larcker (2002) identify that ABC has the potential to improve quality levels and indirectly leads to savings in manufacturing costs. However, they find that on average extensive investment into ABC has not necessarily an effect on profitability. Contradictorily, Cardinaels, Roodhooft and Warlop (2004) investigate the usage of ABC and its value for price setting in a competitive environment. Using a laboratory experiment, they find that pricing decisions profit from ABC data in comparison to decisions based on biased traditional costing information.[6]

---

[5] The publication of Balakrishnan, Hansen and Labro (2011) will be discussed in more detail in chapter 3.1.

[6] See Cardinaels, Roodhooft and Warlop (2004), pp. 6 and 143.

The previously mentioned studies neglect a vital part of cost behavior: According to Noreen and Soderstrom (1994) overhead costs are not strictly proportional to activity. This may lead to sticky cost behavior, a possible source of disturbance for product costing, if the effect is not incorporated into the underlying cost system. There exists only limited literature focusing on optimizing drivers for cost-allocations concerning portfolio decisions, e.g. incorporating effects caused by demand heterogeneity. Homburg (2004) designs a higher-level cost driver, accounting for portfolio based costs resulting in a more precise cost allocation.[7]

Therefore, for investigating the influence of cost-system design on pricing and product-mix decisions, a necessity is targeting the influence of the underlying cost structure, i.e. incorporating sticky cost behavior.

The underlying research framework of the research chapters (3 & 4) depends on data from simulations. The use of non-empirical data results mainly from a lack of existing and applicable data sets in common research databases. This is simply attributable to the fact, that firms are neither willing to implement different cost systems for research purposes, nor are they willing to publish data concerning internal cost systems. Therefore chapter 3 aims at underlining the adequacy of the research method in the field of management accounting and sheds light on the way simulation studies should be conducted.

To address the influence of cost system design on pricing and product-mix decisions, chapter 3 encompasses different market situations and structurally varies cost system designs to estimate the profit loss induced by heuristics in comparison to a pseudo ideal world, using unbiased cost on. The smaller the profit gap – the profit error – the better the performance of a given cost system design.[8] Thereby, one is able to cluster the cost heuristics

[7] See also Babad and Balachandran (1993) or Homburg (2001a) for further approaches to identify better cost drivers.

[8] Decisions based on cost systems approximating cost flows within organizations are biased. The origin of these biases are discussed by Datar and Gupta (1994), pp. 568.

by performance, giving management a tool to choose an adequate accounting system.

Chapter 4 addresses this discussion by adding a cost-stickiness context to the model, incorporating the asymmetry of overhead costs to changes in activity. It can be shown, that by enhancing the cost allocation process using a cost-stickiness driver one is able to reduce the profit error essentially. This finding enables management to assess the implementation alternatives of new cost systems and gives a first insight of how running cost systems can profit from more sophisticated driver selections.

Chapter 5 gives an overview of the main results and indicates directions for future research.

2. Simulation research framework

For this thesis, a simulation approach is used as opposed to analytical models or empirical methods such as survey or archival data. This chapter pursues three goals: Laying a common understanding of simulations, discussing the adequateness of the approach in the field of management accounting research and introducing a research framework to conduct simulation based experiments.

2.1 A basic introduction to simulations

This thesis follows the simulation definition by Kleijnen (2015), defining a simulation model as "a mathematical model that is solved by means of experimentation" and further relates to simulations solved by means of computer algorithms.[9] Hence, a simulation experiment in the scope of this definition can be synonymously seen as a computer experiment. Kleijnen (2015) further differentiates between deterministic vs. random and static vs. dynamic experiments. In contrast to deterministic models, random models incorporate variables based on probability functions. Dynamic models differ from static simulations in modelling time as an independent variable. Both characteristics can be mixed, e.g. a random, static or a deterministic, static model. The term random needs to be explained in detail. Since computer algorithms are deterministic, they are incapable of creating random numbers.[10] Therefore, the terms pseudo random numbers and pseudo random number-generators (PRN) are used. Without laying down the concrete methodology of PRNs, a "good" quality of a PRN is measured upon its capability to generate, firstly uniform, i.e. equally probable and secondly

---

[9] Kleijnen (2015), p. 4.

[10] It should be noted that by the usage of externally applied devices, e.g. measuring radioactive decay, true random number series could be used. The problems are the partially unknown and most-probably not fitting probability distributions, as well as the time to create a fitting series of random numbers, since many of these appliances create random events only by several years. See Niederreiter (2003), p. 2.

independent numbers, meaning that there is "no" relation between drawn values. There exist various generators fitting both prerequisites.[11]

Even deterministic simulations may incorporate (pseudo-)random components and underlie random effects.[12] While the underlying optimization function itself includes only non-random inputs at the time of optimization, the used solver and the input itself can lead to uncertain results. This is the case, when the solution can only be found by approximate procedures and/or the inputs are generated by PRNs.[13]

A simulation is usually embedded in a decision context. Schneeweiß (1992) abstractly models such a decision context, distinguishing between a real world problem, an abstracted real model and a decision generator.[14] A real world problem could be a planning context of a firm. A real model would abstract from this complex problem, e.g. uncertain effects would be modelled by PRNs. The underlying probability distributions of such generators and further simplifications would be evaluated by empirical tests against the real world problem. Since the real model is most likely still not solvable by quantitative measures, a further relaxation – in other words a second simplification – leads to the decision generator. Such a relaxation could be the usage of opportunity costs instead of modelling capacity constraints.[15] Such a decision generator could be implemented as a simulation, solving e.g. an optimization problem. The simulation itself follows an input-process-output model.[16] The simulation input usually consists of parameters to steer the simulation variables, e.g. environmental conditions as firm size, inflation, product range etc. The parameters control hereby the sampling of values from a prior defined distribution function. The process stage is the execution of the simulation yielding the simulation output. It encompasses the relaxed model, which in this case could be based upon a quadratic

[11] See Gentle (2003), p. 63.

[12] See Picheny et al. (2013), p. 3.

[13] See Kleijnen (2015), p. 4.

[14] See also Schneeweiss (2003) for an example of an abstract decision model.

[15] See Homburg (2001b), pp. 51 and 52.

[16] See Hocke, Meyer and Lorscheid (2015), p. 141.

optimization function and a suitable solver. For a given combination of parameters, the underlying model is then subsequently solved. In the introduced planning context, a relaxed model could be a firm's portfolio and pricing decision based on opportunity cost. The decision could be whether to produce, out of two products (*a, b*), both or only one product (*a or b*) and the respective quantities based on a given product price. The yielded output would be the profit for each portfolio combination. According to a set of environmental parameters, one is now able to take a decision on the portfolio question, i.e. take the portfolio with the highest profit. The decision would subsequently be validated against the real model. Referring to the relaxation example of using opportunity costs instead of capacity restrictions, it needs to be checked whether the underlying firm has the capacity and the resources needed to produce the portfolio and the respective quantities.

Figure 1: Abstract simulation model

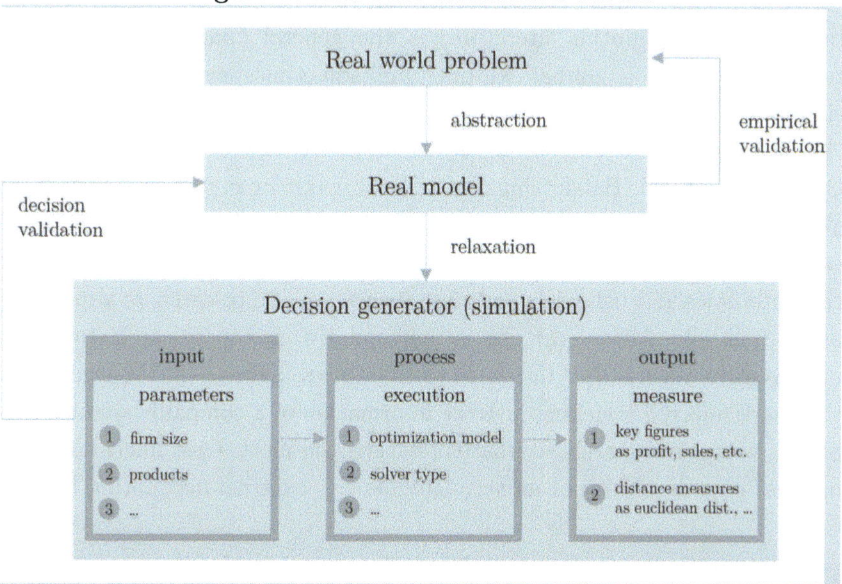

Based on Schneeweiß (1992), p. 4 and Hocke, Meyer and Lorscheid (2015), p. 141.

In addition, the prices set in the simulations could be challenged against market prices, to ensure that such prices would be accepted by customers.

Figure 1 illustrates the previously defined abstract model of a simulation in a decision context. The illustration of the decision generator will be used as a template for the simulation models in chapters 3 and 4.

2.2 On the adequacy of simulations in management accounting research

A comprehensive overview and an analysis of the impact of simulation research in management journals is provided by Harrison et al. (2007) or Reiss (2011). On one hand, both surveys indicate that on average over 10 years only up to 8 percent of the published articles in the evaluated management journals are based on simulations.[17] Labro (2015) critically states that an important factor of the low usage of simulations in management accounting literature, is the general "unfamiliarity of the readership (and of journal editors, and sometimes even referees) with simulation methods".[18]

On the other hand (Balakrishnan and Sivaramakrishnan (2002); Harrison et al. (2007); Reiss (2011); Labro (2015)) highlight the benefits of simulations, especially "because organizations are complex systems and many of their characteristics and behaviors are often inaccessible to researchers, especially over time, simulation can be a particularly useful research tool for management theorists".[19] In regard to this thesis, Labro's (2015) argument, that particularly by lacking internal information of a company, simulations offer a valuable research alternative, weighs the most: Cost allocation and internal cost data are not as accessible as e.g. external accounting figures

[17] See Reiss (2011), p. 246: The proportion of publications using "simulation" or "simulate" either in title or abstract in the field of economic literature for 2005 was less than 3%.
[18] Labro (2015), p. 5.
[19] Harrison et al. (2007), p. 1243.

provided by various databases such as COMPUSTAT[20] or I/B/E/S[21].

In addition, Balakrishnan and Penno (2014) discuss the role of analytical models and the advantages of numerical experiments. They also conclude that simulations belong to the managerial research toolkit, enabling research where analytical approaches are limited. They stress that this might be more useful than a literature based analysis of reality. The biggest advantage they see is that simulation and numerical computation are able to scale: They show that the number of models grow exponentially with the amount of model factors.[22] Hence, given a certain degree of complexity only computational solutions are applicable.

At the same time, this complexity seems to be one of the root causes for the low leverage of simulations. The complexity of such models (numbers of input parameters / variables, justification of variable manifestations, i.e. variable values, statistical distributions, etc.) and the vast output of data tends to mislead research: Labro (2015) states that research tends to go for trees instead of the wood. Each step (input, process, and output) needs to be planned, documented and objectified. Shortcomings in these activities may lead to misunderstandings or rejection of the research method.[23]

There exist various different frameworks (e.g. Sacks et al. (1989); Santner, Williams and Notz (2003); Lorscheid, Heine and Meyer (2012); Kleijnen (2015)). A central method discussed in all approaches is the design of experiments (DOE) framework, which was introduced for farming experiments in the early 20th by Ronald Aylmer Fisher.[24] It typically consists of planning, designing, conducting and analyzing phases to structure

---

[20] Standard & Poor's COMPUSTAT contains financial and price data for active and inactive publicly traded companies.

[21] The Institutional Brokers' Estimate System (I/B/E/S) by Thomson Reuters encompasses mostly (earnings) forecasts.

[22] See Balakrishnan and Penno (2014), p. 532.

[23] See Labro (2015), pp. 3–4.

[24] Fisher documented his approach in his book "The Design of Experiments", see Fisher (1935).

experiments, thereby trying to ensure the quality of experimental data.[25] Whereas Kleijnen (2015) argues that physical experiments differ essentially from computer experiments and calls for a new approach, Sacks et al. (1989) argue that DOE can be applied to computer experiments for two reasons. First, the choice of simulation input is a design question comparable to DOE. Second, the statistical methods applied to physical experiments are also applicable to computer experiments.[26] Lorscheid, Heine and Meyer (2012) extend DOE for computational experiments. Their approach has been chosen deliberately, since the most influential and related research articles leading to this thesis can be structured and thus compared on the basis of the their extended DOE process.[27]

The preceding discussion underlines the necessity to use a standardized and structured approach to enable easier access to the research method and a sound understanding of the simulation process. The discussion revealed that by using DOE the drawbacks of simulations can be mastered and the research method is applicable.

2.3 The underlying research framework

Lorscheid, Heine and Meyer (2012) consider simulations as a state of the art methodology. As introduced in the last section, they develop a methodology to overcome these obstacles based on the systematic design of experiments. Their abstract framework is the subject of this chapter and will be used subsequently in the research chapters (3 & 4).

In general Lorscheid, Heine and Meyer (2012) follow the typical DOE setup but additionally in their approach, each step is linked to either a central objective, which the respective simulation approach can be benchmarked

---

[25] See Antony (2014), p. 40.

[26] Sacks et al. (1989), p. 411.

[27] See Hocke, Meyer and Lorscheid (2015), evaluating among others Labro and Vanhoucke (2007) and Balakrishnan, Hansen and Labro (2011).

against or it is linked to a (statistical) method, used to objectify the experimenter's considerations.

Figure 2: DOE design process

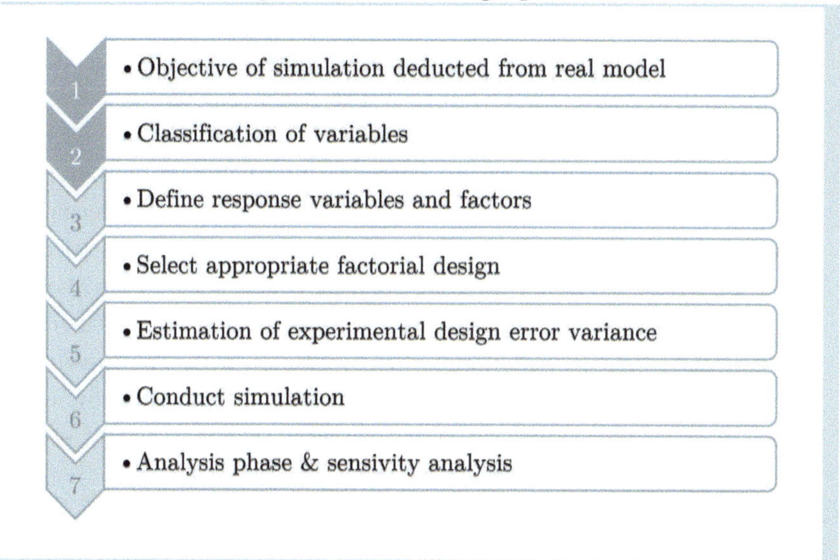

Based on Lorscheid, Heine and Meyer (2012), p. 30.

In this thesis the approach is, as introduced in the previous chapter, embedded into the decision generator model by Schneeweiß (1992). The adjusted DOE design by Lorscheid, Heine and Meyer (2012) as illustrated in Figure 2 consists of the following:

(1) The process of abstraction and relaxation of the real model by Schneeweiß (1992) already takes into account a considerable feedback mechanism to align the decision generator or more precisely enable the simulation to solve the given problem. In addition, Lorscheid, Heine and Meyer (2012) consider theoretical model behaviors such as performance and possible model configurations in their first process step. As stated before, the variety of parameters is positively correlated with the complexity of the model. Hence, the research should focus only on reduced and value creating parameter sets. For the illustration of the adjusted DOE process, let us come back to our portfolio

optimization problem. As illustrated in Figure 1, firm size is such a possible parameter. It needs to be decided if this is a parameter for the simulation, or if it can be neglected because it does not add any insights to the subsequent analysis.

(2) In line with Field and Hole (2003), Lorscheid, Heine and Meyer (2012) see a major advantage in the clustering of variables into dependent, independent and control variables. The dependent variables are the variables of interest. The whole purpose of the simulation is to measure these variables, hence they represent the simulation output. The independent variables should drive the relevant effect on the dependent variables, whereas control variables rather have minor or no effect at all. Additionally control variables are usually not linked to the research question. Independent and control variables are steered via the input parameters of the simulation. To continue with the previously introduced market variable example, consider a parameter, by which the experimenter is able to switch between an initial market size of small, medium and large markets.

(3) The third step includes the transformation of dependent and control variables into factor levels, depending on how the respective variable was modelled in step 2. A possible example could be a market maturity variable, which could be transformed into two factor levels for saturated and growing markets.

(4) The factorial design reflects the possible factor level combinations with the simulation, taking into account also interactional effects between factors.[28] Following Box, Hunter and Hunter (1978) factorial design can be separated in full and fractional. A fractional design limits the degree of interaction between factors. Usually main effects outweigh two-factor effects, and subsequently two-factor effects outweigh three-factor effects and so forth. The idea therefore is to focus only on the important effects.[29] Lorscheid, Heine and Meyer (2012) propose that

---

[28] The term „factorial design“ originates back to Fisher (1935), arguing that experimenters should focus on isolated, elementary factors in an experiment and laying out a structured approach to design experiments.

[29] See Box, Hunter and Hunter (1978), p. 374.

the experimenter should use design points – a minimum set of factor levels – for each factor defined in step 3.[30]

A full-factorial experimental design can be coded as l levels to the power of k factors.[31] A common approach is to indicate a high level of a factor as "+" and his low level as "−"respectively. If more than two levels are used, additional levels are subsequently coded as "+ +" or "− −". If the number of parameters is uneven, "o" indicates the level between "-" and "+". The signs do not necessarily indicate an order of levels, but an indicator of levels, to better separate the levels.

By limiting these factors the model complexity can be reduced, also aiding the runtime of the simulation, because each level combination equals at least one simulation run.

Each iteration to solve the underlying model is also referred to as a "run". Assuming each run is very time consuming (e.g. 30 minutes), a design resulting in a total of e.g. 6 factors each having 2 levels would accumulate to a total of at least 2 to the power of 6 combinations, taking aside multiple runs of the same combination to control for stochastic effects. This would mean the complete simulation would last for at least 32 days.[32] Interaction effects between factors would increase the complexity exponentially.[33] Usually a 2-factor design is a good starting point to obtain a first data-set. From this sparse data-set one is able to decide whether factors are important or if they could possibly be neglected. Computational power is a curse and a savior at the same time. Even if a computer-based simulation can handle high varieties of input factors and model parameters, the size of resulting datasets may become a problem (datasets easily exceed many gigabytes limiting statistical analysis). Additionally, the vast numbers of possible data slices and subsets may add more confusion, than understanding, of the underlying problem.[34]

---

[30] See Lorscheid, Heine and Meyer (2012), pp. 32–33.

[31] See Antony (2014), p. 63.

[32] 32 days = 2^6 combinations * 30 minutes. See Kleijnen et al. (2005), p. 274 for further considerations on efficiency of simulations.

[33] See Sacks et al. (1989), p. 418, stressing that the high cardinality of input factors and interactions needs to be addressed to achieve efficient design and analysis.

[34] Labro (2015), p. 4.

(5) This step aims at measuring the design error: As stated earlier the usage of PRNs and approximate solutions may lead to an unwanted variance in results. To control for this effect, multiple runs by stable inputs need to be conducted. Together with the initial 2-factor design, this leads to a first idea of necessary total simulation runs. A metric to identify the best tradeoff between variance and simulation runs, is considered to be the *coefficient of variance.*

$$CV = \frac{s}{\mu} \quad (1)$$

The CV, calculated by dividing the standard deviation (s) by the mean of the simulation results (μ), is measured for a small set of simulation runs. Subsequently the number of runs is raised until the CV stabilizes.[35]

(6) Having defined design points in the former steps and chosen a fitting number of simulation runs to control for experimental variance, step 6 considers conducting the simulation, where each design point equals a separate experiment.

(7) The final step is the analysis, incorporating sensitivity tests of input parameters. This is achieved by comparing the yielded data for each design point to choose a final set of factors for the experiment and to illustrate the sensitive behavior of the simulation itself. Lorscheid, Heine and Meyer (2012) focus on the application of analysis of variance (ANOVA) for this task.[36]

Based on these findings, adjustments of the model could lead to an iterative procedure of adjusting level choices in step 4. This would also include, adjusting the 2-factor design to a multi-factor design. Coming back to the planning example it could be beneficial to control for more than two levels of market maturity. Santner, Williams and Notz (2003) lay special focus on the analytical methods and robustness tests. The

[35] See Lorscheid, Heine and Meyer (2012), pp. 33. They also discuss the downsides of the CV application.

[36] See Lorscheid, Heine and Meyer (2012), p. 35.

authors suggest using descriptive tests and regression modelling next to ANOVA.[37] This thesis will focus on the first two methods.

2.4 Relevant simulation models in management accounting – A theory review

Whereas DOE lays the foundation for a sound understanding of the methodical approach, the understanding is best supported by non-abstract 'real-life' examples. As a counterpart to the methodical introduction of the last chapter, the proceeding discussion of selected simulation approaches should foster the understanding of the implementation of simulations.

In a way the fundament for state of the art simulations in the field of management accounting has been laid by Balakrishnan and Sivaramakrishnan (2002). The authors investigate a basis model upon which future research can build its simulations and formulate research questions taken up by Balakrishnan, Hansen and Labro (2011); Anand, Balakrishnan and Labro (2013) and this thesis respectively. Since these articles also create the foundation for the developed model in chapter 3 & 4, they are presented subsequently in detail.

2.4.1 The Grand Model

Balakrishnan and Sivaramakrishnan (2002) analytically deduct their 'grand model' for a joint decision upon optimal prices and capacity in an iterative approach. **In short,** with each iteration they extend a basic profit optimization model. The starting point is a simple one-period model, only adjusting the produced quantity based on given prices and variable costs and within the constraints of a given demand and a given capacity. The next extension replaces the given demand, by a demand function dependent on price and price-elasticity. The third extension introduces capacity on a need basis, hence in addition to the given capacity, more expensive flexible capacity can be purchased. The fourth extension enables planning for a

---

37 See Santner, Williams and Notz (2003), pp. 199.

multi-period instead of a one-period setting. While all prior extensions used a deterministic optimization function, the grand model adds a stochastic demand, therefore implementing imperfect information on market behavior.[38]

The grand model derivation by Balakrishnan and Sivaramakrishnan (2002) **in detail**: In this thesis the indexes i, j and t will be used consistently to indicate products ($i \in I$), resources ($j \in J$) and time ($t \in T$), capital letters indicating the total of units.

The fundament for all succeeding models is **model 1**: Prices (P_i) are dictated by the market thus the firm is focused on optimizing production output (Q_i), given a positive marginal income ($P_i - v_i$), v_i beeing the variable costs per product:

$$\max_{Q_i} \sum_{i=1}^{I} (P_i - v_i)\, Q_i \tag{2}$$

$$\text{subject to} \quad \sum_{i=1}^{I} m_{ij} Q_i \leq L_j \qquad \forall\, j$$

$$0 \leq Q_i \leq D_i \qquad \forall\, i$$

See Balakrishnan and Sivaramakrishnan (2002), p. 9.

Setting focus on modelling **demand** and **capacity**: In this model, the simplest way to implement demand (D_i) and capacity (L_j) has been chosen, both being fixed. Obviously, a company's production output (Q_i), is only limited by demand and supplied capacity.[39] The link between quantity and capacity is modeled by the resource consumption matrix (m_{ij}), which maps

[38] See Balakrishnan and Sivaramakrishnan (2002), p. 13.

[39] Presuming an absence of stock keeping of inventories.

the needed resources j for a product i. The needed resources $Q_i m_{ij}$ must not exceed supplied resources L_j.

$$D_i = A_i - b_i P_i \tag{3}$$

By focusing on a monopolistic setting, the given company becomes a price setter and is thus able to adjust the **demand** (D_i): As illustrated in eq. (3) the demand is now modeled as a function of market size (A_i), price elasticity (b_i) and price (P_i).[40] Price elasticity is the responsiveness of demand on price changes. In this thesis only non-luxury goods are considered, hence an increase in prices directly decreases the demand.[41]

By modeling the demand as time-dependent (A_{it}) the question arises, whether the firm has complete knowledge of the demand throughout the planning horizon. The final evolution of the demand function is therefore to incorporate demand uncertainty, expressed by an error term ε_{it}. The error term offsets the expectations of the firm per product and period (see Table 1).

Capacity (L_j) – being the resources supplied – has been neglected as a decision variable so far. Taking a multi-period setting into account Balakrishnan and Sivaramakrishnan (2002) further distinguish between two terms of capacity: long-term capacity (L_j) and capacity on a need basis (R_{jt}). Long-term capacity is available throughout the complete planning horizon (T-periods), whereas short term capacity is only build up and available for period t.

---

40 See Balakrishnan and Sivaramakrishnan (2002), p. 10.

41 See Mankiw and Taylor (2006), p. 88.

Table 1: Evolution of models (cont'd)

Evolution steps	Demand	Capacity
Initial model	$\max\limits_{Q_i} \sum_{i=1}^{I} (P_i - v_i)\, Q_i$	$\sum_{i=1}^{I} m_{ij} Q_i \leq L_j \quad \forall\, j$
• Translates from quantity to demand • Demand depends on prices	$\Rightarrow D_i = A_i - b_i P_i$	
• Time-dependency • Resource costs • Differentiate between long- and short-term capacity	$\Rightarrow D_{it} = A_{it} - b_i P_{it}$	L_j ↗ $T \sum_{j=1}^{J} c_j L_j$ ↘ $\sum_{t=1}^{T} \sum_{j=1}^{J} c_j \phi_j R_{jt}$
• Demand uncertainty	$\Rightarrow D_{it} = A_i + \varepsilon_{it} - b_i P_{it}$	

⇒ **Grand Model:**

$$\max_{P_{it}, R_{jt}, L_j} \; E\left[\sum_{t=1}^{T}\left(\sum_{i=1}^{I}(P_{it} - v_i)(A_i + \varepsilon_{it} - b_i P_{it}) - \sum_{j=1}^{J}\phi_j c_j R_{jt}\right)\right] - T\sum_{j=1}^{J} c_j L_j \tag{4}$$

subject to

$$\sum_{i=1}^{I} m_{ij}(A_i + \varepsilon_{it} - b_i P_{it}) - R_{jt} - L_j \leq 0 \; \forall j, t$$

$$(A_i + \varepsilon_{it} - b_i P_{it}) \geq 0 \; \forall i, t \tag{5}$$

$$P_{it} \geq 0 \; \forall i, t.$$

Table 1: Evolution of models (cont'd)

Decision variables:		Non-decision variables:	
P_{it}	Price for product i in period t	A_i	Market size per product i and period t
		$D_i/(D_{it})$	Demand per product i (and period t)
		$Q_i/(Q_{it})$	Quantity per product i (and period t)
L_j	Initial long-term capacity for resource j (available every period)	ε_{it}	Error term per product i and period t
R_{jt}	Flexible short-term capacity for resource j and period t	b_i	Price elasticity of product i
		v_i	Variable cost of product i
		c_j	Resource costs of resource j
		ϕ_j	Premium price for one capacity of unit j
		m_{ij}	Resource consumption matrix for product i and resource j

See Balakrishnan and Sivaramakrishnan (2002), p. 13.

In this setting both resources become decision variables, since an optimal trade-off between initial setup of resources, in other words the capital employed over the planning horizon and short term investments, due to a heterogeneous demand needs to be found. Now being part of the decision context, capacity costs are no longer sunk.

Therefor resources (j) need to be valued by a cost-price of c_j, identical for short- and long-term resources. Since short-term capacity needs to be purchased on a need basis, a cost-price premium of $\phi_j > 1$ needs to be paid. The premium reflects additional costs, such as higher rates for interim staffing or renting/leasing of production facilities over time. Additionally, a lack of price premium or a premium factor of one, would lead to investments only in short-term capacity.[42] The grand model (see eq. (4)), in comparison to its deterministic predecessors, no longer maximizes the profit itself, but its expectation.[43] Table 1 illustrates the evolution steps from initial to grand model.

The advantage of the grand model is that it can be decomposed into different models and planning scenarios. This is leveraged by Balakrishnan and Sivaramakrishnan (2002) to analytically identify the economic loss of simplified planning approaches in comparison to the grand model. They address simplifications such as separating capacity and price planning, using full costing for capacity approximation, and modeling either hard- or soft-capacity constraints. They also indicate that simulations may enrich the understanding of open research questions such as the influence of cost-pool and cost-allocation design on capacity and pricing issues.

2.4.2 Cost Model

Balakrishnan, Hansen and Labro (2011) take up the idea of investigating the influence of cost-system design on the error of reported costs. The basic idea is to compare a company having full information on cost-consumption with entities only using approximations of the real cost-consumption by products.

In general, full costs of a product can be calculated as the sum of variable costs (v_i) and the costs of consumed capacity ($\sum_{j=1}^{J} m_{ij} c_j$).[44] In the context of Balakrishnan, Hansen and Labro (2011), the central variables are the resource consumption matrix (m_{ij}) and the corresponding cost vector (c_j). In the following, variable costs are neglected. Therefore, following Balakrishnan, Hansen and Labro (2011) the term product cost (PC) is used.

---

42 See Banker and Hughes (1994), p. 481.
43 See Balakrishnan and Sivaramakrishnan (2002), p. 13.
44 See Balakrishnan and Sivaramakrishnan (2002), p. 14.

In an ideal world, a company has full information on resource consumption and resource costs. In reality both information are biased (see Table 2, as indicated by the index *bias* for m_{ij}^{bias}/ c_j^{bias}). The impact of partial and/or biased information on cost reporting, in theory, the delta between both product costs, unbiased (BM) and biased, indicates the quality of an implemented cost system design (see eq. (6) in Table 2).

Where does the bias come from? Naturally, cost systems lack complete information on resource consumption and therefore use algorithms to apply (activity) costs to products. Hence, the resulting product costs are only approximate. In other words, inherit sources of erroneous cost allocation. Cost systems classically use two stage cost allocation processes: on the first stage, costs are allocated to cost pools. On the second stage, the costs accumulated on these pools are allocated to products. The effectiveness of such cost systems is limited by aggregation, measurement and specification errors while pooling and allocating costs.[45]

Aggregation errors usually originate from failures on first layer, i.e. pooling wrong resources into the same cost pools. Specification errors occur on both levels, based on cost driver rates not reflecting the consumption pattern of resources. That could for example be the usage of the labor cost rates for energy overhead, when both are possibly not interrelated. Measurement error – as the last error group – is straightforward: while setting up rates for cost allocation, wrong assumptions of the amount of resource/activity usages are made. E.g. storing inventory lasts not 10 but 15 minutes. If the allocation of overhead costs was based on these time assumptions, the reflected costs would not meet actual process usage.[46]

There exist different basic cost system designs (volume based costing, activity based costing, resource based costing, etc.).[47]

---

[45] See Datar and Gupta (1994), p. 568.

[46] See Labro and Vanhoucke (2007), p. 941.

[47] See Balakrishnan, Labro and Sivaramakrishnan (2012a), p. 4.

Table 2: Derivation of the BHL[48] simulation model

benchmark model		biased model	
1) full information on resource consumption and resource costs	$\sum_{j=1}^{J} m_{ij}^{BM} c_j^{BM} = PC_i^{BM}$	$\sum_{j=1}^{J} m_{ij}^{bias} c_j^{bias} = PC_i^{bias}$	2) biased information on resource consumption and resource costs

$$\Rightarrow \Delta PC_i = PC_i^{BM} - PC_i^{bias} \quad (6)$$

noisy model

$c_j \overset{h1}{\rightarrow} ACP_k$	3) transformation of resource costs into activity cost pools	(7)
$m_{ij} \overset{h2}{\rightarrow} ad_{ki}$	4) transformation of resource into activity consumption	(8)
$\sum_{k=1}^{K} ad_{ki} ACP_k = PC_i^{NM}$	5) product costs based on activity based costing	(9)

$$\Rightarrow \Delta PC_i = PC_i^{BM} - PC_i^{NM} \quad (10)$$

$h1$	heuristic 1: set of algorithms to transform the cost vector of size j into k-activity cost pools	$h2$	heuristic 2: set of algorithms to transform the resource consumption matrix of size i,j into a matrix mapping activities (k) to products (i)
ACP_k	activity cost pool: costs to perform an activity (k)	ad_{ki}	activity driver: maps the costs of activity (k) to a product (i)

[48] The abbreviation BHL identifies in the following the paper Balakrishnan, Hansen and Labro (2011). See also Homburg, Nasev and Plank (2013) p. 9ff.

As already discussed in the introduction, activity based costing is considered one of the best performing alternatives.[49]

Instead of using an abstract "bias" to model the information deficit of cost system designs (see "biased model" in Table 2), Balakrishnan, Hansen and Labro (2011) implement a comparable approach to activity based costing.

The "noisy model" (NM) (see Table 2) simplifies the allocation process in contrast to the "benchmark model" (BM). While the BM allocates resource-costs to products directly, the NM first pools the resource costs on k activity cost pools (ACP_k). Hence, only aggregated costs need to be allocated successively in the second step. The second step accordingly facilitates the allocation process: while the BM has a maximum of I times J allocation rules, the NM only has I times K. It can be expected that the amount of activity cost pools is notably lower than the total resources (J) available. By analogy with eq. (6) the impact of the non-optimal allocation process can be expressed by the delta between BM and NM product costs (see eq.(10))

As introduced in Table 2 the pooling and allocation rules follow specified algorithms. The pooling is defined by heuristic 1 (see eq. (7)), already indicating that the process is only approximate. Likewise, the cost-allocation step is defined by heuristic 2 (see eq. (8)). In the following, the abstract heuristics are illustrated.

2.4.2.1 First-stage heuristics

In detail, the first stage heuristics encompass the following five heuristics:[50] The **random method** (−−) randomly assigns resources to cost pools. This

---

[49] For a comprehensive comparison of different cost-systems and ABC evolutions see Balakrishnan, Labro and Sivaramakrishnan (2012b), p. 24.

[50] See Balakrishnan, Hansen and Labro (2011), p. 527 and also Homburg, Nasev and Plank (2013) in the appendix section p. 26.

method represents the simplest method because it needs information neither about resource costs nor about resource consumption patterns.

In a cost system with, e.g., six activity cost pools, the **size random method** (–) first assigns the six largest resources (in terms of per unit resource costs) to the six cost pools. Subsequently, the remaining resources are randomly assigned to the six cost pools.

In a cost system with six activity cost pools, the **size misc method** (○) assigns the five largest resources (in terms of unit resource costs) to five of the six cost pools. The remaining resources are lumped in the sixth cost pool.

The **correlation random method** (+) groups resources with similar consumption patterns into one cost pool. First, one resource – the base resource - is randomly assigned to each activity cost pool. Then the remaining resources are assigned to activity cost pools based on their correlation with the base resource. The number of resources per cost pool is chosen such that every cost pool has approximately the same number of resources. As this method requires data on consumption patterns, it is informational demanding.

While the correlation random method randomly chooses the base resource, the **correlation size method** (++) chooses the largest resource (in terms of per unit resource costs c_j) as the base resource. The remaining resources are assigned to the cost pools based on their correlation with the base resource. The advantage of this method is the combination of size-based and correlation-based criteria to assign resources to cost pools. It is also informational demanding.

2.4.2.2 Second-stage heuristics

The second-stage heuristics encompass the following four heuristics:[51] According to the **Big Pool Method** (−) the activity driver of a cost pool is the resource consumption coefficient of the largest resource (in terms of per unit resource costs) in the cost pool. The advantage of this method is that it is simple and that the costs of the largest resources are accurately assigned to the products. The disadvantage is that the remaining resources are inaccurately assigned.

For the **Average Method** (+ +) the activity driver of a cost pool is the average of the resource consumption coefficients of all resources in the cost pool. Compared to the big pool method, this method leads to more accurate product costs because it considers more resource consumption information. Nevertheless, the method is associated with relatively high information costs.

The Intermediate Methods Num(2) (−) to Num(4) (+) set the activity driver of a cost pool as the average of the resource consumption coefficients of the largest resources in the cost pool. For example, the activity driver according to the Num(4) method is the average of the consumption patterns of the four largest resources (in terms of per unit resource costs) of a cost pool. While intermediate methods require more information than the big pool method – resource consumption of a single resource vs. resource consumptions of four resources – they require less information than the average method which requires consumption patterns of all resources in a cost pool.

2.4.2.3 Simulation approach

This chapter discusses the general design layout by Balakrishnan, Hansen and Labro (2011). The central research question is the accuracy loss of product costs, by using approximate cost-system designs. Eq. (10) expresses

[51] See Balakrishnan, Hansen and Labro (2011), p. 528 also Homburg, Nasev and Plank (2013) in the appendix section p. 27.

this loss per product, in terms of the delta of product costs ΔPC_i between the benchmark and the noisy model.

To measure the total reported error of such a system, Homburg (2001a) and Balakrishnan, Hansen and Labro (2011) use the Euclidean Distance ($EUCD_s$), as displayed in eq. (11). The subscript s indicates the identifier of the corresponding simulation run. The simulation embeds a catalogue of different environments. Each environment defines the simulation input. In total three parameters (resource cost variation, density of the consumption matrix and correlation of resource consumption) form 48 different environments.

Table 3: BHL simulation process

$$EUCD_s = \sqrt{(\Delta PC_i)^2} \quad s \in S \text{ (simulation runs)} \quad i \in I \text{ (products)} \tag{11}$$

	Input (environment)	Process	Output
Simulation	1. Resource cost variation (*RCV, 3 level*) 2. Density of the consumption matrix (*DENS, 4 level*) 3. Correlation of resource consumption (*COR, 4 level*) ⇒ **48 environments**	1. Calculate product costs in the benchmark model ⇒ **20 samples** 2. For each BM calculate product costs in the noisy model for a combination of a. Heuristic 1 (5 level) b. Heuristic 2 (4 level) c. *ACP* (6 level) d. Measurement error (*ME*) (3 level) ⇒ **360 samples**	⇒ $EUCD_s$ $S =$ 345,600
Example run (*s=1*)	1. Low dispersion (−) 2. High sharing (+) 3. Similar consumption pattern (+)	1. Calculate PC^{BM} 2. Calculate PC^{NM} for a. Random (− −) b. Big Pool (−) c. *2 ACP (− −)* d. ME at 50% (+ + +)	⇒ $EUCD_1$

To cope with the stochastic effect of random number generation, 20 samples of each environment leading to a total number of 960 benchmark models are drawn.[52] A noisy model definition consists out of four parameters (heuristics 1 & 2 combination, the number of activity cost pools, a systematic cost system error and the measurement error) leading to a total number of 360 noisy models, for each BM. The simulation process is summarized in Table 3.

The following paragraph explains the introduced (see Table 3) input parameters used to build the environment. In accordance to the factorial design, the levels for each factor are coded to better visualize the state of the respective factor.[53] The generic design of the parameters works as follows: For each input factor, a distribution function is modeled. The factor level is used as a parameter to steer the distribution, e.g. the boundaries, skewness, etc. Subsequently from this adjusted distribution, a set of random numbers is drawn.

In case of the resource cost variation, a uniform distribution is applied. The level of resource sharing changes the boundaries of the distribution. A low level of cost dispersion limits e.g. the possible drawn random numbers to a corridor of 0 to 0.2 instead of 0 to 1 of the standard uniform distribution. The drawn random numbers are considered the proportion of used costs by each resource of total resource costs. Hence the biggest spread in a low dispersion setting is 20%, in other words each resource will consume approximately the same portion of total resource costs. In a final step, the drawn numbers are normalized. Obviously, only 100% of resource costs are allocable.[54] Table 4 summarizes the interaction between parameters, factors and variables.

---

[52] See DOE design step 6 on page 16 and Lorscheid, Heine and Meyer (2012), pp. 33.

[53] See also step 3 in the DOE process on page 14.

[54] This is an arbitrary example. For the exact algorithm, see the working paper version of BHL, Balakrishnan et al. (2009).

Table 4: BHL Input factors for variables

Factor	Levels & Coding	Functionality	Variable
RCV: Resource cost variation	- Low dispersion 0 Med dispersion + High dispersion	The resource cost variation defines how disperse the total resource costs are distributed over resources. A low dispersion equals a setting where the total resource costs are almost equally distributed. At high dispersion, a small set of resources accounts for a majority of resource costs.	c_j
DENS: Density of the consumption matrix	- Little sharing 0 Medium sharing + High sharing + + Very high sharing	Despite from the complex naming the density parameter is straightforward: The resource consumption matrix is adjusted in a way that settings from little to very high resource sharing are controllable. The most extreme "little sharing" outcome would be a 1:1 mapping between resources and products. On the other side a very high sharing could lead to completely filled matrix m_{ij}, where each	m_{ij}

Table 4: BHL Input factors for variables (cont'd)

Factor	Levels & Coding	Functionality	Variable
		product consumes each resource.	
COR: Correlation of resource consumption	+ Similar consumption 0 Intermediate consumption - Dissimilar consumption -- Very dissimilar consumption	The most complex parameter. It also adjusts the resource consumption matrix. In simple terms, it steers how resource consumption of product *i=1* correlates with product *i=2*. Where DENS steers if two products consume the same resource *j* (binary condition), COR steers if both consume the same amount of *j*, in respect to the chosen level (e.g. similar +).	m_{ij}

See Balakrishnan, Hansen and Labro (2011), p. 525.

2.4.2.4 Results

As proposed in the DOE framework by Lorscheid, Heine and Meyer (2012), Balakrishnan, Hansen and Labro (2011) use an ANOVA regression to analyze the results. In general, the results suggest that more sophisticated allocation methods yield product costs closer to the benchmark, than less advanced methods:[55]

The number of activity cost pools has a marginal effect on the error of product costs. Using more than a moderate number of cost pools only adds a small added value in terms of product cost accuracy. One of the main contradictory findings is, that the more the resource consumption of products varies (i.e. factor COR levels "–" or "– –", see Table 4), the more correlation based methods outperform size based methods.[56]

Important findings, in regard to this thesis, are the influences of cost structure on the performance of the noisy model: for one, even a small reduction of specification errors result in significantly lower reporting errors. For the other, the highest environmental effect originates from the distribution of resource costs.[57]

2.4.3 Margin Model

The *cost model* simulation disconnects from the synchronous profit and capacity optimization problem of the *grand model*, by focusing on optimal product cost determination. Nevertheless, it does not only shed light on one of the research proposals by Balakrishnan and Sivaramakrishnan (2002), identifying the criticality of cost pool design, but also lays the fundament for the *margin model.*

As discussed, a central requirement of cost reporting is the accordance of reported and realized costs. According to Anand, Balakrishnan and Labro (2013), a reporting system is tidy if both figures equal. Obviously, profit-planning tools are only fully reliable by being based on tidy costs. Considering that cost systems are approximations of true cost consumption, in practice cost systems are seldom completely tidy. A central objective of management accounting divisions is therefore to review planned costs based

55 See Balakrishnan, Hansen and Labro (2011), p. 540.
56 See Balakrishnan, Hansen and Labro (2011), p. 537.
57 See Balakrishnan, Hansen and Labro (2011), p. 541 and the results of this thesis on page 66.

on true cost consumption on a regular basis and to adjust allocation methods to close the existing gap.

Leveraging a numerical example / simulation approach Anand, Balakrishnan and Labro (2013) review the heuristics introduced by Balakrishnan, Hansen and Labro (2011) on their capability of yielding tidy costs and the time frame needed to align reported and realized product costs. The underlying model implements a product margin-optimizing firm, given predetermined, static capacity. Different to Balakrishnan and Sivaramakrishnan (2002) and this thesis, the respective optimized company therefore is a price taker and not a (monopolistic) price setter. Price optimization is therefore neglected, as is respectively the quantity produced.[58]

2.4.3.1 Simulation approach

The used profit functions are illustrated in eq. (12) & (16) in Table 5. There is no optimization process because all required variables are known prior to planning. Additionally, the planning process is sequential. This means that at first the product mix is defined and, based on this decision, the capacity L_j^{BM} is set.

As input for the simulation, environmental parameters are used comparative to the *cost model.* Therefore, only the two new parameters for steering markup and quantity are discussed: Anand, Balakrishnan and Labro (2013) calculate the respective product margin (μ_i) leveraging a random number generator using the parameters "average markup" and "variance in markup". The steering concept of the first parameter is straightforward: for the given set of *i*-products, it models the average margin over the portfolio. Comparable to the cost variance parameter (RCV), the variance in markup triggers portfolios with heterogeneous or homogeneous products. For both, 2-levels (high/low) are defined. Quantities (Q_i) are drawn from a uniform

[58] See Anand, Balakrishnan and Labro (2013), p. 7,

distribution.[59] Table 6 illustrates the complete process, while Table 5 describes in detail the underlying model.

Table 5: ABL Margin model definition[60]

BM

$$Profit^{BM} = \sum_{i=1}^{I} \mu_i \lambda_i^{NM} Q_i - \sum_{j=1}^{J} c_j L_j^{BM} \quad (12)$$

$$L_j^{BM} = \sum_{i=1}^{I} m_{ij} \lambda_i^{NM} Q_i \quad \forall_j \qquad PC_i^{BM} = \sum_{j=1}^{J} m_{ij} c_j \quad \forall_i$$

$$\lambda_i^{NM} = \begin{cases} 1 & \mu_i > 0 \\ 0 & \mu_i \leq 0 \end{cases} \quad \forall_i \qquad TC^{BM} = \sum_{j=1}^{J} c_j L_j^{BM}$$

NM

Initial period[61]		Succeeding periods
$TC^{BM} \overset{h1}{\rightarrow} ACP_k^{total}$	(13)	$TC^{NM} \overset{h1}{\rightarrow} ACP_k^{total}$
$m_{ij} \overset{h2}{\rightarrow} ad_{ki}$	(14)	$\frac{ACP_k^{total}}{L_j^{NM}} = ACP_k^{pl} \quad j \subseteq J$
$\frac{ACP_k^{total}}{L_j^{BM}} = ACP_k^{pl} \quad j \subseteq J$	(15)	*ad_{ki} is identical for all periods*

$$PC_i^{NM} = \sum_{k=1}^{K} ad_{ki} ACP_k^{pl} \qquad \lambda_i^{NM} = \begin{cases} 1 & P_i^{NM} > PC_i^{NM} \\ 0 & P_i^{NM} \leq PC_i^{NM} \end{cases} \quad \forall_i$$

$$P_i^{NM} = (1 + \mu_i) PC_i^{NM} \qquad TC^{NM} = \sum_{i=1}^{I} PC_i^{NM} \lambda_i^{NM} Q_i \quad \forall_j$$

$$Profit^{NM} = \sum_{i=1}^{I} \mu_i \lambda_i^{NM} Q_i - TC^{NM} \quad (16)$$

[59] See Anand, Balakrishnan and Labro (2013), p. 11.

[60] The model is not illustrated straight away in Anand, Balakrishnan and Labro (2013), but is derived from various information given in the paper, especially out of the Appendix. ABL will be used as an abbreviation for Anand, Balakrishnan and Labro (2013).

[61] For simplification reasons the time index is neglected.

In the following, both views on the paper are combined: Having used the described inputs, in the process stage firstly the BM profit ($Profit^{BM}$), and secondly the noisy model profit ($Profit^{NM}$) are calculated. This is achieved by initially taking over information from the benchmark model into the noisy model: based on benchmark portfolio (λ_i^{BM}) and benchmark capacity (TC^{BM}) heuristics taken over from the *cost model* are used to allocate costs. [62] Next, building upon these product costs (PC_i^{NM}) the noisy model portfolio (λ_i^{NM}) is derived. Corresponding to this new portfolio, the total costs of the NM are calculated.

If the total costs (TC^{NM}) of the noisy model equal total costs (TC^{BM}) of the benchmark model, i.e. the cost system is tidy, finally the noisy model profit $Profit^{NM}$ is derived, as illustrated in eq. (16).[63] If $TC^{NM} \neq TC^{BM}$, in other words the cost system is untidy, then for t periods, the product costs are refined until either both costs equal or a maximum of T periods is reached.[64]

As metrics for the research (see Table 6, output), the profit efficiency (PF^{eff}, eq. (17)) and mean product cost error ($\overline{PCE}$, eq. (18)) are used. The former being the quality of the noisy model profit estimation, measured upon its relative closeness to the benchmark model. The latter, measuring the mean fit of NM product costs in regard to the benchmark product costs.

---

[62] A subset of heuristics from Balakrishnan, Hansen and Labro (2011) is used.

[63] Different from Balakrishnan, Hansen and Labro (2011) the decision context by Anand, Balakrishnan and Labro (2013) is on product and not on portfolio level. This becomes relevant especially while calculating $Profit^{NM}$: As illustrated in Table 5, corresponding to the *cost model* (see eq. (7) & (9)), the sum of all costs pooled in the activity cost pools (ACP_k^{total}) initially equal the total costs (TC^{BM}) of the benchmark model. Since the *margin model* assesses product costs on item level, the activity costs need to be brought down to this level as well. Eq. (15) documents this process: The total activity costs (ACP_k^{total}) are divided by the total amount of resources j, i.e. the capacity L_j^{BM} of resources j assigned to activity cost pool k. Therefore, the costs ACP_k^{pl} are applicable on product level, expressed by the superscript *pl*.

[64] The „break condition" has been simplified in this summary. For details refer to the appendix of Anand, Balakrishnan and Labro (2013)

Table 6: ABL simulation process

Input	Process	Output	
1. μ_i – For each product, a random 2. markup is generated. (*2x2 levels*) 3. Q_i – For each product a maximum production quantity is drawn.	Benchmark Model 1) Corresponding to the given quantity and markup, capacity L_j^{BM} and $Profit^{BM}$ are calculated. In each period, the benchmark profit is constant. ⇒ **1,000 samples**	$PF_s^{eff} = \frac{Profit^{NM}}{Profit^{BM}}$ $\overline{PCE_s}$ – $\frac{1}{I}\sum_{i=1}^{I}\frac{\lvert PC_i^{BM} - PC_i^{NM}\rvert}{PC_i^{BM}}$	(17) (18)
4. The environmental parameter and factors equal the *cost model* and are neglected in this synopsis. They are only used to build the simulation, but are not used as independent or control variables. ⇒ **4 environments**	Noisy Model 2) Initial period a) To calculate period one noisy model $Profit^{BM}$, as an initial information the noisy model is calculated based on the benchmark portfolio (λ_i^{BM}) and the benchmark capacity (TC^{BM}). b) Calculate difference between TC^{BM} and TC^{NM}.	*convergence rate* $(CR_s) =$ *percentage of NM, where* $TC^{BM} \sim TC^{NM}$ **S = 32,000**	(19)

Additionally for each simulation run, i.e. the combination of input parameters and cost system designs, the rate and time of convergence of total costs between noisy and benchmark model is measured. Hereby the t periods needed until TC^{NM} equals TC^{BM} are determined. If a given time barrier is hit or a level of accuracy is met, the cost system refinement is aborted (CR_S, eq. (19)).

The simulation consists out of S = 32,000 simulation runs. For each market setting (markup average/variance) 1,000 samples are drawn, resulting in 4,000 BM. In line with the cost model, one set of NM is mapped to exact one BM. In the margin model, this leads to 8 NM samples. Instead of using all heuristics known from the cost model Anand, Balakrishnan and Labro (2013) only focus on heuristics on the second stage. For these they reduce the heuristics variation to the big-pool and NUM(2) methods. The number of cost pools is varied by 4 levels (1, 3, 6 and 10).[65]

2.4.3.2 Results

In general Anand, Balakrishnan and Labro (2013) find that the approximate cost-systems (NM) perform quite well in comparison to the BM: They show that on average a convergence rate (CR_s) of approximately 30% to 55% can be reached and that profit efficiency levels PF_s^{eff} of almost 70% are possible.[66]

Counterintuitive is the outperformance of big-pool method compared with the NUM(2) method in 1-pool scenarios. Raising the number of cost-pools leads to a more intuitive result, that superior cost-system design yields better results.[67] Anand, Balakrishnan and Labro (2013) explain this behavior by aggregation errors offsetting specification errors. This explanation is not based on model behavior, but on the findings by Datar and Gupta (1994). This finding can be challenged by reviewing the model characteristics: Big-

65 See Anand, Balakrishnan and Labro (2013), p. 12 and 14.

66 For the definition of the CR see eq. (19). The range of convergence depends on the accuracy level requested. See Anand, Balakrishnan and Labro (2013), pp. 15–16.

67 See panel A by Anand, Balakrishnan and Labro (2013), p. 26.

pool and NUM(2) are almost equal. Both select allocation rates based on the biggest and on the average of the two biggest resources in the cost-pool respectively. Considering environments where the total spread of total resource costs is low and the resource sharing equals between products, both methods should lead to identical decisions. Both, the spread in total resource costs (RCV) and the density (DENS) only vary by 30 percentage-points.[68] Hence, one would assume that both methods would yield comparable results. A detailed analysis on DENS and RCV is not given by Anand, Balakrishnan and Labro (2013).

The mean product cost error ($\overline{PCE_s}$) is reported to be rather high throughout all scenarios: Intuitively, higher markups lead to lower product cost errors and vice-versa. High variance leads to lower product cost errors. [69] While being reported, this finding is not further explained. In light of the markup variable being constructed out of two parameters (variance and average) it is questionable to separate the effects from each other.

Further the markup, following Anand, Balakrishnan and Labro (2013), matters more than cost system design. This is supported by the ANOVA regression. Here, the markup explains more than 30% of mean profit efficiency $\overline{PF^{eff}}$, whereas the cost system design (ACP + Heuristic2) only amounts for approximately 16%.

---

[68] See Anand, Balakrishnan and Labro (2013), p. 29.

[69] See Anand, Balakrishnan and Labro (2013), p. 17.

3. Price and Product-Mix Decisions Under Different Cost Systems

The following chapter is largely based upon my research work "The Impact of Cost Allocation Errors on Price and Product-Mix Decisions".[70] As discussed in chapter 1, in contrast to decision-theory, many firms base portfolio and pricing decisions on cost systems allocating fixed costs to products instead of seeing fixed costs as sunk. A major argument supporting this approach is based on the underlying time frame of the decision process. In the long-run fixed costs can be seen as marginal.[71] Capacity and pricing problems are complex, even more so when jointly solved. Cost systems are approximations, heuristics or broadly speaking means to simplify that joint decision.[72] This simplification leads to less expensive information costs, with the effect that decisions based on heuristics necessarily contain errors.[73] Whereas this has been widely researched with respect to the influence of errors on cost estimates (e.g. Balakrishnan, Hansen and Labro (2011)), there is a need to broaden the focus on the complete pricing and portfolio context. The gap relies upon a pricing context encompassing different market situations and varying cost system designs. Besides investigating whether approximate cost allocation adequately solves the problem in general, the basic idea is to identify scenarios in which a cost system outperforms other alternative systems and to present directions for managers to choose the right accounting alternative.

In the following paragraphs the research design is introduced abstractly. In addition, each design step is classified corresponding to the introduced research framework in chapter 2.3. The first design step, the formulation of the objective, has already been laid in this paragraph. Classification of variables including the appropriate factorial design (steps two to four) and

---

[70] See Homburg, Nasev and Plank (2013).

[71] For a review see Balakrishnan and Sivaramakrishnan (2002) or Cooper and Kaplan (1988) and the discussion on the understanding of long-term variable costs.

[72] See Banker and Hughes (1994); Balachandran, Balakrishnan and Sivaramakrishnan (1997); Balakrishnan and Sivaramakrishnan (2002).

[73] Datar and Gupta (1994), p. 568.

step six - conducting the simulation - is subject of chapter 3.2., information flow between design and result chapters (step 7), the estimation of the experimental design error (step 5) is captured in the robustness section (3.6), subsequent to the results discussion.

As a performance proxy for a cost system design, the profit resulting from price and product mix decisions based on the erroneous cost allocation of the underlying cost system is used. This profit needs to be benchmarked to identify market situations or system design choices especially profitable or preferable. Profits of two erroneous cost system designs cannot be directly compared, since the relation to an optimal, errorless solution is needed.[74] This optimum is referred to as the *benchmark model* (BM), the manifestation of a given cost system design as the *noisy model* (NM). In this sense, the BM can also be seen as the first best, the noisy model as the second best solution.

As is evident from the previous paragraphs, the BM requirements encompass market parameters and a full cost approach. Additionally, the pricing context should be kept independently of competition, to focus solely on the decision process of an individual firm. The best candidate is Balakrishnan and Sivaramakrishnan (2002), developing a multi-product monopolistic firm setting, jointly solving pricing and capacity decisions based on optimal information.

The NM is characterized as a less complex decision generator. On one hand it has less information to solve the problem, on the other hand its decision process is based on heuristics. The decision of how to model the NM is twofold: First, *Activity based costing* is seen as a full costing approach applying costs more correctly in comparison to other allocation forms.[75] It uses a two stage allocation process to assign costs (1) to activities and (2) subsequently activity costs to products.[76] Second, in line with *cost-* and *margin model* the approach by Balakrishnan, Hansen and Labro (2011)

---

[74] See Schmalenbach (1963), p. 447.

[75] See Cardinaels, Roodhooft and Warlop (2004), p. 143.

[76] See Hartgraves and Morse (2015), p. 200.

enables a comprehensive model to systematically alter allocation processes on both stages. Hence ABC is chosen as the base allocation process and the implemented heuristics are based on Balakrishnan, Hansen and Labro (2011).

Putting aside how the models are constructed in detail and how they are computed, at this stage the underlying assumption includes that there exists an optimal (BM) and an approximate (NM) solution. As pointed out the idea is to benchmark the NM profits in reference to the BM profits. Because both models (BM and NM) operate on completely different assumptions[77] another step is necessary to make the profits comparable. A "transfer" of the NM world into the BM world is achieved by using the NM prices as a basis to solve the capacity problem in the BM environment. As a benefit of this model, one is able to compare the solutions eventually. In other words, the NM is a planning model, computing prices on the basis of limited information. Using the NM prices in the benchmark environment (step 3), the realized profits in the "real" world can be calculated and measured upon the BM profits.

Figure 3: Metrics and research questions

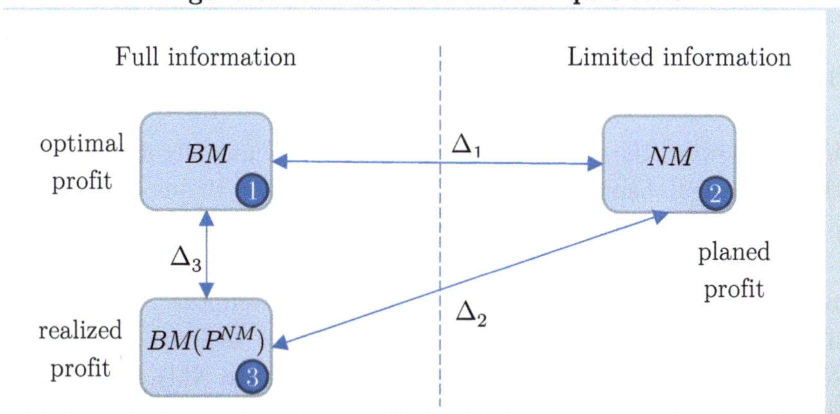

Own depiction.

77 Discussed in detail in chapter 3.1.4.

As depicted in Figure 3, next to the delta (Δ_3) between the optimal solution (1) and the realized profits (3), two other reference points could be chosen. In this thesis Δ_3 has been chosen deliberately, since the difference between BM and NM (Δ_1) yields no information on the NM in terms of "real" performance. Δ_2, the delta between planed and realized profits, on the other hand, gives no indication on the losses towards an optimal solution.

In conclusion, the basic process consists of: (1) computing BM and (2) NM, (3) solving the BM capacity problem under NM prices and finally comparing BM and NM (Δ_3) profits. This process is embedded in a simulation, systematically changing input variables for the BM and the NM. The input variables are classified into production, market and cost system design variables. Whereas production and market variables affect both models, cost system design variables only influence the NM. The systematic variation of production and market parameters forms 8,640 different combinations (BM). Each BM profit is compared to 120 NM profits. This is achieved by altering heuristics on both stages and the number of activities. Therefore a triplet of variables (market, production and cost system design) identifies a unique simulation run. In total, this approach yields 1,036,800 unique combinations.[78]

3.1 Model Details

In the following, the details of the BM and NM are formally illustrated. In the subsequent chapters the simulation approach and the modeling of the production, cost and market variables respectively is described in detail.

Because this chapter focusses on a comprehensive description of the models, it abstracts for a better understanding from the underlying variables. Nevertheless, it is essential that both Models (BM and NM) use the same variable output. At this point, it is further necessary to define the term perfect information against imperfect information in regard to the

---

[78] Due to computational time limits and invalid solutions one obtains less results than optimally possible. This is elabotated in more detail on page 56.

simulation. The BM is based on perfect information (first best) meaning not only that every variable is without bias and deterministic at the point of planning, but also that the core of cost application, the so-called resource consumption matrix, is perfectly known by the modeled company. Hence, resources as well as costs can be traced perfectly to products. In contrast, the NM has limited or *imperfect* information on resource consumption patterns (second best) and hence traces costs imperfectly.

Additionally, for a better understanding of the following chapters it is necessary to come back to the chapter 2.3 distinction of variables and parameters. Parameters govern the simulation of variables by specifying the underlying distributions. Based on these distributions, samples are drawn for each variable using pseudo random number generators.

3.1.1 Model design choices

As mentioned earlier, the idea is to focus on the direct relation of cost system (accuracy) and pricing decision. Hence, competition-based models as the *margin model* by Anand, Balakrishnan and Labro (2013) are out of focus.[79] Next, the BM should also incorporate the capacity decision. Both inevitably lead to the *grand model* by Balakrishnan and Sivaramakrishnan (2002)[80], which differentiates this study from Hwang, Evans and Hegde (1993) and Anand, Balakrishnan and Labro (2013).

In contrast to Hwang, Evans and Hegde (1993) the cost allocation heuristics and the number of activity cost pools differ considerably. Particular attention must be paid to whether or not the number of cost pools matters in terms of profit accuracy as it does for cost allocation accuracy.[81] Anand, Balakrishnan and Labro (2013)'s model is based on a competitive market situation where no real pricing context is given and only different gross margin levels are simulated. Hence, the isolated effect of cost systems affecting pricing decisions is not in the focus. Nevertheless, both articles

[79] See chapter 2.4.3.

[80] See *grand model* in chapter 2.4.1.

[81] Balakrishnan, Hansen and Labro (2011), p. 534.

illustrate what choices are available while designing the simulation and could have great impact on the design.

Turning to the NM the question is which cost system to choose and how to structurally modify it. There exists a larger literature body especially on cost heuristics: Balachandran, Balakrishnan and Sivaramakrishnan (1997) measure the impact of cost allocation heuristics on capacity decisions. Stating that prices are known, they first solve the capacity problem and subsequently the product-mix problem. Homburg (2004) brings a portfolio based cost allocation into play, taking into account the cost interplay between resources. He finds that ABC systems using higher-level cost drivers (on portfolio level) are able to improve the ABC performance[82].

Balakrishnan, Hansen and Labro (2011)'s was identified as the best reference for a cost model for two reasons: First, as indicated, ABC seems to be the most sophisticated cost allocation model. Balakrishnan, Hansen and Labro (2011) base their heuristics on ABC. Second, the introduced heuristics use multiple activity cost pools, which can be used to control for cost system complexity. In comparison to a multiple pool system, a one pool system is regarded as a less complex system. Additionally, they incorporate strategies to alternate between different production environments.

3.1.2 The Benchmark Model

This section is based upon the economic rationale decomposing the joint pricing and capacity planning problem into a set of pricing decisions on individual product level and capacity planning problems for individual resources.[83] The used reference model is a simplification of the *grand model* by Balakrishnan and Sivaramakrishnan (2002).[84]

---

[82] This idea is taken up in chapter 4 illustrating the "Extended Decision Model Incorporating Cost-Stickiness".

[83] See Banker, Hwang and Mishra (2002), p. 79.

[84] See chapter 2.4.1.

To recapitulate, the aim of their study is to evaluate under which conditions the use of full costs is economically sufficient. Following Balakrishnan and Sivaramakrishnan (2002), two factors are crucial to limit the economic loss resulting from full-costing: The ability of the firm to adjust capacities and prices on a need basis.[85] For that purpose they consider different economic models. Starting point of their discussion is a classic product-mix problem, allocating fixed capacity to a portfolio of products for a price-taking firm in a one-period setting. Subsequently the focus is moved on a monopolistic setting, hence a price-demand relation characterizes the market. This price setting model is extended by joint capacity decisions, and finally transformed from a static one-period into a multi-period, multi-product setting optimizing profits under uncertain demand reactions: *grand model.* The model assumes a centralized decision making process based on available future cost and demand information.[86] In the following uncertainties are excluded for the sake of simplification.[87]

In the BM decision context, the firm optimizes prices P_{it}^{BM}, short- and long-term capacities (R_{jt} and L_j) simultaneously for products $i=1,...,I$ and resources $j=1,...,J$ over *a* planning horizon of $t=1,...T$ periods to achieve the highest possible $Profit^{BM}$.[88]

Whereas L_j is available over the T periods, R_{jt} is used to fill short-term capacity needs per period. Long-term capacity commitments are priced at c_j per unit of capacity. Since short-term capacity purchasing is more expensive, ϕ_j models the premium on capacity unit costs.

[85] See Balakrishnan and Sivaramakrishnan (2002), p. 28.

[86] See Banker and Hughes (1994), p. 489 and Gupta and King (1997), p. 102.

[87] See Balakrishnan and Sivaramakrishnan (2002), p. 12. Model 4a is used, which is identical to the grand model, except for uncertainty.

[88] In the following, the superscripts BM and NM identify if a given variable belongs to the BM or NM.

As mentioned the BM operates on full information (first best), meaning that the underlying resource consumption matrix (m_{ij}) traces errorless resource demand of product i to the resource j.

$$\begin{aligned}
\max_{P_{it}^{BM}, R_{jt}, L_j} \quad & \sum_{t=1}^{T} \left(\sum_{i=1}^{I} (P_{it}^{BM} - v_i)(A_{it} - b_i P_{it}^{BM}) - \sum_{j=1}^{J} \phi_j c_j R_{jt} \right) \\
& - T \sum_{j=1}^{J} c_j L_j \\
\text{subject to} \quad & \sum_{i=1}^{I} m_{ij}(A_{it} - b_i P_{it}^{BM}) - R_{jt} - L_j \leq 0 \;\forall j, t \\
& (A_{it} - b_i P_{it}^{BM}) \geq 0 \;\forall i, t \\
& P_{it}^{BM} \geq 0 \;\forall i, t.
\end{aligned} \tag{20}$$

Decision variables:

P_{it}^{BM}	Optimal price for product i in period t of the BM
L_j	Initial long-term capacity for resource j
R_{jt}	Flexible short-term capacity for resource j and period t

Non-decision variables:

A_{it}	Market size per product i and period t
b_i	Price elasticity of product i
v_i	Variable cost of product i
c_j	Resource costs of resource j
ϕ_j	Premium price for one on capacity unit j
m_{ij}	Resource consumption for product i,resource j

Based upon Balakrishnan and Sivaramakrishnan (2002), p. 12.

Beside the non-negative constraint of prices, it is obvious that *installed capacity* ($R_{jt} + L_j$) must at least equal *used capacity* ($\sum_{i=1}^{I} m_{ij}(A_{it} -$

$b_i P_{it}^{BM}$)) per resource and period (see constraint I). Finally, the market size must equal or exceed the number of produced products i (constraint II). In other words, market size limits the possible sales.

3.1.3 The Noisy Model

The NM abstracts in many ways from the powerful planning mechanism from the BM. This is a means for aligning the NM to a more practical situation. First, in practice the usage of joint pricing and capacity planning is almost impossible due to limited information or organizational means.[89] Second, one of the major drawbacks in practice is the lack of knowledge about the true resource consumption. To cope with the lack of information, full cost methods are used as heuristic.

The implemented NM optimizes only P_{it}^{NM}. Capacity decision are not (directly) incorporated in the model. In contrast to the BM, activity based costing is used to allocate cost of resources. The allocation process refers to the *cost model* and its two-stage approach: first, assigning resources to activities and second assigning activities to products.[90]

On each stage, heuristic decisions are used for the allocation process. From this point onwards these are referred to as first-stage and second-stage heuristics. The research idea is to investigate the performance of these heuristics under different model regimes. Whereas in the BM the resource allocation is based on perfect consumption information (m_{ij}), the approach by Balakrishnan, Hansen and Labro (2011) enables an approximate allocation of costs to products (via first- and second-stage heuristics) under imperfect information. The outcome of the cost allocation process is the activity costs (ABC_i) per product.

89 See Balakrishnan and Sivaramakrishnan (2001), p. 1; Deng and Yano (2006), p. 753.

90 See chapter 2.4.2 for details.

Table 7: The noisy model

$$\max_{P_{it}^{NM}} \sum_{t=1}^{T} \sum_{i=1}^{I} (P_{it}^{NM} - v_i - ABC_i)(A_{it} - b_i P_{it}^{NM}) \tag{21}$$

$$subject\ to \quad (A_{it} - b_i P_{it}^{NM}) \geq 0 \ \ \forall i, t$$

$$P_{it}^{NM} \geq 0 \ \ \forall i, t.$$

To investigate the influence of cost allocation under limited information, only part of the resource consumption information in m_{ij} is used to allocate resource costs to products. Two linear transformations are used to first map resource costs to activity cost pools and secondly activity costs to products, the first is based on (c_j) the second based on (m_{ij}).[91] In the following the heuristics are only described methodological, without repeating the detailed discussion of fist-stage and second-stage heuristics from chapters 2.4.2.1 and 2.4.2.2.

3.1.3.1 First-stage heuristics

In general the first transformation $c_j \xrightarrow{Heuristic\ 1} ACP_k$ uses fist-stage heuristics to assign resource costs to activity cost pools. The heuristics on the first stage choose resource drivers (rd_{jk}) that allocate resource costs c_j to $k=1,...,K$ activity cost pools. Resource drivers are rules that assign resource costs to activity cost pools, e.g., the random method randomly assigns resource costs to activity cost pools, alternatively the correlation method groups resources with similar consumption patterns into one cost pool. Hence, instead of detailed resource cost information (c_j), the NM has aggregated information about the costs of activity cost pools (ACP_k). An example for assigning costs to activity pools could be assigning all marketing

---

[91] Various prior studies use cost allocation heuristics, e.g. Hwang, Evans and Hegde (1993); Balachandran, Balakrishnan and Sivaramakrishnan (1997); Homburg (2001a), (2004); Balakrishnan, Hansen and Labro (2011). The advantage of the approach suggested by Balakrishnan, Hansen and Labro (2011) is that it covers simple as well as complex cost systems that are relatively easy to implement in simulations.

costs to a marketing activity cost pool together with other overhead costs related to marketing activities.

3.1.3.2 Second-stage heuristics

In general the second transformation $m_{ij} \xrightarrow{Heuristics\ 2} ad_{ki}$ is based on heuristics that use some of the information in (m_{ij}) to determine activity drivers (ad_{ki}) that are used to assign activity costs to products. In detail, activity drivers are rules that assign activity costs to products, e.g., the big pool method uses the resource consumption of the largest resource (in terms of per unit resource costs c_j) to assign the activity costs to products. Hence, instead of full information about (m_{ij}), the NM has information about the activity drivers (ad_{ki}), i.e., aggregated consumption across resources, which is just a subset of the resource consumption matrix (m_{ij}). Keeping to the marketing activity example, the chosen activity driver could be the overhead rate of the marketing costs, subsequently used for all other overhead costs in the pool.

Taken together, both the aggregation of resources in activity cost pools (ACP_k) (the first transformation) and the aggregation of consumption across resources reflected in the activity drivers (ad_{ki}) (the second transformation), bias the allocation of resource costs to products in the NM.

3.1.4 Alternatives of modeling capacity in the NM

One of the main differences between BM and NM is the capacity decision. At the time of planning, the NM considers no pre-installed capacity. By solving the NM, a pseudo capacity is built: $L^{NM} = \sum_{i=1}^{I} \sum_{k=1}^{K} (ad_{ki})(A_i - b_i P_i^{NM})$. The sum $\sum_{k=1}^{K} (ad_{ki})$ illustrates the activity consumption of product i over k activities. The total resources L^{NM} needed to meet a demand of $(A_i - b_i P_i^{NM})$ results from multiplying demand with the activity consumption.

Obviously installed capacity of BM and NM differ $(L^{NM} \neq L^{BM})$. Therefore the profits of BM and NM are not comparable. Two modeling alternatives arise to achieve comparable profits: First, constraining the NM cost of capacity ($ACP_kL_k{}^{NM}$) to be equal to BM cost of capacity ($c_jL_j{}^{BM}$), second, keeping the model as defined but using the NM pricing decision as a basis for comparison. Therefore the NM prices are used in the BM to obtain the NM capacity (under BM conditions). This yields a NM profit that is comparable to the BM profit.

Both alternatives have pros and cons. A conditional approach would imply that the NM relies on optimal information about the costs of capacity ($c_jL_j{}^{BM}$). The other alternative introduces another „model", hence adding complexity. Since the basic idea is to let the NM decide, as independently as possible from the BM, the second option is implemented.

3.2 The Simulation Approach

To this point the focus was on the formal part of both models (BM and NM). This section clarifies how the models are embedded in the simulation, meaning how variables become alive by building up different market & production environments and cost system designs.[92] In line with the introduced research framework by Lorscheid, Heine and Meyer (2012) the classification of variables and their factorial design (stages two to four) are subject of this chapter.

3.2.1 Market & production parameters

The first set of independent variables are the market & production variables, steered via their corresponding sets of parameters, as defined in the following. While the market & production conditions have an impact on the performance of the benchmark model and respectively on the noisy models, the choice of cost system design only affects the NM performance.

Following a monopolistic setting, price elasticity (b_i) and market growth are the key parameters affecting demand. Price elasticity was chosen to be a

---

[92] The variations are comparable to Hwang, Evans and Hegde (1993); Balachandran, Balakrishnan and Sivaramakrishnan (1997); Balakrishnan, Hansen and Labro (2011); Anand, Balakrishnan and Labro (2013).

constant factor (-1.3), hence not being systematically altered, to keep the simulation framework as simple as possible.[93] For robustness reasons, different price elasticity levels are discussed in section 3.6. The market variable A_{it}, explicitly the market size in period one ($t = 1$), is modeled as a uniform distribution with bounds [5500, 5600]. Based on this "initial" demand, the subsequent periods follow different auto-regressive processes (AR(1), $\varepsilon_t \sim N(0,1)$):

$$\text{Decreasing Market } (-) \qquad A_{it} = 0.9A_{it-1} + 200\varepsilon_t \tag{22}$$

$$\text{Saturated Market } (\circ) \qquad A_{it} = A_{it-1} + 200\varepsilon_t \tag{23}$$

$$\text{Increasing Market } (+) \qquad A_{it} = 500 + A_{it-1} + 200\varepsilon_t \tag{24}$$

$$A_{it} < 0 \text{ are set to } 0$$

A saturated market has 0%, a decreasing market grossly -9% and an increasing market 8% of mean period growth rate.[94]

To determine the **cost structure** of the production environment, the following parameters are used: the density of the resource consumption matrix, the size and variance of variable costs and the size and variance of resource costs.[95]

[93] A price elasticity of (-1.3) implies that a 1% increase in price reduces demand by 1.3%. Price elasticities smaller (larger) than (-1) indicate elastic (inelastic) demand, i.e., changes in price have a large (small) effect on demand. The elasticity of (-1.3) is comparable to price elasticities in the automotive industry in particular in the Economy and Small segments (Bordley (1993), p. 460). Note that in eq. (20), the absolute value of (-1.3) is used following the model specification of Balakrishnan and Sivaramakrishnan (2002).

[94] In its (2013) World Economic Outlook the IMF reports GDP growth rates for the advanced economies between -2% and 4%, for Developing Asia between 3% and 11% and for Latin America between 0% and 8% over the period 2010 and 2014 (forecast).

[95] The base algorithm to generate the individual variable outcomes described in the following paragraphs is built upon Balakrishnan, Hansen and Labro (2011). Please also see the variable definitions on page 31 and Table 4.

According to Balakrishnan, Hansen and Labro (2011) the resource consumption matrix can either be sparse or full. Economically this separates firms into groups where either few or many resources are shared between products. In other words, the resource consumptions of all products equal or are diverse. To model this, the parameter *resource sharing* can be varied between four states: From very few resource sharing (−), over zero (∘) to a maximum of sharing (+ +). (−,∘, +, ++).

Two parameters steer size and variance of resource costs. Resource costs amount between either 40000 or 60000 units (−,+). Three levels (−, ∘, +) determine the variance of resource costs, reflecting situations of homogeneous (−) or heterogeneous (+) costs, i.e. some very expensive resources against many inexpensive ones. The size (−,+) and variance of variable (−,+) costs are equally simulated, whereas the levels are different.

To complete the picture of environmental parameters throughout the simulation, fixed settings of 20 products, 20 resources and 5 periods are used. The penalty costs for short term resources amount to $\phi = 1.2$. Meaning that for additional short-term resources, a premium of 20% needs to be payed.[96]

3.2.2 Cost system design & parameters

This chapter concentrates on the different cost system designs and the origination of errors within cost system designs. A crucial effect on the accuracy of cost systems is attributed to errors in aggregation, specification and measurement.[97] Aggregation errors can arise when heterogeneous resource costs are pooled and allocated to products via a single cost driver. This cost driver is unable to reflect the different resource consumption patterns. Specification error arises from incorrect cost identification

[96] Note that Balakrishnan, Hansen and Labro (2011) use 50 products and 50 resources in their simulation. Since a higher number of combinations is simulated, e.g., because market parameters are added, in the main specification 20 products and 20 resources are used to keep the number of models (8,640 BMs and 1,036,800 NMs) computationally feasible. For a detailed annotation of variables please refer to Appendix (B: Variable and Parameter declaration).

[97] Datar and Gupta (1994) introduce these effects.

methods, where allocated costs and the true resource consumption differ extensively. An example could be the usage of a volume driver for setup costs, where setup costs do not rise with an increase in volume. Measurement errors refer to errors in measuring resource or activity consumption, e.g., set up costs involve estimates of the time spent on set up activities which are typically estimated with questionnaires or interviews that are prone to measurement error.[98]

Aggregation & Specification errors are inherited in the used heuristics – also explained in chapter 2.4.2. The measurement error is modeled in line with Labro and Vanhoucke (2007) and Balakrishnan, Hansen and Labro (2011). The errors are applied to cost driver rates used in the different NMs. They are systematically varied by levels of 10% (−), 30% (∘) and 50% (+). As an example, assume that the true resource consumption of product i of resource j is 20%. If the systematic error parameter is set to low (−), a uniformly distributed error between ±10 %, with a mean of zero is added to the 20%.

The cost system design choices are mainly based on Balakrishnan, Hansen and Labro (2011). Because the central model body (the resource consumption matrix) implies a volume-based resource planning and application, heuristics aiming at the correct cost allocation of batch resources are neglected.[99] The two stage cost allocation process has been discussed in the previous chapters. In sum, five heuristics (random, size random, size misc, correlation random, correlation size) are used in the first stage, four (big pool, num 2, num 4, average) heuristics are implemented in the second stage. This leads to a total of 20 possible combinations. As discussed, activity cost pools connect heuristics one and two – first assigning resource costs to activity cost pools and later charge those pooled costs to products. Hence another system parameter is the amount of ACP's used. Balakrishnan, Hansen and Labro (2011)'s analysis reveals only small

[98] Datar and Gupta (1994), p. 568.

[99] Batch resources were also neglected to reduce model complexity. In the robustness section (3.6) batch resources are nevertheless included to see whether results are stable.

increases in accuracy by using more than six cost pools. This leads to a total of 120 different cost system design choices.

3.2.3 Information & simulation flow and data

The following depiction (Figure 4) summarizes the previous chapter. It also classifies the variables, input encompassing the independent variables, output generating the dependent variable. The variables used on the process stage while simulating the NM are also input variables and therefore classified as independent. It is important to stress again, that no information from the BM is used in the NM. The combination of market and production parameters yields 864 BMs = 3 levels of market growth * 4 levels of resource sharing * 2 levels of total resource costs * 3 levels of resource costs variance * 2 levels of total variable costs * 2 levels of variable costs variance * 3 levels of measurement error.

As can be seen in the Simulation and Optimization Box, there are 10 model variations / samples for each of these parameters from each of the 864 BMs, totaling 8,640 BM observations. For each of the BMs, the combination of two-stage heuristics and the number of activity cost pools yields 120 NMs = 5 first-stage heuristics * 4 second-stage heuristics * 6 different numbers of activity pools, totaling 120 NM observations * 8,640 BM observations = 1,036,800 observations. While solving the quadratic optimization of eq. (20), it can happen that either no optimum is found or the optimization timed out, resulting in 896,909 observations (87% of the 1,036,800 possible observations).

The simulation is coded in the programming language C++ using the NAG C library. One of the total 8,640 simulation runs (incorporating the NM processing time) can last up to 10 minute, yielding a total simulation time, on a one core / non-parallel processing architecture, of approximately 60 days. Since this would be hardly feasible, the simulation is run on CHEOPS, the cologne high performance computer cluster. Using CHEOPS and a distributed calculation approach, the processing time is brought down to approx. 2h. A completed simulation creates 32 gigabytes of data. The data has been analyzed using the statistical program R.[100]

Figure 4: Information and simulation flow

$$\Delta Profit_s = Profit_s^{BM} - Profit_s^{NM} \quad s \in S \text{ (simulation runs)} \tag{25}$$

	Input	Process	Output
Simulation	1. Variable costs variance (VCV, *2 level*) 2. Variable costs (*2 level*) 3. Resource cost variance (*RCV, 3 level*) 4. Resource costs (*2 level*) 5. Measurement error (*3 level*) 6. Market growth (*3 level*) 7. Resource sharing (*4 level*) $\Rightarrow level^{factor}$ $= 2^3 3^3 4^1$ = 864 combinations	1. Optimize profit benchmark model, see eq. (20). ⇒ 10 samples 2. For each BM calculate profit noisy model see eq. (21) for a combination of a. Heuristics 1 (5 level) b. Heuristics 2 (4 level) c. *ACP* (6 level) $\Rightarrow level^{factor}$ $= 5^1 4^1 6^1$ = 120 combinations	⇒ $\Delta Profit_s$ $S =$ BM*NM = 864*10*120 = 1,036,800
Example run (*s=1*)	1. Low variable costs variance (–) 2. Low variable costs (–) 3. High resource cost variance (+) 4. High resource costs (+) 5. Medium measurement error (○) 6. Saturated market (○) 7. Very high resource sharing (+ +)	1. Optimize $Profit_1^{BM}$ 2. Optimize $Profit_1^{NM}$ for a. Random (– –) b. Big Pool (–) c. *2 ACP**	⇒ $\Delta Profit_1$

Own depiction, * The coding of the variables is in line with chapter 2.4.2.3.

[100] For a detailed description of CHEOPS see RRZK (2014). The NAG library version used is Mark 24, see NAG (2015)

3.2.4 Simulation Example

The following example aims to clarify the information structure and flow, by explaining the simulation for a setting of one-period ($T=1$), three resources ($J=1$) and two products ($I=2$). To simplify readability, the number of digits is reduced and parameters modified as follows: A_i~ U(2000,2100), $\sum v_i$=100 and $\sum c_j$=100.

3.2.4.1 Stage one: BM joint price and capacity decision

For the given setting, Table 8 additionally outlines the randomly generated inputs and the optimized output variables.

Table 8: Example of simulation input & output for the BM

Input									Output		
A	v	c	m				b	ϕ	P^{BM}	L^{BM}	R^{BM}[101]
i_1 2039	i_1 55.6	j_1 25.2		j_1	j_2	j_3	1.3	1.2	i_1 *841.9*	j_1 *979.0*	j_1 *0*
i_2 2068	i_2 44.4	j_2 40.3	i_1	0	0.63	1			i_2 *837.7*	j_2 *957.2*	j_2 *0*
		j_3 34.5	i_2	1	0.37	0				j_3 *944.5*	j_3 *0*

Since a one-period setting is used, short-term adjustments are not needed and allocating resources only into long-term capacity (L^{BM}) is optimal.

Adjusting eq. (20) of the BM for one period, two products and three resources (see Table 9) and using Table 8 as input, a profit for the BM of $\mathbf{1,423,523.13}$ is calculated. Having calculated the BM, the NM profit needs to be computed.

[101] As profits are maximized for one period only all resource capacities are reflected in L and not R.

Table 9: Profit calculation

$\underset{P_{it}^{BM}, R_{jt}, L_j}{max}$	$\sum_{i=1}^{2} (P_i^{BM} - v_i) * (A_i - b_i P_i^{BM})$	$-\sum_{j=1}^{3} \phi_j c_j R_j$	$-\sum_{j=1}^{3} c_j L_j$
$Profit^{BM}=$	(841.9 – 55.6) * (2039 – 1.3 * 841.9) + (837.7 – 44" " .4) * (2068 – 1.3 * 837.7)	$-\begin{pmatrix} 0 \\ +0 \\ +0 \end{pmatrix}$	–(25.2 * 979 +40.3 * 957.2 +34.5 * 944.5)

$$= \mathbf{1,423,523.13}$$

3.2.4.2 Stage two: NM price decision

Regarding the underlying cost system for this example, a two-activity cost pool system is assumed and the random method as a first-stage heuristic and the big pool method as a second-stage heuristic is used. In the first stage, the random method randomly allocates the costs of resource j to a cost pool k. Here, resources j_1 and j_3 are allocated to cost pool k_1 and resource j_2 is allocated to cost pool k_2. In the second stage, the big pool method allocates the activity costs of an activity cost pool using the resource consumption pattern (m) of the most expensive resource in the pool. The most expensive resource in cost pool k_1 is j_3 and in cost pool k_2 it is resource j_2.

Hence, the costs of pool k_1 (59.7, see gray, dotted lines in Figure 5) are assigned to products i_1 and i_2 based on the consumption coefficients of resource j_3 ($m_{13} = 1$ and $m_{23} = 0$) and the costs of pool k_2 (40.3 see blue, solid lines in Figure 5) are assigned to products i_1 and i_2 based on the consumption coefficients of resource j_2 ($m_{13} = 0.63$ and $m_{23} = 0.37$, see Table 8 for the corresponding resource consumption matrix values). Since the interest lies on the pricing decision of the NM in the second stage, here just the optimal prices $P_1 = 856.45$ and $P_2 = 823.16$ are reported.

Figure 5: Example, two stage allocation process

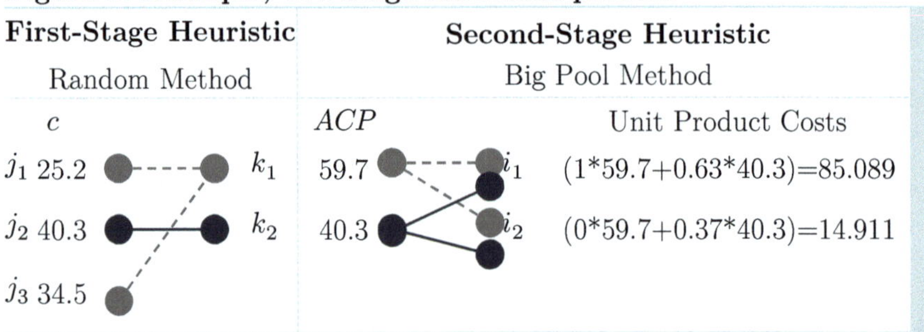

Own depiction.

3.2.4.3 Stage three: NM capacity decision

To obtain the capacity of the NM (L and R), the NM prices from stage two are inserted in the BM (the corresponding input/output is illustrated in Table 10) to obtain $Profit^{NM}$. Subsequently the profit gap between NM and BM is calculated.

Table 10: Example of simulation input & output for the NM

Input						Output		
A	v	c	m	b	ϕ	P^{NM}	L	R
i_1 2039	i_1 55.6	j_1 25.2	j_1 j_2 j_3	1.3	1.2	i_1 856.45	j_1 998	j_1 0
i_2 2068	i_2 44.4	j_2 40.3	i_1 0 0.63 1			i_2 823.16	j_2 952.33	j_2 0
		j_3 34.5	i_2 1 0.37 0				j_3 925.61	j_3 0

$$Profit^{NM} = (856.45 - 55.6) * (2039 - 1.3 * 856.45) + (823.16 - 44.4) * (2068 - 1.3 * 823.16) - (25.2 * 998 + 40.3 * 952.33 + 34.5 * 925.61) = \mathbf{1,422,935.1}$$

$$\Delta Profit = Profit^{BM} - Profit^{NM} = 1{,}423{,}523.13 - 1{,}422{,}935.1 = \mathbf{588.03}.$$

Hence, the usage of a simple allocation method leads to a total profit error of just 588 units, a small gap in comparison to a 1.4 million profit. This example abstracted from many assumptions and from model details to enable a better access to the mechanics of the simulation. In the result section (see page 69ff.), using more complex environmental settings, i.e. increasing the number of products and periods, the influence of cost system design decisions on profit errors is substantially more pronounced.

3.3 Hypotheses Development

Thus far the focus was placed on the model and the simulation, while the core questions underlying the simulation have mainly been discussed in the introduction. In this section, the focus lies on the differentiation of the research question and the development of three hypotheses. The first hypothesis (H1) relates to the question of which cost systems minimize profit errors. A first definition of the profit error is $\Delta Profit = Profit^{BM} - Profit^{NM}$ (see eq. (25)), being the difference between the BM profit and the cost system's profit (NM profit). Reflecting prior research (Hwang, Evans and Hegde (1993); Anand, Balakrishnan and Labro (2013)), the hypothesis is defined as follows:

(H1) *More complex cost systems are associated with lower profit errors.*

The second hypothesis (H2) is related to the question of when, i.e., under which market conditions cost systems minimize profit errors. The aim is to test whether market growth influences the effect that more complex cost systems reduce profit errors. Market growth may strengthen or weaken the effect depending on which profit error type dominates. To explain this, notice that two profit error types may occur: production quantity errors (PQE) and product portfolio errors (consisting of drop error (DE) and keep error (KE)). While the errors are introduced in detail later on, production quantity and portfolio errors are separated. For now, PQE is the error resulting from identical portfolio decisions (i.e. identical products) between BM and NM, but with different pricing decisions. The portfolio error, i.e. BM and NM produce different products, originates from false keep and drop decisions. A "false keep" describes the situation that the BM drops a product, but the NM **keeps** the product in the portfolio. The DE can be seen vice versa.

On one hand, market growth should strengthen the effect that more complex cost systems reduce profit errors if production quantity errors dominate. The intuition is that growing markets are characterized by larger production quantities and that product cost errors accumulate as production quantity increases. Hence, more complex cost systems should reduce profit errors related to production quantity errors as markets grow. On the other hand, market growth should weaken the effect that more complex cost systems reduce profit errors if product portfolio errors dominate. According to the model mechanics, when markets grow, i.e., demand increases, profit margins rise because the monopolistic firm can require higher prices while full costs at the product level remain constant. As profit margins and profits increase, profit errors related to keeping unprofitable products or dropping profitable products due to cost allocation distortions should decrease. Consequently, more complex cost allocation heuristics should matter less for product portfolio errors when markets grow. In short, market growth will strengthen the effect that more complex cost systems reduce profit errors if the production quantity error dominates the product portfolio errors and vice versa. The prediction therefore is:

(H2)	*The effect that more complex cost systems are associated with lower profit errors is strengthened by market growth if the production quantity error (PQE) dominates the product portfolio errors (keep error (KE) and drop error (DE)).*[102]
(H2a)	*In growing markets more complex cost systems should reduce production quantity errors (PQE) more than in shrinking markets.*

[102] (H2) refers to second-stage heuristics only because Balakrishnan, Hansen and Labro (2011) document that first-stage heuristics have considerably less impact on cost allocation errors than second-stage heuristics.

(H2b) *In shrinking markets more complex cost systems should reduce product portfolio errors (keep error (KE) and drop error (DE)) more than in growing markets.*

The third hypothesis (H3) focuses on why some cost systems yield lower total profit errors than others. It can be conjectured that if more complex cost systems improve cost allocation, they should lead to lower production quantity errors (PQE) and lower product portfolio errors, i.e., lower keep and drop errors (KE and DE):

(H3) *More complex cost systems are associated with lower production quantity errors (PQE), lower keep errors (KE) and lower drop errors (DE).*

3.4 Key metrics and analysis method

The first goal of this section is to explain which key metrics are used and how they are derived – respectively how they are calculated. Building on that section I illustrate with which methods the research question is evaluated.

Since, as discussed in the hypothesis section, it is necessary to decompose the profit error into different explanatory parts, the focus lies first on the four profit error types, followed by a section on the used regression analysis. Which builds on the simulation section as well as on the different profit error types.

3.4.1 Derivation of Profit Error Types

The delta between BM and NM profits - the total profit error ($\Delta Profit = Profit^{BM} - Profit^{NM}$) – can also be seen as the sum of 4 errors: (1) the production quantity error, (2) the drop error, (3) the keep error, and (4) the capacity error (CE): $\Delta Profit = \Delta Profit_{PQE} + \Delta Profit_{DE} + \Delta Profit_{KE} + \Delta Profit_{CE}$.

It is possible to rewrite eq. (20) (see p. 48) of the BM to illustrate full unit costs and idle capacity. Variable and resource costs $(v_i + \sum_{j=1}^{J} m_{ij}c_j)$ sum up to full product unit costs FC_i. Idle capacity[103] is defined as the gap between resources supplied (RS) and resources used (RU). In the BM, resources supplied equal the sum of long term and short term capacity commitments across all resources $(\sum_{t=1}^{T}\sum_{j=1}^{J}(L_j + R_{jt}))$. In contrast, the resources consumed by the production process are defined as the resources used: $RU_{jt} = \sum_{i=1}^{I} m_{ij}q_{it} \quad \forall j,t,$ and $q_{it} = (A_{it} - b_i P_{it}^{BM})$ being the produced quantity. Therefore, eq. (20) can be restated as follows:[104]

$$\max_{P_{it}^{BM},R_{jt},L_j} \sum_{t=1}^{T}\sum_{i=1}^{I}\left(\begin{array}{l}(P_{it}^{BM} - FC_i)(A_{it} - b_i P_{it}^{BM}) - \\ \sum_{j=1}^{J} c_j[\,(\phi-1)R_{jt} + (L_j + R_{jt} - RU_{jt})]\end{array}\right)\begin{array}{l}Profit_{product}^{BM} \\ Profit_{capacity}^{BM}\end{array} \tag{26}$$

In eq. (26), one can differentiate between a product related part and a capacity related part. It is vital for understanding to remember that in order to gain comparable profits, the NM prices are used in the BM environment. Since both profit functions ((20) & (26)) are equal, it is also possible to apply NM prices in eq. (26). Hence, it is also possible to restate the total profit error ($\Delta Profit$) in the context of eq. (26). This results in a delta profit for product related decisions ($\Delta Profit_{product}$) as well as for capacity related decisions ($\Delta Profit_{capacity}$). Coming back to the idea to decompose the profit error even further, by restating the $\Delta Profit_{capacity}$ as the capacity error (CE) one has already assembled one of the four error types. The next step is to further separate the $\Delta Profit_{product}$ into $\Delta Profit_{PQE} + \Delta Profit_{DE} + \Delta Profit_{KE}$, representing errors resulting from different production quantity and product portfolio decisions.[105]

---

[103] Idle costs occur for example if productive workers will be unoccupied. See Datar et al. (2015), p. 46.

[104] A detailed derivation of the given equation can be found in the Appendix A.

[105] From here on the abbreviations PQE, DE & KE are used instead of the long form, e.g. $\Delta Profit_{PQE}$.

Usually quantity differences result from different portfolio decision between BM and NM. In terms of cause & effect, portfolio errors are the cause and quantity errors represent the effect. In a price setting environment one can argue that for identical portfolios, differences in pricing decisions lead inevitably to quantity differences, i.e. errors. It is therefore crucial to isolate quantity errors from portfolio errors. The three boxes in Figure 6 illustrate (left) the benchmark profitability evaluation of a given set of products, the noisy model profitability evaluation (middle) and the joint view (right). In the BM bucket a product is profitable (grey) or unprofitable (white). Correspondingly, the portfolio illustrated in the NM bucket separates a profitable product (doted bars) and an unprofitable product (solid bars). Overlaying both boxes (NM over BM), the different error types are identifiable (right box). The grey area with dotted bars indicates products the NM correctly identified, but possibly assessed a wrong quantity, for its portfolio.

Figure 6: Production Quantity, Drop and Keep Error

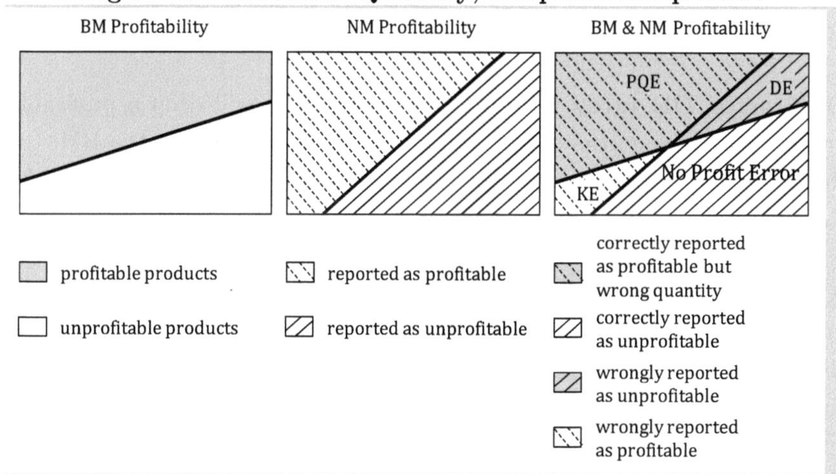

Own depiction.

The area with white and solid bars indicates a correct portfolio exclusion of products (BM and NM decision are equal). The true portfolio errors lie within the grey and solid bars area (falsely dropped products) and the white and dotted bars section (falsely kept products).

To conclude the BM and NM portfolio differences, respectively the profit errors, can be explained by three questions which are answered differently by both models:

1. Is a product profitable in the BM? In the monopolistic setting a product is profitable in the BM if its profit margin is positive, i.e., the prohibitive product price (A_{it}/b_i) exceeds its full unit product costs (FC_i). Hence, a product is profitable in the BM if the profit margin is positive $a_{it}/b_i > FC_i^{BM}$.

2. Does the NM overestimate full costs of a product? The full cost difference between BM and NM can be defined as $\Delta FC_i = FC_i^{NM} - FC_i^{BM}$. Hence, the NM overestimates full costs if the difference in full costs between NM and BM is positive $\Delta FC_i > 0$.

3. Is the product profitable in the NM? The product is profitable in the NM if the full cost difference between NM and BM is smaller than the profit margin $\Delta FC_i < |A_{it}/b_i - FC_i^{BM}|$.

Drop error DE (grey & solid lines): The NM will drop a profitable product from the portfolio if: (1) the product is profitable in the BM, (2) the NM overestimates the cost of the product in such a way that (3) the NM evaluates the product as unprofitable.

Keep error KE (white & dotted lines): The NM will falsely keep an unprofitable product in the portfolio if: (1) the product is unprofitable in the BM, (2) the NM underestimates the costs of the product in such a way that (3) the NM evaluates the product as profitable.

Production quantity error PQE (grey & dotted lines): If the NM keeps a profitable product in its portfolio, its production quantity may deviate upwards or downwards compared to the BM. The NM will produce less (more) units of a product compared to the BM if (1) the product is profitable in the BM, (2) the NM overestimates (underestimates) the costs of the profitable product but not to an extent that it decides to drop the product, i.e. (3) the NM evaluates the product as profitable. Hence, it keeps the product in the portfolio but due to its higher (less) costs it evaluates it as less (more) profitable compared to the BM so that the quantity it produces is less (more) compared to the BM.

No profit error (white & solid lines): No profit error between BM and NM arises only if both models evaluate a product as unprofitable and hence do not include it in the portfolio. The NM will drop an unprofitable product if (1) the product is unprofitable in the BM, (2) the NM overestimates (underestimates) the costs of the unprofitable product but not to an extent that it decides to keep the product and hence (3) the NM evaluates the product as unprofitable.

The **capacity error (CE)** is not illustrated in Figure 6. It arises because the production quantity error (PQE) and the product portfolio errors (DE and KE) lead to differences in capacity requirements between BM and NM as well as to differences in how BM and NM trade off short and long term capacity.

3.4.2 Regression Specification

Up to now the focus lied on a deeper understanding of the used metrics and the simulation. This section discusses how the metrics and simulated data will be used to assess the developed hypotheses. To address the first question about which cost systems minimize profit errors (H1), the following OLS regression is estimated:[106] As discussed the profit error is the difference between BM and NM profits ($\Delta Profit = Profit^{BM} - Profit^{NM}$). The three factors combined to characterize different cost systems are: ACP (the number of activity cost pools ranging from one to six), Heuristics1 (five different first-stage heuristics) and Heuristics2 (four different second-stage heuristics). The other variables are market and production environment parameters. Respectively, the coefficients of the variables ACP, Heuristics1

[106] For a description of the OLS method refer to Moosmüller (2008), p. 92.

and Heuristics2 show the effect of different cost systems on the profit error after controlling for market and production parameters.

$$\begin{aligned}\Delta Profit_i = \alpha + &\beta_1 ACP_i + \beta_2 Heuristics1_i + \beta_3 Heuristics2_i \\ &+\beta_4 Market\ growth_i + \beta_5 Market\ growth_i * Heuristics2_i \\ &+\beta_6 Resource\ sharing_i \\ &+\beta_7 Resource\ cost\ variance_i + \beta_8 Total\ resource\ cost_i \\ &+\beta_9 Total\ variable\ cost_i + \beta_{10} Variable\ cost\ variance_i \\ &+\beta_{11} Measurment\ error_i + \varepsilon_i\end{aligned} \tag{27}$$

Two specifications of eq. (27) are estimated: In the **first** regression specification, a coefficient per categorical variable (Table 13) is obtained. In the **second** regression specification, one coefficient for each category per variable (Table 14) is obtained to assess the monotonicity of these results. As all variables are categorical, each category is coded as a dummy. To avoid the dummy trap, the lowest category is always chosen as the reference category dummy that is omitted.[107] For example, the lowest ACP category is one activity cost pool. To omit the dummy for one ACP, only five dummies for two to six ACPs are included. The effect of the omitted reference category dummy is captured by the intercept. The coefficients of the included ACP dummies reflect the effect compared to the reference category dummy. Therefore, the beta of the dummy that is one for five activity cost pools and zero otherwise shows the profit error change of switching from one to five activity cost pools.

In addition, to estimate the two versions of eq. (27) with profit error as the dependent variable, the equation is assessed with the BM profit and with the NMs profits individually as dependent variables. Hereby, one is able to

[107] See Tutz (2011), p. 16.

assess whether cost systems affect profit errors via the BM profit, NM profit or both.

The regression results related to market growth from estimating eq. (27) are used to address the second question about when, i.e., under which market conditions cost systems minimize profit errors (H2).

Finally, to address the third question about why some cost systems produce lower profit errors (H3), the impact of cost systems on four profit error types are estimated by replacing the dependent variable $\Delta Profit$ in eq. (27) with the different profit error components: the production quantity error (PQE), the "drop error" (DE), the "keep error" (KE) and the capacity error (CE).

3.5 Results

3.5.1 Descriptive Results

Table 11 shows distributions of the BM and NM profits and the profit error (the difference between BM and NM profit). While all 8,640 BMs[108] are profitable with profits ranging from 5.9 million to almost 400 million with a median of about 107 million, about 14% of the 896,909 NMs are unprofitable with a median of about 60 million. The resulting profit error lies between about 400 thousand and 500 million with a median of approx. 23 million.

Table 11: Profit and Cost Errors Distributions

	Min.	1. Quant.	Median	Mean	3. Quant.	Max.
Profit BM	5,910 k	54,400 k	107,000 k	119,000 k	157,000 k	393,000 k
Profit NM	-293,000 k	21,400 k	59,200 k	80,000 k	129,000 k	381,000 k
Profit Error	433 k	12,000 k	22,500 k	39,200 k	48,300 k	496,000 k
EUCD*	156	1,950	3,580	5,510	7,040	58,300

* Observations: 896,909, in thousands (k).

[108] For the derivation of the number of BM see p. 56.

Table 12 describes product portfolio decisions by heuristics (big pool vs. average method). On average, the BM produces 87.2% of the 20 possible products. While the NM produces fewer products than the BM under the simple big pool method (78.58%), it produces more products under the more complex average method (84.05%). Consistent with this observation, the false drops for the big pool method (11.82%) are more than the false keeps (4.27%). Respectively false drops for the average method (3.99%) are less than the false keeps (1.77%). The last column of the panel shows that the overlap between the BM and NM product portfolio is higher for the average method than the big pool method (90% vs. 80%). These descriptive statistics indicate that the average method outperforms the big pool method in terms of product portfolio decisions.

Table 12: Portfolio Decisions in BM and NM by Heuristics

Heuristic	Units	Average Portfolio BM	Average Portfolio NM	False Drops	False Keeps	Equal Portfolio
BigPool	Ratio	0.872	0.7858	0.1182	0.0427	0.7969
INT1	Ratio	0.872	0.8002	0.0927	0.0329	0.8321
INT2	Ratio	0.872	0.8176	0.0670	0.0242	0.8671
AVG	Ratio	0.872	0.8405	0.0399	0.0177	0.9016

3.5.2 Cost-System Complexity (H1)

To examine the first hypotheses (H1), that more complex cost systems have lower profit errors, the mean profit errors across different cost systems and an OLS regression are presented. The advantage of the regression is that it allows controlling for the impact of market and production parameters on the profit error.

3.5.2.1 Mean Profit Errors across Different Cost Systems

Figure 7 illustrates profit errors. The focus is on the second-stage heuristics because the impact of first-stage heuristics is negligible. The figure shows the mean profit error measured as the NM profit divided by the BM profit on the y-axis and the number of activity cost pools on the x-axes, i.e. the mean profit error for each of the 24 heuristic and cost pool combinations (24 = 6 ACPs * 4 second-stage heuristics) over 896,909 NMs. The figure indicates that consistent with H1, more complex cost systems lead to lower profit errors.

Figure 7: Profit Errors by Heuristic

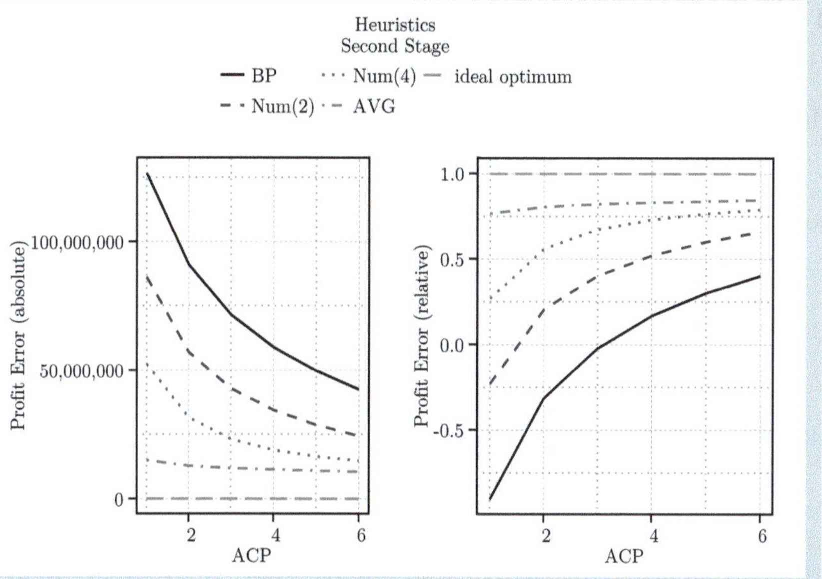

Based upon Balakrishnan, Hansen and Labro (2011), p. 532. See also Homburg, Nasev and Plank (2013) p. 34.

In addition to that, the figure indicates that the reduction in profit error from adding additional ACPs decreases. Finally, it is surprising that for the average method (AVG) a higher number of cost pools, i.e., higher cost system complexity does not significantly reduce profit errors.

3.5.2.2 Regression Results for Profit Errors across Different Cost Systems

Table 13 presents the estimation of eq. (27) according to the first regression specification, i.e., one coefficient for each categorical variable. To assess the profit error impact of more complex cost systems the focus lies on the variables ACP, Heuristics1 and Heuristics2 after controlling for market and production parameters: (1) adding one activity cost pool, i.e., increasing cost system complexity, reduces profit error by about 8.7 million on average, (2) more complex first-stage cost allocation heuristics reduce profit error by about 0.4 million and (3) more complex second-stage cost allocation heuristics reduce profit error by about 15 million.

Table 13: Regression Results Non-Dummy Specification

	Profit Error	BM profit	NM profit
(Intercept)	61,455,419.28***	200,942,132.88***	139,486,713.60***
	(172.68)	(650.95)	(308.41)
ACP	-8,716,460.26***	-1,049.16	8,715,411.10***
	(-464.43)	(-0.064)	(365.42)
Heuristics1	-398,092.30***	1,222.65	399,314.95***
	(-17.54)	(0.062)	(13.85)
Heuristics2	-15,398,743.38***	13,639.83	15,412,383.21***
	(-207.79)	(0.21)	(163.66)
Market growth	13,532,968.19***	78,785,165.96***	65,252,197.78***
	(142.30)	(955.14)	(539.94)
Market growth * Heuristics2	-2,466,500.05***	-8,713.43	2,457,786.62***
	(-71.03)	(-0.29)	(55.69)
Resource sharing	-19,482,036.54***	-24,711,075.20***	-5,229,038.66***
	(-509.05)	(-744.42)	(-107.52)
Resource costs variance	-7,421,789.63***	5,881,161.06***	13,302,950.69***
	(-47.41)	(43.31)	(66.87)
Total resource costs	843.54***	-4,032.15***	-4,875.70***

Table 13 (cont'd)	**Profit Error**	**BM profit**	**NM profit**
	(263.40)	(-1,451.62)	(-1,198.06)
Total variable costs	-358.06***	-4,793.98***	-4,435.92***
	(-11.20)	(-172.88)	(-109.18)
Variable costs variance	-144,981.16	1,590,302.81***	1,735,283.97***
	(-1.13)	(14.34)	(10.68)
Measurement error	10,590,225.10***	1,153,770.00***	-9,436,455.10***
	(54.10)	(6.79)	(-37.93)
R^2	0.55	0.90	0.82
Adj. R^2	0.55	0.90	0.82
Num. obs.	896,909.00	896,909.00	896,909.00

***p < 0.001, **p < 0.01, *p < 0.05

These findings indicate that the second-stage heuristics have a larger impact on profit errors than the first-stage heuristics. In sum, the findings of Table 13 support H1, that more complex cost systems are associated with lower profit errors.

Table 14, Panel A presents the estimation of eq. (27) according to the second regression specification, i.e., one coefficient for each category of each variable by using category dummies. This specification allows assessing the monotonicity of results. Again, the focus lies on the variables ACP, Heuristics1 and Heuristics2. In Table 14, Panel B, the percentage effects for the categories of these variables relative to the reference category are calculated.

The findings are: A switch from one activity cost pool (the reference dummy category) to two activity cost pools reduces profit error by about 21.8

million, see Panel A (= 20 % reduction, see Panel B). Changing from the reference to three ACPs results in a lower profit error by about 32.4 million etc. Finally, switching from one to six ACPs reduces profit error by about 46.7 million (= 50 % reduction). Summing up, more activity cost pools, i.e. higher cost system complexity in terms of cost pools, monotonically reduces profit error.

Next, the impact of more complex first-stage heuristics on the profit error compared to the least complex reference heuristic (random method) is as follows: The size random heuristic reduces profit error by about 0.9 million (= 1 % reduction), the size misc heuristic increases profit error by about 15 million, the correlation random heuristic reduces profit error by about 1.1 million and the correlation size heuristic (the most complex first-stage heuristic) reduces profit error by about 1.8 million (= 1 % reduction). In sum, the monotonic effect of more complex first-stage heuristics on profit error is interrupted by the size misc method that performs worse than the reference heuristic (the random method), which is the simplest first-stage heuristic. This finding is consistent with the results of Table 13 where only a small effect of first-stage heuristics on profit errors can be seen. This result is also in line with Balakrishnan, Hansen and Labro (2011) who find similar effects regarding the impact of first-stage heuristics on cost errors.

Table 14: Regression Results Dummy Specification

Panel A: Regression Results

	Profit Error	BM profit	NM profit
(Intercept)	107,916,792.34***	130,150,162.26***	22,233,369.92***
	(653.95)	(973.95)	(105.03)
ACP2	-21,806,134.46***	0.0000033	21,806,134.46***
	(-210.38)	(0.00000000004)	(164.01)
ACP3	-32,496,611.96***	-986.31	32,495,625.65***
	(-313.50)	(-0.012)	(244.40)
ACP4	-38,889,264.84***	3,699.06	38,892,963.90***
	(-374.97)	(0.044)	(292.35)
ACP5	-43,340,540.92***	-9,355.63	43,331,185.29***
	(-416.95)	(-0.11)	(324.99)
ACP6	-46,763,729.19***	-6,747.45	46,756,981.74***

Panel A: Regression Results (cont'd)

	Profit Error	**BM profit**	**NM profit**
	(-447.65)	(-0.08)	(348.93)
Size Random (Heuristics1)	-872,868.85***	11,158.61	884,027.46***
	(-9.14)	(0.14)	(7.21)
Size Misc (Heuristics1)	15,070,326.75***	11,158.61	-15,059,168.15***
	(157.76)	(0.14)	(-122.90)
Cor. Random (Heuristics1)	-1,172,073.09***	11,158.61	1,183,231.70***
	(-12.27)	(0.14)	(9.66)
Cor. Size (Heuristics1)	-1,860,797.97***	11,158.61	1,871,956.58***
	(-19.48)	(0.14)	(15.28)
Num(2) (Heuristics2)	-24,679,139.52***	2,947.81	24,682,087.33***
	(-173.13)	(0.026)	(134.99)
Num(4) (Heuristics2)	-41,429,579.56***	9,627.04	41,439,206.61***
	(-290.66)	(0.083)	(226.65)
AVG (Heuristics2)	-53,490,336.94***	8,227.22	53,498,564.16***
	(-375.28)	(0.071)	(292.61)
Market Growth (saturated)	3,352,654.31***	60,231,674.78***	56,879,020.47***
	(22.92)	(508.44)	(303.11)
Market Growth (increasing)	22,936,969.12***	158,033,698.66***	135,096,729.54***
	(157.19)	(1,337.42)	(721.77)
Market growth (saturated) * Num(2) (Heuristics2)	-3,326,045.22***	8,213.58	3,334,258.80***
	(-16.08)	(0.049)	(12.57)
Market growth (saturated) *	-6,316,423.82***	-6,384.92	6,310,038.89***

Panel A: Regression Results (cont'd)

	Profit Error	BM profit	NM profit
Num(4) (Heuristics2)			
	(-30.53)	(-0.038)	(23.78)
Market growth (saturated) * AVG(Heuristics2)	-8,754,553.24***	4,152.50	8,758,705.73***
	(-42.32)	(0.025)	(33.01)
Market growth (increasing) * Num(2) (Heuristics2)	-6,098,612.95***	12,224.25	6,110,837.19***
	(-29.55)	(0.073)	(23.08)
Market growth (increasing) * Num(4) (Heuristics2)	-11,039,104.81***	-37,998.30	11,001,106.51***
	(-53.49)	(-0.23)	(41.56)
Market growth (increasing) * AVG(Heuristics2)	-14,741,715.44***	-34,827.15	14,706,888.30***
	(-71.43)	(-0.21)	(55.55)
Resource sharing (○)	-19,280,825.38***	-39,036,271.78***	-19,755,446.40***
	(-231.66)	(-579.20)	(-185.05)
Resource sharing (+)	-34,741,276.76***	-52,978,524.70***	-18,237,247.94***
	(-411.45)	(-774.83)	(-168.39)
Resource sharing (+ +)	-43,408,522.77***	-56,553,841.81***	-13,145,319.04***
	(-508.48)	(-818.08)	(-120.04)
Resource costs variance (○)	-2,074,707.35***	1,343,439.03***	3,418,146.38***

Panel A: Regression Results (cont'd)

	Profit Error	BM profit	NM profit
	(-28.20)	(22.55)	(36.22)
Resource costs variance (+)	-3,736,520.74***	2,879,563.53***	6,616,084.27***
	(-50.81)	(48.36)	(70.14)
Total resource costs (+)	17,034,787.46***	-80,376,328.22***	-97,411,115.68***
	(283.03)	(-1,649.13)	(-1,261.74)
Total variable costs (+)	-718,801.55***	-9,599,418.08***	-8,880,616.53***
	(-11.97)	(-197.35)	(-115.26)
Variable costs variance (+)	-145,549.56*	664,363.47***	809,913.03***
	(-2.42)	(13.66)	(10.51)
Measurement Error (○)	1,578,289.13***	239,000.04***	-1,339,289.10***
	(21.46)	(4.01)	(-14.19)
Measurement Error (+)	4,286,505.19***	567,558.98***	-3,718,946.21***
	(58.27)	(9.53)	(-39.41)
R^2	0.60	0.92	0.83
Adj. R^2	0.60	0.92	0.83
Num. obs.	896,909.00	896,909.00	896,909.00

*** $p < 0.001$, ** $p < 0.01$, * $p < 0.05$

Table 14: Regression Results Dummy Specification (cont'd)
Panel B: Effects Related to H1 & H3 based on Regr. Coefficients in Panel A

Base	Change		
ACP	**ACP = 2**	**ACP = 6**	
Intercept: ACP = 1	$\frac{ACP2}{Intercept} = \frac{-21.8}{107.9}$ $\approx$ **−20** %	$\frac{ACP6}{Intercept} \approx$ **−43** %	
Heuristics1	**Size Random**	**Correl. Size**	
Intercept: Random	$\frac{Size\ Rand.}{Intercept} = \frac{-0.9}{107.9}$ $\approx$ **−1** %	*Correel. SizeIntercept* $\approx$ **−1** %	
Heuristics2	**Num (2)**	**Num (4)**	**AVG**
Intercept: BP	$\frac{Num(2)}{Intercept} = \frac{-24,7}{107.9}$ $\approx$ **−23** %	$\frac{Num(4)}{Intercept} \approx$ **−38** %	$\frac{AVG}{Intercept}$ $\approx$ **−50** %

Finally, the impact of more complex second-stage heuristics on the profit error compared to the least complex reference heuristic (big pool) is as follows: the Num(2) heuristic reduces profit error by about 24.7 million (= 23 % reduction), the Num(4) heuristic reduces profit error by about 41.4 million (= 38 % reduction) and the average heuristic (the most complex second-stage heuristic) reduces profit error by about 53.5 million (= 50 % reduction). Hence, more complex second-stage heuristics decrease profit errors monotonically. In line with Balakrishnan, Hansen and Labro (2011)'s cost error findings, the impact of second-stage heuristics on the reduction of profit errors is higher compared to the first-stage heuristics.

The regression results of Table 13 support hypothesis H1, that more complex cost systems (in terms of the number of activity cost pools and the choice of the first- and second-stage heuristics) are associated with lower profit errors. Taking aside the first stage-heuristics, a monotonic for the number of activity cost pools and second-stage heuristics can be found.

3.5.3 Market Growth (H2, H2a & H2b)

To test (H2), whether market growth reinforces the effect that more complex cost systems reduce profit errors (the result of H1), the coefficient of the interaction between the variables Market growth and Heuristics2 in the first column of Table 13 is an indicator. The coefficient is negative and significant, indicating that for a mean[109] market growth of 2, switching to a more complex second-stage heuristic reduces profit error by 2.5*2=5 million.

The regression in Table 14, Panel A tests whether the effect is monotonic across market growth categories. The focus lies on the interaction coefficients between second-stage heuristics and market growth categories: The reference category is a decreasing market and the big pool method (simplest heuristic). The interactions between a saturated market and second-stage heuristics are negative and increasing in magnitude (-3.3 million, -6.3 million and -8.7 million). The interactions between a growing market and second-stage heuristics are also negative, increasing in magnitude and the magnitude is higher relative to the saturated market (-6 million, -11 million and -14.7 million). Both, the interactions for the saturated and increasing market, indicate an additional profit error reduction by more complex cost systems as markets grow.

Taken together, in Table 13 it can be shown that as markets grow, more complex cost systems reduce profit errors, supporting (H2) and suggesting that production quantity errors (PQE) dominate product portfolio errors (keep or drop errors) as explained in the hypotheses section. With (H2a) and (H2b), this conjecture is tested more directly.

While the dependent variable in Table 13 is the total profit error, in Table 15, the dependent variable in the first column is the production quantity error (PQE) and in the second column the product portfolio error (comprising the drop and keep errors DE and KE).

---

[109] Market growth is a categorical variable that is 1 for shrinking markets, 2 for saturated markets and 3 for growing markets. The sample mean of that categorical variable is (1+2+3)/3=2.

Table 15: Regression Results by PQE & DE+KE

	PQE	DE+KE
(Intercept)	32,504,186.94***	27,301,903.39***
	(164.76)	(117.48)
ACP	-5,276,219.16***	-3,450,782.63***
	(-507.16)	(-281.58)
Heuristics1	-213,194.67***	-179,157.40***
	(-16.95)	(-12.09)
Heuristics2	-5,417,584.07***	-9,113,080.63***
	(-131.89)	(-188.33)
Market growth	14,061,609.50***	-2,910,015.44***
	(266.75)	(-46.86)
Market growth * Heuristics2	**-3,665,531.93*** **	**727,660.76*** **
	(-190.42)	(32.09)
Resource sharing	-10,783,579.24***	-9,951,261.61***
	(-508.32)	(-398.21)
Resource costs variance	-3,864,172.85***	-3,314,494.12***
	(-44.53)	(-32.42)
Total resource costs	276.11***	473.72***
	(155.54)	(226.54)
Total variable costs	-338.23***	124.10***
	(-19.09)	(5.94)
Variable costs variance	-79,170.66	-93,144.46
	(-1.12)	(-1.12)
Measurement error	7,954,385.51***	2,999,760.31***
	(73.30)	(23.47)
Adj. R^2	0.59	0.34
Num. obs.	896,909.00	896,909.00

*** $p < 0.001$, ** $p < 0.01$, * $p < 0.05$

Let us focus on the first column in Table 15 related to the production quantity error (PQE). (H2a) hypothesizes that in growing markets more complex cost systems should reduce production quantity errors (PQE) more than in shrinking markets. The negative and significant coefficient of the interaction between market growth and Heuristics2 in Table 15 supports (H2a) indicating that for a mean market growth of 2, switching to a more complex second-stage heuristic reduces PQE by 3.6 * 2 = 7.2 million.

Finally, the second column in Table 15 is related to the product portfolio errors (DE and KE). (H2b) hypothesizes that in shrinking markets more complex cost systems should reduce product portfolio errors (DE and KE) more than in growing markets.

The positive and significant coefficient of the interaction between market growth and Heuristics2 in Table 15 supports (H2b) indicating that for a mean market growth of 2, switching to a more complex second-stage heuristic increases product portfolio errors by 0.6 * 2 = 1.2 million. Conversely, as markets shrink, switching to a more complex second-stage heuristic would reduce product portfolio errors.

In conclusion, findings indicate that (a) as markets grow complex cost systems monotonically reduce profit errors supporting hypothesis (H2), (b) in growing markets complex cost systems reduce production quantity errors (PQE) more than in shrinking markets supporting hypothesis (H2a) and (c) in shrinking markets complex cost systems reduce product portfolio errors (DE and KE) more than in growing markets supporting hypothesis (H2b).

3.5.4 Profit Error Types

Using hypothesis (H3) the idea is to test whether more complex cost systems cause lower production quantity errors (PQE) and lower product portfolio errors, i.e., lower keep and drop errors (KE and DE).

Let us focus on the mean plots since regression results are similar but not as intuitive. Figure 8 illustrates the impact of different second-stage heuristics on the four different error types (production quantity error

(PQE), drop error (DE), keep error (KE) and capacity error (CE)). The left and right diagrams differ only with respect to the y-axis: in the left diagram, it is the magnitude of each profit error type and in the right diagram, it is the ratio between profit error type and total profit error.

Figure 8: Profit Errors Types

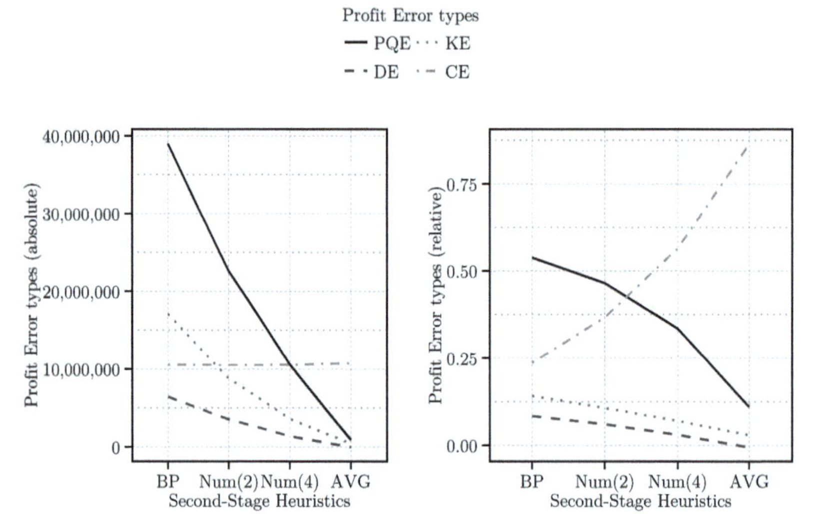

Based upon Balakrishnan, Hansen and Labro (2011), p. 532.

Figure 8 shows the following: First, among all error types, the production quantity error (PQE) is the highest and has the highest fraction of the total profit error. Second, and most interesting, the keep error is higher than the drop error indicating that on average cost systems tend to underestimate costs more often and therefore keep unprofitable products than they tend to overestimate costs resulting in the drop of profitable products. The implication of this finding is that simple cost heuristics have higher total cost errors because they keep more unprofitable products. Third, consistent with results for the total profit error, it can be shown that more complex cost systems have lower values for each error type, except for the capacity error (CE) that is similar for all cost systems.[110] The capacity error (CE) is similar in magnitude for all cost heuristics (left diagram) because the noisy model (see Table 7 on p. 50) does not permit heuristics to adjust full costs over time. Finally, the average method, which is the most complex heuristic, dominates all other heuristics in terms of having the lowest profit errors across all profit error types.

In conclusion, the profit error type analysis shows that more complex cost systems have lower production quantity errors (PQE) and lower product portfolio errors (KE and DE). In addition, the largest errors are production quantity errors. Also, on average, cost systems tend to keep more unprofitable products than drop profitable products indicating that cost systems tend to underestimate full costs.

3.6 Robustness

Simulations are based on the parametric algorithms and on the manifestation of randomly distributed variables. They need to be tested against different parameter choices. The sensitivity of the results against these alterations needs to be documented. Additionally – since the heuristic algorithms are based on Balakrishnan, Hansen and Labro (2011) – it is also necessary to test whether the algorithmic implemented yields comparable results: Therefore, in the next paragraphs the focus lies on parameter choice and the performance of heuristics.

3.6.1 Parameter fit and sensitivity against alteration of parameter choice

As introduced in chapter 3.2, it is differentiated between market, production and cost system parameters. Table 16 reports descriptive statistics related to the two most important production parameters for a comparison with

[110] The capacity error (CE) is similar across cost heuristics in the left diagram but increases with more complex cost systems in the right diagram of Figure 8. This is because more complex cost systems have lower total profit errors (equal to the sum of the four errors in the left diagram). Since the capacity error is similar in magnitude across all cost systems (left diagram), as a fraction of total profit error it increases for more complex cost systems.

Balakrishnan, Hansen and Labro (2011): resource cost variance and resource sharing.

An indicator for the fit of variable manifestations at identical parameter choice is the comparability of the result set. In line with Balakrishnan, Hansen and Labro (2011) an increase of resource cost variance leads to: First, the ratio of percentage costs in the largest divided by the smallest cost pool increases. Second, the percentage cost in the top 5% of resources increases. Third, the cost errors of the big pool method decline, while the cost errors of the average method increase. The intuition here is that size based heuristics like the big pool method perform better the higher the fraction of one resource is relative to total resource costs.

Table 16: Parameter fit

Variation in resource costs (using parameter RCV)	**Units**	**Global Average**	**dispersion**		
			Low	**Med**	**High**
	Observations	7,529	2,514	2,505	2,510
Percentage of cost in largest pool / percentage of cost in smallest pool	Ratio	3.21	1.59	2.66	5.4
Percentage of costs in top 5 resources [TRC = 40,000]	Percent	0.34	0.29	0.34	0.39
EUCD using BigPool	Cost Unit	9,753	1,953	2,611	1,295
EUCD using AVG	Cost Unit	1,846	2,252	3,083	2,594

Based upon Balakrishnan, Hansen and Labro (2011), p. 530.

As reported by Balakrishnan, Hansen and Labro (2011) an increase in resource sharing yields: First, the percentage of zero entries in the resource consumption matrix decreases. Second, the average range of consumption of a resource across products decreases too.

For the environment parameters (independent from Balakrishnan, Hansen and Labro (2011)) first, the price elasticity is changed: In comparison to the main specification, where $b = -1.3$ indicates that a 1% increase in price reduces demand by 1.3%, simulation results are robust against runs with a value of -1.0 implying a proportional reaction of volume to price changes or price elasticity modeled as a uniformly distributed random variable $b = U(-0.5; -1.5)$.[111] Second, the modeling of saturated markets is varied. Replacing the random walk process ($A_{it} = A_{it-1} + 200\varepsilon_t$, $\varepsilon \sim N(0,1)$) with a white noise ($A_{it} = A_0 + 200\varepsilon_t$, $\varepsilon \sim N(0,1)$) does not materially change the results.[112]

Third, increasing the short term resource costs penalty parameter ϕ (in main specification being $\phi = 1.2$) to $\phi = 1.5$ leads to stable results as well as modeling $\phi = U(1.1; 1.5)$ as a uniformly distributed random variable.[113] Taken together, the results are robust to varying the main parameters of the simulation.

3.6.2 Mean Cost Errors across Different Cost Systems

Figure 9 illustrates cost errors for the first-stage heuristics (left diagram) and second-stage heuristics (right diagram). The diagram display mean cost errors measured as the mean Euclidian distance (EUCD) in costs on the y-axes and the number of activity cost pools on the x-axes, i.e., the average of cost errors for each heuristic and cost pool combination.[114]

---

[111] See Appendix C, Table 19.

[112] See Appendix C, Table 20.

[113] See Appendix C, Table 21.

[114] For the left diagram the average cost error over 896,909 NMs (see data section) for each first stage-heuristic and cost pool combination is calculated: 30 combinations=6ACPs*5 first-stage heuristics. For the right diagram average of cost errors over 896,909 NMs for each second stage-heuristic and cost pool combination is measured: 24 combinations=6ACPs*4 second-stage heuristics.

The cost error ranking of heuristics and cost pool combinations that is obtained is similar to the ranking documented in Balakrishnan, Hansen and Labro (2011). A difference occurs in two ways: First, a worse cost error for the size misc (Size_M) method is obtained. Second, the differences in cost errors between heuristics are less pronounced.[115]

Figure 9: Cost Error of First & Second Stage Heuristics

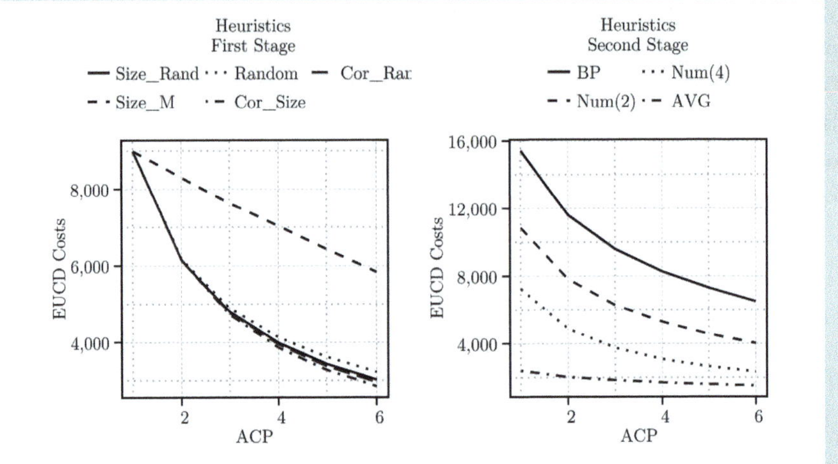

Based upon Balakrishnan, Hansen and Labro (2011), p. 532.

3.6.3 Distributions of Cost and Profit Errors: Graphical Analysis (Box Plots) and Formal Tests (Pearson Correlation, Rank Test and Regression)

In line with Balakrishnan, Hansen and Labro (2011) the order of the heuristics in terms of their performance is equal. This section aims at ranking the performance against the cost error in contrast to the subsequent section ranking performance against the profit error. To illustrate that the heuristic performance equals in a cost as in a pricing context, graphical

[115] Note that the EUCD values differ from Balakrishnan, Hansen and Labro (2011) because they work with full costs at the product portfolio level of 1 million while the work at hand is built with full costs at the individual product level of 60,000. This is because Balakrishnan, Hansen and Labro (2011) do not have a decision context, while this thesis has a pricing decision context where full costs at the product portfolio level are initially unknown.

analysis and formal tests are used. For the graphical examination of distributions of cost and profit errors, the 120 heuristics and cost pool combinations (120 = 6 ACPs * 5 firs t-stage heuristics * 4 second-stage heuristics) are ranked separately based on their cost and profit errors. For example, for the cost error ranking, the cost error for each of the 120 combinations for the first of the 8,640 BMs is estimated. Subsequently, the 120 combinations are ranked such that the combination with the highest cost error is ranked 0 and the combination with the lowest error is ranked 120. Repeating these steps for the second, third ... and 8,640th BM conclusively 8,640 cost error rankings from 0 to 120 are obtained. In the same way the profit error ranking is constructed.

Figure 10: Box Plot of Heuristic Ranking

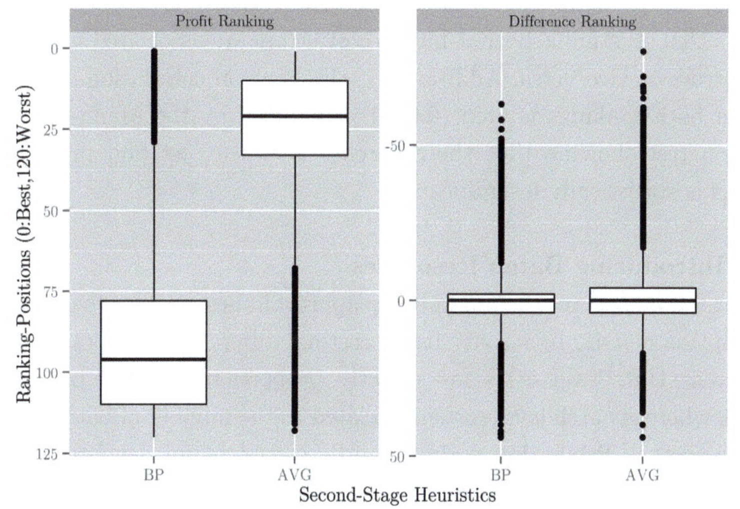

Own depiction.

Figure 10 comprises four box plots.[116] The first box plot illustrates the distribution of the 8,640 profit error rankings of the big pool method.

[116] The first quartile of the distribution ends at the bottom of the box, the box covers the second quartile and the third quartile begins at the top of the box. The bar in the box is the median and the dots are outliers.

Similarly, the second box plot reflects the distribution of the 8,640 profit error rankings of the average heuristic (AVG). A comparison of the plots indicates that profit errors of the average heuristic are lower than profit errors of the big pool heuristic across the whole distribution: median, highest, lowest value and variance. The median profit error of the average heuristic (rank 21) is lower than the median profit error of the big pool heuristic (rank 96). While the big pool method ranks on the lower end positions (ranks 78 to 110) about 50% of the time, the average method ranks on the higher end positions (ranks 10 to 33) about 50% of the time.

The third (fourth) box plot refers to the difference between the cost and profit error rankings of the big pool method (average method). Both plots indicate that differences in the distribution of cost and profit error rankings are small: the median is close to zero and the variance is low. This finding suggests that it is unlikely that higher cost errors are associated with lower profit errors or vice versa. Additionally, the Pearson correlation coefficient between both rankings is high (0.9794) supported by the Mann-Whitney-Wilcoxon test showing that the difference between cost and profit error rankings is statistically insignificant.

3.6.4 Introducing Batch Resources

Another difference in the underlying approach lies within the resource consumption matrix. In activity based costing, different cost hierarchies are considered: Unit level costs are directly proportional to the production volume, whereas batch level costs are related to the number of batches, such as setup costs.[117] While this study primarily considers unit-level resources / costs, Balakrishnan, Hansen and Labro (2011) also consider batch-level resources. They split the resource consumption matrix into volume and batch resources.[118] To test whether this affects the simulation, this adjustment is applied. Neither descriptive nor the regression results are affected by this refinement.

---

[117] See Hartgraves and Morse (2015), p. 48.

[118] For details on this method see the Appendix B of the earlier working paper by Balakrishnan et al. (2009).

In conclusion, robustness tests indicate that neither parameter adjustments nor core simulation method changes affect the result set.

3.7 Preliminary conclusion of cost system influences on decision making

The used simulation approach enables the assessment of the impact of fixed cost allocation via different cost systems on pricing and product-mix decisions and hence on profits. The main findings in short: more complex cost systems - characterized by a higher number of activity cost pools and more complex first- and second-stage cost allocation heuristics, are associated with lower profit errors. More specifically, the most complex cost system reduces profit errors by 50% compared to the simplest cost system. Also, while cost system related variables explain 36% of the variance in profit error, the market and production environment explains 18%, suggesting that cost systems are the most important factor affecting profit errors. The market conditions analysis completes the drawn picture as complex cost systems reduce profit errors more when markets grow. Lastly the decomposition of the profit error into (a) error in production volume, (b) error related to dropping profitable products, (c) error related to keeping unprofitable products and (d) the capacity error gives reason why some cost systems perform better than others: The largest errors result from distortions in production quantity, the second largest errors arise from keeping unprofitable products and the third largest errors result from dropping profitable products.

The main takeaway is: On average, cost systems tend to underestimate full costs. Results also imply more complex cost systems profiting from lower total profit errors across all error types (except for the capacity error (CE), which is similar across all heuristics). This finding implies that more complex cost systems help reducing production quantity errors, as well as underestimating full costs. Alternatively, firms can consider applying a correction factor to reduce the cost underestimation arising from simple cost systems.

This adds to the existing literature a pricing context in which cost system effects on pricing and product-mix decisions can be measured, thus giving firms a tool to assess optimal prices and product-mixes in markets where firms have pricing power, setting prices and choosing the product-mix. It also lays the fundament for a different kind of analysis: the influence of sticky costs on the performance of heuristic decision making in a pricing context. This is taken up in the following chapter.

4. Extended Decision Model Incorporating Cost-Stickiness

In 1994 Noreen and Soderstrom formulated two important statements:[119] First, the relation between overhead costs and activities is **not** strictly proportional and second, whereas the design of more sophisticated cost systems incorporating the non-proportional cost behavior may be costly, in an environment where costs are decision relevant, the implementation of such accounting methods is recommended.

This phenomenon has already been targeted in Germany in the early thirties of the last century, e.g. Strube (1936) investigated and documented cost behavior patterns. The asymmetry of overhead costs to changes in activity has been documented since then in many publications.[120] Naming the phenomenon *"sticky"*, Anderson, Banker and Janakiraman (2003) refer with this term to differences in the extent of increases and decreases in costs corresponding to equivalent in-/decreases in activity. A good example is the German economy, where labor costs can more easily be increased than decreased in times of economic downturn, because of union power and strict labor laws.[121]

Up to this point managerial research has focused on discovering and explaining the sticky costs phenomenon. Homburg (2004) develops a method for binary portfolio decisions, incorporating asymmetric cost-behavior. Building on this methodology, this chapter widens the focus on pricing decisions incorporating sticky cost-behavior. The assumption is, that costing systems neglecting cost stickiness are, for one, unable to reflect real cost consumption and therefore, for the other, lead to biased decisions.

[119] See Noreen and Soderstrom (1994), pp. 273-274.

[120] E.g. Noreen and Soderstrom (1997); Anderson, Banker and Janakiraman (2003); Banker, Byzalov and Plehn-Dujowich (2014).

[121] See Banker and Chen (2006), p. 26, or Calleja, Steliaros and Thomas (2006), p. 133.

To find evidence for this assumption the research framework of the previous chapter is changed in the following: Cost-stickiness is included in the benchmark model. But instead of having only one type of noisy models, this approach uses two different noisy models: one neglecting and one incorporating cost-stickiness.[122] The details of the sticky implementation will be covered in depth later. For now let's assume the BM considers cost stickiness and the performance of non-sticky noisy models, i.e. the heuristics are kept unchanged, is measured analogously to the approach of chapter 3. In accordance with the above formulated assumption the performance of the noisy model should drop.

The line of argument is as follows: Demand changes lead to short-term capacity changes over time, in addition to the installed and per period available long-term capacity. It can be assumed, that due to cost-stickiness, these capacity adjustments are costly and short-term installed capacity can only be disinvested, if needed, at a premium. Based on the mechanics of the (unchanged) NM, the NM is unable to adjust its cost allocation process to changes in demand over time. Additionally it is unable to cope with different costs for capacity buildup and divestment. The NM allocates costs via heuristics directly to products. The heuristics yield activity costs which are stable over time and are therefore unable to reflect changes in demand nor to align costs in respect to the direction of resource adjustment. Therefore, leaving the heuristics unchanged, the NM should yield lower profits.

Whereas it is a first goal of this chapter to show, that the performance of the NM drops, the main idea is to install NMs that are able to cope with the cost-stickiness effect. The key for this lies with the short-term capacity adjustments, as they are mainly driven by cost-stickiness. The size of short-term adjustments itself is driven by fluctuations in market size (A_{it}). Hence the NM adjustment should focus on these changes. It will be later discussed

[122] Since the research framework is identical in terms of how the research is conducted methodologically, a detailed description of the DOE phases as in Lorscheid, Heine and Meyer (2012) is neglected in the following.

how this adjustment takes place, but the - enhanced - new NM should therefore be able to yield lower profit errors.

While the previous paragraphs abstractly touched on the approach, in the following the basic metrics will be introduced to answer the research questions of this chapter:

(1) How big is the lever of the new NM? This is covered by comparing the new BM profits with the enhanced NM profits.
(2) How severe is the loss in cost-system performance by neglecting cost-stickiness? This is achieved by comparing the result of research question (1) with the delta in profits of the new BM against the old NM, i.e. the usage of the old heuristic set.
(3) And lastly it can be shown how a NM hast to be designed to control for cost-stickiness.

The answer to these questions are very important to researchers and practitioners, as this enables them for the first time to measure the loss caused by cost-stickiness and gives them a starting point of how to adjust their cost-systems in the future.

The remainder of this chapter gives a broader introduction on cost-stickiness, followed by how the research framework is transformed to model sticky cost behavior introducing an enhanced cost allocation process.

4.1 A Side Note on Cost-Stickiness and its model implications

The fundamentals behind cost-stickiness have been shortly addressed in the previous chapter. This chapter aims at backing the intuition of integrating cost stickiness into the decision model and documents its contribution to the literature body. Additionally it is also identified which source of cost-stickiness will be implemented. It is neither a comprehensive overview of cost-stickiness nor a discussion of its empirical evidence, since this would only add limited value for the development of the enhanced simulation model.

Since Anderson, Banker and Janakiraman (2003) developed one of the central concepts to measure cost-stickiness, empirical evidence has been found also in cross country studies (e.g. Banker and Chen (2006)) or as an effect of incentive systems (Dierynck, Landsman and Renders (2012)).[123] A new discussion led by Balakrishnan, Labro and Soderstrom (2014) and Banker and Byzalov (2014) on the used methodology and the role of cost structure towards sticky costs will be taken up in the discussion of the results.

Independent of all the research efforts on finding evidence and explaining cost-stickiness, neither in practice nor in theory, traditional costing has been explicitly modified to control for sticky behavior in the relation between activity levels in the current, past or future period.[124]

Where traditional costing only distinguishes between fixed and variable costs related to changes in activity volume, the sticky model adds costs resulting from resource commitment decisions.[125] Because of their partly lumpy character the latter category cannot be changed as an immediate response to demand changes. Considering the question "why are costs lumpy", prior research has come up with multiple considerations.

Following Mahlendorf (2009) two basic differentiations group the source of sticky costs due to adjustment delays (unavoidable) and managers' deliberate decisions (avoidable). The adjustment delay theory is straight forward: costs cannot be adjusted (mostly declined) in the same period as volume changes occur.[126] This leads inevitably to idle capacity costs. On the other hand, the deliberate decisions theory clusters entrepreneurial intended and unintended cost sources. Unintended costs result from agency issues.

[123] For a detailed discussion of the cost-stickiness literature body I refer to Baumgarten (2012).
[124] See Banker, Byzalov and Plehn-Dujowich (2014), p. 840.
[125] See Anderson, Banker and Janakiraman (2003), p. 48.
[126] See Baumgarten, Bonenkamp and Homburg (2010), p. 3.

Instead of optimizing shareholder value, management maximizes its personal value. The buzz word in this context is empire building, meaning self-centered management uses sales growth periods to build up capacity in their domain (i.e. employer stock in their own department), whereas they refrain from giving up these resources in periods of sale declines.[127] The source of this behavior can be manifold: one possible argument is misleading incentive systems.[128]

Incentive schemes are not the only factor driving the decision process. Another factor is expectations of future developments and the inherent consideration if an adjustment of capacity economically makes sense, i.e. the costs of adjustment are below the costs resulting from idle capacity. Whether adjustments have to be made in the first place, depends therefore on the prediction of future sales. It is more likely that management is willing to adjust capacity upwards in times of sales growth than in periods of economic distress. In the latter environment, management decision is not consequently a reduction of capacity, if the persistence of sales declines is expected to be short. Whereas managers aim to reduce adjustment costs, they trade off capacity utilization and respectively their cost over a longer period of time, against adjustment costs in the actual period.[129]

Both, benchmark and noisy model do not incorporate agency theory elements. Therefore only the adjustment delay theory is reflected in the new approach. The following chapter covers the extension.

4.2 The Extended Model Approach

The aim of this chapter is to develop the extended model and clarify the design decisions. Recapitulating the introduced research questions, the

[127] See Chen, Lu and Sougiannis (2012); Kama and Weiss (2013), p. 203.

[128] See Dierynck, Landsman and Renders (2012), p. 1220; Banker, Byzalov and Plehn-Dujowich (2014), p. 847.

[129] See Banker, Byzalov and Plehn-Dujowich (2014), p. 860.

approach has to measure both, the effect of neglecting cost stickiness and the gain by incorporating it into decision making.

The task of the BM model still is to reflect optimal decisions in an environment of perfect information. As it is the reference point, performance of the NM will be measured against it, it is obvious that this model has to incorporate cost stickiness. To separate it from the former BM, the cost-stickiness enhanced BM will be identified by the index "ext" (BM^{ext}). In addition we need two NM: one is the unchanged NM of the last chapter, from here on classified as the standard NM (NM^{std}). The second one is the new NM (NM^{ext}), extended to control for cost-stickiness. Therefore the simulation process also has to be adjusted, first calculating the BM^{ext}, followed by the NM^{std} and subsequently the NM^{ext}. This alignment of the simulation will be the subject of chapter 4.2.3.

4.2.1 The BM adjustment

Following the cost-stickiness introduction, adjustments in capacity follow demand fluctuations. Moreover, reducing installed capacity is more costly than installing additional capacity. Lastly, built up resource costs of previous periods need to have an impact on the resource costs in the current period. This is basically what separates the standard *BM* (chapter 3) from the extended BM^{ext}.[130]

$$\max_{P_{it}^{BM}, R_{jt}, L_j} \sum_{t=1}^{T} \left(\sum_{i=1}^{I} (P_{it}^{BM} - v_i)(A_{it} - b_i P_{it}^{BM}) - \sum_{j=1}^{J} \phi_j c_j R_{jt} \right) - T \sum_{j=1}^{J} c_j L_j \tag{28}$$

Equation (28) displays the standard benchmark model. One could argue that the term $\sum_{j=1}^{J} \phi_j c_j R_{jt}$ already covers sticki-costs. Adjustments in

[130] See Banker, Byzalov and Plehn-Dujowich (2011), pp. 2–3.

capacity (R_{jt}) are time dependent and one unit of additional capacity costs the standard costs c_j plus a premium rate in costs ($\phi_j > 1$).

This only partially reflects the sticky-cost function. First, it does not differentiate between premiums for investing and divesting capacity. Second, capacity is only installed for one period.

Hence the adjustment is threefold:

(1) The premium ϕ_j is split into a premium for costs of building up capacity (ϕ_j^+) and one for reducing capacity (ϕ_j^-). Obviously the premium for divestments needs to be greater than the premium for investments ($\phi_j^- > \phi_j^+$). Consequently the costs for a short term capacity divestment of resource j ($c_j^- = \phi_j^- c_j$) is higher than the costs for investments ($c_j^+ = \phi_j^+ c_j$).

(2) The buildup of short-term capacities R_{jt} is now persistent, meaning that adjustments are still periodically possible, but built capacities from one period are now kept until they are used or divested. Therefore R_{jt} is the sum of resources of previous periods (R_{jt-1}), the current invest (R_{jt}^+) and the divest (R_{jt}^-). Hence, it is better to refer to these resources as mid-term capacity, instead of short-term capacity.

(3) Due to the split in the cost premium and the resulting differences in costs for mid-term investments and respectively divestments, the profit function (see eq. (29)) needs to be adjusted. The sum $\sum_{j=1}^{J}(c_j R_{jt} + c_j^+ R_{jt}^+ + c_j^- R_{jt}^-)$ reflects these changes, incorporating costs for the already built up resources ($c_j R_{jt}$), as well as for investments and divestments ($c_j^+ R_{jt}^+ + c_j^- R_{jt}^-$).

The optimal solution renders $Profit^{BM^{ext}}$:

$$\max_{P_{it}^{BM^{ext}}, R_{jt}, R_{jt}^{+}, R_{jt}^{-}, L_j} \sum_{t=0}^{T} \left(\sum_{i=1}^{I} \left(P_{it}^{BM^{ext}} - v_i\right)\left(A_{it} - b_i P_{it}^{BM^{ext}}\right) - \sum_{j=1}^{J} \left(c_j R_{jt} + c_j^{+} R_{jt}^{+} + c_j^{-} R_{jt}^{-}\right) \right) - T \sum_{j=1}^{J} c_j L_j \quad (29)$$

$$\begin{aligned}
\textit{subject to} \quad & \sum_{i=1}^{I} m_{ij}\left(A_{it} - b_i P_{it}^{BM^{ext}}\right) - R_{jt} - L_j \leq 0 && \forall j, t, \\
& \left(A_{it} - b_i P_{it}^{BM^{ext}}\right) \geq 0 && \forall i, t, \\
& R_{jt} = R_{jt-1} + R_{jt}^{+} - R_{jt}^{-} && \forall j, t, \\
& c_j^{+} = \phi_j^{+} c_j && \forall j, \\
& c_j^{-} = \phi_j^{-} c_j && \forall j, \\
& P_{it}^{BM^{ext}}, R_{jt}, R_{jt}^{+}, R_{jt}^{-}, L_j \geq 0 && \forall i, j, t.
\end{aligned}$$

Decision variables:		**Non-decision variables:**	
$P_{it}^{BM^{ext}}$	Optimal price for product i in period t of the BM	A_{it}	Market size per product i and period t
L_j	Initial long-term capacity for resource j (available every period)	b_i	Price elasticity of product i
R_{jt}	Flexible mid-term capacity for resource j and period t	v_i	Variable cost of product i
R_{jt}^{+}	Invest in mid-term capacity for resource j and period t	c_j	Base resource costs of resource j
R_{jt}^{-}	Disinvestment in mid-term capacity for resource j and period t	c_j^{+}	Resource costs for additional resources
		c_j^{-}	Resource costs for divested resources
		ϕ_j^{+}	Premium price for investing in additional capacity of j
		ϕ_j^{-}	Premium price for disinvesting capacity of j
		m_{ij}	Resource consumption matrix for product i and resource j

Based upon Balakrishnan and Sivaramakrishnan (2002), p. 12.

Aside from these changes the extended benchmark model follows the mechanics of the BM of chapter 3. Over a planning horizon of $t=1,\dots T$ periods the BM^{ext} optimizes prices and capacities simultaneously for products $i=1,\dots,I$ and resources $j=1,\dots,J$.

4.2.2 The NM adjustment

As discussed in the introduction of this chapter, we need two noisy models, the standard NM^{std} and the extended NM^{ext}. The extension itself has only been shortly addressed and is the subject of this chapter.

As already stated, the allocation process of costs needs to be refined. If one follows this line of thought, two elements need to be incorporated into the NM: The change in demand over time and the direction of resource changes, i.e. buildup or reduction of capacity.

An obvious starting point would be the heuristics, which steer the allocation process. This is maybe an intuitive starting point for the adjustment. But for two reasons it is hardly possible to control for cost-stickiness at this level.

$$\max_{P_{it}^{NM^{std}}} \sum_{t=1}^{T} \sum_{i=1}^{I} (P_{it}^{NM^{std}} - v_i - ABC_i)(A_{it} - b_i P_{it}^{NM^{std}}) \tag{30}$$

The heuristic output is essentially the activity cost vector ABC_i. According to the profit function of the standard NM^{std} (30), these costs are independent of the produced quantity $q_{it} = (A_{it} - b_i P_{it}^{NM^{std}})$. Setting the activity costs for product i, the NM^{std} subsequently optimizes the prices $P_{it}^{NM^{std}}$ and consequently also the production quantity. Hence at the time the NM^{std} sets activity costs, the production quantity has not been determined. In addition, as covered in section 3.1.4, the capacity decision has not taken place. A distinction between costs of resource increase and decrease is therefore impossible.

Focusing on the capacity decision another aspect comes into play: Resources are used across products, therefore only the complete portfolio decision determines the needed resource quantities. Ceteris paribus, a sticky cost-factor taking into consideration changes in resource consumption triggered by changes in market size, can only be applied on a portfolio level.

Further, it needs to be considered, that the higher the fluctuations in market size, the higher the fluctuations in demand are and the lesser the standard NM^{std} is able to cope with the effect.

Homburg (2004) calls demand fluctuation, demand heterogeneity and develops a portfolio based driver, which controls for costs induced by these fluctuations. In the following a driver is developed to enhance the standard NM^{std}, enabling the resulting extended NM^{ext} to cope with cost stickiness.

Homburg (2004)'s profit function is based on the alternation of different portfolio constellations, which are binary decisions: include a certain product in the mix or not. In this publication the price determines the product mix, therefore the approach is different to the underlying publication by Homburg (2004).

The basic idea is to estimate the cost gap resulting from neglecting cost-stickiness in the NM^{std} in comparison to the BM^{ext}. By closing this costing gap, the extended model NM^{ext} should also be able to reduce the profit error towards the BM^{ext}. The question is, whether there exists a functional relation between the costs induced by demand heterogeneity and the resulting cost gap, emerging from capacity differences between the NM^{std} and the BM^{ext}?

The demand heterogeneity can be expressed as the change in demand between the actual and the previous period valued by the costs for these resources. More explicitly for the complete time frame the delta in quantity can be expressed as $\sum_{t=2}^{T}\left|\sum_{i=1}^{I} m_{ij}\left[(q_{it})-(q_{it-1})\right]\right|$. The resource consumption matrix is used to trace back the quantity to resources. To economically quantify the heterogeneity, this delta needs to be valued by a cost factor incorporating the different cost-components for investments and divestments $(\phi_j^+ c_j + \phi_j^- c_j - c_j)$. In sum the resulting heterogeneity driver $h_{cs}(P_{it})$ can be expressed as:[131]

$$h_{cs}(P_{it}) = \sum_{j=1}^{J} (\phi_j^+ c_j + \phi_j^- c_j - c_j) \sum_{t=2}^{T} \left| \sum_{i=1}^{I} m_{ij} \left[(A_{it} - b_i P_{it}) - (A_{it-1} - b_i P_{it-1}) \right] \right| \quad (31)$$

Based upon Homburg (2004), p. 338

In other terms, the heterogeneity driver expresses the error the standard NM^{std} makes by neglecting the costs of demand changes. By using the yielded prices P_{it}^{std} by the NM^{std}, one is able to calculate the error for each noisy model, i.e. calculating $h_{cs}(P_{it}^{std})$.

Hereby one component of the functional relation between NM^{std} and BM^{ext} has been identified. The other component is the capacity difference emerging from the inability of the NM^{std} to cope with the demand heterogeneity. To measure the capacity difference by the NM^{ext} the pseudo capacity estimation of section 3.1.4 is used. In other terms, it is the economic valuation of the produced quantity x_{it} by the activity costs ABC_i. The costs of capacity of the BM^{ext} is obviously the sum of medium term and long term capacity valued by the corresponding cost vectors. The delta in costs between both models can therefore be expressed as:

$$\Delta C(P_{it}^{NM^{std}}) = \sum_{t=1}^{T} \sum_{j=1}^{J} (c_j L_j + R_{jt} c_j + c_j^+ R_{jt}^+ + c_j^- R_{jt}^-) - \sum_{t=1}^{T} \sum_{i=1}^{I} ABC_i \left[(A_{it} - b_i P_{it}^{NM^{std}}) \right] \quad (32)$$

Based upon Homburg (2004), p. 338

[131] The subscript ‘cs’ identifies variables as cost-stickiness enhanced.

To recapitulate, the idea is to develop an extended NM^{ext} that is able by closing the costing gap (in comparison to the BM^{ext}) caused by cost-stickiness to yield better pricing decisions and hence higher profits. It was considered that therefore a cost driver on portfolio level needs to be developed. Generally speaking, the cost driver rate should reflect the structural error the NM^{std} generates. This error can be expressed as the resulting false capacity decision based on neglecting the demand heterogeneity. In addition one can state, that the higher the demand heterogeneity the higher the capacity error. In line with Homburg (2004), assuming the functional relation between h_{cs} and ΔC is linear, the slope of this function can be considered the cost driver rate. Therefore in accordance with eq. (33) the slope π_{cs} describes how intense a change in heterogeneity (h_{cs}) effects the cost gap or in other words the cost error (ΔC) of the NM^{std}.

Following Homburg (2004) the functional relation between the demand heterogeneity and the delta in costs can therefore be expressed as follows:

$$\Delta C(P_{it}^{NM^{std}}) = \beta_0 + \pi_{cs} h_{cs}(P_{it}^{NM^{std}}) + \varepsilon \tag{33}$$

Having identified π_{cs} two questions arise: How can π_{cs} be used to extend the standard noisy model and how will it be estimated. A detailed discussion of the method to estimate π_{cs} is the subject of section 4.2.3.

Abstracting from the method to determine the cost driver rate π_{cs}, the noisy model extension should value at the time of planning the demand heterogeneity for a given production program. In other words while setting the price $P_{it}^{NM^{ext}}$ the extended NM^{ext} needs to incorporate the costs of the demand heterogeneity caused by setting the price $P_{it}^{NM^{ext}}$. The demand heterogeneity for the current production program can be calculated by using eq. (31) and inserting $P_{it}^{NM^{ext}}$ into h_{cs}. The costs of the heterogeneity are reflected in the cost driver rate π_{cs}. These costs reduce the estimated profit of the profit function known from the NM^{std}:

$$\max_{P_{it}^{NM^{ext}}} \sum_{t=1}^{T}\sum_{i=1}^{I}(P_{it}^{NM^{ext}} - v_i - ABC_i)(A_{it} - b_i P_{it}^{NM^{ext}}) - \pi_{cs} h_{cs}(P_{it}^{NM^{ext}}) \tag{34}$$

$$\text{subject to } (A_{it} - b_i P_{it}^{NM^{ext}}) \geq 0 \ \forall i,t$$

$$P_{it}^{NM^{ext}} \geq 0 \ \forall i,t.$$

Based upon Homburg (2004), p. 339

Eq. (34) illustrates the extended noisy model NM^{ext}. As discussed in section 3.7, the heuristics tend to systematically underestimate full costs. This error is overcome in the NM^{ext} by limiting the profits using sticky-costs factor equaling $\pi_{cs} h_{cs}(P_{it}^{NM^{ext}})$.

4.2.3 Information & simulation flow and data

To wrap up the previous sections, the steps to calculate the extended NM^{ext} are:

1. Calculate the BM^{ext} & NM^{std}
2. Estimate the cost driver rate π_{cs} based on step 1
3. Calculate the NM^{ext}

The common thread running through the simulation is almost the same as in chapter 3; first the benchmark system is simulated followed by the noisy models.

The combination of market and production parameters has been kept equal to the former simulation. The total of parameters still yields 864 BMs, whereas the number of model variations for each of the 864 BMs has been inclined to have a broader information base for the regression. Additionally in comparison the former simulation used 10 model variations per parameter combination, this time 40 variations are processed - resulting in 34,560 BM observations.

Since the focus of this research is no longer on the heuristics only, the set of heuristics has been minimized, leaving only the random and correlation size method on the first stage and big pool as well as the average heuristic on the second stage. Since the number of activity pools has a monotonic relation to the delta in profits, for this approach only 3 levels of activity pools are used. This gives a total of 12 models (2 heuristics1 * 2 heuristics2 * 3 ACPs). Figure 11 provides an overview of the simulation flow, illustrating also the regression approach being outlined in the following.

Let us focus on step 2 (see above). Basically a regression approach (the regression function is defined in eq. (33)) is used to determine the cost driver rate π_{cs}. For simplification reasons - up to this point - it was abstracted from the method to calculate the cost driver rate π_{cs}. To restate: the cost driver rate reflects the structural error a set of standard NM^{std} generates, by neglecting demand heterogeneity and cost-stickiness. The set of NM^{std} is defined by identical variable outputs and usage of heuristics. Hence for this set, π_{cs} quantifies how severe the demand heterogeneity is undervalued. The set of NM^{std} encompasses capacity cost differences (ΔC) between a BM^{ext} and a number of NM^{std}, as well as the demand heterogeneity (h_{cs}) for each NM^{std}.

Finally, π_{cs} is calculated using a linear regression between ΔC and the heterogeneity driver h_{cs}. As data points, the results from the standard (32) noisy models are used, across identical heuristic combinations and activity cost pools using the 40 simulation runs. The hereby estimated π_{cs} is subsequently used in the extended NM^{ext} noisy model to estimate $PF^{NM^{ext}}$.

The following example should clarify the approach:

1. First choose a type of NM^{std} definition: hold the choice of heuristic combination (random + average) and the number of activity pools (3 pools) static.
2. For market and production parameters choose static parameters, e.g. a decreasing market, resource cost vector level eq. 0.5, etc. This yields comparable variable outputs and distributions.
3. Use the resulting 40 BM^{ext} and NM^{std} combinations to estimate π_{cs}.

Figure 11: Information and simulation flow (2nd simulation)

$$\Delta PF_s^{NM^{std}} = PF_s^{BM^{ext}} - PF_s^{NM^{std}} \quad * \tag{35}$$

$$\Delta PF_s^{NM^{ext}} = PF_s^{BM^{ext}} - PF_s^{NM^{ext}} \quad * \tag{36}$$

	Input		Process	Output
Simulation	1. Variable costs variance (VCV, *2 level*) 2. Variable costs (*2 level*) 3. Resource cost variance (RCV, *3 level*) 4. Resource costs (*2 level*) 5. Measurement error (*3 level*) 6. Market growth (*3 level*) 7. Resource sharing (*4 level*) $\Rightarrow level^{factor} = 2^3 3^3 4^1 = 864$ combinations	Standard	1. Optimize profit extended benchmark model, see eq. (29). $\Rightarrow$ 40 samples 2. For each BM^{ext} calculate profit std. noisy model see eq. (30) for a combination of a. Heuristics 1 (2 level) b. Heuristics 2 (2 level) c. ACP (3 level) $\Rightarrow level^{factor} = 2^2 3^1 = 12$ combinations	$\Rightarrow \Delta PF_s^{NM^{std}}$ $\Rightarrow \Delta PF_s^{NM^{ext}}$
		Extension	3. Out of these 480 BM^{ext}/NM^{std} data points, calculate for each NM^{std} configuration the 40 capacity cost differences (ΔC) and demand heterogeneity (h_{cs}). 4. Using this subset asses the cost driver rate π_{cs} by means of a linear regression, see eq. (33). 5. Optimize the profit NM^{ext}. 6. Repeat steps (3) to (5) for each NM^{std} configuration (12 times).	$S =$ BM*NM = 864*40*12 = 414,720

*$s \in S$ (simulation runs), own depiction.

Finally, as in the standard simulation of chapter 3, the obtained prices are used to calculate the corresponding profit errors, by using them in the BM as input variables and calculating the respective truly needed capacities. This is also an identical procedure as in the standard simulation used in chapter 3.2.

In total this approach yields - by combining the 34,560 BM with 12 NM combinations of heuristics and cost pools - 414,720 observations. As in the previous chapter the optimization sometimes timed out, or no optimal solution was found, resulting in 348,000 observations (84% of the 414,720 possible observations) in total.

4.3 Hypothesis Development

At the beginning of chapter 4 the basic research questions and motivation has been introduced. A central question is, if the enhanced noisy model (NM^{ext}) is able to yield higher profits than the ordinary noisy model (NM^{std}) and if so, how great is lever of the enhanced approach. Homburg (2004) has already shown that the higher level cost driver is able to enhance the ABC performance. In theory, taking the results of the former simulation model into account, it is indicated that NM^{std} performance is highly correlated with product and demand heterogeneity: Looking again at Table 13, it can be deducted that resource sharing and market growth have the first and third biggest effect on the profit error. As discussed in the "Based upon Balakrishnan and Sivaramakrishnan (2002), p. 12.

Aside from these changes the extended benchmark model follows the mechanics of the BM of chapter 3. Over a planning horizon of $t=1,\dots T$ periods the BM^{ext} optimizes prices and capacities simultaneously for products $i=1,\dots,I$ and resources $j=1,\dots,J$.

The NM adjustment" section, the NM^{ext} is designed to counter these profit decreasing effects. Hence (H1) is defined as follows:

(H1) *The extended noisy model outperforms the standard noisy model*

In addition, as discussed, the introduced driver takes the portfolio decision into account. The Heuristics on first- and second-stage are not changed in their implementation. Therefore the performance of both heuristics should not be affected, and hence the prediction is:

(H2) *The performance of heuristics on first- and second-stage is comparable between both noisy models*

Lastly, since the new driver aims at better portfolio decisions, the differentiation of the product error into its four parts should indicate that DE and KE errors differ between both noisy models. As cost allocation on portfolio level should also lead to a better resource handling of the extended model, the CE error should be lower in the extended model.

(H3) *The extended model reduces DE, KE and CE in comparison to the standard noisy model*

4.4 Research framework: Key metrics and analysis method

The basic research setting is equal to chapter 3.4, including the definition of profit errors. The fundament still is an OLS regression, which will be presented subsequently. In addition a new metric is used in the descriptive section to compare the performance of the noisy models against each other.

4.4.1 Variance of Profits

This metric is used to capture the variance of the suboptimal noisy model profits, based on Labro and Vanhoucke (2007).[132] The reference of this method is the maximum difference between noisy and benchmark model.

[132] Labro and Vanhoucke (2007) (p. 953) use this metric to control for the importance of a product and its allocated costs with respect to the portfolio. As closer the metric is to 1, only a few products account for the majority of cost in the portfolio, whereas the other products can be neglected.

This difference is set in relation to the sum of all differences between the benchmark profit and the noisy models' profits:

$$Var\_PF^{NM^{std}} = \frac{\sum_{h=1}^{H}\left(PF^{BM^{ext}} - PF_h^{NM^{std}}\right)}{max_{h=1}^{H}\left(PF^{BM^{ext}} - PF_h^{NM^{std}}\right)} \quad (37)$$

$$Var\_PF^{NM^{ext}} = \frac{\sum_{h=1}^{H}\left(PF^{BM^{ext}} - PF_h^{NM^{ext}}\right)}{max_{h=1}^{H}\left(PF^{BM^{ext}} - PF_h^{NM^{ext}}\right)} \quad (38)$$

$h = 1, \dots, 12$ indicating (2 H1 * 2 H2 * 3 ACPs)
$n = 1, \dots, 34{,}560$ indicating the number of BM

4.4.2 Regression Specifications

In contrast to chapter 3.4.2 the regression models slightly differ from each other. Three different regression results are compared, (39) the environment and production parameter influences on the BM, (40) in addition to these parameters, the cost system design choices on both noisy models and (41) the impact of the new driver on the extended noisy model:

$$\begin{aligned} PF^{BM^{ext}} = {} & \beta_0 + \beta_1 Market\ growth_i + \beta_2 Resource\ sharing_i \\ & + \beta_3 Resource\ cost\ variance_i + \beta_4 Total\ resource\ cost_i \\ & + \beta_5 Total\ variable\ cost_i + \beta_6 Variable\ cost\ variance_i \\ & + \beta_7 Measurment\ error_i + \varepsilon_i \end{aligned} \quad (39)$$

$$\begin{aligned} \Delta PF_i^{NM^{std}} = {} & \beta_0 + \beta_1 Market\ growth_i + \beta_2 Resource\ sharing_i \\ & + \beta_3 Resource\ cost\ variance_i + \beta_4 Total\ resource\ cost \\ & + \beta_5 Total\ variable\ cost_i + \beta_6 Variable\ cost\ variance_i \\ & + \beta_7 Measurment\ error_i \\ & + \beta_8 ACP_i + \beta_9 Heuristics1_i + Heuristics2_i + \varepsilon_i \end{aligned} \quad (40)$$

$$
\begin{aligned}
\Delta PF_i^{NM^{ext}} = \; & \beta_0 + \beta_1 Market\ growth_i + \beta_2 Resource\ sharing_i \\
& + \beta_3 Resource\ cost\ variance_i + \beta_4 Total\ resource\ cost \\
& + \beta_5 Total\ variable\ cost_i + \beta_6 Variable\ cost\ variance_i \\
& + \beta_7 Measurment\ error_i \\
& + \beta_8 ACP_i + \beta_9 Heuristics1_i + \beta_9 Heuristics2_i \\
& + \pi_{cs} + \varepsilon_i
\end{aligned} \tag{41}
$$

The regression specification encompasses one coefficient per categorical variable. The variable output can be found in Appendix B; results are illustrated in Table 18.

4.5 Results

4.5.1 Descriptive Results (H3)

First of all, in comparison to the results of the simulation approach in chapter 3.5 the results in Table 17 (Panel A) indicate that both noisy models decline in overall performance. Even by reducing - in contrast to the first approach - variable as well as resource costs (see Appendix B), comparing on average the individual NM profits, there is a gap of approx. 20 million (PF^{NM} of 80 mio.[133]; $PF^{NM^{std}}$ of 58 mio.; $PF^{NM^{ext}}$ of 60 mio.). The descriptive results also show that the extended NM^{ext} on average yields higher profits, roughly 2 million. In addition, the NM^{ext} is more volatile, suggested by the first and third quantile results as by the $Var\_PF^{NM^{ext}}$, which is for almost every quantile higher than the $Var\_PF^{NM^{std}}$. These first results support hypothesis (H1), indicating that the performance of the extended noisy model is superior to the standard model.

Panel B documents the separation of the profit error for each noisy model into the four error types: product quantity error, drop error, keep error and capacity error. On first sight one might ask, how some of the key figures can be negative? Would that not imply, that the NM performs better than the BM. But this would only be the case, if the total (profit error) is negative, which it is not.

[133] See page 64.

Table 17: Profit and Profit Error Distributions

Panel A: Standard Descriptives

	Min.	1. Quant,	Median	Mean	3. Quant,	Max.
$PF^{BM^{ext}}$	56,378 k	104,310 k	160,802 k	179,540 k	252,675 k	379,536 k
$PF^{NM^{std}}$	-292,486 k	-1,586 k	28,798 k	57,549 k	122,811 k	320,617 k
$PF^{NM^{ext}}$	-292,487 k	-3,152 k	31,648 k	59,665 k	124,322 k	320,617 k
$Var\_PF^{NM^{std}}$	0.09	0.31	0.34	0.33	0.37	0.39
$Var\_PF^{NM^{ext}}$	0.17	0.32	0.35	0.34	0.37	0.39

Panel B: Profit Error by Type

	Profit Error	PQE	DE	KE	CE
NM^{std}	122,029 k	-36,838 k	-20,581 k	-12,027 k	191,476 k
NM^{ext}	120,108 k	-35,839 k	-4,628 k	-9,049 k	169,623 k

* Observations: 348,000, in thousands (k).

In contrast Panel B documents, that both models achieve higher sales at the costs of over proportional high capacity costs. This finding is in line with the lower performance of both NM due to the cost sticky environmental setting. Supporting (H3) all profit error types are lower in the NM^{ext}.

4.5.2 Regression Results (H1 & H2)

The focus of this section lies on hypothesis (H1) and (H2). Therefore a deeper look into the drivers of the NM performance and the related heuristics is necessary. This is achieved by using the introduced regression (see section 4.4.2). The results are illustrated in Table 18, covering the BM profit and the profit errors of the standard and extended noisy models.

Table 18: Regression Results Non-Dummy Specification incl. the extended NM

	$PF^{BM^{ext}}$	$Profit^{NM^{std}}$ $Error$	$Profit^{NM^{ext}}$ $Error$
(Intercept)	91,979,159.34***	99,078,213.67***	94,459,091.06***
	(690.59)	(161.40)	(188.58)
Market growth	104,307,246.24***	18,466,718.09***	16,143,203.91***
	(4,213.44)	(82.13)	(88.26)
Resource sharing	-3,244,638.69***	-2,774,168.08***	-2,426,465.79***
	(-136.73)	(-40.35)	(-42.39)
Resource costs variance	1,094,118.94***	-3,844,235.98***	-3,889,407.49***
	(11.26)	(-13.65)	(-16.98)
Total resource costs	-2,490.87***	2,674.71***	2,812.55***
	(-1,254.20)	(464.88)	(598.75)
Total variable costs	-8,140.47***	-3,397.68***	-3,271.41***
	(-410.04)	(-59.08)	(-69.93)
Variable costs variance	452,538.60***	18,553.31	-33,014.78
	(5.70)	(0.081)	(-0.18)
Measurement error	-141,359.70	6,747,575.75***	6,820,814.84***
	(-1.16)	(19.17)	(23.82)
ACP		-4,104,133.10***	-5,429,943.91***
		(-146.69)	(-238.53)
Heuristics1		-5,465,248.36***	-1,251,959.70***
		(-47.52)	(-13.38)
Heuristics2		-28,404,768.17***	-27,433,893.62***
		(-97.46)	(-115.28)

Table 18: Regression Results Non-Dummy Specification incl. the extended NM (cont'd)

	$PF^{BM^{ext}}$	$Profit^{NM^{std}}$ Error	$Profit^{NM^{ext}}$ Error
Market growth * Heuristics2		-4,507,298.45***	-4,982,185.75***
		(-31.41)	(-42.56)
cost driver rate (π_{cs})			-7,475,117.69***
			(-13.55)
Adj. R^2	0.98	0.52	0.64
Num. obs.	348,000.00	348,000.00	348,000.00
			*p < 0.001, **p < 0.01, *p < 0.05

The findings are in line with the descriptive results, indicating that the overall performance of the extended noisy model is superior to the standard model, by ~5% points.[134]

Also the rather poor overall performance using the basic random method and big pool (incorporated in the intercept) of both models is striking. Since the delta is greater than the $PF^{BM^{ext}}$, in both cases the NM effectively yields negative profits. This underlines the hypothesis (H1) that the extended system outperforms the standard model.

The outlined results also in favor of H2 – heuristics perform equally in the standard and extended model - since the whole cost system design yields comparable results across both NM models: The heuristics on stage two, as well as the activity cost pools and the measurement error are on the same level.

[134] The relative performance is measured by dividing the profit error by the extended BM profit ($\frac{PF^{NM^{ext}}}{PF^{BM^{ext}}}$~1,0772; and $\frac{PF^{NM^{std}}}{PF^{BM^{ext}}}$~1,027;) using the intercepts.

The only real outlier are heuristics on the first stage. This result can be interpreted as the minor relevance of these heuristics because of the portfolio driver. Since the first-stage heuristic is responsible for the allocation of costs to activities, wrong cost allocation is healed on the portfolio level by the sticky cost driver rates and the heterogeneous driver (h_c). The slightly bigger effect of the number of activity cost pools could be traced back to eq. (32): Activity costs have a direct impact on ΔC and subsequently cause a "double effect" (indirectly via the sticky costs π_{cs} and directly in eq. (33)) on the extended model results.

Overall the results also suggest, that the model extension works as designed: One reason to incorporate the new driver was to improve the noisy models' robustness against changes in market situations. This is supported by the less important influence of (approx. 2 million) market growth on the delta profits. In addition the sticky cost driver rate reduces the profit error (NM^{ext}) essentially by approx. 7.5 million. However it needs to be stated, that the highest impact on profit errors lies with the usage of more sophisticated second-stage heuristics (i.e. the usage of the average instead of the big pool method). In contrast to the 7.5 million gain of the sticky drivers, advanced second-stage heuristics alone account for a lever of approx. 27.5 million, not incorporating the interaction effect between better second-stage heuristics and changes in market growth.

4.5.3 The influence of cost structure

Even if not directly comparable in absolute terms, but in direction, the simulation results of chapter 3 and the sticky simulation differ essentially. Whereas in the non-sticky simulation mainly the production parameters drove the performance of the models (resource sharing had the biggest effect), the sticky model is driven by the cost system design choices and market growth (accounting for the top 5 performance drivers only subsequently followed by production parameters).

The higher effect of cost system related influences goes along with the design of the economic environment. Prior decisions on capacity have a higher persistence, and hence changes in cost allocation have ceteris paribus a higher impact on profits. In addition costs are less controllable over time, since a decline in capacity is costly due to adjustment costs. Hence the cost structure becomes more important in a sticky environment, and has, as the results indicate a higher impact on profits.

Balakrishnan, Labro and Soderstrom (2014) discuss in their work "Cost Structure and Sticky Costs" the influence of cost structure (neglection) on prior research results. They argue, that in the data samples used to measure cost stickiness, especially in the approach by Anderson, Banker and Janakiraman (2003), costs of resources are incorporated which are only partly or not at all adjustable over the considered time horizon. Whereas the assumption of their used metrics dictates that all costs need to be fully adjustable.

While the simulation study in this chapter is far from fully incorporating these raised concerns, it also outlines the dependency of the profit realization on the underlying cost structure and supporting the raised concern by Balakrishnan, Labro and Soderstrom (2014).

4.6 Discussion of the limitations of the new approach

One may argue that even if the NM^{ext} yields higher profits, to calculate the costs of the demand heterogeneity, one needs the optimal capacity decision of the BM^{ext} and the NM^{std} pricing decisions and therefore the approach would be artificial.
Simulations analyzes are artificial by heart, but never the less able to give answers to practical questions[135]: The idea is to outline the inefficiencies by neglecting the cost-stickiness effects in planning decisions. Moreover, the aim is to introduce a basic fundament of how cost-systems need to be refined to be able to control for cost-stickiness.
Whereas the presented simulation approach is able to answer the design question, the above mentioned criticism points at the practical implication. By abstracting from the given approach a possible practical modeling

[135] See Harrison et al. (2007), p. 1243.

alternative could be measuring the information on demand heterogeneity and its inherent costs by an ex-post analysis of cost-systems. It is therefore possible to analyze planed and used capacity and their adjustment costs. Hereby a sticky factor as the heterogeneity cost driver rate can be estimated. Even an ex-ante analysis is possible, extrapolating the ex-post information to future periods. Hence a practical relevant implementation is possible. The simulation results underline, that this course of action could be profitable, because of more reliable profit forecasts.

5. Conclusion

What impact has the performance of the underlying cost-system and its design on the quality of pricing and product-mix decisions? By using a full-cost based simulation approach, this thesis sheds light upon the question raised by Balakrishnan and Sivaramakrishnan (2002). The previous research by Hwang, Evans and Hegde (1993); Homburg (2004); Balakrishnan, Hansen and Labro (2011); Anand, Balakrishnan and Labro (2013) is extended by laying a special focus on pricing decisions in a dynamic model, considering different market and environment situations and integrating cost-stickiness into the decision problem.

The most important findings are listed hereafter: More complex cost systems are able to reduce profit errors extensively (52%). This effect is even more pronounced in environments of growing markets. The decomposition into the four error types reveals that distortions in production quantity are notably higher than errors arising from wrong portfolio decisions. In addition, keep errors exceed drop errors indicating a systematic underestimation of full costs by all heuristics.

Having led the basic fundament for a generic research model, the research question is modified to incorporate cost-stickiness. The basic idea behind this approach is bridging the gap between cost system design and cost stickiness. It could be shown, that enhancing cost systems by sticky drivers is possible and advisable, since these systems are capable of yielding higher profits. Nevertheless, implementation costs of such drivers need to be considered, since the results also document, that enhanced standard methods are also capable of closing the profit gap considerably. The exact lever of sticky cost drivers therefore needs to be measured in future work.

In addition, the reliance of the model on the underlying cost structure has been shown and therefore broadens the understanding of cost stickiness and adds to the discussion on its relevance in used cost stickiness metrics. To the author's best knowledge there exists no implementation of a sticky cost driver in practice. The only theoretical model to build on is proposed by

Homburg (2004). Therefore, this thesis also adds an argument and a means of how to include a sticky driver in a decision based pricing context.

Using a simulation approach, the results necessarily underlie the axioms of the model and the distribution assumptions of the used random number generators. While the robustness section focused on different parameter settings, displaying a stability of the simulation against changes, the core model is not modified, therefore limiting the results by only considering monopolistic settings. Taking into account the results by Hwang, Evans and Hegde (1993); Anand, Balakrishnan and Labro (2013), a more dynamic model would represent a straightforward extension, changing the ability of the firm to set prices in varying competitive environments.

My thesis contributes to the academic literature on errors from inefficient cost systems in capacity and pricing decisions. The added pricing context to Balakrishnan, Hansen and Labro (2011) is an important enhancement since in markets where firms have pricing power, setting prices and choosing the product-mix belongs to the most important decisions that determine firms' performance. Besides, in practice, pricing discretion frequently arises outside monopolistic settings from a lack of transparency and comparability.

The simulation approach further provides hypotheses that can be tested empirically. For example, researchers could use surveys to test (a) whether cost system complexity increases profits, (b) whether the profit benefit from more complex cost systems is more pronounced in growing markets, (c) whether firms tend to keep more unprofitable products than they drop profitable products and (d) whether firms with more complex cost systems make less product portfolio and production quantity errors.

Lastly, the implementation of cost-stickiness into a decision context is also relevant to managers who wish to select and implement a new cost system or to assess and improve a running cost system. In addition to the standard model (chapter 4), practice can consider the results regarding the performance of different cost systems under different market and production environments.

6. References

Altomonte, C. / Barattieri, A. / Basu, S. (2015): *Average-cost pricing: Some evidence and implications.* European Economic Review, 281–296.

Anand, V. / Balakrishnan, R. / Labro, E. (2013): Profit Effcets of Errors in Cost Systems : A Numerical Experiment, Working Paper.

Anderson, M.C. / Banker, R.D. / Janakiraman, S.N. (2003): *Are Selling, General, and Administrative Costs "Sticky"?* Journal of Accounting Research, 47–63.

Antony, J. (2014): *Design of Experiments for Engineers and Scientists,* 2nd ed. Elsevier Science, London.

Babad, Y.M. / Balachandran, B. V. (1993): *Cost driver optimization in activity-based costing.* The Accounting Review, 563–575.

Balachandran, B. V. / Balakrishnan, R. / Sivaramakrishnan, K. (1997): *On the efficiency of cost-based decision rules for capacity planning.* The Accounting Review, 599–619.

Balakrishnan, R. et al. (2009): *Evaluating Heuristics Used When Designing Product Costing Systems.* Working Paper.

Balakrishnan, R. / Hansen, S. / Labro, E. (2011): *Evaluating Heuristics Used When Designing Product Costing Systems.* Management Science, 520–541.

Balakrishnan, R. / Labro, E. / Sivaramakrishnan, K. (2012a): *Product Costs as Decision Aids: An Analysis of Alternative Approaches (Part 1).* Accounting Horizons, 1–20.

Balakrishnan, R. / Labro, E. / Sivaramakrishnan, K. (2012b): *Product Costs as Decision Aids: An Analysis of Alternative Approaches (Part 2).* Accounting Horizons, 21–41.

Balakrishnan, R. / Labro, E. / Soderstrom, N.S. (2014): *Cost Structure and Sticky Costs.* Journal of Management Accounting Research, 91–116.

Balakrishnan, R. / Penno, M. (2014): *Causality in the context of analytical models and numerical experiments.* Accounting, Organizations and Society, 531–534.

Balakrishnan, R. / Sivaramakrishnan, K. (2001): *Sequential Solutions to Capacity-Planning and Pricing Decisions.* Contemporary Accounting Research, 1–26.

Balakrishnan, R. / Sivaramakrishnan, K. (2002): *A critical overview of the use of full-cost data for planning and pricing.* Journal of Management Accounting Research, 3–31.

Banker, R. / Byzalov, D. / Plehn-Dujowich, J. (2011): Sticky cost behavior: Theory and evidence, Working Paper.

Banker, R. / Chen, L. (2006): Labor market characteristics and cross-country differences in cost stickiness, Working Paper.

Banker, R.D. / Byzalov, D. (2014): *Asymmetric Cost Behavior.* Journal of Management Accounting Research, 43–79.

Banker, R.D. / Byzalov, D. / Plehn-Dujowich, J.M. (2014): *Demand Uncertainty and Cost Behavior.* The Accounting Review, 839–865.

Banker, R.D. / Hughes, J.S. (1994): *Product Costing and Pricing.* The Accounting Review, 479–494.

Banker, R.D. / Hwang, I. / Mishra, B.K. (2002): *Product costing and pricing under long-term capacity commitment.* Journal of Management Accounting Research, 79–97.

Baumgarten, D. (2012): *The Cost Stickiness Phenomenon.* Gabler Verlag, Wiesbaden.

Baumgarten, D. / Bonenkamp, U. / Homburg, C. (2010): *The Information Content of the SG&A Ratio.* Journal of Management Accounting Research, 1–22.

Bordley, R.F. (1993): *Estimating Automotive Elasticities from Segment Elasticities and First Choice/Second Choice Data.* The Review of Economics and Statistics, 455–462.

Box, G.E.P. / Hunter, W.G. / Hunter, J.S. (1978): *Statistics for experimenters: an introduction to design, data analysis, and model building.* Wiley, New York.

Calleja, K. / Steliaros, M. / Thomas, D.C. (2006): *A note on cost stickiness: Some international comparisons.* Management Accounting Research, 127–140.

Cardinaels, E. / Roodhooft, F. / Warlop, L. (2004): *The Value of Activity-Based Costing in Competitive Pricing Decisions.* Journal of Management Accounting Research, 133–148.

Chen, C.X. / Lu, H. / Sougiannis, T. (2012): *The Agency Problem, Corporate Governance, and the Asymmetrical Behavior of Selling, General, and Administrative Costs*.* Contemporary Accounting Research, 252–282.

Christensen, J. / Demski, J.S. (1997): *Product costing in the presence of endogenous subcost functions.* Review of Accounting Studies, 65–87.

Cooper, R. / Kaplan, R.S. (1988): *How Cost Accounting Distorts Product Costs.* Management Accounting, 20–27.

Datar, S. / Gupta, M. (1994): *Aggregation, specification and measurement errors in product costing.* The Accounting Review, 567–591.

Datar, S.M. et al. (2015): *Cost Accounting: A Managerial Emphasis,* 15th ed. Pearson Higher Education AU, Boston.

Dearman, D.T. / Shields, M.D. (2001): *Cost Knowledge and Cost-Based Judgment Performance.* Journal of Management Accounting Research, 1–18.

Deng, S. / Yano, C.A. (2006): *Joint Production and Pricing Decisions with Setup Costs and Capacity Constraints.* Management Science, 741–756.

Dierynck, B. / Landsman, W.R. / Renders, A. (2012): *Do Managerial Incentives Drive Cost Behavior? Evidence about the Role of the Zero Earnings Benchmark for Labor Cost Behavior in Private Belgian Firms.* The Accounting Review, 1219–1246.

Drury, C. / Tayles, M. (1994): *Product costing in UK manufacturing organizations.* European Accounting Review, 443–470.

Field, A.P. / Hole, G. (2003): *How to Design and Report Experiments.* Sage publications Limited, London.

Fisher, R.A. (1935): *The Design of Experiments.* Oliver and Boyd, Edinburgh.

Gentle, J.E. (2003): *Random Number Generation and Monte Carlo Methods*, Statistics and Computing. Springer-Verlag, New York.

Gupta, M. / King, R.R. (1997): *An Experimental Investigation of the Effect of Cost Information and Feedback on Product Cost Decisions*.* Contemporary Accounting Research, 99–127.

Hall, R.L. / Hitch, C.J. (1939): *Price Theory and Business Behaviour.* Oxford Economic Papers, 12–45.

Harrison, J.R. et al. (2007): *Simulation modeling in organizational and management research.* Academy of Management Review, 1229–1245.

Hartgraves, A.L. / Morse, W.J. (2015): *Managerial Accounting*, 7th ed. Cambridge Business Publishers.

Hocke, S. / Meyer, M. / Lorscheid, I. (2015): *Improving simulation model analysis and communication via design of experiment principles: an example from the simulation-based design of cost accounting systems.* Journal of Management Control, 131–155.

Homburg, C. (2001a): *A note on optimal cost driver selection in ABC.* Management Accounting Research, 197–205.

Homburg, C. (2001b): *Hierarchische Controllingkonzeption.* Physica-Verlag HD, Heidelberg.

Homburg, C. (2004): *Improving activity-based costing heuristics by higher-level cost drivers.* European Journal of Operational Research, 332–343.

Homburg, C. / Nasev, J. / Plank, P. (2013): The Impact of Cost Allocation Errors on Price and Product-Mix Decisions. Working Paper, University of Cologne.

Hwang, Y. / Evans, J.H.I.I.I. / Hegde, V.G. (1993): *Product Cost Bias and Selection of an Allocation Base.* Journal of Management Accounting Research, 213–242.

International Monetary Fund (2013): *World Economic outlook - Transitions and Tensions.* International Monetary Fund, Washington.

Ittner, C.D. / Lanen, W.N. / Larcker, D.F. (2002): *The Association Between Activity-Based Costing and Manufacturing Performance.* Journal of Accounting Research, 711–726.

Kama, I. / Weiss, D. (2013): *Do Earnings Targets and Managerial Incentives Affect Sticky Costs?* Journal of Accounting Research, 201–224.

Kennedy, T. / Affleck-Graves, J. (2001): *The Impact of Activity-Based Costing Techniques on Firm Performance.* Journal of Management Accounting Research, 19–45.

Kleijnen, J.P.C. et al. (2005): *State-of-the-Art Review: A User's Guide to the Brave New World of Designing Simulation Experiments.* INFORMS Journal on Computing, 263–289.

Kleijnen, J.P.C. (2015): *Design and Analysis of Simulation Experiments*, International Series in Operations Research & Management Science. Springer International Publishing, Cham.

Labro, E. (2015): *Using simulation methods in accounting research.* Journal of Management Control, 99–104.

Labro, E. / Vanhoucke, M. (2007): *A simulation analysis of interactions among errors in costing systems.* The Accounting Review, 939–962.

Lorscheid, I. / Heine, B.-O. / Meyer, M. (2012): *Opening the "black box" of simulations: increased transparency and effective communication through the systematic design of experiments.* Computational and Mathematical Organization Theory, 22–62.

Lucas, M. (1999): *economists versus accountants.* Management Accounting: Magazine for Chartered Management Accountants, 34–35.

Lucas, M.. (2003): *Pricing decisions and the neoclassical theory of the firm.* Management Accounting Research, 201–217.

Mahlendorf, M. (2009): *Sticky Cost Issues — Kostenremanenz bei Nachfrageschwankungen.* Controlling & Management, 193–195.

Mankiw, N.G. / Taylor, M.P. (2006): *Economics*, Economics. Thomson Learning, London.

Moosmüller, G. (2008): *Methoden der empirischen Wirtschaftsforschung.* Pearson Deutschland GmbH.

NAG (2015): The NAG C Library [WWW Document]. URL: http://www.nag.co.uk/numeric/CL/CLdescription.asp (accessed 2015-03-29).

Niederreiter, H. (2003): *Random Number Generation and Monte Carlo Methods*, Statistics and Computing. Springer-Verlag, New York.

Noreen, E. / Soderstrom, N. (1994): *Are overhead costs strictly proportional to activity?* Journal of Accounting and Economics, 255–278.

Noreen, E. / Soderstrom, N. (1997): *The accuracy of proportional cost models: evidence from hospital service departments.* Review of Accounting Studies, 89–114.

Picheny, V. et al. (2013): *Quantile-Based Optimization of Noisy Computer Experiments With Tunable Precision.* Technometrics, 2–13.

Reiss, J. (2011): *A Plea for (Good) Simulations: Nudging Economics Toward an Experimental Science.* Simulation & Gaming, 243–264.

Robinson, J. (1933): *The Economics of Imperfect Competition.* Macmillan, London.

RRZK (2014): High Performance Computing (HPC) [WWW Document]. URL: http://rrzk.uni-koeln.de/hpc.html (accessed 2015-03-29).

Sacks, J. et al. (1989): *Design and Analysis of Computer Experiments.* Statistical Science, 409–423.

Santner, T.J. / Williams, B.J. / Notz, W.I. (2003): *The Design and Analysis of Computer Experiments*, Springer Series in Statistics. Springer New York, New York.

Scapens, R.W. (1994): *Never mind the gap: towards an institutional perspective on management accounting practice.* Management Accounting Research, 301–321.

Schmalenbach, E. (1963): *Kostenrechnung und Preispolitik*, 8th ed. Köln und Opladen.

Schneeweiß, C. (1992): *Planung*, Springer-Lehrbuch. Springer Berlin Heidelberg, Berlin, Heidelberg.

Schneeweiss, C. (1998): *On the applicability of activity based costing as a planning instrument.* International Journal of Production Economics, 277–284.

Schneeweiss, C. (2003): *Distributed Decision Making.* Springer, Berlin, Heidelberg.

Shim, E. / Sudit, E.F. (1995): *How manufacturers price products.* Strategic Finance, 37–39.

Strube, E. (1936): *Kostenremanenz und Beschäftigungsschwankungen.* Zeitschrift für Handelswissenschaftliche Forschung, 505–541.

Tutz, G. (2011): *Regression for Categorical Data.* Cambridge University Press, New York.

7. Appendix

A. Error Derivation

$$\max_{P_{it}^{BM},R_{jt},L_j} \sum_{t=1}^{T}\left(\sum_{i=1}^{I}(P_{it}^{BM}-v_i)(q_{it})-\sum_{j=1}^{J}\phi_j c_j R_{jt}\right)-T\sum_{j=1}^{J}c_j L_j$$

Enhance by $\sum_{t=1}^{T}\sum_{i=1}^{I}\sum_{j=1}^{J}m_{ij}c_j q_{it}-\sum_{t=1}^{T}\sum_{i=1}^{I}\sum_{j=1}^{J}m_{ij}c_j q_{it}$

$$\rightarrow \max_{P_{it}^{BM},R_{jt},L_j} \sum_{t=1}^{T}\left(\sum_{i=1}^{I}(P_{it}^{BM}-v_i)(q_{it})-\sum_{j=1}^{J}\phi_j c_j R_{jt}\right)-\sum_{t=1}^{T}\sum_{i=1}^{I}\sum_{j=1}^{J}m_{ij}c_j q_{it}$$
$$-T\sum_{j=1}^{J}c_j L_j+\sum_{t=1}^{T}\sum_{i=1}^{I}\sum_{j=1}^{J}m_{ij}c_j q_{it}$$

Set $q_{it}=(A_{it}-b_i P_{it}^{BM})$

$$\rightarrow \max_{P_{it}^{BM},R_{jt},L_j} \sum_{t=1}^{T}\left(\sum_{i=1}^{I}(P_{it}^{BM}-v_i)(q_{it})\right)-\sum_{t=1}^{T}\sum_{i=1}^{I}\sum_{j=1}^{J}m_{ij}c_j q_{it}$$
$$-T\sum_{j=1}^{J}c_j L_j+\sum_{t=1}^{T}\sum_{i=1}^{I}\sum_{j=1}^{J}m_{ij}c_j q_{it}-\sum_{t=1}^{T}\sum_{j=1}^{J}\phi_j c_j R_{jt}$$

$$\rightarrow \max_{P_{it}^{BM},R_{jt},L_j} \sum_{t=1}^{T}\left(\sum_{i=1}^{I}\left((P_{it}^{BM}-v_i)(q_{it}-q_{it}\sum_{j=1}^{J}m_{ij}c_j\right)\right.$$
$$\left.-\left(\sum_{j=1}^{J}c_j L_j-\sum_{j=1}^{J}c_j\sum_{i=1}^{I}m_{ij}q_{it}+\sum_{j=1}^{J}\phi_j c_j R_{jt}\right)\right)$$

$$\rightarrow \max_{P_{it}^{BM},R_{jt},L_j} \sum_{t=1}^{T}\left(\sum_{i=1}^{I}\left((P_{it}^{BM}-v_i)(q_{it})\ -q_{it}\sum_{j=1}^{J}m_{ij}c_j\right)\right.$$
$$\left.-\left(\sum_{j=1}^{J}c_j L_j-\sum_{j=1}^{J}c_j\,RU_{it}+\sum_{j=1}^{J}\phi_j c_j R_{jt}\right)\right)$$

Set $RU_{it}=\sum_{i=1}^{I}m_{ij}q_{it}$ and $FC_i=v_i+\sum_{j=1}^{J}m_{ij}c_j$

$$\rightarrow \max_{P_{it}^{BM},R_{jt},L_j} \sum_{t=1}^{T}\left(\sum_{i=1}^{I}((P_{it}^{BM}-FC_i)(q_{it}))\right.$$
$$\left.-\left(\sum_{j=1}^{J}c_{j[}[(\phi_j-1)R_{jt}+(L_j+R_{jt}-RU_{it})]\right)\right)$$

B. Variable and Parameter declaration

Variable	Definition	Categories
Profit error	$\Delta Profit = Profit^{BM} - Profit^{NM}$	Continuous
Cost error	$EUCD = \sqrt{\sum_{i=0}^{I}(FC_i^{BM} - FC_i^{NM})^2}$	Continuous
Heuristics1	1=Random 2=Size random 3=Size misc 4=Correlation random 5=Correlation size	
Heuristics1 (Size-Based)	0=(Non size based: Random, Correlation random) 1=(Size based: Size random, Size misc, Correlation size)	
Heuristics2	1=Big Pool) 2=Num(2) 3=Num(4) 4=Average	
ACP	Number of activity cost pools	(1, 2, 3, 4, 5, 6)
Price elasticity	A price elasticity of (-1.3) implies that a 1% increase in price reduces demand by 1.3%. Price elasticities above (below) the absolute value of one indicate elastic (inelastic) demand, i.e., changes in price have a large (small) effect on demand.	(-1.3)
Market growth	A_{it}: Market size (maximum quantity) of product i in period t, with starting volume $A_{i1} = U(5500{,}5600)$, ε_t: $N(0{,}1)$ $A_{it} = 0.9A_{it-1} + 200\varepsilon_t$ $A_{it} = A_{it-1} + 200\varepsilon_t$ $A_{it} = 500 + A_{it-1} + 200\varepsilon_t$	Decreasing = 1 Saturated = 2 Increasing = 3

Variable and Parameter declaration (cont'd)

Variable	Definition	Categories
Resource sharing	The resource sharing level refers to the zeros in the resource consumption matrix that define whether a product i consumes resource j. Few zeros indicate homogeneous resource consumption, i.e., high resource sharing.	(-0.75, 0, 0.75, 1.50)
Total resource costs (TRC)	The sum of unit resource costs across all resources.	(40000, 60000)
Resource costs variance (RCV)	At a level of 0.25 the J resources have similar costs, whereas at a level of 0.75 few resources have a large fraction of total resource costs.	(0.25, 0.50, 0.75)
Resource costs (c_j)	J elements are drawn from a uniform distribution with bounds 1 ±RCV. This vector is normalized and then multiplied with TRC.	
Total variable costs (TVC)	The sum of unit variable costs across all products.	(5000, 7000)
Variable costs variance (VCV)	At a level of 0.25 the I products have similar costs, whereas at a level of 0.75 few products have a large fraction of total variable costs.	(0.25, 0.75)
Variable costs (v_i)	I elements are drawn from a uniform distribution with bounds 1 ±VCV. This vector is normalized and then multiplied with TVC.	
Measurement error	Errors in measuring resource or activity consumption, e.g., set up costs involve estimates of the time spent on set up activities which are typically estimated with questionnaires or interviews that are prone to measurement error (Datar and Gupta, 1994).	(0.1, 0.3, 0.5)

See also Homburg, Nasev and Plank (2013) p. 9ff.

C. Robustness Tables

Table 19: Regression Results (Non-Dummy), price elasticity uniformly distributed

	Profit error	BM profit	NM profit
Intercept	60,987,674.20***	222,515,480.45***	161,527,806.25***
	(156.97)	(577.72)	(306.92)
ACP	-8,571,460.87***	-1,553.50	8,569,907.36***
	(-462.53)	(-0.085)	(341.40)
Heuristics1	-388,422.17***	4,553.55	392,975.72***
	(-6.53)	(0.077)	(4.88)
Heuristics2	-15,195,088.80***	6,856.91	15,201,945.71***
	(-207.90)	(0.095)	(153.55)
Market growth	13,207,532.24***	89,672,260.08***	76,464,727.84***
	(140.71)	(963.70)	(601.41)
Market growth * H2	-2,443,777.51***	-2,848.94	2,440,928.57***
	(-71.30)	(-0.084)	(52.58)
Resource sharing	-19,437,865.85***	-24,350,883.64***	-4,913,017.79***
	(-514.60)	(-650.30)	(-96.02)
Resource costs variance	-7,008,433.21***	4,742,616.02***	11,751,049.24***
	(-19.15)	(13.07)	(23.70)
Resource costs variance*H1	-6,203.84	-6,907.46	-703.62
	(-0.056)	(-0.063)	(-0.0047)
Total resource costs	854.23***	-4,394.32***	-5,248.55***
	(269.93)	(-1,400.71)	(-1,224.39)
Total variable costs	-526.66***	-5,164.91***	-4,638.25***
	(-16.68)	(-165.04)	(-108.47)
Variable costs variance	-210,940.62	1,561,360.29***	1,772,300.91***
	(-1.67)	(12.47)	(10.36)
Measurement error	11,033,799.79***	-492,203.42*	-11,526,003.21***
	(57.11)	(-2.57)	(-44.04)
Adj. R^2	0.55	0.90	0.83
N	890,471.00	890,471.00	890,471.00

$^{***}p < 0.001$, $^{**}p < 0.01$, $^{*}p < 0.05$.

Price elasticity is modeled as: $b = u(1.0; 1.5)$

Table 20: Regression Results (Non-Dummy), Robust White Noise

	Profit error	BM profit	NM profit
Intercept	61,023,438.38***	203,485,298.46***	142,461,860.08***
	(152.87)	(590.74)	(281.57)
ACP	-8,787,429.60***	-348.47	8,787,081.13***
	(-463.02)	(-0.021)	(365.28)
Heuristics1	-446,577.17***	-4,287.54	442,289.63***
	(-7.36)	(-0.082)	(5.75)
Heuristics2	-15,472,464.78***	-1,268.52	15,471,196.26***
	(-206.95)	(-0.02)	(163.26)
Market growth	13,970,040.15***	78,562,146.98***	64,592,106.83***
	(145.50)	(948.22)	(530.76)
Market growth * Heuristics2	-2,534,290.23***	2,986.21	2,537,276.44***
	(-72.29)	(0.099)	(57.10)
Resource sharing	-19,739,165.38***	-24,493,992.44***	-4,754,827.06***
	(-510.17)	(-733.62)	(-96.95)
Resource costs variance	-8,046,467.72***	7,055,175.61***	15,101,643.33***
	(-21.51)	(21.85)	(31.85)
Resource costs variance * Heuristics1	94,952.96	10,035.44	-84,917.52
	(0.84)	(0.10)	(-0.60)
Total resource costs	857.58***	-4,033.78***	-4,891.36***
	(264.73)	(-1,442.99)	(-1,191.24)
Total variable costs	-302.51***	-5,064.92***	-4,762.42***
	(-9.36)	(-181.53)	(-116.20)
Variable costs variance	-204,857.61	1,088,860.25***	1,293,717.86***
	(-1.58)	(9.76)	(7.89)
Measurement error	10,589,856.48***	-1,785,573.99***	-12,375,430.46***
	(53.44)	(-10.44)	(-49.27)
Adj. R^2	0.55	0.90	0.82
N	887,077.00	887,077.00	887,077.00

*** $p < 0.001$, ** $p < 0.01$, * $p < 0.05$.

Table 21: Regression Results (Non-Dummy), higher penalty parameter[136]

	Profit error	BM profit	NM profit
Intercept	61,235,374.55***	196,950,672.54***	135,715,297.99***
	(139.80)	(567.33)	(254.28)
ACP	-8,822,321.09***	-877.75	8,821,443.34***
	(-422.01)	(-0.053)	(346.29)
Heuristics1	-455,790.45***	15,393.11	471,183.56***
	(-6.79)	(0.29)	(5.76)
Heuristics2	-16,686,573.27***	12,209.71	16,698,782.98***
	(-199.95)	(0.18)	(164.21)
Market growth	15,199,162.75***	79,590,526.93***	64,391,364.18***
	(143.89)	(950.71)	(500.28)
Market growth * H2	-1,915,088.38***	-6,999.62	1,908,088.75***
	(-49.66)	(-0.23)	(40.61)
Resource sharing	-17,518,094.39***	-25,688,361.57***	-8,170,267.17***
	(-410.71)	(-759.90)	(-157.20)
Resource costs variance	-9,076,911.91***	7,114,972.66***	16,191,884.56***
	(-22.05)	(21.81)	(32.28)
Resource costs variance * H1	86,164.08	-29,697.62	-115,861.70
	(0.70)	(-0.30)	(-0.77)
Total resource costs	1,040.76***	-4,016.11***	-5,056.87***
	(291.72)	(-1,420.34)	(-1,163.22)
Total variable costs	-206.11***	-4,725.13***	-4,519.02***
	(-5.79)	(-167.37)	(-104.12)
Variable costs variance	-422,661.09**	589,366.06***	1,012,027.15***
	(-2.97)	(5.22)	(5.83)
Measurement error	10,310,747.27***	603,916.65***	-9,706,830.62***
	(47.37)	(3.50)	(-36.59)
Adj. R^2	0.52	0.90	0.80
N	848,351.00	848,351.00	848,351.00

$^{***}p < 0.001$, $^{**}p < 0.01$, $^{*}p < 0.05$.

[136] Penalty parameter at $\phi = 1.5$.

MIX
Papier aus verantwortungsvollen Quellen
Paper from responsible sources
FSC® C105338

If you have any concerns about our products,
you can contact us on
ProductSafety@springernature.com

In case Publisher is established outside the EU,
the EU authorized representative is:
Springer Nature Customer Service Center GmbH
Europaplatz 3, 69115 Heidelberg, Germany

Printed by Libri Plureos GmbH
in Hamburg, Germany

Studien zur Neuen Politischen Ökonomie

Herausgegeben von
T. Bräuninger, Mannheim, Deutschland
G. Schneider, Konstanz, Deutschland

Eva Bernauer

Identities in Civil Conflict

How Ethnicity, Religion and Ideology Jointly Affect Rebellion

Springer VS

Eva Bernauer
Mannheim, Germany

Dissertation zur Erlangung des Doktorgrades der Sozialwissenschaften an der Universität Mannheim unter dem Titel "Civil Conflict in Three Dimensions - Ethnic, Religious and Class-Based Support of Rebel Groups in the National and International Domain"

Tag der mündlichen Prüfung: 02.10.2015

Erstgutachter: Professor Dr. Thomas Bräuninger
Zweitgutachter: Professor Sabine Carey, Ph.D.
Drittgutachter: Professor Nicolay Marinov, Ph.D.

Studien zur Neuen Politischen Ökonomie
ISBN 978-3-658-14151-6 ISBN 978-3-658-14152-3 (eBook)
DOI 10.1007/978-3-658-14152-3

Library of Congress Control Number: 2016939109

Springer VS

Printed on acid-free paper

This Springer VS imprint is published by Springer Nature
The registered company is Springer Fachmedien Wiesbaden GmbH

Acknowledgments

Having worked for more than four years on this dissertation while studying at the Graduate School of Economic and Social Sciences at Mannheim University, I would love to thank many people.

First and foremost, I want to thank my supervisor Prof. Dr. Thomas Bräuninger, who combines excellent academic and analytic skills with a great personality, and who let me pursue my own research interests. I am extremely grateful for the time and patience that he afforded, especially at the beginning of this dissertation project, when there was most need for it. As my original interest was primarily in civil conflicts and quantitative methods, I very greatly thank Thomas for broadening my horizon by insisting on thorough — at best formal — theorizing. Last but not least, I thank Thomas for assisting me in gaining financial support throughout the entire research period.

I am thankful to Prof. Dr. Gerald Schneider who supported me in applying for the Graduate School of Economic and Social Sciences in Mannheim in the first place. I also thank Prof. Sabine Carey, Ph.D., who shares my interest in civil conflicts, for serving as a secondary reviewer, and Prof. Nikolay Marinov, Ph.D., for serving as a tertiary reviewer.

I would love to thank all my colleagues and friends from the CDSS and from the Chair of Political Economy at Mannheim University for their great companionship. It was good to have so many fellows struggling with the same challenges when writing a dissertation, being able to discuss technical issues at workshops or in D7, and at the same time spending a great non-academic time over lunch or at night. I especially thank Susanne Michalik and Nathalie Giger for a joyful time in Mannheim and very good friendship.

Most of all, I thank my husband Andreas for providing me with moral and practical support. In difficult times, Andreas placed his trust in me, while at the same time holding my ambitions in check. Andreas also had helpful tips regarding programming, the R Language and Latex, for which I am grateful. Our three wonderful children were born during the time of writing this dissertation. It was great that Andreas went on parental leave for one year so that I was able to finish this book.

Finally, I am deeply indebted to the Graduate School of Economic and Social Sciences (GESS) in Mannheim and the Mannheim Centre for European Social Research (MZES) for their generous financial support. Without their support, this research would not have been possible.

Contents

List of Tables

List of Figures

Summary

This book is interested in the prediction of civil conflicts based upon the political exclusion of identity groups and their transnational links to external governments. The innovation lies in a simultaneous consideration of three identities — ethnicity, religion and class-based ideology — according to which groups may differ, be excluded and have links to external governments. Previous research has almost exclusively focused on ethnic exclusion or ethnic transnational links when predicting civil conflicts. However, empirical case studies provide ample support that civil conflicts are not only started by ethnic groups, but also by religious and class-based ideological groups, while external support patterns also run along all three lines of identity. That said, I spell out in detail what it means if all three identity lines are taken into account. Most importantly, such a focus implies a shift to a society's unique three-dimensional identity setup, based upon which the excluded population and their transnational links can be determined. The goal is to assess whether a three-dimensional perspective on exclusion and transnational links is superior to a purely one- or two-dimensional perspective when predicting civil conflicts.

The book comprises two parts: the first part focuses exclusively on national identity constellations and exclusion patterns, while the second part additionally takes transnational links to external governments into account. In the first part, based upon survey data, I assemble an original dataset on the three-dimensional identity setup of each society for 57 countries and — with given data on the government's ethnic, religious and class-based ideological identity — I subsequently determine two key independent variables: the size of the excluded population and the size of the largest excluded three-dimensional subgroup. I analyze the effect of these variables on the onset of civil conflict in quantitative analyses, as well as assessing the performance of a three-dimensional perspective vis-à-vis a one- or two-dimensional one. Recognizing the a-theoretical nature of both key independent variables, I subsequently develop a game-theoretic model that determines the most likely rebel group and its size based upon expected utility calculations by all individuals in the three-dimensional identity setup. The resulting variables are again tested in quantitative analyses. Ultimately, the first part shows that the shift to three dimensions yields valuable insights.

In the second part, I assemble additional data on the number of ethnic, religious and class-based ideological links that the excluded population has to external governments. Following the argumentation of the first part, I develop precise theoretical expectations concerning the effect of each of these variables on the risk of civil conflict, including in interaction with other variables such as a country's regime type and the size of the excluded population. The quantitative analysis examines the merit of considering religious and class-based ideological links in addition to ethnic links and — again — assesses the superiority of a three-dimensional perspective vis-à-vis a one- or two-dimensional one. One key finding is that in non-democratic regimes the sum of ethnic and religious links significantly increases the risk of civil conflict onset for all levels of exclusion, while ideological links surprisingly have no conflict-enhancing effect. By contrast, in democratic regimes, ethnic and religious links only have a conflict-enhancing effect for low levels of exclusion, as expected, whereas ideological links are again insignificant. The analysis reveals the value of combining ethnic and religious linkages, as well as conditioning the effect of linkages on regime type, thereby confirming key theoretical expectations that have been formulated — yet not proven — in previous studies.

Put briefly, this book predicts civil conflicts based upon the unique ethnic, religious and ideological demographic identity setup of a country, the government's identity, the resulting exclusion patterns and the transnational links that the excluded population has to external governments. With the current conflicts in the Middle East and North Africa, this book deals with a highly relevant and up-to-date topic. It additionally makes a crucial contribution to the research literature, which has increasingly focused on exclusion patterns and transnational links in recent years when predicting civil conflicts, albeit almost exclusively with a mere ethnic focus and thus neglecting religion and ideology.[1]

[1] Note that this book uses the expressions class-based ideology, ideology, and class interchangeably.

Chapter 1.

Introduction

A **civil conflict** is a contested incompatibility between a government and an internal opposition group where the use of armed force results in a certain number of battle-related deaths on both sides in a year (cp. Wallensteen and Sollenberg 2001).[1] Civil conflicts are a ubiquitous phenomenon. With civil conflicts currently (2014) being waged in several Middle Eastern countries — most prominently in Iraq, Syria, Yemen and Libya — as well as countries of other world regions, including in Ukraine, Southern Sudan, Nigeria, Somalia, Mexico, Colombia, Pakistan, Afghanistan, India and Myanmar, the question immediately arises concerning how to explain these and other civil conflicts. For only if we could understand how these conflicts came about and what the underlying issue of contestation is, we could possibly start to think about how to end the conflicts and even prevent the eruption of such conflicts in the first place. After all, civil conflicts claim a huge number of deaths and refugee flows and they imply large-scale suffering for the civilian population. Moreover, a huge percentage of civil conflicts involves external states as participants, sometimes on the government's and sometimes on the rebels' side, often contributing to a prolongation, aggravation and spread of the conflict. Although the overall number of civil conflicts has declined from 1990 onwards, when it reached a temporal peak, it is not yet clear whether the declining trend will continue or reverse in the near future (cp. Themnér and Wallensteen 2012). Moreover, the number of civil conflicts per year has steadily varied between 31 and 37 in recent years, whereas so-called internationalized civil conflicts — those with outside intervention — have been on the rise (Themnér and Wallensteen 2012, 2013, 2014).

In the media and elsewhere, it is well recognized that many civil conflicts run along different ethnic, religious or class-based ideological lines of identity. Thus, it is frequently mentioned that Sunni Arabs rebel in Iraq, Syria and Yemen against the Shiite governments, that ethnic Russians challenge the

[1] The Uppsala Armed Conflict Database requires a minimum of 25 battle-related deaths on both sides per year. Note that this book uses interchangeably the expressions of civil conflict and (internal) armed conflict.

government in Ukraine, Christian Black Leftists in Southern Sudan have long opposed the Muslim Arab Rightist government, and left-wing guerrillas stand against the government in Colombia, to mention just a few examples. At the same time, it has been realized that the different identity groups do not naturally clash — contradicting a view that often prevailed several years ago — but rather that many of the clashing groups already lived peacefully together in the past. Thus, it is well recognized that it is not *ancient ethnic hatred* but rather *political discrimination* that drives the respective groups to rebellion (cp. Horowitz 1985; Petersen 2002). Moreover, third states providing support to rebel groups often have identity linkages to the groups, with the standard explanation being that co-identity groups at home pressure their governments to act on behalf of their excluded brethren abroad.

Emotional factors figure prominently in the current explanations for violent rebellion and external support. Political discrimination is assumed to generate frustration and hatred, which motivates individuals towards violent political action. External support is supposed to be generated by sympathy between people of the same ethnicity in different countries. However, it is rarely if ever discussed why we see political discrimination in the first place, why it should run along identity lines at all, and why people should actually suffer with their co-identity groups elsewhere without ever having been in contact with them. This lack of a deeper understanding of the mechanisms in place results in many international actors simply advising the incorporation of all identity groups into the government. However, given that the local governments almost never adhere to these recommendations, frustration, anger and incomprehension on the side of the international advisor typically result.

Other scholars hold that different identity lines in civil conflicts are merely epiphenomenal; instead, they see narrow strategic motivations such as looting, the acquisition of territory or the control of governmental spoils on the rebels' side as well as the securing of economic spheres of influence on the side of the third-party intervenor as the main motivating factors (cp. Collier and Hoeffler 2004). The civil war in the Democratic Republic of Congo (1996–1997, 1998–) often serves as an illustrative example, where Uganda and Rwanda supposedly only intervened on the rebels' side to profit from the looting of diamonds, gold and coltan (Olsson and Fors 2004). Quantitative studies following this view use natural resources, GDP and mountainous terrain as proxies for the spoils, opportunities and opportunity costs arising from violent rebellion, and although some of these factors —

especially GDP — emerge as important predictors for civil conflict onset, much about the onset of civil conflict remains unexplained (cp. Fearon and Laitin 2003; Collier and Hoeffler 2004; Fearon 2005). While such studies also include variables on differing identities as proxies for the so-called *grievance* approach — most prominently the fractionalization and the polarization index — the insignificance of these variables is interpreted as evidence for the allegation that identities are not the decisive factor when predicting the onset of civil conflict.

This book adopts a different view and holds that strategic motivations and differing identities are perfectly reconcilable: political exclusion, violent mobilization and transnational support very often occur along different identity lines exactly out of *strategic* motivations, on part of both the political leader and the mass population. While political leaders first and foremost want to remain in office, the mass population is primarily interested in the acquisition of private goods (cp. Bueno de Mesquita et al. 2003). I argue that political exclusion, mobilization and support along identity lines lend themselves perfectly to fit these goals. This explains why governments are so resistant to the advice of simply including all identity groups into the government. While a few previous theoretical studies have recognized that political exclusion may be driven by strategic motivations (Fearon 1999; Caselli and Coleman II 2006), the mechanisms have never been spelled out in detail, and the focus has only been placed upon *ethnic* groups. Quantitative studies on the onset of civil conflict have recently turned to identity-based political exclusion and transnational linkages, although they likewise have only focused on *ethnic* exclusion and *ethnic* ties (e.g. Wimmer et al. 2009; Cederman et al. 2009, 2010, 2013). Given these research gaps, my book spells out in further detail the mechanisms underlying the strategic identity account, whereby the study extends this account — in both the theoretical and empirical analyses — beyond ethnicity to also encompass religion and class-based ideology.

Including religion and class-based ideology as two additional dimensions alongside ethnicity has a straightforward reason: while half of civil conflicts in the last fifty to one hundred years have indeed been fought between groups of different ethnic identity, the other half have pitted different religious or ideological groups (or a combination of identities) against each other. Among the examples of religious groups challenging the government are Muslims in Lebanon, Egypt, Iran, Indonesia, India and Nigeria, Christians in Uganda and Northern Ireland, or Sikhs in India. Examples of ideological leftist groups challenging the government can be found in El Salvador, Peru,

Greece, the Philippines, Nepal, South Korea and Madagascar (Cunningham et al. 2009). Rebel groups often even exhibit a combination of identities being ethnic-ideological (TPFL in Ethiopia, Fretilin in Indonesia, or FAR/URNG in Guatemala), ethnic-religious (VRS in Bosnia, SPLM in Sudan, or LRA in Uganda), religious-ideological (NSF in Romania, Royalists in the Yemen Arab Republic, MEK in Iran), or even ethnic-religious-ideological (Timorese-Catholic-Marxist Fretilin in Indonesia, Palestinian-Muslim-Leftist INM in Lebanon, Black-Christian-Leftist ANC in South Africa, Eritrean-Christian-Marxist EPLF in Ethiopia).

However, despite the overwhelming case study evidence for the multidimensional nature of civil conflicts, quantitative studies have overwhelmingly tried to predict even non-ethnic conflicts only with ethnic exclusion and ethnic linkages. Some authors have recognized this shortcoming and tried to address it, by either focusing on the dependent variable *ethnic* civil conflict or shifting to *ethnic groups* as the unit of analysis. Thus, group-based analyses on ethnic groups examine whether large excluded ethnic groups are more likely to rebel than small ethnic groups (Cederman et al. 2010), as well as whether the relationship is contingent upon the existence of transnational ethnic ties (Cederman et al. 2013). While a group-based analysis certainly has its merits, I argue that it comes with a certain shortcoming. If, in the respective societies, other than ethnic cleavages are additionally salient, these cleavages might actually divide the ethnic groups, ultimately rendering them less cohesive than one might think upon first consideration. These divisions might even inhibit ethnic groups from effectively challenging the government in the first place, or they might undermine the ethnic groups' fighting power. One example is ethnic Kurds in Iran, who have been divided religiously into a Sunni and a Shia faction. While Sunni Kurds are completely excluded from political power and have repeatedly challenged the government, Shiite Kurds profit from the Shiite Persian/Azeri government in Iran and thus have no incentive to rebel (Abrahamian 2008). Thus, it would be wrong to designate all ethnic Kurds as a potential rebelling force. That said, even group-based analyses on ethnic groups might obtain erroneous results, namely if other identity dimensions are salient and cross-cut ethnic groups.

I go as far as arguing that all three dimensions — ethnicity, religion and class-based ideology — are present as *latent* dimensions in all countries over the world all the time. These dimensions are activated and turned *salient* through the self-definition of political entrepreneurs like the government or the rebel force, from which certain patterns of inclusion and exclusion emerge. That said, the country-specific three-dimensional identity setup emerges as the key quantity of interest. As data on this quantity is not yet readily available, it is generated for the first time in this book, based upon survey data. Together with the government's self-definition, different variables are then generated, most importantly, the size of the excluded population and the size of the largest excluded three-dimensional subgroup.[2] While the latter variable — namely the size of the largest excluded three-dimensional subgroup — appears to be uninformed and ad-hoc upon first glance, a formal part provides a more theoretical foundation for this variable, which emerges in the quantitative analyses as a good predictor for the onset of civil conflict outperforming one- and two-dimensional indices.

The implicit assumption behind the aforementioned variables is that "power is in the numbers" (DeNardo 1985), whereby larger excluded groups are more likely to effectively challenge the government with violent means than small ones. While rebel groups certainly gain strength from the number of people participating in the rebellion, they also require weapons, which are often provided with outside help, mostly by external states. Interestingly, transnational rebel support also often runs along all three identity lines of ethnicity, religion and class-based ideology, whereby rebels are supported by those governments nearby that belong to the exactly same ethnic, religious or ideological denomination. The strategic motivations for third states providing support may include the goal of unifying countries to increase the respective favored ethnic, religious or ideological constituency (through annexation or secession), or the goal of establishing as many like-minded governments as possible in the region to reduce the risk of themselves being toppled. In contrast to previous studies, this book not only looks at ethnic ties, but also considers religious and class-based ideological ties, given that the proposed mechanism should likewise hold for these two additional dimensions. As data on religious and class-based ideological ties has not yet been available, this book constructs these data based upon the unique three-dimensional identity setup and the governments' ethnic, religious or ideological denomination. Quantitative empirical analyses partly confirm the expectations, especially providing support for the conflict-enhancing effect of ethnic and religious ties in non-democratic and democratic regimes, whereas ideological ties do not exhibit the expected positive effect on conflict onset, possibly because the effect is contingent about other factors being present.

This book comprises two parts: the first part addresses the issue of

[2]The term 'subgroup' is used when referring to a multidimensional group (for a formal definition see page 111).

identity-based political exclusion and rebel support, thus focusing entirely on national configurations; while the second part extends the analysis to identity-based transnational support, thereby taking international configurations into account. Chapter 2 discusses the related literature and motivates with case study evidence that ethnicity, religion and class-based ideology are the three key latent dimensions for political contestation. Chapter 3 elaborates why favoritism and conflict run along identity lines at all and generates first expectations about the most likely challenger. It also conceptualizes the three-dimensional identity setup and presents the key hypotheses in a multidimensional setting. Chapter 4 examines the influence of the informally derived variables on the onset of civil conflict in quantitative analyses, before Chapter 5 provides a more formal underpinning for these variables, motivates the argument with case studies, and tests alternative, formally derived variables in additional quantitative analyses. The second part on transnational support introduces the related literature in Chapter 6 and motivates with two episodes that not only ethnic, but also religious and ideological links facilitate rebellion. Chapter 7 discusses why transnational support is based upon identity criteria and generates hypotheses, before Chapter 8 evaluates the claims empirically. The study concludes in Chapter 9 by relating the findings to the recent uprisings in the Middle East and North Africa and summarizing the results.

Part I.

National Political Exclusion and Support of Rebel Groups

Chapter 2.

Ethnic, Religious and Class-Based Civil Conflicts

The first part of this book focuses on national political exclusion and rebel support along identity lines, namely ethnic, religious or class-based ideological lines, as well as any combination thereof. In this context, **political exclusion** or **discrimination** refers to actions of the government that exempt certain parts of the population from the distribution of governmental resources. Political exclusion is the reverse of **political inclusion** or **favoritism**, referring to governmental actions that privilege and support certain parts of the population (Grim and Finke 2006, 15f.). Furthermore, following Chandra (2006, 400), I define **identity** as "any social category in which an individual is eligible to be a member." The main research question is whether it is possible to predict the onset of civil conflict based upon exclusion patterns along all three lines of identity — ethnicity, religion and class-based ideology — as well as whether such a three-dimensional perspective on political exclusion is superior to a one- or two-dimensional perspective. The following two sections show that this research makes an important contribution to the literature, and that ample empirical case study evidence points to the necessity of considering all three — rather than only one or two — of the three identity dimensions of ethnicity, religion and class-based ideology.

2.1. The Literature

By focusing on the exclusion of large, multidimensional identity groups as a predictor for civil conflict, this book ties in with extant research on the relationship between demography and civil conflict (Esteban and Ray 1994; Alesina et al. 2003; Montalvo and Reynal-Querol 2005), as well as political exclusion and civil conflict (Horowitz 1985; Gurr 1993; Wimmer et al. 2009; Cederman et al. 2010). I add a theoretical foundation to existing studies and deviate from the focus on a single identity category by looking at three dimensions. This book also extends existing studies by conditioning the effect of exclusion on regime type: an aspect that has previously not been in the focus. The following paragraphs show what we can learn from existing studies by sketching both the demographic and the exclusion perspective, as well as by briefly introducing findings on regime type and civil conflict.

As the examples in the introduction illustrate, civil conflicts run along ethnic, religious and class-based ideological lines as well as any combination thereof. Some consider these identity-based differences between rebel groups and governments as epiphenomenal (e.g. Collier and Hoeffler 2004). Others try to account for these differences assuming that groups of a different identity are more likely to experience grievances, more likely to become mobilized and thus more likely to clash (Gurr 2000). The question thus arises concerning whether it is possible to predict the onset of civil conflict with demographic measures of social identity. Given the prevalence of *ethnic* civil conflict, the most prominent demographic indicator has become the ethnic fractionalization index as a measure of ethnic diversity (Easterly and Levine 1997), which is assumed to increase the risk of civil conflict onset. However, quantitative support for this indicator has been absent or weak (Collier and Hoeffler 2004; Fearon and Laitin 2003; Miguel et al. 2004; Hegre and Sambanis 2006).[1]

One deficiency of the fractionalization index is that the choice for fractionalization is rather arbitrary. While a higher number of mobilized ethnic groups may clash more often, an opposite stance holds that it is very difficult for small ethnic groups to mobilize in the first place, with the implication being that the risk of civil conflict should be highest if two almost equally sized groups — rather than many small groups — oppose each other (cp. Montalvo and Reynal-Querol 2005; Esteban and Schneider 2008). On top of that, it may be argued that very different, distant ethnic groups are more likely to clash than very similar groups, wherefore the distance between ethnic groups should also be taken into account (see Fearon 2003). That said, authors recommend using a measure of polarization — rather than fractionalization — although the support for this is likewise ambiguous (see Schneider and Wiesehomeier 2010). Given these opposing views, Esteban and Ray (2011) develop theoretical expectations about the conditions under which one or the other indicator — fractionalization or polarization — should apply in determining the severity of civil conflict (not its onset). With public goods, preferences with respect to the implemented policy and thus distances between groups are more relevant, thus privileging the polarization index. With private goods, when goods are distributed on

[1] There is more support for the fractionalization index if non-linear effects or lower-level violence are taken into account (cp. Cederman et al. 2009; Hegre and Sambanis 2006).

an individual basis, relative group size matters most, thus privileging the fractionalization index (Esteban and Ray 2011, 1364). Empirical tests on conflict incidence (Esteban et al. 2012) provide support for this perspective.

A second weakness of demographic indices like the fractionalization index is that they neglect the institutional context, most importantly, patterns of political inclusion and exclusion (see Cederman and Girardin 2007; Fearon et al. 2007). In a seminal work, Horowitz (1985) most prominently introduces the idea that ethnic favoritism and its downside of ethnic political exclusion are the main causes of violent ethnic conflict, providing numerous case study examples for the assumed relationship (similarly Petersen 2002). From a theoretical perspective, political exclusion may lead to conflict via social-psychological mechanisms, whereby politically excluded groups develop low self-esteem and a feeling of subordination, which motivates them to violently reverse the status quo (cp. Tajfel and Turner 1979). Others like Caselli and Coleman II (2006) and Fearon (1999) provide a more strategically motivated underpinning for ethnic rebellion.

Empirically, the Minorities at Risk project sets out to test the grievance perspective by collecting systematic world-wide data on excluded ethnic minorities and their risk for rebellion, although it is often criticized for its selection bias (Fearon 2003, 196; Hug 2003). The most recent and elaborate data collection exercise comes from Cederman et al. (2010), with a dataset on supposedly all politically relevant ethnic groups in over 155 countries and their relative political status.[2] Quantitative analyses of these data show that the size of the excluded ethnic population (Wimmer et al. 2009) and the political exclusion of large ethnic groups (Cederman et al. 2010) significantly increase the risk of civil conflict onset. Theoretically, the authors informally refer to a mixture of social-psychological grievances and strategic calculations, which motivate individuals to resort to violent means (Wimmer et al. 2009, 321).

While the simultaneous consideration of demographic characteristics and political exclusion in more recent studies is desirable, one shortcoming is that these studies constrain their focus to ethnicity in the form of either ethnic demographics or ethnic exclusion. However, this exclusive focus on *ethnicity* has been criticized in recent years and is the main peg of this book. Although civil conflicts frequently run along ethnic lines, other identity lines — most prominently religion and class-based ideology — are also present, sometimes in isolation, sometimes in combination. However, if civil conflicts

[2]Ethnic groups are politically relevant if they are active in national politics or if they are discriminated against, according to expert codings.

are multidimensional, running not only along ethnic but also religious or class-based ideological lines, predicting civil conflict merely with an ethnic demographic indicator or ethnic exclusion falls short of the reality. Ignoring these other dimensions implies that we occasionally try to predict class-based or religious conflict with an ethnic demographic or exclusion pattern rather than the more plausible alternative of class-based or religious divisions. It also implies that we ignore all lines of identity that emerge in addition to ethnic divisions and that might be able to predict any kind of civil conflict, whether ethnic, religious or class-based ideological. Put differently, given that civil conflicts are often non-ethnic and multidimensional — as case studies show — shouldn't we take all relevant dimensions into account when predicting civil conflict? The literature thus far has only partly recognized this problem of the non-ethnic and multidimensional nature of civil conflict, providing tentative solutions, which I will recapitulate in turn.

One solution when acknowledging the multidimensional nature of civil conflict is to focus on ethnic conflict as a dependent variable rather than civil conflict per se (see Sambanis 2001; Fearon and Laitin 2003, 79), or to focus on ethnic groups as the unit of analysis (Cederman et al. 2010). The idea is that the ethnic demographic or exclusion variables should at least be able to predict the particular kind of ethnic civil conflict, if not all kinds of conflict. However, this approach is deficient in two respects: first, we are mainly interested in civil conflicts per se, and not in one very narrow kind; and second, adopting an exclusively ethnic lens obscures that divisions other than ethnic ones might influence and modify the demographic setup. Therefore, another common solution in the literature has been to include religious or class indicators alongside ethnic indicators to predict civil conflict as such. Most prominently, Collier and Hoeffler (2004) and Fearon and Laitin (2003) include the ethnic fractionalization index in addition to a religious fractionalization index and a Gini coefficient on income or land inequality, although they find little support for any of them. Alternatively, these and other authors construct multiplicative indices like the social fractionalization index[3] (Collier and Hoeffler 2004), albeit they are likewise problematic (Stoll 2007). Therefore, the quest has been to ascertain a single variable that captures the multidimensional nature of social diversity to predict civil conflict, which might ultimately run along one dimension or

[3]According to Collier and Hoeffler (2004, 595), the social fractionalization index is "the product of the ethno-linguistic fractionalization and the religious fractionalization index plus the ethno-linguistic or the religious fractionalization index, whichever is the greater."

many.

Selway is exceptional in that he follows the quest for a single multidimensional variable by constructing a two-dimensional index of overlappingness or crosscuttingness (cp. Selway 2011; Gubler and Selway 2012). His implicit assumption is that if two cleavages strongly overlap, the diverging identities of the respective groups and their opposing interests become more salient, whereby the groups are more likely to clash than if cleavages are crosscutting. However, Selway's index is constrained to two dimensions, the issue of political inclusion and exclusion is completely neglected, and empirical support for the index has been inconclusive (see Selway 2011). Others (cp. Østby 2008) likewise recognize the importance of characteristics other than ethnic ones. However, they maintain the assumption about the predominance of ethnic groups and consider — in addition to the ethnic groups' political status — their economic endowments. The principal argument is similar to that of Selway: if ethnic groups not only differ in their political status, but also in their economic endowments, there are more reasons for antagonism, meaning that they are more likely to violently oppose each other. While these latter studies at least take patterns of inclusion and exclusion into account, class only serves as an attribute of ethnic groups, rather than an extra dimension. Moreover, religion is subsumed under the banner of ethnicity rather than being conceptualized as an extra dimension. This forfeits the possibility of predicting pure class-based ideological or religious conflicts.

Finally, previous studies on political exclusion have failed to account for an interaction between exclusion and regime type. Regime type has been examined — if at all — as an independent predictor of civil conflict onset yielding the following findings: regime type, measured with the Polity IV index, seemed to exert an inverse u-shape relationship on armed conflict onset, whereby regimes in the middle categories — often called anocratic regimes — were found to be more likely to experience armed conflict onset than autocratic or democratic regimes (cp. Hegre et al. 2001; Fearon and Laitin 2003). However, Vreeland (2008) convincingly showed that this effect was due to the fact that — by definition in Polity IV — anocratic regimes are often politically instable, thus making the alleged relationship between anocracy and conflict tautological. When removing this aspect of political instability for the coding of anocracies, anocratic regimes are no more likely and democratic regimes no less likely to experience armed conflict onset than other regimes (Hegre 2014), wherefore no specific regime type effect was found. This book contributes to the research on regime types in that it shows that the effect of political exclusion and transnational links varies for non-competitive/autocratic and competitive/democratic regimes. One argument is that large excluded groups only have a strong incentive and a numerical advantage of violently mobilizing against the government in non-competitive regimes. By contrast, in competitive regimes, large excluded groups can realistically hope to win the next election. Small groups might miss out in both regimes alike, although it is unclear whether these groups — given their small size — have the potential to violently challenge the government without external help.

In sum, there is no study at present — to my knowledge — that makes an argument about a social diversity measure that accounts for all three dimensions of ethnicity, religion and class-based ideology and additionally takes the political exclusion patterns along all three lines into account, thereby being able to predict civil conflict of any kind, whether ethnic, religious or class-based ideological. Accordingly, this book intends to fill this gap. It conceptualizes ethnicity, religion and class-based ideology as three latent dimensions within one identity space, where political entrepreneurs — whether the government or the rebel group — can position themselves. The self-definition of the respective entrepreneurs comes along with certain patterns of political inclusion and exclusion, which give rise to rebellion in more than one dimension. However, the effect of exclusion on armed conflict crucially depends on the type of the political regime.

2.2. Patterns of Favoritism and Conflict

This section provides ample empirical case study evidence showing that both political favoritism and the violent mobilization of rebel groups run along all three lines of identity — ethnicity, religion and class-based ideology — often even exhibiting a combination of two or three dimensions. Furthermore, there is good reason to assume that there is neither a regional pattern nor a time trend in the latent dimensionality of political competition implying that ethnicity, religion and class-based ideology can be assumed to be latently present in all societies all the time. With these arguments being established in further detail in the following paragraphs, the subsequent chapter develops an informal strategic theoretical underpinning concerning why we observe these identity-based patterns of political favoritism and violent mobilization in the first place.

Favoritism and Conflict along Ethnic Lines

Favoritism and mobilization along *ethnic* lines has hugely been discussed in the African context (Arriola 2009; Padró i Miquel 2007; Posner 2005). Typically, one or more ethnic groups tend to be in power favoring co-ethnics via the distribution of governmental posts and assets, while other ethnic groups are politically excluded. Ethnic groups vie to get into office to secure and distribute governmental spoils (Bates 1983; Posner 2005; Fearon 1999; Caselli and Coleman II 2006), via either electoral (see Posner 2005; Chandra 2007), or non-electoral means (see Wimmer et al. 2009; Cederman et al. 2010). Private goods are distributed in the form of road development (Burgess et al. 2011), education and health policies (Franck and Rainer 2012; Kramon and Posner 2013) or — most importantly — via governmental posts (Padró i Miquel 2007). Prominent African examples of an ethnic group controlling the government and favoring co-ethnics are Bemba in Zambia, Ovimbundu in Angola, Kikuyus and Kalenjin in Kenya, Northern groups in Nigeria and Uganda, Tutsis in Burundi, M'Boshi in the Republic of the Congo and Tigreans in Ethiopa. However, ethnic favoritism is by no means constrained to the African continent. Examples of ethnic dominance outside Africa include Sinhalese in Sri Lanka, Pashtuns in Afghanistan, Bengali in Bangladesh, Burmese in Myanmar, Whites in Bolivia, Persians in Iran, Turks in Turkey and Serbs in Yugoslavia (cp. Chandra 2007, 84; Horowitz 1985).

While case study examples are abound, quantitative evidence that governments tend to be captured by ethnic groups and that these groups actually favor their co-ethnics is more scarce. Indirect evidence for ethnic favoritism has been found in early quantitative studies examining the relationship between ethnic diversity and economic and political performance like public goods provision, with highly diverse countries performing rather poorly (see Easterly and Levine 1997; La Porta et al. 1999; Alesina et al. 2003; Alesina and Ferrara 2005; Habyarimana et al. 2007; Desmet et al. 2009; Casey and Owen 2014). Direct evidence has been provided in recent studies with the availability of data on the identity of political leaders and the dominant ethnic composition of the executive. These studies explicitly show that ethnic groups actually benefit from having their co-ethnics in power: road development in Kenya seems to be driven by ethnic favoritism (Burgess et al. 2011), and an ethnic political leader positively affects primary education and infant health of its co-ethnics as examined for 18 Sub-Saharan Africa countries over the last 50 years (Franck and Rainer 2012; also see Kramon and Posner 2012, 2013).[4]

Given the politics of ethnic favoritism, excluded ethnic groups have an incentive to challenge the ethnic group in power, via either electoral or non-electoral means.[5] Ethnic clientelism during elections has been documented by Posner (2005), Chandra (2005), Wantchekon (2003), and Cederman et al. (2013). The mobilization of excluded ethnic groups in rebellions has been shown in various case studies (see Collier and Sambanis 2005 or the seminal study by Horowitz 1985). To relate back to the examples above, almost every ethnic group in power has experienced counter-mobilization by excluded ethnic groups like by Lozi in Zambia, Bakongo and Cabinda in Angola, Luo in Kenya, Southern groups in Nigeria and Uganda, Hutus in Burundi, Lari in the Republic of the Congo, Afars, Amhara, Oromo, and Somalis in Ethiopia, Tamils in Sri Lanka, Hazaras and Tajiks in Afghanistan, Biharis and Chittagong Hill Tribes in Bangladesh, Kachins, Karens, Mons and Shans in Myanmar, indigenous people in Bolivia, Kurds in Iran and Turkey and Bosniaks and Croats in Yugoslavia. Furthermore, quantitative examinations reveal that the size of the excluded ethnic population or the size of an ethnic group positively predict the onset of civil conflict (Wimmer et al. 2009; Cederman et al. 2010).

Favoritism and Conflict along Religious Lines

The importance of religion in politics has become an issue in recent years (Thomas 2000; cp. Philpott 2007), with the role of religion in conflict being one aspect of it, whereas religious favoritism has received much less

[4]Adverse results on ethnic favoritism can be found for taxation in Kasara (2007) and infant mortality in Guinea in Kudamatsu (2009). However, see the cautionary note by Kramon and Posner (2013) concerning any conclusions when focusing on one private good only.

[5]The question of whether governments are indeed captured by certain ethnic groups providing spoils to only the core constituency (see Cederman et al. 2010) does not yet seem to be completely settled. Francois et al. (2012) find evidence for a proportionate representation of ethnic groups. Alubo (2008, 51) considers ethnic favoritism to be mere window-dressing stating that "politicians refer to unequal representation, and seem to manipulate the view and use it strategically — in the end, however, both sit together and share the spoils". By contrast, other authors attribute the presence of several ethnic groups in government to the cooptation of single individuals, but not to real group representation (see Faksh 1984, 147). Moreover, still others hold that the core constituency of one ethnic group can still be convinced that it receives most goods of all, despite the presence of other ethnic groups in government (see Chandra 2007, 101).

attention.[6] In religious conflicts, often different religious groups oppose each other, but sometimes it is also a secular government versus a religious uprising, or liberals versus radicals of the same denomination (see Blaydes and Linzer 2012; Stewart 2009, 3).[7] Religious favoritism seems to come in a similar vein as ethnic favoritism: political and military posts are distributed to co-religious groups and the government budget flows to co-religious people, often via regional development projects or education programs that favor the respective religious groups over the political exclusion of other religious groups (cp. Grim and Finke 2011, 49f., 51, 207; Toft 2006, 19; Akbaba 2009). Prominent examples of regimes of religious favoritism are the prevailing cases of the Alawite Syrian regime or the Sunni governments in Bahrain, Saudi Arabia or under Hussein in Iraq. Other examples include the Northern Muslim governments in Nigeria and Sudan, the Buddhist governments in Thailand and Sri Lanka, the Hindu government in India, the Jewish government in Israel or the Protestant Northern Ireland government.

In all these cases, absent other channels of political contestation, religious favoritism led to the violent uprising of the excluded religious groups, mobilizing the respective population with the explicit goal to control the government. Thus, Muslim Sunnis stood up in Syria, Shiites in Bahrain, Saudi Arabia, and Iraq, Southern Christians in Nigeria and Sudan, Southern Muslims in Thailand, Hindus in Sri Lanka, Muslims in India and Israel and Catholics in Northern Ireland. To take up the Syrian case as an example of religious favoritism and violence, the Alawite religious minority constituting 12 percent of the population, once excluded, succeeded in entering the Syrian army in substantial numbers in the 1960s. By staging a military coup, it was able to control the government and completely reshuffle the composition of the government, appointing a high number of Alawites in key political and military positions and channeling substantial resources to the Alawite region (King 2007, 454; Faksh 1984, 146). This preferential treatment triggered the opposition of the Sunni majority, leading to violent uprisings against the Alawite government during the 1970–1980s (Muslim Brotherhood), and again from 2011 onwards (Svensson 2013, 418, 422f.). Despite these numerous case study examples, quantitative data on religious

[6]One exception is Stewart (2009) analyzing the issue of religious favoritism under the terminology of political as well as social, economic and cultural horizontal inequalities. See also Henne (2012, 755f.).

[7]The relationship between state and religion is complicated by the fact that religious actors often emerge as a very potent, independent force, wherefore one has to understand the special relationship between the state and the church (cp. Finke and Martin 2012, 12).

favoritism is scarce (exceptional is Grim and Finke 2011, who code religious favoritism as one category in their data, but do not explore it in much detail), instead privileging the issue of religious discrimination (Grim and Finke 2006; Fox 2013).[8] To my knowledge, there are no quantitative studies explicitly examining the relationship between religious discrimination/favoritism and the provision of public goods or armed conflict onset.[9]

Favoritism and Conflict along Class Lines

Class-based ideological favoritism in developing countries typically sets landowners and capitalists on one side against peasants and workers on the other side.[10] Both groups seek to distribute state assets among themselves (cp. Scott 1969; Acemoglu and Robinson 2005).[11] If landowners/capitalists are in power, typically under the banner of right-wing politics, we generally observe politics dominated by a *landed elite* facing a huge impoverished and uneducated peasant population (very typical in Latin America like in Brazil, Nicaragua, El Salvador, Colombia, and Guatemala (see Booth 1991), as well as in the Philippines (Holden 2009; Quimpo 2005, 2009), Nepal (Misra 2002; Joshi and Mason 2011), and South Africa (Ntsebeza 2011)), or politics dominated by a *capitalist elite* colluding with state bureaucrats while exploiting the labor force of the urban poor (exemplary are Iran,

[8] Religious discrimination encompasses restrictions on buildings (most prominently, the construction of mosques and churches), punishment of conversion, mandatory education in the religion of the majority, confiscation of property, exclusion from the social pension system, etc. (see Fox 2013, 460ff.). Religious favoritism in Grim and Finke (2006) "refers to the actions of the state that provide one religion or a small group of religions special privileges, support, or favorable sanctions" (Grim and Finke 2006, 15f.).

[9] Many studies focus on the relative frequency of religious conflicts and their duration or intensity (see Lindberg 2008; Tusicisny 2004) or on the relationship between religious fragmentation/polarization and performance/conflict (see Montalvo and Reynal-Querol 2003; Akdede 2010; Dincer 2008). Religious conflicts have also been indirectly examined under the heading of ethno-religious violence.

[10] Matters are complicated by the often dependent relationship between landlords and peasants, whereby landlords have extensive monitoring and sanctioning capacities over peasants thereby preventing a violent uprising (see Joshi and Mason 2011; Schmidt et al. 1977, 305).

[11] While rich people certainly do not have the same propensity for the provision of pork like poor people ("a dollar is not worth the same", see Calvo and Murillo 2004; Magaloni et al. 2007, 187; Dixit and Londregan 1996), rich people still have a strong interest in government favoritism in the sense that their wealth is preserved. Moreover, direct payments have been documented at least for middle-income people in Mexico (see Magaloni et al. 2007).

with a period of accelerated capitalist industrialization between 1965 and 1975 (Petras et al. 1981, 60ff.), South Africa from 1958 onwards (Petras et al. 1981, 56ff.), or Brazil under the military dictatorship from 1964 to 1985 (Petras et al. 1981, 50ff.)). In either case, government resources are distributed among a small group of people based upon class criteria. By contrast, if peasants/workers come into power, typically under the banner of left-wing politics, we observe land distribution to the poor, micro credit programs, low interest loans, the nationalization of firms, the granting of labor rights and extensive public education programs — in actuality that assets are distributed among the rural and urban poor masses (exemplary are Chile under Allende (1970–1973), Brazil under Goulart (1961–1964), Iran under Mossadegh (1951–1953), Syria under Baath (1950–1960s) and Thailand under Thaksin (2001–2006)). Quantitative evidence for whether inequality impairs good governance is mixed (see Easterly 2007 vs. Casey and Owen 2014). However, the tendency of right-wing governments to favor a small wealthy elite and of left-wing governments to empower the poor is confirmed in quantitative analyses showing that inequalities tend to reduce under left-wing governments (Ha 2012), as exemplified in recent years for several leftist Latin American countries (Ortiz and Cummins 2011, 27).[12]

Depending on which side is in power, the other side tries to mobilize forces to topple the government: exemplary are the leftist insurgencies in Nicaragua (1977–1979), El Salvador (1979–1991), Colombia (1964–), Guatemala (1963–1995), the Philippines (1946–1954, 1969–), Nepal (1960–1962, 1996–2006), South Africa (1981–1988) and Iran (1979–2001) (see Booth 1991; Parsa 2000), as well as violent topplings and uprisings through rightists — often with the help of the military (see Sklar 1979, 540f.) or external forces, like in Chile (toppling of Allende in 1973), Brazil (toppling of Goulart in 1964), Iran (toppling of Mossadeq in 1953) and Thailand (toppling of Thaksin in 2006). Quantitative examinations of whether the uneven distribution of income or land increases the risk of rebellion long found only mixed support, probably due to poor data (see Russett 1964; Muller 1985; Weede 1986; Lichbach 1989; Collier and Hoeffler 2004; Fearon and Laitin 2003; Besançon 2005).[13]

[12]Once the poor get to power and have access to wealth, they sometimes tend to change their 'ideology' from leftist to rightist — see Mbeki in South Africa (Vale and Barrett 2009) — although this is not necessarily the case.

[13]For a skeptical view that vertical inequalities matter for conflict, see Esteban et al. (2012, 1310): "The clear economic demarcation across classes is a two-edged sword: while it breeds resentment, the very poverty of the have-nots militates against a successful insurrection, and even then the different skill and occupational niches occupied by capitalist and worker makes effective redistribution across classes a

However, a recent study by Bartusevičius (2014) uses much better data on income inequalities (Solt 2009) and educational inequalities (Benaabdelaali et al. 2012) and finds that inequality increases the risk of civil conflict.

Multidimensionality of Favoritism and Conflict

As documented thus far, case studies suggest and quantitative studies presuppose that ethnic groups in government face ethnic rebellions, religious groups face religious rebellions and rightist/leftist groups face leftist/rightist rebellions. While this 'same-dimensionality' of favoritism and rebellion might be true for some cases, it is not true for all cases. Different empirical examples show that government favoritism can run along one dimension and rebellion along another. Exemplary are the Islamic government in Iran (under Khomeini) opposed by a predominantly leftist insurgency (MEK) (Svensson 2013, 465), the Socialist regime in Ethiopia (under Derg) faced by several ethnic rebel groups (Oromo, Tigray, Amhara), or the ethnic regime of Acholi and Langi in Uganda (under Obote) opposed by a religious movement (NRA). Moreover, case studies suggest that different identity dimensions are frequently combined, in both favoritism and rebellion. Thus, the Syrian government defined itself not only in religious terms (Alawite) but also in class terms (Leftist), the Sri Lankan government not only referred to its distinct ethnic identity (Sinhalese) but also to its religion (Buddhist), and the Mexican government under the PRI was not only characterized by its ideological stance (Centrist) but also by its ethnicity (White). Rebel groups likewise refer to categories from different dimensions constituting themselves as ethnic-ideological (FAR/URNG in Guatemala), ethnic-religious (VRS in Bosnia) or religious-ideological (NSF in Romania).

Quantitative studies have long recognized that rebel groups can often not been coded along one dimension only, rather exhibiting the characteristics of many (Fearon and Laitin 2003; Fearon 2003). This book's descriptive data likewise supports a multidimensional nature of favoritism and rebellion: of all non-democratic governments, 34% were ethnic, 9% ideological (left-right) and 54% were ethnic-ideological (the remainder being ethnic-religious, religious-ideological, or ethnic-religious-ideological). Of

more indirect and difficult prospect." In a similar vein, some studies have turned to horizontal, instead of vertical inequalities, largely focusing on the inequality within and between ethnic groups (Baldwin and Huber 2010; Stewart 2009; Østby 2008; Cederman et al. 2011; Cederman et al. 2013; Kuhn and Weidmann 2013; Huber and Mayoral 2013).

all rebel movements, 28% were ethnic, 2% religious, 17% ideological, 5% ethnic-ideological, 26% ethnic-religious, 3% religious-ideological and 3% ethnic-religious-ideological (with 17% being nothing at all). Despite its prevalence, the multidimensionality of favoritism and conflict has almost completely been neglected in the formal, quantitative and analytical case study literature. Given this lack of attention, the contribution of this book is to take all three identity dimensions — ethnicity, religion and class-based ideology — simultaneously into account. My argument is that all three dimensions are *latent* in every society all the time and can be activated by political entrepreneurs instrumentally for political purposes thus rendering one or the other dimension *salient*. Trends in saliency might be due to differing underlying demographic characteristics or different outside support patterns. However, the assumption of three latent dimensions presupposes that there is neither a regional pattern nor a time trend: an objection one might raise at first sight, but that has to be declined upon further inspection, as the following paragraphs show.

Regional Pattern

One might object that certain dimensions are present in some regions, but not in others, with the class dimension being confined to Latin America, the ethnic dimension to Sub-Saharan Africa and the religious dimension to the Middle East. This possibly Western European perspective might arise from the fact that Latin America is associated with leftist revolutions and governments, Sub-Saharan Africa is known for its ethnic political competition and civil conflicts, and the Middle East attracts much attention for the role of religion in politics, like in the recent uprisings with a prominent role of the Muslim Brotherhood in Egypt, an Islamist government in Tunisia, Sunni Islamist violence in Libya and Syria, as well as Shia-Sunni struggles in Iraq, Saudi Arabia and Bahrain (Fox 2013, 408). However, I argue that this view is misleading. While it might be true that certain dimensions are more salient in some regions than others, this is not the case for the underlying *latent dimensions.* Thus, although many conflicts in Latin America definitely center on class issues, ethnicity and religion nevertheless serve as important additional dimensions. This becomes visible in the ethnic discrimination and mobilization of black, colored and indigenous people (Hooker 2005; Van Cott 2007, 129f.; Madrid 2005; do Valle Silva 2000), the debated role of the Catholic church during the military dictatorships (Gill 1994), or the recent steep rise in Protestant activism (Burdick 2005; Vásquez and

Williams 2005; Freston 2004). Likewise, it holds for Sub-Saharan Africa that despite the prevalence of civil conflicts along ethnic lines, class and religion are also important dimensions. During the Cold War, often due to superpower support, many African governments and movements took a socialist or a capitalist stance[14] (cp. Bates 1981), while religion intermingles as a potent force in many of its conflicts (see Basedau et al. 2011), like in the recent case of the Ivory Coast (cp. Stewart 2009, 25).[15] In the Middle East/North Africa (MENA) region, the prominence of religion unjustifiably hides ethnicity and class dimensions. For one, there are numerous well-organized *ethnic* groups in the MENA region like Kurds in Iraq and Iran, Baluchis in Iran, Palestinians in Israel, Lebanon, and Jordan, as well as Berbers in Algeria and Morocco, the political discrimination of which has been answered with revolt (Asal et al. 2012). For another, class has been a crucial force in the recent Arab Spring uprisings and before: starting in the 1970s, former socialist regimes slowly re-transformed into liberal, capitalist societies empowering economic and landed elites vis-à-vis the excluded lower and middle class (King 2007; Kandil 2012, 203f.). The severe rent-seeking behavior of a minor upper class — expressed in low price purchases of national firms, loans without guarantees, an upward distribution of land and the positioning of businessmen in political office (see King 2007, 439ff. for Egypt, Algeria, Tunisia) — resulted in severe inequalities and alienated huge parts of the population, certainly contributing a great deal to the recent uprisings (cp. Campante and Chor 2012). Disregarding this class aspect during the Arab Spring and before seems to be 'indefensible' (Kandil 2012, 198).[16]

[14]While the class issue became important with some retard, due to colonial politics fostering ethnic rather than class differences (see Posner 2005), during the Cold War, class came to divide Socialist regimes like Guinea, Guinea-Bissau, the Congo People's Republic, Angola, Mozambique, Tanzania, Somalia and Ethiopia (see Sklar 1979) on the one hand, and Capitalist regimes with an emerging indigenous owning class like Nigeria (Kieh and Agbese 1993), Kenya (Gordon 1995), Uganda (Fatton 1988) and Zambia (Baylies and Szeftel 1982) on the other hand.

[15]Studies focusing on the prevalent instrumental purpose of ethnicity during elections nevertheless recognize the presence of class and religion as additional important dimensions (cp. Eifert et al. 2010).

[16]Note that from 1975 to 1980, only 7 per cent of armed conflicts in the MENA region had a religious incompatibility (see Svensson 2013, 419).

Time Trend

A second objection might be that certain dimensions are present at some time point but not at another. Thus, one might suspect that the left-right divide was prominent during the Cold War, ethnicity came to the forefront in the 1990s, and religion emerged in the 2000s (see Brubaker and Laitin 1998, 424f.; Huntington 1993, 26, 29; Gartzke and Gleditsch 2006, 55f.). Some stylized facts seem to support this view: indeed, many ideological conflicts were terminated with the end of the Cold War, like in Honduras in 1990 or Guatemala in 1996 (see Kalyvas and Balcells 2010; Kanet 2006, 342) or leftist movements became a right-ward shift like in South Africa (Bauer and Taylor 2011, 259f., 280f.), thus nurturing the view of declining leftist violence. Instead, numerous ethnic conflicts like in Rwanda, Congo, Yugoslavia, Kosovo, Chechnya, and Sri Lanka came to dominate the media in the 1990s, whereas religious favoritism and violence has received increasing attention with the recent Middle Eastern uprisings, as documented above. However, the perceived trend of religious violence replacing ethnic violence replacing ideological violence is most likely due to a changing focus in media and scholarly attention (see Fox 2013, 407f.; Fox 2004, 717f.). Ethnicity, religion and class have been present all the time, at least as underlying latent dimensions. Although it might be less beneficial nowadays to call oneself Marxist as a rebel group, class-based differences giving rise to leftist/rightist dichotomies remain as topical as ever. There remain leftist groups challenging governments like in Venezuela (1992: Chavez), Turkey (1991: Devrimci Sol), Russia (1993: leftist forces), Nepal (1996: Maoists) or Colombia (1946–: Farc, ELN, EPL, M-19), and the continued or even increasing inequalities between rich and poor do not suggest a reversing trend.[17] Moreover, in-depth analyses of the Middle Eastern violence will certainly contribute to a revival of the class issue. Unsurprisingly, scholarly attention has very recently refocused on class-based differences as a potent mobilizing force (see Bartusevičius 2014).

While class thus continues to be a relevant dimension after 1990, ethnicity already played a crucial role well before 1990, as amply documented. Authors have found that the share of ethnic conflicts started to increase since the

[17] Although inequality in Sub-Saharan Africa and Latin America slightly decreased between 1990/2000 and 2008, it remains huge. In other regions, such as Eastern Europe and Asia, inequality is even increasing (see Ortiz and Cummins 2011). Note that conflict-ridden Colombia, Nepal, Russia and Zambia have the highest level of inequality.

1960s and even declined in the mid-1990s (see Gurr 1993), thus rendering the Cold War a "non-significant determinant of ethnic war onset" (Sambanis 2001, 275). Similarly, the political relevance of religion has not been constrained to the very recent years. Although there might be a "slight increase of people who believe in God" (Grim and Finke 2011, 203), religious conflicts existed well before 1990 (Fox 2004). Thus, if there was any time trend at all, this effect is certainly not due to shifting latent dimensions. At most, temporal changes in the *saliency* of dimensions might be due to changing governmental favoritism or changing transnational support patterns rendering one dimension more salient during one period than another (see Kanet 2006, 342).

To conclude, this chapter has established that ethnicity, religion and class-based ideology are the three latent political dimensions present in all regions of the world for all the time since 1945 (at least). The next chapter develops the argument that political entrepreneurs position themselves along these dimensions based upon strategic calculations, thus rendering one or the other — or even a combination of dimensions — salient.

Chapter 3.

Favoritism and Conflict along Identity Lines

This chapter builds upon the previous allegation that ethnicity, religion and class-based ideology are the three latent dimensions underlying political competition, providing a strategic argument for why this is the case. Subsequently, the chapter generates first expectations about the most likely challenger in a rebellion and its relative size. These quantities of interest will be adapted to a multidimensional perspective, before being tested as predictors for civil conflict onset in subsequent quantitative analyses.

3.1. The Argument

The argument for why favoritism and conflict run along identity lines goes as follows. Politicians need the support of parts of the population to get into office and remain there. So-called patronage politics is perfectly apt for getting this support, all the more if patronage politics is group-based.[1] From a theoretical standpoint, ethnicity, religion and class-based ideology lend themselves very well as stable and visible group criteria for government favoritism and rebel mobilization, thus explaining why we observe empirically that political favoritism and conflict run along all three lines of identity. The cornerstones of the argument are sketched in Figure 3.1 and shall be developed in further detail in the following paragraphs.

Vying for Office

Like many others (most prominently Bueno de Mesquita et al. 2003, cp. Pickering and Kisangani 2010, 480), I start with the assumption that political entrepreneurs above all vie to get into office and remain there, whereby they

[1] The argument about group-based patronage follows a similar reasoning to Chandra (2007) (also compare Posner 2005). However, I strongly diverge from Chandra in assuming that not only ethnicity but also religion and class lend themselves well for favoritism and mobilization, as well as by focusing on a different mode of contestation, namely violent competition, rather than electoral competition.

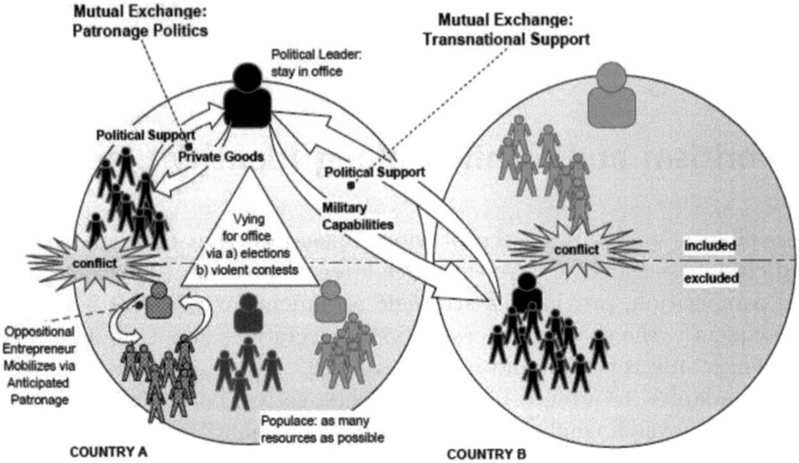

Figure 3.1.: *Schematic representation of the argument. A political leader favors its co-identity group via the provision of private goods to secure the group's political support, which in turn helps him to remain in office (patronage). Oppositional entrepreneurs vie for office via elections or violent contests and mobilize the excluded population through anticipated patronage. The political leader may also provide support to co-identity people in a nearby country if this support serves his primary interest in staying in office (see Part II).*

need the support of parts of the population to achieve this goal. Accordingly, entrepreneurs have to offer something in return or credibly promise to do so in the future.[2] The amount of support that political entrepreneurs need from the population and the kind of offers they make vary in different institutional systems. One major distinction is between democracies and autocracies (see Acemoglu and Robinson 2005). In democracies, politicians vie for office via elections and thus they need a majority or a quite substantial mass to win the election. In autocratic political systems, characterized by the absence or irrelevance of elections, politicians vie for office mainly via violent contests

[2]For alternative assumptions about the relationship between political leaders and their constituencies, see Franck and Rainer (2012, 296).

like coups and civil conflicts. Success in these violent modes of competition is not achieved deterministically by reaching a certain critical threshold, but rather probabilistically, whereby the probability of success largely depends on the number of people mobilized (DeNardo 1985; Akcinaroglu 2012, 892).

The Provision of Goods

It was long assumed that democratic states provide public goods, while autocratic states provide private goods (see Bueno de Mesquita et al. 2003; Lake and Baum 2001). The argument was that democratic leaders have to reach a larger group of potential supporters than autocratic leaders to remain in office. With a large support base, public goods are more efficient than private goods, as the latter imply that the gains per person diminish with an increasing number of profiteers, eventually becoming negligibly small. In comparison, the value of public goods is relatively independent of the number of profiteers, up to the point when congestion occurs. By contrast, in autocratic systems, it was assumed that politicians have to reach a smaller group of people to remain in office wherefore private goods are the means of choice (cp. Bueno de Mesquita et al. 2003).

Meanwhile, it has been recognized that such a conceptualization of democracies and autocracies is too simplistic, and that some refinements are pending. First, even in democratic systems, political leaders target certain well-defined audiences with special privileges — rather than the entire population — to win an election. Thus, it would be more appropriate to conceive of the respective goods as club goods characterized by non-rivalry and excludability rather than public goods characterized by non-rivalry and non-excludability (see Arena and Nicoletti (2014) for a refinement of Bueno de Mesquita et al. (2003)). Second, when private goods are distributed probabilistically rather than deterministically, as explicated in the following paragraphs, a much larger audience can be reached. This allows even politicians in democratic systems to remain in office through the distribution of private goods (cp. Chandra 2007), and explains why, empirically, even democratic states (especially the newly established ones) make extensive use of private goods provision (Keefer and Vlaicu 2008). With private goods being distributed in both democratic and autocratic systems, the distinction between these two types of systems tends to blur. Thus, private goods like subsidized food, reduced school fees or payments for attendance, government-built housing, electrification, health support in the form of immunization, drugs or birth attendance, government contracts, the building of roads and market places, and — perhaps most importantly — the appointment of supporters to political offices (see Magaloni et al. 2007, 186; Arriola 2009, 1340f.; Posner 2005, xif.; Franck and Rainer 2012, 297; Kramon and Posner 2013, 464ff.) are relevant in both autocracies *and* (new) democracies.[3]

Patronage Politics

The exchange of private goods for political support in elections (Chandra 2007; Stokes 2005; Magaloni et al. 2007, 183) or violent contests (Padró i Miquel 2007; Burgess et al. 2011) is well known in the literature under the terminology of **patronage politics.**[4] Characteristic for patronage politics is the dyadic reciprocal transaction, whereby politicians seek to ensure that those people favored by them tend to vote for them or support them in a violent struggle, and civilians in the population seek to ensure that those entrepreneurs who they support in an election or a violent contest deliver on their promises (see Hicken 2011). Whether this reciprocal relationship works or not largely depends on a repetition of the transaction that implies a mechanism of reputation, whether politicians and civilians have monitoring capacities overlooking whether one or the other side delivers, as well as the availability of sanctioning devices (Keefer and Vlaicu 2008; Stokes 2005, 316f.). It is well known for democracies that if a politician does not deliver on her electoral promises, she is likely to be sanctioned by the public in the next election by not being voted for (cp. Chandra 2007, 94). Vice-versa, if a politician favors a certain clientele with club goods but people from that clientele do not vote for her, the favoritism is likely to be withdrawn and redirected (cp. Chandra 2007, 90). In autocracies, a political entrepreneur in office who reneges on her promises is likely to be removed through a coup or rebellion (Gandhi and Przeworski 2007, 1280). On the other hand, rebel leaders try to establish their credibility ex ante by delivering during the struggle (see Fjelde and Nilsson 2012, 607; Humphreys and Weinstein

[3]Note that favoritism does not always have to come in the form of goods provision, but it may also appear as an absence or reduction of extraction. Thus, leaders may extract from everyone, but less from a certain group, which thus supports the politician because the group fears that it will be extracted even more under an alternative leader (see Padró i Miquel 2007).

[4]Patronage is similar to clientelism and pork-barrel politics with possible differences being that clientelism only uses traditional dyadic ties, whereas pork-barrel politics applies to legislation rather than implementation (see Hicken 2011; Chandra 2007, 86f.).

2008, 439, 441; Goodwin and Skocpol 1989, 494). The population is tightly overseen by either kind of political entrepreneur, often facing harsh sanctions if it does not comply (Humphreys and Weinstein 2006, 431; Fearon and Laitin 1996; Kalyvas et al. 2006; Lilja and Hultman 2011). Given their excludability, targeted goods in the form of club goods or private goods lend themselves well for such a direct transaction between political entrepreneurs and their clientele, much better than public goods. As the name suggests, targeted goods are targeted to a special audience, thereby carrying the opportunity and the risk that the target can be changed. Public goods are less apt, as people cannot be punished if they withhold their support: people gain irrespective of whether they supported a political entrepreneur or not.

Group-Based Patronage Politics

Theoretically, patronage politics could occur on a personal level based upon affinity criteria (Bueno de Mesquita et al. 2003, 60ff.; Magaloni et al. 2007, 185). However, this kind of personal patronage implies that only those people who directly gain something feel favored, whereas all others are excluded and have an incentive to topple the government. Extending the basis of support comes at a high cost: the gains per person diminish quickly when distributing a fix government budget. Thus, if the threat of a revolutionary uprising is seen as real, it will be favorable to distribute goods alternatively, whereby more people feel favored. One valuable option is to distribute goods based upon well-defined group criteria (see Chandra 2007, 91ff. for a similar argument; Francois et al. 2012, 3; Alubo 2008, 48). Thus, private goods are distributed *probabilistically* to the members of a well-defined group, whereby everyone within the group has a fair chance of getting something out of the lottery, while everyone outside the group has no chance of getting anything. Although individuals from within the group might miss out in one round, they at least have a chance of gaining in the next round (see Chandra 2007, 92), or gaining indirectly through in-group members.[5] Two conditions are necessary for this group-based favoritism to work (cp. Chandra 2006, 414-417): first, it is necessary that group boundaries are *stable/sticky* so that the intrusion of outsiders is prevented, otherwise, the initial goal of preventing individual gains becoming diminishingly small would be eroded;

[5]Evidence for the latter mechanism is found in Markussen and Tarp (2014), showing that farmers tend to invest more in land improvement if relatives are in power, probably due to strengthening property rights and informal access to credit.

and second, it is crucial that group boundaries are *visible*, given that once patronage politics transcends the personal level and gets to the group level, it becomes all the more important to establish mechanisms that allow for the mutual observability of politicians and citizens. Do politicians deliver on their promised gains? Do citizens support a politician by whom they are favored? Visible group criteria help ensure that the reciprocal transaction works: citizens can check in person whether individuals from a certain group are exclusively represented in government, as well as whether private goods reach only those individuals fulfilling certain group criteria as established by the government. Vice-versa, politicians can check whether those groups favored actually deliver on their support (cp. Chandra 2007, 95). This kind of monitoring is more difficult in democratic systems with support being expressed in the form of elections, where — at least theoretically — the secrecy of the ballot prevents the monitoring of individuals' voting behavior.[6] Monitoring is easier in autocratic systems where participation in rebel movements can be directly observed.

Ethnic, Religious and Class-Based Patronage

According to existing studies, ethnicity lends itself well for group-based patronage and mobilization because ethnicity fulfills the two criteria of stickiness and visibility (see Chandra 2007, 96-98; Chandra 2006, 415; Fearon 1999; Caselli and Coleman II 2006; Horowitz 1985, 45ff.). Ethnic groups typically differ in their natural outer appearance like facial traits, height, hair type and skin color, as well as in their surnames, language and place of residence (see Chandra 2006; Harris and Findley 2014), thus exhibiting characteristics that are generally difficult to change and clearly visible (see Chandra 2006, 2007; Gurr 1993, 167).[7] Other criteria such as religion and class are typically seen as less apt for group-based favoritism and mobilization. For one, it is assumed that religion and class can be changed more easily; for another, they are seen as less visible (Chandra 2006, 415).

My book partly deviates from this argumentation. First, the identifiability of ethnicity is not as clear-cut as it might seem upon first consideration. In fact, experimental research shows that it is quite difficult for the average

[6] In practice, there are many ways to circumvent these constraints, see Magaloni et al. (2007, 186) or Chandra (2007, 89ff.).

[7] Note that there are a few rare examples for changes in peoples' ethnicities, however, at extremely high costs and only in case of critical disruptures or over a very long period (Chandra 2012, 161).

individual to identify others' ethnicity correctly, while only individuals with a strong own ethnic identity do a better job (Habyarimana et al. 2007 on Uganda; Harris and Findley 2014 on South Africa). Second, religion and class are more sticky and visible than one might first think.[8] Despite being theoretically possible, it seems very difficult in practice to change one's religion given the generally strong psychological attachment to it.[9] Moreover, religious groups are often clearly discernible. They differ in their outer appearance — often imposed in the form of facial markers like the Hindu red dot or clothings like the Muslim scarf — and their surnames, as well as their place of residence (cp. Chandra 2006, 416), thus guaranteeing a similar amount of visibility like ethnicity. Likewise, class and economic status seem to be quite sticky, inhibiting individuals from easily moving upward economically.[10] Chandra (2006, 415) herself recognizes that "[c]hanging one's initial endowment of economic resources, acquiring more land for instance, can in some contexts be almost as difficult as changing one's skin color." Finally, economic groups are also distinguishable based upon their outer appearance, visible through clothing and the holding of land and companies, as well as by their accents and places of residence (see Chandra 2006, 416f.). Although economic cues probably have to be more "dramatic" to be seen, as Chandra (2007, 97) notes, they at least allow deciding "whether the observed comes from an upper-class or working-class background" (which is completely sufficient for this book's perspective). Thus, from a theoretical standpoint, not only ethnicity but also religion and class lend themselves well for group-based favoritism and mobilization as they are characterized by stickiness and visibility.[11]

[8]Although the identifiability of religion and class has received much less scholarly attention, at least one experimental study to my knowledge shows that individuals take religious cues like Muslim caps and beards of political leaders as indicators for expected in-group favoritism (see Chhibber and Sekhon 2013, 7).

[9]This does not preclude that religious adaptation sometimes occurs (Posner 2004, 11). For a more cautionary note on the stickiness of ethnicity and religion, see Fedderke et al. (2008, 273, 275).

[10]Although individuals could voluntarily move downward economically to gain from a leftist government, the abandonment of wealth certainly does not compensate for the benefits gained from an anti-poverty leftist policy.

[11]The question arises whether there are not even more dimensions fulfilling the two criteria of stickiness and visibility, like gender, age and eye color, for example. While there is some empirical support for the first two criteria (see Caprioli 2005; Melander 2005; Urdal 2006), the evidence is much sparser than for ethnicity, religion and class-based ideology. Even in the electoral politics literature, ethnicity, religion and class have been identified as the major cleavages, next to an urban-rural divide, differing foreign policy positions, a postmaterialist cleavage and support for the democratic

Group-Based Mobilization

The previous subsections delineated the mechanisms that explain why political favoritism runs along ethnic, religious and class-based ideological lines of identity in patronage societies. However, why does electoral or violent political mobilization also run along these lines? Moreover, who will be the most likely or severest challenger? In order to answer these questions, it is important to realize that in both democracies and autocracies, it is puzzling upon first glance why individuals participate in elections or rebellions at all considering that the own contribution is negligibly small, voting or rebellion is associated with costs, and one gains irrespective of whether one has contributed to the endeavor or not (cp. Olson 1965; Kalyvas and Kocher 2007). The problem is all the more puzzling, once we recognize that the anticipated costs of rebel participation far exceed the costs of voting, as a rebellion implies substantial risks like imprisonment or death (cp. Kalyvas and Kocher 2007, 181). This so-called collective action problem has long concerned scholars on electoral politics and violent competition, and it has not yet been completely solved. Tentative solutions point to special incentives that are tied to actual participation, in order to explain why participation pays off at all. In elections, an inherent value of voting has been posited to explain why people vote, whereas in rebellions it has been stressed that rebel leaders often incentivize their followers by direct payments during the rebellion (Humphreys and Weinstein 2008). While direct payments certainly apply, indirect incentives like the prospect of being favored once the rebelling group successfully captures the government, are likewise important (Bueno de Mesquita et al. 2003); otherwise, the rebels would have no interest in ever ending the fighting. Thus, group-based patronage politics — and the prospect thereof — not only benefits the leader and the group in government; likewise, it helps the opposition to mobilize the population in the first place. Finally, participation via group-based politics should work all the better if different groups compete closely, whereby the own participation is seen as decisive (cp. Powell 1986; Jackman 1987; Aldrich 1993; Gelman et al. 1998). Moreover, mobilization should be easier if many people participate. A high number of participators reduces the cost of participation, as individuals are less likely to be singled-out by the government as a target, and it increases the cost of non-participation as peer pressure rises (see Kalyvas and Kocher 2007). Thus, one can assume that large identity groups have a comparative advantage in mobilizing support;

regime (see Stoll 2007, 1445; Potter 2014, 13).

indeed, this assumption is supported by empirical evidence (see Oliver and Marwell 1988).

3.2. Hypotheses

The previous section provided an explanation why favoritism and conflict run along identity lines, as well as formulating a first expectation according to which large identity groups should have a comparative advantage in mobilizing support. Based upon these allegations, the present section informally generates — in reference to existing studies — hypotheses about the most likely challenger and its relative size. However, divergent from previous studies, the section argues that the effect of the variables of interest should depend on the type of the political regime.

The theoretical and empirical literature on civil conflicts long acted upon the implicit assumption that governments were confronted by a single unitary rebel group (Akcinaroglu 2012, 881). Part of the reason for this perspective was pragmatic: for one, it was easier to develop game-theoretic models with only two actors, one being the government and the other the rebel group (see Hirshleifer 1989; Acemoglu and Robinson 2001); for another, empirical analyses were conducted on the national — rather than group — level, thus requiring parsimonious country-level indicators (see Fearon and Laitin 2003; Collier and Hoeffler 2004). With a strong focus on ethnic discrimination as a driving force for rebellion (Gurr 1993; Sambanis 2001, 262f.), the assumption was that *excluded ethnic people* would resort to violent means (Horowitz 1985; Petersen 2002). However, the literature was silent concerning whether all excluded people would collaborate beyond ethnic group boundaries to topple the government, or whether ethnic groups would act separately. In either case, the size of the politically excluded ethnic population was taken as a proxy for the level of societal discontent, which would translate into violent action, thus determining the risk of civil conflict. Quantitative analyses focusing on the excluded ethnic population as a predictor for civil conflict provide support for this perspective (Wimmer et al. 2009). Following this reasoning, it is possible to formulate a first expectation:

Hypothesis 1: The risk of civil conflict onset is higher, the larger the excluded population.

However, the notion that the excluded population acts together to topple the government has been challenged. First, it is held that the excluded population is also divided along ethnic lines and that these divisions make inter-ethnic cooperation impossible. The reasons for this view vary from primordial arguments pointing to ancient ethnic hatreds (Vanhanen 1999), over high coordination and transaction costs between ethnic groups (Weidmann 2009) to purely instrumentalist reasonings focusing on the incompatibility of the goals of different ethnic groups (Posner 2005; Chandra 2007, 2012). In either case, the expectation is that politically excluded ethnic groups will act separately. Second, it is argued that not every excluded group actually becomes mobilized. Generally, civil conflicts do not engulf entire states but rather occur in clearly confined areas (Cederman and Gleditsch 2009, 487). After all, in about 50 percent of all conflict years, the government is confronted by *one* rebel group only. This group typically refers to an ethnic, religious or class category thus having a clear-cut identity that does *not* comprise the entire excluded population but only parts of it. In the other 50 percent of cases more than one rebel group confronts the government, whereby splits are rarely due to different identities[12], but rather due to divisions concerning different stances in the degree of radicalism, different notions of whether secession is sought or not, or in struggles over leadership (cp. K. Cunningham 2011; K. Cunningham et al. 2012).[13] That said, the largest excluded identity group most likely emerges as the severest challenger to the government (cp. Cederman et al. 2010).[14] Accordingly, the second

[12]Only in some cases do rebel groups refer to distinct categories from one dimension — like in Afghanistan, Angola, Bosnia or Ethiopia (ethnic dimension) — or categories from different dimensions — like in India (eth-rel-ideo), Indonesia (eth-rel), Lebanon (rel-ideo) or the Philippines (MNLF and NPA).

[13]Based upon a rebel group dataset by Cunningham et al. (2009), one can show that among the cases with only one rebel group at a time, the rebel group has high mobilization capacity in 15 percent of the cases; while with more than one rebel group, the second largest rebel group has high mobilization capacity only in 1.5 percent of the cases.

[14]Note that some scholars propagate a disaggregation of civil conflict looking at the different groups as the unit of analysis. Although a disaggregation of civil conflict analyses certainly has its merits (Cederman and Gleditsch 2009), it is crucial to be aware of the weaknesses of group-level analyses. Most importantly, dyads are treated as if they were isolated from one another when in fact rebel groups act simultaneously and are highly interdependent (Akcinaroglu 2012, 880ff.; see Bapat and Bond 2012; Fjelde and Nilsson 2012). These simultaneities and interdependencies have severe consequences for the rebels' relative fighting force: on the one hand, the simultaneous action of rebel groups implies that a government cannot devote its entire resources to fighting each single group off, but rather has to take a decision about the distribution of resources to the different groups with the course being by no means clear. On the other hand, rebel groups are highly interdependent as they form alliances, split groups and even fight each other. Moreover, it is also unclear how these interactions

hypothesis reads as follows:

Hypothesis 2: The risk of civil conflict onset is higher, the larger the largest excluded group.

However, existing studies fail to condition the effect of exclusion on the type of the political regime. The neglect of regime types is surprising as the argument advanced thus far explicitly refers to *autocratic* or *non-competitive* regimes, in which the primary mode of contestation is the violent struggle and excluded groups *cannot* expect to get into office via elections. In these regimes, large excluded groups are a potent force to violently challenge the government. Once functioning elections are introduced, like in *democratic* or *competitive* regimes, large excluded groups can in fact hope to be represented after the next electoral round. Starting a civil conflict very likely does not pay off. At most, one can expect that small excluded groups have an incentive to violently challenge the government, as their prospects of becoming represented might be diminishingly small. That said, the conditioning effect of regime type should be accounted for in the above hypotheses, which subsequently read as follows:

Hypothesis 1a: The risk of civil conflict onset in non-competitive regimes is higher, the larger the excluded population.

Hypothesis 2a: The risk of civil conflict onset in non-competitive regimes is higher, the larger the largest excluded group.

Hypothesis 1b: The risk of civil conflict onset in competitive regimes is lower, the larger the excluded population.

Hypothesis 2b: The risk of civil conflict onset in competitive regimes is lower, the larger the largest excluded group.

With an ethnic perspective, the two quantities of interest refer to the size of the excluded ethnic population and the size of the largest excluded ethnic group. The next section considers how these quantities change with a multidimensional perspective.

---

translate into the rebels' relative capabilities vis-à-vis the government.

3.3. A Multidimensional Perspective

The previous sections established that ethnicity, religion and class-based ideology are the three key latent dimensions of political contestation, developing an argument for why favoritism and mobilization run along identity lines at all and formulating first expectations about the most likely challenger. The present section adapts these expectations to the multidimensional perspective adopted in this book. For this purpose, the chapter first informally conceptualizes the three-dimensional identity setup, then determines the coverage of the government's self-definition and finally derives expectations about the size of the most likely challenger in a multidimensional setup. Underlying assumptions will be justified. The resulting expectations are tested in the following chapter, before a more formal stance on these questions is taken.

The Three-Dimensional Identity Setup

In order to derive the three-dimensional identity setup underlying this book's perspective, let us start with a fictionalized example of a girl named Ayla who lives in Wonderland. Wonderland has two ethnic groups, Black and White people; two religious groups, Muslim and Protestant people; and two economic groups, lower-class and upper-class people corresponding to a leftist and a rightist orientation. Let us assume the following relative population shares: the two ethnic groups — for simplicity, let us call them e_1 (Black) and e_2 (White) — comprise 30% and 70% of the population, the two religious groups, r_1 (Muslim) and r_2 (Protestant), comprise 50% and 50% of the population, and the two ideological groups, i_1 (Leftist) and i_2 (Rightist), comprise 20% and 80% of the population.

I assume that Ayla belongs to exactly one group from each of the three dimensions of ethnicity, religion and class-based ideology. Her ethnicity is Black, her religion is Protestant, and she belongs to the economic upper class, having a conservative, rightist orientation. In short, Ayla is characterized by a three-dimensional repertoire of identity attributes being Black-Protestant-Rightist. Ayla probably shares this repertoire with other people in the population, although the number is not discernable from the marginal distributions: it might be anything between zero people and half the population. Other people have one of the eight possible three-dimensional identity repertoires, being Black-Protestant-Leftist, White-Protestant-Rightist, White-Protestant-Leftist, etc.

Table 3.1.: How the Identity Setup Changes with the Underlying Dimensionality.

i_1	e_1	e_2
r_1	3%	7%
r_2	3%	7%

i_2	e_1	e_2
r_1	12%	28%
r_2	12%	28%

(a) *Three-dimensional identity setup*

e_1	e_2
30%	70%

r_1	r_2
50%	50%

i_1	i_2
20%	80%

(b) *One-dimensional identity setups: ethnic, religious, ideological*

	e_1	e_2
r_1	15%	35%
r_2	15%	35%

	e_1	e_2
i_1	6%	14%
i_2	24%	56%

	r_1	r_2
i_1	10%	10%
i_2	40%	40%

(c) *Two-dimensional identity setups: ethnic-religious, ethnic-ideological, religious-ideological*

For simplicity, let us assume that the population is proportionately distributed over all possible eight identity repertoires. This setup can nicely be illustrated with a cube, whereby each of the three vectors corresponds to one dimension and people are assumed to sit inside the cube according to their combination of identity categories from each dimension. However, once we drop the assumption of equal or proportionate distribution, it is better to illustrate the demographic identity setup of a country in a three-dimensional cross-table, like Table 3.1 (a) does for our fictionalized example. What differs from country to country are the number and kinds of groups per dimension, the distribution of the population over the different identity repertoires, and the degree to which the dimensions are correlated (cp. Selway 2011).

Some authors challenge the notion of having ethnicity, religion and class-based ideology as three latent dimensions (as previously discussed). Table 3.1 (a)–(c) traces the change of the demographic setup for our fictionalized example if only a subset of dimensions is taken into account. Most prominently, others consider ethnicity to be the only relevant dimension (see Table 3.1 (b)). Dropping religion and class skips all crosscuttingness, whereby the only quantities of interest are the separate ethnic groups with their relative population shares. Alternatively, despite being advocated much less frequently — if at all — one can focus exclusively on religion or ideology (also see Table 3.1 (b)). Finally, it is possible to consider only two of three dimensions (see Table 3.1 (c)), whether ethnicity and religion, ethnicity and ideology, or religion and ideology. In order to establish the superiority of having three dimensions, it is crucial to set the three-dimensional perspective in comparison to the one- or two-dimensional perspective.

The Coverage of the Government's Self-Definition

Next, let us discuss the coverage of the government's self-definition. Who is included and who is excluded when a government defines itself? If we start with the simple one-dimensional case, things are easy. Let us assume that an actor refers in its self-definition to certain ethnic categories, then all people belonging to these ethnic categories are assumed to be included, while all others are excluded. Relating back to the above example: if a government is Black, then Black Ayla will certainly be included. Deciding who is included and who is excluded is likewise easy if a government refers in its self-definition to one of the other two dimensions, namely religion or class-based ideology.

How does the reasoning change once we adopt a two- or three-dimensional perspective rather than a purely one-dimensional one? If the government refers in its self-definition to categories from different dimensions, things become a little more complicated given the overlappingness of dimensions: are only those people who fulfill *all* criteria represented, or are all people who fulfill *at least one* criterion represented? Let me illustrate this problem by returning to our fictionalized example: assume that the government is Black and Muslim. Are only those people who are Black *and* Muslim at the same time included, or all those people who are Black *or* Muslim? I take the latter view, whereby all people falling under at least one criterion of a government's self-definition gain to some degree and are assumed to be included, whereas all others are excluded. The reasons are two-fold. First, the government's reference to more than one dimension is often due to a coalition of actors. As it is plausible to assume that each coalition partner wants to benefit its core constituency, all people somehow falling under the definition should gain to some degree.[15] Second, when a government favors people on more than one dimension, it is probably difficult for the government to determine for each person individually whether it fulfills all criteria or just one criterion of the government's self-definition. Instead, it seems more plausible to assume in the above example of a Black-Muslim government that some amount of money is distributed to all Black people while another amount is distributed to all Muslim people, whereby people who are Black and Muslim gain relatively more while people like Ayla — being only Black — or others only being Muslim gain relatively less yet are still included.

Multidimensional Quantities of Interest

Once we adopt a multidimensional perspective on political exclusion and conflict, the theoretical expectations have to be adapted. After all, a three-dimensional perspective yields other quantities of interest than a one- or two-dimensional perspective. Thus, the present section determines the size of the excluded population and of the largest group according to Hypotheses 1a and 2a for all seven different identity setups (1x 3-D, 3x 1-D, 3x 2-D) separately. If ethnicity is taken into account as the only relevant dimension, the quantity of interest reduces to the size of the excluded ethnic population or the size of the largest excluded ethnic group, as hypothesized in Wimmer et al. (2009). If religion or ideology is the only latent dimension, the interest shifts to the size of the excluded religious or ideological population or the size of the largest excluded religious or ideological group, respectively. With a two- or three-dimensional view, the focus proceeds to the size of the population not fulfilling at least one of the government's identity criteria.

Let me illustrate the consequences of using different underlying dimensions for the quantities of interest with our fictionalized example of Wonderland (see Table 3.2). Assume that the government in Wonderland is Black and Muslim. This implies that all Black or Muslim people are included and that people who are neither Black nor Muslim are excluded. The excluded population in a three-dimensional setting comprises the White-Protestant-Leftist subgroup (e_2-r_2-i_1) with 7% and the White-Protestant-Rightist subgroup (e_2-r_2-i_2) with 28%, thus totaling 35% of the population, as Table 3.2 (a) demonstrates. Assuming that all identity lines are dividing,

[15]Often, two or more ethnic groups are represented within a government. If the requirement were that all included people would have to fulfill all criteria, the favored population would reduce to zero.

the largest excluded subgroup in a three-dimensional setting is the White-Protestant-Rightist subgroup with 28%. Once we reduce the focus to one (Table 3.2 (b)) or two dimensions (Table 3.2 (c)), the quantities of interest change. With a mere ethnic focus, only the ethnic categories matter for the identity setup and the self-definition of the government. Consequently, as the government is Black, all White people (e_2) — totaling 70% of the population — are excluded. In this case, the excluded population and the largest excluded subgroup are the same (70%). With a mere religious focus, only the religious categories matter. Consequently, as the government is Muslim, all Protestant people (r_2) — totaling 50% of the population — are excluded. Again, the excluded population and the largest excluded subgroup are the same (50%). With a mere class-based ideological focus, finally, only the ideological categories matter. As the government does not define itself in ideological terms, one has to make a decision concerning how to treat this case: do we assume a missing value because ideology is irrelevant (cp. Wimmer et al. 2009)? Alternatively, do we assume that all people are included or excluded? In order to ensure comparability with the multidimensional perspective (guarantee the same number of observations), I assume for these cases that no one is excluded. However, in order to ensure robustness in the quantitative analysis, I also construct the other two versions of a missing value and everyone being excluded. Last but not least, let us consider the two-dimensional case. With an ethnic-religious focus (Black-Muslim government), the White-Protestant subgroup (e_2-r_2) — totaling 35% — defines the excluded population and the largest excluded subgroup; with an ethnic-ideological focus (Black government), the White-Leftist subgroup (e_2-i_1) — with 14% — and the White-Rightist subgroup (e_2-i_2) — with 56% — form the excluded population, totaling 70% of the population, with the latter subgroup being the largest one. Finally, with a religious-ideological focus (Muslim government), the Protestant-Leftist subgroup (r_2-i_1) — with 10% — and the Protestant-Rightist subgroup (r_2-i_2) — with 40% — form the excluded population, totaling 50% of the population, with the latter subgroup being the largest one. As this example clearly shows, the quantities of interest change with the underlying dimensionality.

Generally, it holds that if the focus lies on the *excluded population*, the quantity of interest changes as soon as any one of the categories of a government's self-definition does not appear as an underlying dimension. If the focus lies on the *largest excluded subgroup*, the quantity of interest changes with any additional dimension, independent of whether it appears

Table 3.2.: How the Quantities of Interest Change with the Underlying Dimensionality (Included Groups Underlined).

i_1	e_1	e_2
r_1	3%	7%
r_2	3%	7%

i_2	e_1	e_2
r_1	12%	28%
r_2	12%	28%

(a) *Three-dimensional identity setup*

e_1	e_2
30%	70%

r_1	r_2
50%	50%

i_1	i_2
20%	80%

(b) *One-dimensional identity setups: ethnic, religious, ideological*

	e_1	e_2
r_1	15%	35%
r_2	15%	35%

	e_1	e_2
i_1	6%	14%
i_2	24%	56%

	r_1	r_2
i_1	10%	10%
i_2	40%	40%

(c) *Two-dimensional identity setups: ethnic-religious, ethnic-ideological, religious-ideological*

in the government's self-definition. Thus, it seems crucial to consider all potential dimensions that a government might realistically use for its self-definition. Given that, empirically, governments refer to any one of the three dimensions of ethnicity, religion and class-based ideology, often even combining them, adopting a three-dimensional perspective seems to provide the most complete picture. However, this claim regarding the superiority of a three-dimensional perspective has to be established empirically. Therefore, the revised hypotheses read as follows:

Hypothesis 1a: The risk of civil conflict onset in non-competitive regimes is higher, the larger the excluded population. This effect should be more pronounced for a three-dimensional perspective compared to a one- or two-dimensional perspective.*

Hypothesis 2a: The risk of civil conflict onset in non-competitive regimes is higher, the larger the largest excluded group. This effect should be more* *pronounced for a three-dimensional perspective compared to a one- or two-dimensional perspective.*

Hypothesis 1b: The risk of civil conflict onset in competitive regimes is lower, the larger the excluded population. This effect should be more pronounced for a three-dimensional perspective compared to a one- or two-dimensional perspective.*

Hypothesis 2b: The risk of civil conflict onset in competitive regimes is lower, the larger the largest excluded group. This effect should be more pronounced for a three-dimensional perspective compared to a one- or two-dimensional perspective.*

Underlying Assumptions

Before testing the hypotheses, let me discuss and defend three possibly controversial assumptions underlying this book's three-dimensional perspective. The first assumption concerns the conceptualization of a dimension as an accumulation of nominal categories rather than a range of continuous attributes. The second assumption conceptualizes ethnicity as one single dimension rather than a collection of multiple dimensions. Finally, the third assumption holds that ethnicity, religion and class-based ideology are three distinct dimensions, rather than one dimension being an attribute of another.

Nominal categories

One assumption with the above conceptualization is that each dimension has nominal categories rather than being characterized by a continuum of attributes (see Chandra 2012; Esteban and Ray 2011). This is certainly a simplifying assumption as a continuum would capture reality much better. Ethnicity, in racial terms, might vary from completely black skin color over different degrees of brown tones to being completely white, while the religiosity of people might go from being extremely religious with respect to one denomination — let us say Protestantism — over being moderately religious to being radically Muslim, and class typically ranges from the very poor over medium income people to the very rich (which is assumed to be correlated with a positioning on the left-right axis). That said, it seems difficult at first sight to set arbitrary thresholds unanimously classifying people as Black, White, Protestant, Muslim, Leftist or Rightist. On the other hand, people all over the world use these clear-cut categories and act as if boundaries between groups can clearly be drawn. When asking about people's ethnicity, religion or class, surveys typically use nominal categories and people generally have not much difficulty in assigning themselves to one of the categories. Thus, nominal categories become manifest and structure political and societal life, which is why it also seems completely justifiable to use them in this book.

The One-Dimensionality of Ethnicity

Another assumption underlying this book's perspective is that ethnicity, religion and class themselves are one-dimensional. This view is challenged by authors who contend that ethnicity itself should be considered multidimensional, comprising race, language, tribe, clan, caste and religion (Posner 2005; Chandra 2012).[16] Adherents of the multidimensional view of ethnicity ask why in some countries race, and in other countries language, tribe, clan, caste, or religion become politically salient, as well as why the saliency of one or the other ethnic dimension might even vary temporarily within a country (cp. Wilkinson 2008). For example, Posner (2005) wonders why at some time point language and at another time point tribal affiliations came to dominate the political arena in Zambia.

While there is a point to the objection of ethnicity being multidimensional, I nevertheless argue for a unidimensional conceptualization of ethnicity in this book for the following reasons. First, not all ethnic categories are present all over the world; for example, tribe, clan and caste are region-specific (and a varying number of dimensions by region would complicate matters). Second, there is sound evidence that the activation of one or the other category depends on the level of competition, whereby race and language tend to be activated on the national level and tribe and clan tend to be activated on the local level (Posner 2005, 8f., 143ff.). As this book focuses on political competition at the national level, race and language seem to be the main ethnic categories of interest.[17] That said, the question arises concerning why one should not consider race and language as two separate dimensions in addition to religion and class, rather than pooling

[16]Chandra (2012, 51) includes language, dialect, race, physical differences, tribe, clan, nationality, region, religion, sect and caste as identity categories associated with ethnicity.

[17]In a dataset by Alesina et al. (2003, 159), "the definition of ethnicity involves a combination of racial and linguistic characteristics", and the resulting indicator closely correlates with Fearon's one (Fearon 2003, 196).

them under the banner of ethnicity. Despite possibly being desirable in principle, practical reasons and theoretical considerations speak against it: first, four dimensions are more difficult to analyze than three; second, separate data on race and language is not necessarily available; and third, considering that generally only one of the two concepts race *or* language becomes politically activated in a country at a time, deciding for either of them on a case-by-case basis seems well defensible.[18] Fortunately, when using survey data as this book does, this decision has already been made by country-experts before conducting a national survey on the individuals' ethnicity.

Ethnicity, Religion and Class as Distinct Dimensions

A third assumption underlying this book's three-dimensional identity setup is that ethnicity, religion and class are indeed three distinct dimensions. This view is challenged on two fronts. As indicated above, some authors contend that religion is an ethnic sub-dimension and not a separate dimension because the defining characteristic of ethnicity — namely that it is descent-based (Chandra 2012, 51ff.) — also seems to hold true for some religions (Horowitz 1985, 53; Fearon 2003, 200; Posner 2005; Wimmer et al. 2009: Online Appendix; Chandra 2007, 2; Chandra 2012, 9; Wilkinson 2008, 273).[19] However, recognizing that several religions are precisely not descent-based, the authors at the same time argue for a differentiation between religions that *are* descent-based and those that are *not* (Chandra 2012 9, 63f.; Fearon 2003, 200). In my view, however, such non-uniform treatment of religion makes it problematic to conceptualize religion as an ethnic sub-dimension per se. I argue that ethnicity and religion capture two different things: while ethnicity is about descent-based physical features, religion deals with specific assumptions about the supernatural, which subsequently become manifest in certain group-based habits. That said, the more common notion would be to consider religion as an extra dimension alongside ethnicity, as done in this book and likewise in Alesina et al. (2003, 159), Chandra (2012, 67) and Esteban et al. (2012, 1311), as well as in

[18] Posner and others show that language tends to be activated in Africa, and race in Latin America. If both concepts are relevant, classifications in common datasets on ethnicity reflect the judgment of anthropologists and ethnologists (Alesina et al. 2003, 159).

[19] However, if religion is descent-based, there tends to be a strong overlappingness of religion and ethnicity, whereby the descent-based notion is likely due to the ethnic — rather than the religious — component (cp. Gubler and Selway 2012, 212f.).

several population surveys asking separately for the respondents' ethnicity and their religion.[20]

The other challenge emerges from scholars who reject class as a separate dimension of political competition and argue instead for economic inequalities being an attribute of ethnic groups (Cederman et al. 2011; Stewart 2009). As a justification, the respective scholars refer to the empirical non-findings on vertical inequalities and violent conflict, theoretically pointing to the difficulty of the poor to mobilize (Esteban et al. 2012). However, as documented above, vertical inequalities emerge as a significant predictor of violent conflicts with the availability of better data (Bartusevičius 2014), and numerous case study examples of leftist groups violently challenging governments all over the world conflict with the theoretical objection. Thus, in my view, conceptualizing ethnicity, religion and class as separate dimensions is completely defensible.

[20]Interestingly, Posner (2004, 3) shows that "the pairwise correlation between religious and linguistic fractionalization is just 0.27."

Chapter 4.

Testing the Argument on Exclusion and Conflict

This chapter derives the key variables of the empirical analyses and discusses the methods that will be used to analyze the variables in subsequent quantitative tests.

4.1. Definitions, Data and Variables

This book collects original data on the three-dimensional identity setup of a country and matches these data with existing datasets on the political exclusion and inclusion of identity groups. The goal is to determine the size of both the excluded population and the largest excluded three-dimensional subgroup so that the above hypotheses can be tested. The following paragraphs introduce the different steps in further detail.

Defining and Operationalizing Ethnicity, Religion and Class

As previously discussed, the defining characteristic of ethnicity is its descent-based character (Fearon 2003, 200; Chandra 2006, 400). While this is common sense, more controversy arises concerning the question of the multi-dimensional nature of ethnicity. Should language, dialect, race, nationality, tribe, clan, religion, sect and caste all be part of a definition of ethnicity (cp. Horowitz 1985, 52f.; Fearon 2003, 200; Wimmer et al. 2009, 325; Chandra 2012, 51)? As already explicated in further detail before, there is good reason to assume that on the *national* level — which is the focus here — ethnicity can well be defined based upon two characteristics only, namely race and language (cp. Posner 2005). Fortunately, such a view combines well with the availability of data. While early data collection attempts focused purely on linguistic differences when delineating ethnic groups, later approaches took both linguistic and racial distinctions into account, arguing that — in some countries — people perceive the ethnic landscape more in terms of language, while in other countries it is about race (Alesina et al. 2003; Fearon 2003).

This book separates religion from the definition of ethnicity. While ethnic identity is largely established by descent-based physical features, religion deals with specific beliefs in the supernatural, which manifest themselves on earth in group-specific habits. Therefore, I follow the definition by Finke and Martin (2012, 1) and define "religion as explanations of existence based on supernatural assumptions that include statements about the nature and workings of the supernatural and about ultimate meaning" and "religious groups as 'collectives that promote religious beliefs, symbols and practices that support these supernatural assumptions' " (Henne 2012 cit. Smith 1996, 5). Operationalizing religion seems easier than operationalizing ethnicity, given that there is only one 'dimension'. However, problems about the correct level of aggregation likewise apply. Should Protestants and Catholics be grouped under a major category of Christians? Should Shia and Sunni Muslims be considered separately or grouped under a joint category of Muslims? Ideally, I would opt for as much disaggregation as possible, and subsequently allow in the theoretical model for the building of coalitions. However, in practice, data constraints apply, whereby religious groups are often aggregated.

Finally, class refers to the economic situation of individuals, mainly considering the amount of income that they possess (cp. Van der Waal et al. 2007, 406).[1] Operationalizing this concept seems straightforward by simply asking for the individuals' level of income, or, alternatively, directly for their subjectively felt class belonging. However, this book chooses a different, less forward operationalization of class, namely the self-classification of people along the left-right-ideological axis.[2] This classification is taken as a proxy for their income situation assuming a correlation between low income and leftist redistributive attitudes, as well as between high income and rightist conservative attitudes (cp. Cusack 1997, 375). Extensive support for such a correlation and the continued relevance of economic class as a determinant for an individual's position on the left-right axis is provided in Wiesehomeier and Doyle (2012, 21, 23) for Latin America, and in Van der Waal et al. (2007) for 15 developed countries (cp. Morton et al. 2011). Despite ample evidence that when development levels are increasing, the issue of income is

[1]Others have operationalized class in terms of occupation, thereby inappropriately confounding the issue of economic and educational status (see Van der Waal et al. 2007, 409).

[2]The reason is that data on the government's self-definition are available for its ethnic, religious and ideological left-center-right identity, but not for its class identity. Therefore, it makes most sense to already code the people on the left-right, rather than the class dimension.

supplemented by other considerations and topics influencing the left-right position (Benoit et al. 2006), at least in developing countries, a positioning on the left-right axis seems to mainly rest on income and its political implications as the most pressing need. Given that this book's primary focus is on these latter types of regimes, it is completely defensible to assume a high correlation between individuals' income and their positioning on the left-right-axis, as well as using the ideological left-right positioning as an operationalization of class.[3]

The Three-Dimensional Identity Setup of a Society

This book uses the World Values Survey (WVS) to operationalize the different identity concepts and determine the three-dimensional identity setup of a society.[4] The WVS is a world-wide survey based upon a representative sample of the adult population in over 87 countries, totaling more than 256.000 interviewees and covering — up to 2014 — five waves between 1981 and 2009.[5] In most countries, the sampling method has been some form of multistage stratified random sampling with a required minimum sample size of 1,000 respondents.[6]

The WVS contains data on the individual's ethnicity ($x051$), religion ($f025$) and class/ideology ($e033$). The WVS largely conforms to the view of ethnicity, religion and ideology taken in this book. Ethnicity is defined in terms of race — skin color or national background — or language, while religion refers to various religious denominations, and ideology is measured on a left-right scale. The different categories for ethnicity, religion and

[3]In developed countries, education emerges as an additional determinant of voting behavior along the left-right axis, often cross-cutting the class dimension, with highly educated people tending to vote leftist (Gerber et al. 2010; Van der Waal et al. 2007; Wiesehomeier and Doyle 2012, 22). However, in developing, poor countries, class seems to be the key determinant of left-right voting behavior.

[4]"World Values Survey," `http://www.worldvaluessurvey.org/wvs.jsp` on: [2011/2/1].

[5]The waves are: 1981–1984, 1990–1994, 1995–1998, 1999–2004 and 2005–2009. Recently, there has been a new wave available covering 2010-2014.

[6]The WVS uses the following sampling procedure: "In the first stages, a random selection of sampling points is made based on the given society statistical regions, districts, census units, election sections, electoral registers or voting stations and central population registers. In most countries the population size and/or degree of urbanization of these Primary Sampling Units are taken into account. In some countries, individuals are drawn from national registers" (`http://www.worldvaluessurvey.org/WVSContents.jsp?CMSID=FieldworkSampling` on: [2014/4/15]). With the sampling points given, the random route procedure and the last birthday method are typically used to identify the individuals to be interviewed.

ideology are pre-specified in the survey and they differ by country in the case of ethnicity and religion. Thus, individuals interviewed in the survey can decide to which category they belong from a list of given ones. Overall, the WVS contains more than 190 different ethnic groups, more than 80 different religious groups and 10 categories for positioning oneself on an ideological left-right scale. I use these categories as they are given, apart from the 10 categories on the left-right scale, which are recoded, whereby categories 1-5 represent leftist attitudes and categories 6-10 represent rightist attitudes. If the category of centrism has become salient in the respective country at some time point between 1975 and 2005, the categories 5 and 6 are recoded as centrist attitudes.

As individuals choose exactly one category from each of the three dimensions of ethnicity, religion and ideology, it is possible to construct the three-dimensional identity repertoire for each individual and group individuals with the same identity repertoire into one "three-dimensional subgroup". This ultimately allows determining the three-dimensional identity setup, which is the distribution of the population over all possible three-dimensional identity repertoires in a country.[7] To my knowledge, the resulting dataset is completely novel.

Data from the WVS is used to the extent that information on all three identities — ethnicity, religion and ideology — is available. Ultimately, this book's dataset contains information on 57 countries[8] and uses the WVS's last three waves (Wave 3, 4, and 5). For many countries, demographic data is only available for one time point, while there are two or three time points for others. In either case, information on the subgroups' population shares is used for the entire time period for which information on all other variables

[7] General problems with survey data apply. Researchers might impose their knowledge about conflict processes asking, in the worst case, only for the two groups involved in a conflict. Individuals may lie and assign themselves to another group than their real one, favorably the included group, based upon strategic calculations, as reported in Alesina and Ferrara (2005, 790) for two examples taken from Wilkinson (2002). If this tendency of the population to associate with the government is wide-spread, the excluded population will be underestimated systematically; however, I am not aware of evidence for such a systematic bias.

[8] The 57 countries are Albania, Argentina, Armenia, Australia, Azerbaijan, Bangladesh, Belarus, Bosnia and Herzegovina, Brazil, Bulgaria, Burkina Faso, Canada, Chile, Dominican Republic, Finland, France, Georgia, Ghana, Guatemala, India, Iraq, Italy, Japan, Jordan, Kyrgyzstan, Latvia, Macedonia, Mali, Mexico, Moldova, Morocco, Nigeria, Pakistan, Peru, Poland, Romania, Rwanda, Slovakia, Slovenia, South Africa, South Korea, Spain, Sweden, Switzerland, Taiwan, Thailand, Trinidad and Tobago, Uganda, Ukraine, United Kingdom, United States of America, Uruguay, Venezuela, Vietnam, Yugoslavia, Zambia and Zimbabwe.

in the dataset is available. This is the time period from 1975 to 2005.

Representativeness of the Demographic Setup

While the WVS aims to be a representative sample, one should be aware that the categories per dimension are chosen by research teams, whereby the typical selection problems may apply. Additionally, various restrictions impeded researchers from taking full probability samples in most cases. Nonetheless, why can we be confident that the kinds of groups and their relative population shares are sufficiently representative? Other authors who also use the World Values Survey to extract information about demographics conduct some cross-checking to ensure that the data provided are representative. For example, Selway correlates fractionalization indices based upon the WVS with fractionalization indices from Alesina et al. (2003), Fearon (2003) and Reynal-Querol (2002) and finds relatively high correlations, thus concluding that we can have "confidence in the surveys' categorization" (Appendix to Selway 2011, 2). Selway also compares ethnic groups from the WVS (and other surveys) with those from a study by Posner (2005), finding that the WVS generally includes more groups than Posner. Finally, Elkins and Sides (2007) aim to ascertain whether the ethnic groups in the WVS largely correspond to the ethnic groups in the Minorities at Risk dataset. In their 51 countries covered by the WVS, they find that 90 out of 155 Minorities at Risk appear in the WVS: while the 65 left-out groups are rather small and very concentrated, they do not exhibit other differences from the included groups.

Non-Random Sample of Countries

The analysis is based upon a non-random sample of 57 out of potentially about 193 countries. The reason for this restriction is that the WVS does not include data for all countries all over the world, while there are missing values on the variables of interest for some countries included. One might suspect that those countries not included are either highly restrictive — thus not allowing the survey to be conducted, which possibly makes them less conflict-prone — or they are so highly conflict-prone that the conduct of a survey becomes impossible. In either case, there might be a selection on the dependent variable, which raises the question of a selection bias. This question has already been tackled by other authors, generally concluding that there is no matter of concern. Selway (2011) shows that constraining the analysis to countries from the WVS does not introduce a bias in the quantitative analysis, given that the conflict propensity of countries from the WVS is comparable to the overall conflict propensity. Additionally, Gubler and Selway (2012, 218) find that for the 80 out of 159 countries, the means and standard deviation of the dependent variable civil war onset are very similar to those for the excluded countries.

Time-Invariant Demographic Indicators

For most of the countries, I use a single demographic indicator regardless of the year.[9] Note that this implies that the level of conflict in a year is often predicted by the demographic setup from a subsequent year, which might introduce an endogeneity problem. Therefore, choosing this option is only defensible if the demographic setup can be assumed to be stationary, whereby the setup from 1970 largely corresponds to the setup from 1980, 1990 or 2000, and if it is exogenous to the conflict process. I argue that the stationarity of the three-dimensional identity setup is generally given for the period of about 30 years under consideration (cp. Alesina et al. 2003; Fearon 2003; Chandra 2012). Although the number of dimensions, the categories per dimension, and the population shares in each category theoretically might change over time, these changes seem to be rare, at least in the short term (Chandra 2012). Evidence for the contrary is scarce. In the literature, one example of Somalia is frequently cited as evidence that a new dimension — the tribal dimension — became salient after a conflict (Fearon 2003, 198), while another example, Yugoslavia, is used to show that two previously united groups — Serbs and Croats — came to perceive each other as separate groups (Gartzke and Gleditsch 2006, 60). Moreover, two further examples, Lapps in Norway and Russians in Estonia, are taken as evidence that population shares within groups can dramatically change due to assimilation or migration processes (Posner 2004). However, the respective authors candidly contend that such cases are truly exceptional.[10]

However, what does change in the short term are the coalitions between groups and the activated dimensions (cp. Chandra 2012), but neither the coalitions nor the activated dimensions are presupposed in the three-dimensional demographic setup. Accounting for these two factors is something that this book explicitly allows for in the formal theoretical part.

[9]Others have taken a similar approach, see Gubler and Selway (2012, 216f.).

[10]A study by Fletcher and Iyigun (2010) is divergent, holding that conflict influences demographics.

The Political Exclusion of Identity Groups

Finally, data on the three-dimensional identity setup of a society is harmonized with information on the government's self-definition to ascertain which three-dimensional subgroups in a society are politically included or excluded. Based upon the Ethnic Groups in Power (EPR) dataset by Wimmer et al. (2009) and the government's religious and ideological orientation from the Database of Political Institutions (DPI), the study first determines whether each ethnic, religious and ideological group of the WVS is politically included or excluded. Ethnic inclusion is determined by the degree of "executive-level power, that is, representation in the presidency, cabinet, and senior posts in the administration, including the army" (Wimmer et al. 2009, 326), while religious and ideological inclusion is determined by the current party in power and its religious (Christian, Catholic, Islamic, Hindu, Buddhist, Jewish) or ideological (left, right, centrist) self-definition. If the party in government explicitly stands for a certain religion or ideology, this book assumes that it favors the population with the same religion or ideology. Given the information on the exclusion and inclusion of ethnic, religious and ideological groups, it is possible to determine whether each three-dimensional subgroup is currently represented in government or not.[11]

Key Independent Variables on Exclusion

I use two types of key independent variables, one on the size of the excluded population and the other on the size of the largest excluded subgroup. In order to assess the performance of the so-called three-dimensional indicators in comparison to one- and two-dimensional indicators, the study constructs variables for all three-, one- and two-dimensional settings. This finally yields fourteen variables: seven variables on the excluded population (1x 3-D, 3x 2-D, 3x 1-D) and seven variables on the largest excluded subgroup (1x 3-D, 3x 2-D, 3x 1-D). Finally, the study also compares the performance of these variables vis-à-vis two ethnic variables from Wimmer et al. (2009): one on

[11]Note that the categories in the World Values Survey do not necessarily accord with the categories in Wimmer et al. (2009) or the DPI. While matching for the ideological categories worked perfectly, matching for the ethnic and religious categories was less straightforward (details can be obtained from the author). One major problem was that the religious categories in the DPI are much less fine-grained than in the WVS. Most prominently, the WVS often differentiates between Shia and Sunni Islamic groups, whereas the DPI only includes Islamic governments, without further differentiating them.

Table 4.1.: Key Independent Variables on Exclusion

Variable	Abbrev.	Avg. (%)	Mdn. (%)
excl. three-d. pop.	ERI_{all}	11.1	4.6
excl. ethnic pop.	E_{all}	12.5	7.1
excl. relig. pop.	R_{all}	6.1	1.7
excl. ideol. pop.	I_{all}	49.4	49.5
excl. eth-relig. pop.	ER_{all}	11.8	7.1
excl. eth-ideo. pop.	EI_{all}	11.6	4.7
excl. rel-ideol. pop.	RI_{all}	45.9	48.7
largest excl. three-d. group	ERI_{max}	5.4	1.8
largest excl. ethnic group	E_{max}	9.0	5.0
largest excl. relig. group	R_{max}	5.4	1.7
largest excl. ideol. group	I_{max}	43.0	45.3
largest excl. eth-relig. group	ER_{max}	5.9	3.3
largest excl. eth-ideol. group	EI_{max}	7.8	2.2
largest excl. rel-ideol. group	RI_{max}	28.9	31.0
excl. eth. pop (Wimmer)	W_{all}	12.5	4.0
largest excl. eth. group (Wimmer)	W_{max}	9.4	2.0

the excluded ethnic population and the other on the largest excluded ethnic group (see Table 4.1).[12]

Let us consider summary statistics for some of the key independent variables (cp. Table 4.1). On average, the size of the largest excluded three-dimensional subgroup is around 5.4% (median: 1.8%), the largest excluded ethnic group is around 9% (median: 5%), the largest excluded religious group is around 5.4% (median: 1.7%) and the largest excluded ideological group is around 43% (median: 45.3%). Box plots (see Figure 4.1) reveal that despite a substantial number of cases with ethnic and ideological exclusion, religious exclusion is rare.[13] Thus, one has to be cautious when drawing inferences about religious exclusion.

Finally, the correlation between the variables is generally low, with some exceptions (cp. Table 4.2 and Table 4.3). The highest correlation exists for the three-dimensional and the ethnic-ideological variable (0.97, 0.90).

[12] Like the control variables, all these independent variables will be lagged in the analyses.

[13] This pattern might be due to the fact that the Database of Political Institutions uses rather large encompassing religious categories, like Christian or Islamic. Note that for the box plots, I also consider the cases where the respective category is not relevant.

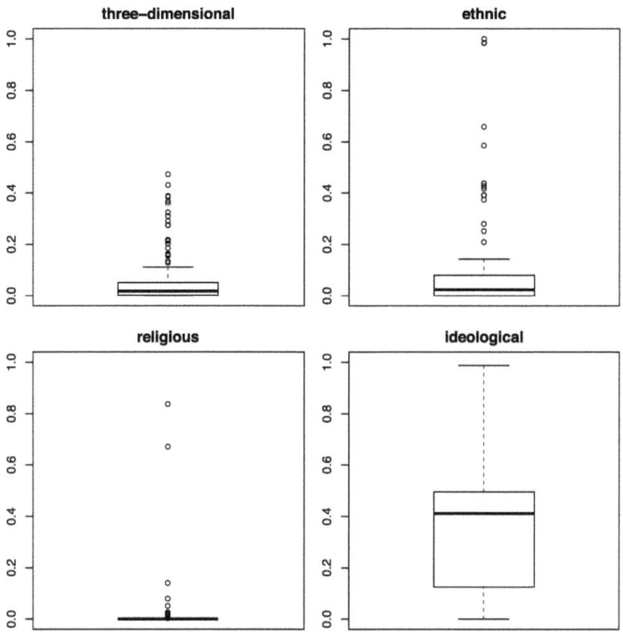

Figure 4.1.: *Box plots on the size of the largest excluded (sub-)group. A box plot displays numerical data through their quartiles. The bottom of the box is the first quartile, the top of the box is the third quartile, and the band inside the box is the median. Lines extending vertically from the boxes are whiskers, which extend, maximally, to 1.5 times the interquartile range from the box. Dots beyond the end of the whiskers are outliers.*

Thus, one would expect rather similar results for these two variables. High correlations also hold for the ethnic-religious and the ethnic variable, as well as the religious-ideological and the ideological variable. Given the rareness of religious exclusion, these correlations were to be expected. Finally, the excluded three-dimensional population and the largest excluded three-dimensional subgroup are also highly correlated, exhibiting a correlation coefficient of 0.88.

Table 4.2.: Correlation Table for the Excluded Population

	three	*eth*	*rel*	*ideo*	*ethrel*	*ethideo*	*relideo*
eth	0.25						
rel	−0.05	−0.03					
ideo	0.21	−0.01	−0.07				
ethrel	0.22	0.95	−0.04	−0.02			
ethideo	0.97	0.23	−0.04	0.21	0.20		
relideo	0.26	0.04	0.03	0.90	0.04	0.22	
Wim	0.05	0.57	−0.04	−0.23	0.52	0.03	−0.18

Table 4.3.: Correlation Table for the Largest Excluded (Sub-)Group

	three	*eth*	*rel*	*ideo*	*ethrel*	*ethideo*	*relideo*
eth	0.15						
rel	−0.04	−0.03					
ideo	0.15	0.03	−0.06				
ethrel	0.10	0.85	−0.03	0.01			
ethideo	0.90	0.23	−0.04	0.15	0.11		
relideo	0.23	−0.00	0.03	0.83	0.04	0.12	
Wim	−0.00	0.55	−0.03	−0.23	0.45	0.04	−0.20

Key Independent Variable on Regime Type

According to this book's expectations, the effect of exclusion on civil conflict onset depends on the type of the political regime. In the theoretical part, I argued that exclusion works differently in so-called competitive regimes — regimes with functioning elections — and non-competitive regimes — regimes without functioning elections. The standard regime type variable in the literature is the Polity IV index. However, Polity IV is a composite index ranging from -10 to +10, which captures various aspects of political life (Marshall et al. 2002). Alongside the competitiveness of political participation and executive recruitment, it contains aspects of the openness of recruitment and constraints on the executive, which makes it unapt for testing a hypothesis that rests exclusively on the competitiveness of regimes (cp. Hyde and Marinov 2011; Vreeland 2008; Cheibub et al. 2010).[14]

[14] According to Hyde and Marinov (2011, 201f.), "[t]he main challenge in using such aggregated measures is that they are at best noisy approximations of elections and

This book thus constructs a new regime type variable on the non-competitiveness of regimes (*noncl*) based upon NELDA data (Hyde and Marinov 2011). This variable is a dichotomous indicator that takes a value of 1 if there was no election in a country for more than four years (legislative or executive), or if there was an election, within which either no opposition was allowed or the election was not free and fair.[15] I assume that the opposition cannot hope to get into power via constitutional means in these so-called non-competitive regimes without functioning elections, but rather has to resort to extra-constitutional means if it wants to come into power. However, in order to test for the robustness of the results, I also construct a variable on autocracy (*autocl*), based upon Polity IV data. This dichotomous indicator takes a value of 1 if a country takes a value between −10 and −6 on the Polity IV scale (standard conceptualization). The two variables *noncl* and *autocl* are positively correlated by a factor of 0.5. Most regimes (82.3%) are non-competitive and autocratic or competitive and non-autocratic (as one would expect), although some regimes are non-competitive and non-autocratic (7%) or competitive and autocratic (10.7%).[16]

Dependent Variable: The Onset of Internal Armed Conflict

In the first run of my analyses, I use the dependent variable from Wimmer et al. (2009) on the onset of internal armed conflicts (*onset*1).[17] This variable is based upon the UCDP Armed Conflicts Dataset (ACD, version 3-2005b,

competition. [...] Thus, by design, even though the Polity data set is one of the most widely used sources of data on variation in democratic and authoritarian political institutions, it does not draw a distinction between elections that allow competition and those that do not."

[15] For this purpose, I use the *nelda*3 and *nelda*11 variables.

[16] Cederman et al. (2013, 388) also consider competitive elections with and without (alleged) fraud based upon NELDA. They regard elections as competitive if the following three questions are answered in the affirmative: (1) Was opposition allowed? (2) Was more than one party legal? (3) Was there a choice of candidates on the ballot? (*nelda*3, *nelda*4, *nelda*5), thereby following Hyde and Marinov (2011, 194).

[17] Note that Wimmer's study contains two dependent variables: one where ongoing civil conflicts are coded as missing values, and the other where ongoing civil conflicts are coded as zero and an extra ongoing variable is introduced. Note that new onsets that occur while another conflict is ongoing are omitted in both versions. While this book mainly uses the first version (ongoing conflicts are coded as missings), which takes the name of *newonset*2 in Wimmer, it conducts additional robustness tests with the second version (ongoings as zero and extra ongoing variable). Note that taking new onsets while others are ongoing into account does not change the results.

Gleditsch et al. 2002). It takes a value of 1 if an internal armed conflict with more than 25 battle deaths breaks out in a certain year *for the first time or after ten years elapse*, and it assumes that ongoing conflicts are coded as missings. By using this variable, I intend to ensure the comparability of results with respect to Wimmer et al.'s original study (Wimmer et al. 2009).

However, in further analyses, I replace *onset*1 with a more recent and up-to-date variable on internal armed conflict onset based upon the UCDP ACD version 4-2010 (Gleditsch et al. 2002). This new onset variable takes a value of 1 if an internal armed conflict with more than 25 battle deaths breaks out in a certain year *for the first time or after two years elapse.* I remove coups d'état according to Powell and Thyne (2011) from the list of armed conflicts to better fit the theoretical expectations. The variable comes in two versions, one for which ongoing conflicts are coded as missings (*onset*2) and another one for which ongoing conflicts are coded as zero (*onset*3), while an extra variable for ongoing conflicts is introduced (*ongoingl*). The two dependent variables *onset*1 and *onset*2 are correlated by a factor of 0.81. Using the more recent *onset*2 variable has clear advantages: with the dependent variable by Wimmer et al. (2009), there are only 25 onsets of internal armed conflicts in my data. By contrast, when applying the new onset variable with a more up-to-date two year elapse between conflicts, I record 54 onsets of internal armed conflict, despite the removal of coups d'état.[18]

Governmental versus Territorial Conflicts

The theoretical part has thus far assumed that the government and the rebel group vie for the control over government. While two-thirds of all internal armed conflicts are indeed so-called **governmental conflicts**[19], one-third are **territorial conflicts**, whereby the rebels' goal is not control over the government but rather autonomy or secession (Buhaug 2006). While these

[18] Another difficulty in using the dependent variable by Wimmer et al. (2009) is that they modified the original ACD data, thereby making their dependent variable less transparent.

[19] According to the Uppsala Armed Conflict Database, governmental conflicts involve incompatibilities concerning "the type of the political system, the replacement of the central government or the change of its composition", whereas territorial conflicts are about "the status of a specified territory, e.g. the change of the state in control of a certain territory (interstate conflict), secession or autonomy (intrastate conflict)" ("UCDP," `http://www.pcr.uu.se/research/ucdp/definitions/` on: [2014/10/7].)

two types of conflicts may differ in certain respects (Buhaug 2006), the theoretical logic advanced in this book is the same. In both governmental and territorial conflicts, rebel groups vie for the control over the state — whether all or part of it — to implement policies that are favorable to themselves. If rebel groups succeed in governmental conflicts, they will be able to decide about the division of the given 'national pie' — and according to this book's logic, the pie will be distributed among themselves. If rebel groups succeed in territorial conflicts and become independent, they will also be able to decide about the division of a 'pie', although this is a 'new national pie' and — again — this will most likely be distributed among themselves. The difference between the two scenarios is, first, that the size of the pie may vary, and, second, that the resulting excluded population is larger in successful governmental than in successful territorial conflicts. However, only the first of these two differences is consequential for the rebels' expected gains. That said, this book includes both governmental and territorial conflicts within the dependent variable of armed conflict onset.

Control Variables

In order to make this book comparable to existing studies, it includes well-established control variables. In determining the controls, it follows prominent studies by Fearon and Laitin (2003), Hegre and Sambanis (2006) and Wimmer et al. (2009). The control variables are GDP per capita (*gdpcapl*) and size of the population (*lpopl*) (cp. Wimmer et al. 2009), oil production per capita (*oilpcl*) (Wimmer and Min 2006), mountainous terrain (*lmtnest*) (cp. Fearon and Laitin 2003; Wimmer et al. 2009), and a variable on three-dimensional identity fractionalization ($fracl$) based upon the WVS (in reference to the typical ethnic fractionalization variable, like in Fearon and Laitin (2003)).

First, GDP is typically used as a proxy for a state's capabilities in financial, administrative and military terms (Fearon and Laitin 2003, 76). The higher these capabilities are, the easier it is to control and contain potential rebel movements or prevent them from emerging from the outset by accommodating the critical groups in time (Wimmer et al. 2009). Thus, the expectation is that the higher the GDP, the lower the risk of civil conflict onset, which is why GDP should exert a negative influence on civil conflict onset. GDP data generally come from Penn World Tables (Wimmer et al. 2009). Second, population size is usually used as a proxy for state cohesion. The assumption is that more populous countries are less cohesive, meaning that rebels can more easily be recruited and hidden, thereby making these countries more prone to civil conflicts (Wimmer et al. 2009, 323; Fearon and Laitin 2003, 81). In short, population size should exert a positive influence on civil conflict onset, and it is usually measured with World Bank data. Third, mountains are used to measure rough terrain, which likewise is expected to reduce the state's control and help the rebels to retreat (Fearon and Laitin 2003, 76), thus facilitating civil conflict onset. As a measure for rough terrain, Fearon and Laitin (2003, 81) use the "proportion of the country that is 'mountainous' according to the codings of geographer A. J. Gerard." Fourth, it is assumed that oil producers have a weaker state apparatus than other states because there is not such a great need for a strong, intrusive apparatus to raise revenues (Fearon and Laitin 2003, 81). Thus, oil should exhibit a positive influence, and it is measured as 'oil production per capita' from data by Mitchell (cp. Wimmer and Min 2006, 885). Finally, fractionalization is supposed to measure the degree of potential conflict between groups. The assumption is that the more groups there are, the more likely they are to clash and thus the more likely the emergence of "barriers to upward mobility for minority groups", who in turn are likely to revolt (Fearon and Laitin 2003, 78). Thus, fractionalization should increase the risk of civil conflict onset. This book adapts the generally used ethnic fractionalization index to a three-dimensional view. Thus, fractionalization is the probability that two randomly drawn individuals belong to two different ethnic, religious or ideological groups. Overall, former quantitative studies have found GDP and population size to exert a substantial and significant influence on civil conflict onset, while there is less systematic evidence for the other variables (Hegre and Sambanis 2006, 508ff.).

4.2. Coverage and Methods

This book's dataset covers 57 countries on a yearly basis from 1975 to 2005, containing up to 1553 observations. In the following, I examine whether a three-dimensional perspective is superior to a one- or two-dimensional perspective. The key independent variables focus on the size of the excluded population and the largest excluded subgroup. As the informal theoretical part established that the positive effect of these variables on the onset of internal armed conflict should only be prevalent in non-competitive regimes, the main interest lies in the interaction effects of the key independent variables with non-competitive regimes. In order to examine and compare these effects, I use a standard approach in the conflict literature of *logistic regression analysis*, due to the binary character of the dependent variable armed conflict onset. Given the time series cross-sectional nature of the data, leading to dependencies between observations, I include a natural cubic spline function and report robust standard errors.[20]

Before interpreting a model and drawing valid inferences, one has to ensure that the model itself is correctly specified (King and Roberts 2014; Esarey and Pierce 2012). Specification errors might result from an incorrect distributional assumption, an incorrect stochastic component or — most prominently — an incorrect functional form (King and Roberts 2014, 11). Functional form misspecification concerns the systematic component of the regression equation, often resulting from an independent variable not being correctly transformed (unaccounted nonlinearities and interaction effects) or even being completely neglected (omitted variable bias). If such problems exist but are not appropriately addressed, inferences about point estimates, significance levels and predicted probabilities might be incorrect (King and Roberts 2014; Esarey and Pierce 2012). Although it is a well-known textbook advice that specification error has to be addressed before results can meaningfully be interpreted, applied research has very often neglected this advice. Recently, Esarey and Pierce (2012) have taken up the issue again and proposed a method for logistic regression analysis that allows identifying whether a model is correctly specified. Their approach extends the suggestion by Gelman et al. (2004) to separate ranked predicted probabilities into fixed bins and compare the mean predicted probability to the observed empirical frequency m of positive outcomes for each bin (Esarey and Pierce 2012, 486; see also Hosmer and Lemeshow (1980)). However, rather than arbitrary binning, Esarey and Pierce propose non-parametric smoothing. Subsequently, they plot empirical probabilities in the sample against the in-sample predicted probabilities in a so-called *heat map plot* and assess via confidence intervals generated from parametric bootstrapping whether inaccuracies in prediction can be attributed either to random sampling variation or true misspecification (see Esarey and Pierce 2012, 486ff.). The heat map statistic reports the percentage of observations with a one-tailed p-value less than or equal to a certain threshold (usually 0.1). If this percentage becomes too high (≥ 0.2), whereby the heat map plot strongly deviates from the 45 degree line, model specification is problematic and has to be addressed (Esarey and Pierce 2012, 491). This book follows

[20]Note that classical and robust standard errors should not diverge, otherwise misspecification is a problem (King and Roberts 2014).

Esarey and Pierce's advice and uses heat map plots and heat map statistics to assess whether the models are correctly specified.

However, model misspecification is not the only cause leading to wrong inferences, with perfect prediction and multicollinearity reflecting other frequent problems in logistic regression analysis. First, extremely high point estimates and significance levels might alert us to perfect prediction, a numerical problem due to a covariate pattern with only one outcome. As this problem is often the result of sparse data and missing variation on the independent variable, it can best be accounted for by extending the dataset. Second, multicollinearity — which can also lead to wrong parameter estimates with implausible magnitude — stems from a very high correlation between the independent variables. It is typically assessed via tolerance or variance inflation factor (VIF) values with VIF values above 10 typically seen as problematic (O'Brien 2007). Transforming independent variables, combining them or increasing the number of observations are among the favorite solutions, whereas simply dropping variables or using the technique of 'residualization' are seen as problematic (York 2012).

Point estimates and significance levels in standard logistic regression tables give a hint about which individual independent variables are relevant. However, for substantive interpretation, it is much more important to analyze whether changes in independent variables from one value to another translate into significant changes in predicted probabilities for the outcome variable holding all other variables at fixed values. This focus on first differences in logistic regression analysis is all the more relevant once interaction terms are included, because for these terms, the significance in first differences cannot be deduced from the significance of the interaction terms (Berry et al. 2012, 8; Brambor et al. 2006). As a continuous independent variable (exclusion) is interacted with a dichotomous variable (non-competitive regime) in the present analysis, first difference analyses are crucial. Moreover, it will be illustrative to plot predicted probabilities and confidence intervals for the entire range of the continuous independent variable separately for non-competitive and competitive regimes (see Brambor et al. 2006) and to assess whether changes in predicted probabilities are indeed substantive (cp. Berry et al. 2012, 7).

Knowing that a model well predicts probabilities and that a single variable is a significant predictor does not yet tell us much about whether the model successfully separates cases/outcomes. Here, one typically relies on classification-based approaches that transform predicted probabilities into expected values with predicted probabilities above a certain threshold

(t) being transformed into 'ones' and predicted probabilities below that threshold being transformed into 'zeros'. Upon comparing observed values to expected values, it is possible to determine the rate of true positives and false positives, as typically known from a classification table. The receiver operating characteristic (ROC) curve generalizes this approach by calculating and plotting the rate of true positives against the rate of false positives for every possible threshold t (Ward et al. 2010, 4). If predicted probabilities were assigned randomly, the model would produce true and false positives at an equal rate, resulting in a straight 45-degree ROC line, yielding an area below the curve of 1/2, the value of the Area Under the Curve (AUC) statistic. By contrast, a perfect model with a 100% true positive rate would trace the upper outer bounds of the square plot, yielding an AUC value of 1 (cp. Ward et al. 2010, 4f.). AUC values below 0.65 are typically seen as poor, while those above 0.85 are seen as excellent. Note that while it is possible that a heat map plot points to a perfect model fit with respect to predicted probabilities, the ROC curve might yield a more moderate or even poor result with respect to the separation of cases/outcomes. This kind of deviation between heat map plot and ROC curve especially occurs when the dependent variable is rare and error-dominated, like in the case of armed conflict onset, where most predicted probabilities are clustered in a very narrow range of low values implying that a separation of outcomes below or above a certain threshold becomes difficult (cp. Esarey and Pierce 2012, 498).[21] While the ROC curve allows assessing the contribution that all independent variables jointly make in separating outcomes, the ROC approach likewise allows assessing the contribution of a single independent variable (in-sample prediction). Ward et al. (2010, 5f.)) suggest excluding each single independent variable from a fully specified model and observing how the AUC value changes. The variable with the largest contribution is deleted and the procedure is repeated over and over again. This allows determining the sequence of importance for all independent variables.

Once the goodness-of-fit of a model and the significance and substantial influence of key independent variables has been established, it is possible to compare different models with each other. Model comparison is highly relevant in the current analysis, which seeks to examine whether a three-dimensional exclusion perspective is superior to a one-dimensional or a two-dimensional exclusion perspective. Different approaches have been

[21]In this case, the ROC curve understates the quality of a model and one should not give too much attention to it.

suggested to make non-nested model comparison. The simplest approach would be to include all independent variables of different models into one joint model and subsequently assess via nested model comparison whether the variables that differ from one model to another jointly contribute to model amelioration. However, this approach is highly problematic and has been rejected in all major textbooks (Clarke 2011, 7). Instead, non-nested model comparison is typically conducted via likelihood-based statistics, like the information criteria (AIC) by Akaike (1973), the Bayesian information criteria (BIC) by Schwarz et al. (1978), the Vuong test (Vuong 1989) or the Clarke test (Clarke 2007).[22]

The AIC and the BIC assess the quality of a model by balancing model fit with an adjustment for parsimony. Model comparison is simply achieved by comparing the AIC or BIC statistics of two different models and choosing the one with the lower statistic. However, AIC and BIC provide no probabilistic statements concerning model selection (see Clarke 2003). By contrast, the Vuong test assesses which one of two different models is closer to the true — but unknown — specification. While this sounds complicated, it is simply "the average log-likelihood ratio suitably normalized" (Clarke 2001, 734). Finally, compared to Vuong, which is based upon the normal distribution assumption, Clarke (2001, 2003, 2007) develops a non-parametric test. This test compares the individual log-likelihoods of two models — corrected for their dimensionality — and assesses the frequency of one model having higher log-likelihoods than the other. Clarke shows that if the individual log-likelihood ratios are not distributed normally (assessed via the kurtosis[23] of the respective distribution), which is often the case, then his test outperforms the Vuong test.[24] Thus, it ultimately seems most appropriate for model comparison to choose between the Vuong and the Clarke test based upon a prior assessment concerning the distribution of the individual log-likelihood ratios.

[22]Despite not being appropriate for the comparison of logistic regression models (see Imai and Tingley 2012; Davidson and MacKinnon 1981), some authors nevertheless use a J-Test (see Collier and Hoeffler 2004).

[23]Clarke 2007: "Kurtosis measures whether a symmetric distribution has, relative to the Normal, thicker tails and higher peaks or not (Spanos 1999, 119). The Normal is a mesokurtic distribution and has a kurtosis of 3. The double exponential has thicker tails and is more peaked than the Normal, and thus is a leptokurtic distribution with a kurtosis of 6."

[24]While the Vuong test is a conservative test tending to reject neither model in favor of the other, the Clarke test more often decides between the models, but tends to make a wrong decision. Nonetheless, one can trade these effects off and show that the Clarke test is very often the better choice.

Once the best model of a set of alternatives has been identified, one can corroborate the findings with robustness checks to assess the sensitivity of results with respect to alternative operationalizations of variables, influential observations and alternative methods. Concerning the operationalization of variables, this book uses a different, theoretically less plausible — yet more established — independent variable on political institutions, *autocl* (see page 73), which is interacted with the key one- and multidimensional variables. Second, this book uses a more up-to-date dependent variable for armed conflict onset, *onset2* (see page 74). Finally, influential observations have a high leverage on one or more of the coefficients, in the worst case implying that a variable is only significant due to a few influential observations. A high Pregibon leverage value allows us to identify these observations before excluding them from the analysis and examining whether the results still hold. Once identified, influential observations can be further examined to determine whether they are simply a result of a coding error or whether these observations are truly different from the rest of the data (Pregibon 1981).

4.3. Empirical Results

I first report the results when regressing the dependent variable internal armed conflict onset according to Wimmer et al. (2009) (*onset1*) on the key independent variables and important controls without interaction terms focusing separately on the excluded population (Table 4.4) and the largest excluded subgroup (Table 4.5). In seven separate models without interaction terms, I include the three-dimensional variable (Model 1), the one-dimensional variables (Model 2-4), and the two-dimensional variables (Model 5-7), as well as the ethnic variable by Wimmer (Model 8) and all control variables. Table 4.4 and Table 4.5 report the results for the key independent variables, while the control variables are neglected due to space constraints (complete results in Appendix A). When focusing on the excluded population, Table 4.4 shows that neither of the one-, two- or three-dimensional variables proves significant. The same holds true when considering the largest excluded subgroup, as shown in Table 4.5. The heat map statistic reveals that the models are properly specified: on the one hand, the percentage of observations with p-values larger than 0.2 is zero, which is perfect; on the other hand, the fitted heat map line — as shown in Figure 4.2 for one of the two three-dimensional exclusion variables (ERI_{max}) — slightly deviates from the 45 degree line, especially for observations with high predicted probabilities. This fit can potentially be ameliorated via a transformation of the independent variables or via the introduction of interaction effects. Perfect prediction is only an issue for the religious exclusion variable (coefficient estimates and standard errors not displayed). However, difficulties with this variable were to be expected given the infrequence of religious exclusion in the present sample. Overall, the results of Table 4.4 and Table 4.5 confirm the expectations from the theoretical section, namely that the exclusion variables do not significantly predict the onset of armed conflict if all regimes are considered, regardless of their competitiveness. Of the control variables (see Appendix A), GDP per capita significantly reduces the risk of civil conflict onset in all models, as one would expect. Oil significantly increases the risk of civil conflict onset, and the other control variables — population size, mountainous terrain, fractionalization and peace years — exert no systematic significant conflict-reducing effect.

To account for the potentially differing effect of the exclusion variables across regime types, I next interact each of the exclusion variables with the independent variable on non-competitive regimes (*noncl*), resulting in another two tables with eight models each. Table 4.6 and Table 4.7 display the coefficient estimates and their significance of both the interaction terms and the constitutive terms. Model specification seems to be good. The heat map plot on the three-dimensional exclusion variable ERI_{max} — as shown in Figure 4.3 — reveals a slightly better fit with an interaction term than without an interaction term: zero percent of the observations are problematic and the fitted heat map line better approximates the 45 degree line.[25] Again, perfect prediction is only an issue for the one-dimensional religious exclusion variables. By contrast, multicollinearity is never a problem. With misspecification being highly unlikely, one can proceed to making valid inferences.

Table 4.6 and Table 4.7 reveal that the interaction terms on the three-dimensional exclusion variable ERI_{max}, the ethnic-ideological exclusion variable EI_{max} and the two Wimmer variables (W_{max}, W_{all}) are positive and significant. In order to assess whether exclusion significantly and substantially increases the risk of civil conflict onset in non-competitive or

[25] The heat map statistic is similarly good for the ethnic, the ethnic-ideological, and the Wimmer models; and it is slightly problematic for the ideological, the ethnic-religious, and the religious-ideological models. While the percentage of problematic observations is not too high, the fitted heat map line strongly deviates from the 45 degree line for high predicted probabilities.

Table 4.4.: Logit Estimations: Effect of Excluded Population Without Interaction on Conflict Onset

	Dependent variable:							
	onset1							
	(1)	(2)	(3)	(4)	(5)	(6)	(7)	(8)
noncl	−0.489	−0.545	−0.485	−0.533	−0.470	−0.489	−0.536	−0.513
	(0.502)	(0.510)	(0.509)	(0.510)	(0.510)	(0.502)	(0.511)	(0.501)
ERI_{all}	0.789							
	(1.079)							
E_{all}		1.555						
		(1.048)						
R_{all}			–					
			–					
I_{all}				−0.893				
				(0.638)				
ER_{all}					0.791			
					(1.252)			
EI_{all}						0.751		
						(1.088)		
RI_{all}							−0.923	
							(0.618)	
W_{all}								0.570
								(0.910)
Observations	1,247	1,247	1,247	1,247	1,247	1,247	1,247	1,247
Log Likelihood	-111.077	-110.225	-111.001	-110.484	-111.071	-111.093	-110.413	-111.084
Akaike Inf. Crit.	248.154	246.450	248.002	246.969	248.142	248.187	246.825	248.167

Note: *p<0.1; **p<0.05; ***p<0.01
robust standard errors in parentheses

Table 4.5.: Logit Estimations: Effect of Largest Excluded Subgroup Without Interaction on Conflict Onset

	Dependent variable:							
	onset1							
	(1)	(2)	(3)	(4)	(5)	(6)	(7)	(8)
noncl	−0.500	−0.557	−0.485	−0.514	−0.475	−0.492	−0.515	−0.483
	(0.493)	(0.511)	(0.509)	(0.510)	(0.514)	(0.499)	(0.509)	(0.509)
ERI_{max}	1.704							
	(2.625)							
E_{max}		1.674						
		(1.274)						
R_{max}			−					
			−					
I_{max}				−0.747				
				(0.796)				
ER_{max}					0.828			
					(2.488)			
EI_{max}						0.648		
						(1.687)		
RI_{max}							−0.896	
							(1.094)	
W_{max}								−0.261
								(1.123)
Observations	1,247	1,247	1,247	1,247	1,247	1,247	1,247	1,247
Log Likelihood	-111.087	-110.364	-111.001	-110.854	-111.197	-111.185	-110.929	-111.226
Akaike Inf. Crit.	248.174	246.728	248.002	247.707	248.394	248.371	247.857	248.453

Note: *p<0.1; **p<0.05; ***p<0.01
robust standard errors in parentheses

Table 4.6.: Logit Estimations: Effect of Excluded Population With Interaction on Conflict Onset

	Dependent variable:							
	onset1							
	(1)	(2)	(3)	(4)	(5)	(6)	(7)	(8)
noncl	−0.830	−0.724	−0.485	−0.752	−0.467	−0.836	−0.776	−1.325*
	(0.572)	(0.592)	(0.509)	(0.581)	(0.548)	(0.573)	(0.581)	(0.755)
ERI_{all}	−0.279							
	(1.168)							
noncl:ERI_{all}	2.639							
	(1.814)							
E_{all}		1.032						
		(1.251)						
noncl:E_{all}		1.155						
		(1.741)						
R_{all}			–					
			–					
noncl:R_{all}			–					
			–					
I_{all}				−1.112				
				(0.763)				
noncl:I_{all}				0.789				
				(1.354)				
ER_{all}					0.797			
					(1.295)			
noncl:ER_{all}					−0.040			
					(3.480)			
EI_{all}						−0.339		
						(1.171)		
noncl:EI_{all}						2.693		
						(1.817)		
RI_{all}							−1.158	
							(0.733)	
noncl:RI_{all}							0.877	
							(1.357)	
W_{all}								−0.677
								(1.199)
noncl:W_{all}								3.283*
								(1.780)
Observations	1,247	1,247	1,247	1,247	1,247	1,247	1,247	1,247
Log Likelihood	-110.506	-110.030	-111.001	-110.357	-111.071	-110.502	-110.256	-109.566
Akaike Inf. Crit.	249.012	248.059	250.002	248.714	250.141	249.005	248.513	247.132
Note:	*p<0.1; **p<0.05; ***p<0.01							
	robust standard errors in parentheses							

Table 4.7.: Logit Estimations: Effect of Largest Excluded Subgroup With Interaction on Conflict Onset

	Dependent variable:							
	onset1							
	(1)	(2)	(3)	(4)	(5)	(6)	(7)	(8)
noncl	−1.087*	−0.764	−0.485	−0.668	−0.730	−1.013*	−0.416	−0.963
	(0.615)	(0.579)	(0.509)	(0.599)	(0.629)	(0.582)	(0.579)	(0.631)
ERI_{max}	−3.631							
	(3.351)							
noncl:ERI_{max}	10.456**							
	(4.785)							
E_{max}		0.684						
		(1.795)						
noncl:E_{max}		1.645						
		(2.070)						
R_{max}			–					
			–					
noncl:R_{max}			–					
			–					
I_{max}				−0.933				
				(0.975)				
noncl:I_{max}				0.612				
				(1.507)				
ER_{max}					−0.036			
					(2.087)			
noncl:ER_{max}					4.438			
					(6.352)			
EI_{max}						−3.067		
						(2.113)		
noncl:EI_{max}						6.449**		
						(2.788)		
RI_{max}							−0.751	
							(1.296)	
noncl:RI_{max}							−0.592	
							(2.016)	
W_{max}								−1.650
								(1.328)
noncl:W_{max}								3.319*
								(1.931)
Observations	1,247	1,247	1,247	1,247	1,247	1,247	1,247	1,247
Log Likelihood	-109.519	-110.063	-111.001	-110.792	-110.850	-109.593	-110.900	-110.162
Akaike Inf. Crit.	247.038	248.126	250.002	249.584	249.699	247.185	249.800	248.324

Note: *p<0.1; **p<0.05; ***p<0.01
robust standard errors in parentheses

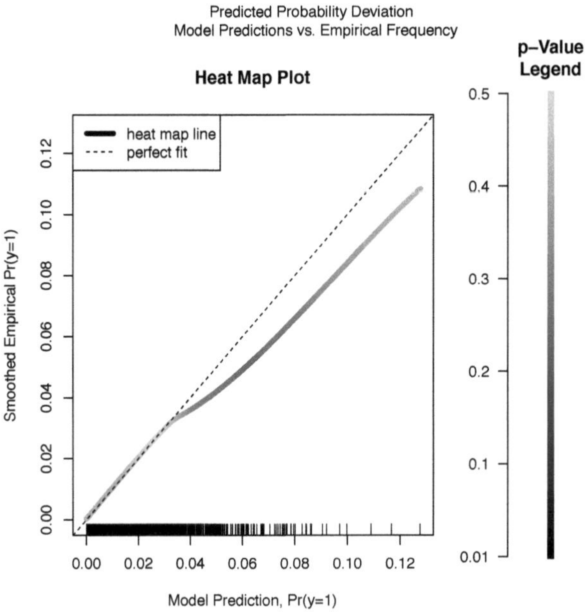

Figure 4.2.: *Fitted heat map line for Model 1 in Table 4.5. This model includes* ERI_{max} *as the key independent variable not interacted with regime type.*

competitive regimes, first difference (FD) analyses are necessary.[26] Figure 4.4 displays FD effects for non-competitive regimes when increasing key independent variables from zero to their third quartile.

The figure reveals that the change in predicted probabilities is positive and clearly significant at the 10-percent level for the three-dimensional exclusion variable ERI_{max}. When increasing ERI_{max} from zero to the third quartile (0.051), the predicted probability of armed conflict onset rises from 4.1% to 5.3% (by 25% or by over 1.2 percentage points, 90-percent-CI: [0.1; 3.0]). Thus, one key expectation (Hypothesis 2a*) from the theoretical part is

[26] In these and all following analyses on first difference effects and predicted probabilities, the control variables are set to the following values: *gdpcapl* to the first quartile, *lpopl*, *oilpcl*, *lmtnest* and *fracl* to the third quartile, *peaceyrs* at a value of three (with the respective splines), and *year* to 1980.

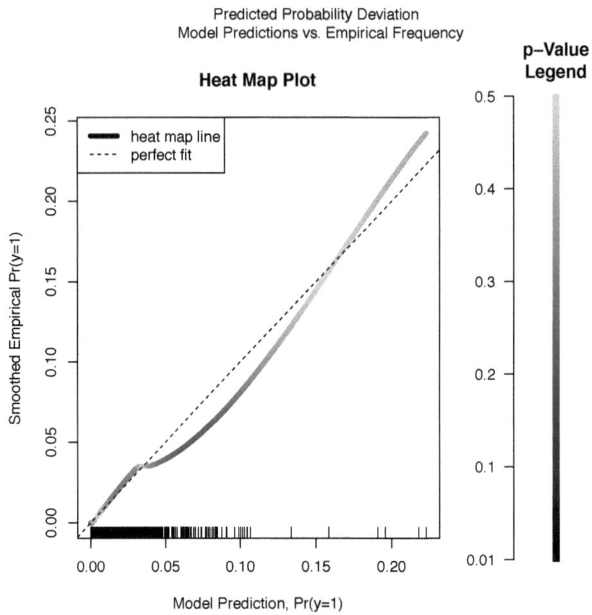

Figure 4.3.: *Fitted heat map line for Model 1 in Table 4.7. This model includes ERI_{max} as the key independent variable interacted with regime type.*

confirmed: when considering political exclusion in three dimensions, the size of the largest excluded three-dimensional subgroup positively, significantly, and substantially predicts the onset of civil conflict in non-competitive regimes. The change in predicted probabilities is insignificant for most one-dimensional and two-dimensional variables, apart from one Wimmer variable (W_{all}), and the ethnic-ideological (EI_{max}) exclusion variable, for which the effect is marginally significant. When increasing these two variables from zero to the third quartile, the predicted probability increases from 3% to 4.2% (by 1.2 percentage points, CI: [0.1; 3.1]), and from 4.4% to 5.2% (by 0.8 percentage points, CI: [0; 2]).[27] Unexpectedly, the variable on the excluded population in three dimensions (ERI_{all}) is not significant, which implies

[27] For the other ethnic variable by Wimmer (W_{max}), the predicted probability increases from 4.6% to 5.1% (by 0.5 percentage points, CI: [-0.5; 1.6]).

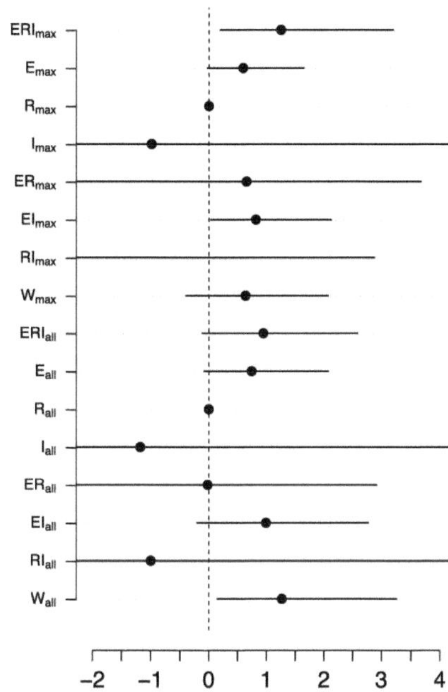

Figure 4.4.: *First difference analyses of the effect of exclusion in non-competitive regimes. In each case, the value of the key independent variable is increased from zero to the third quartile and the effect on the change in predicted probabilities, including 90% confidence intervals, is displayed.*

that the other key expectation (Hypothesis 1a*) does not receive empirical backing.[28]

Figure 4.5 to Figure 4.7 display the effects of exclusion on the predicted probability of armed conflict onset graphically for all three models with significant FD effects, for both non-competitive and competitive regimes. The figures confirm the positive effect of exclusion on armed conflict onset in non-competitive regimes for all three models. For competitive regimes, the effect of exclusion on armed conflict onset seems to be negative suggesting that with higher levels of exclusion, the risk of armed conflict onset reduces,

[28]Note that with a different specification, *onset*2 and *autocl*, first difference effects in autocratic regimes are also significant for the variable ERI_{all}.

which is in line with the expectations from Hypotheses 1b* and 2b*. However, this effect is never clearly significant when increasing the level of exclusion from zero to the third quartile (cp. Figure 4.8). It is notable that with no or minimal exclusion in three dimensions (Figure 4.5), competitive regimes have a higher risk of armed conflict onset (10.1%) than non-competitive regimes (4.4%), pointing to the interpretation that very small groups can mobilize more easily in competitive than in non-competitive regimes; with slightly higher exclusion levels, non-competitive and competitive regimes are about equally likely to experience armed conflict onset; and with substantially higher exclusion levels, non-competitive regimes more likely experience armed conflict than competitive regimes. These differences reach marginal statistical significance for the case of no exclusion, as Figure 4.9 shows for a comparison of non-competitive and competitive regimes, and statistical significance once exclusion goes beyond 0.3.

While the three-dimensional exclusion variable ERI_{max} is a positive and significant predictor for armed conflict onset in non-competitive regimes, this finding says little about how well the entire model succeeds in classifying outcomes, as well as the individual contribution of the three-dimensional exclusion variable to this fit. Here, the ROC curve/AUC statistic is informative: when looking at it, we see that a model that includes the three-dimensional exclusion variable ERI_{max} and its interaction term fits decently well (see Figure 4.10). The AUC value for such a model is 0.765 compared to an AUC value of 0.749 for a model without the three-dimensional exclusion variable and its interaction term.[29] Not very surprisingly given the similarity of models apart from one independent variable, the AUC statistic for the other models with significant interaction effects (EI_{max} and W_{all}) take about the same value like the one with the three-dimensional exclusion variable (0.764, 0.761, differences not statistically significant).[30] In order to determine the influence of single independent variables to the AUC, Figure 4.11 subsequently excludes the most influential predictors to the AUC statistic. It clearly shows that GDP is most influential for being dropped in the first place. This result could be expected, as GDP also proves to be by far the most influential predictor in other studies (see Ward et al. 2010, 6). Remarkably, the three-dimensional exclusion variable ERI_{max} and its interaction term already rank in second place, thereby supporting

[29]Note that this value is decent given the difficulty of correctly classifying outcomes for a rare events error-dominated dependent variable like civil conflict onset.

[30]Thus, the AUC statistic does not help to discriminate between the models, but that was not the purpose of this exercise anyway.

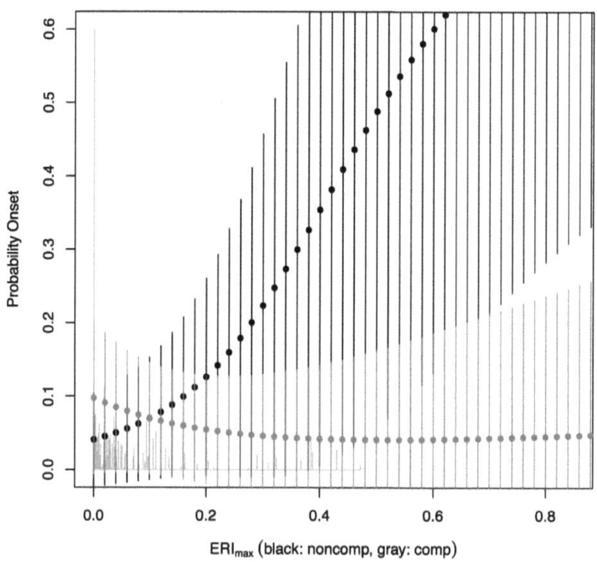

Figure 4.5.: *Predicted probability of armed conflict onset and 90% confidence interval for varying values of the variable ERI_{max}, separately for non-competitive and competitive regimes. (Relative frequencies of the values of the independent variable are displayed along the x-axis in gray.)*

the relevance of the three-dimensional exclusion variable for model fit in terms of outcome classification.[31]

As discussed in the previous section, the significance of independent variables and their contribution to the AUC statistic help little in determining whether one model is superior to another. In order to compare our three models with significant interaction effects, it is more suitable to refer to likelihood-based statistics like the Vuong and Clarke test. The decision for one or the other test is based upon the distribution of the individual log-likelihood ratios: if these ratios are distributed normally, the Vuong test is

[31]The same holds true for the ethnic-ideological (EI_{max}) and the Wimmer (W_{all}) variable.

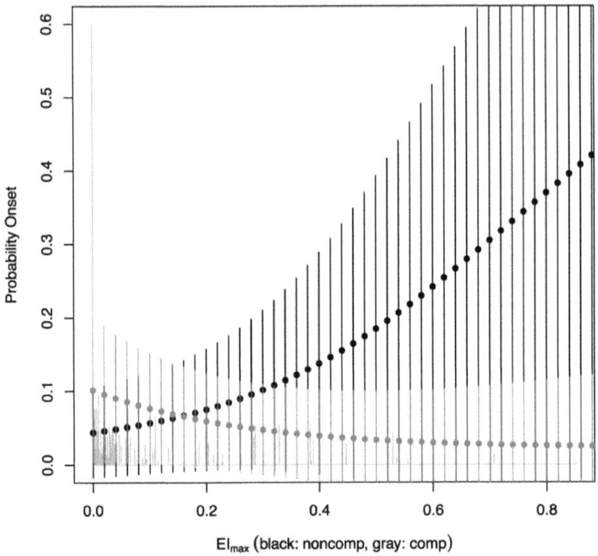

Figure 4.6.: *Predicted probability of armed conflict onset and 90% confidence interval for varying values of the variable EI_{max}, separately for non-competitive and competitive regimes. (Relative frequencies of the values of the independent variable are displayed along the x-axis in gray.)*

more appropriate; otherwise, in case of a non-normal distribution, the Clarke test prevails. If we look at the kurtosis value for all three combinations of the three models, it is clearly visible that the individual log-likelihood ratios are not distributed normally, thereby favoring the Clarke test. When comparing the models, the Clarke test favors a three-dimensional (ERI_{max}) model over an ethnic-ideological (EI_{max}) model, although it cannot discriminate between the three-dimensional (ERI_{max}) model and the Wimmer model (W_{all}). However, there are other reasons for preferring the three-dimensional exclusion variable over the ethnic exclusion variable by Wimmer, as the following section on robustness tests shows.

First, however, let me summarize the results. As the heat map plots

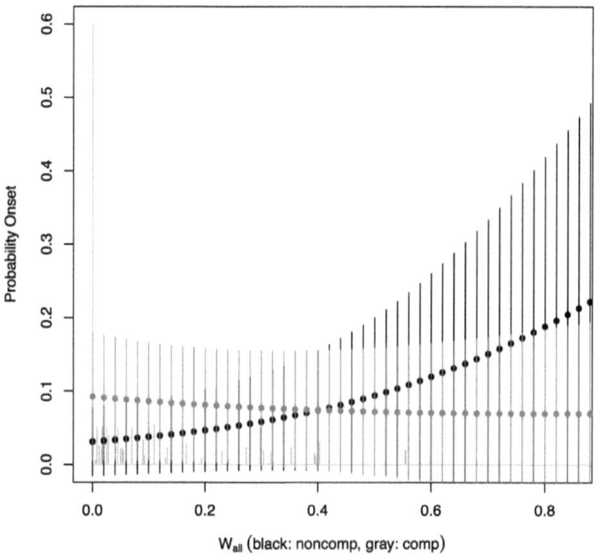

Figure 4.7.: *Predicted probability of armed conflict onset and 90% confidence interval for varying values of the variable W_{all}, separately for non-competitive and competitive regimes. (Relative frequencies of the values of the independent variable are displayed along the x-axis in gray.)*

reveal, all models are well specified. First difference analyses (from zero to the third quartile) are clearly significant only for the size of the largest excluded three-dimensional subgroup and for the size of the excluded ethnic population according to Wimmer, and marginally significant for the size of the largest excluded ethnic-ideological subgroup. Tests on the ROC curve support the relevance of these variables, as they already rank in second place after GDP in terms of importance and dropping them substantially reduces the AUC statistic. Finally, the Clarke test establishes a superiority of the three-dimensional over an ethnic-ideological variable, although it cannot discriminate between the three-dimensional exclusion variable and the Wimmer variable on the excluded ethnic population. Let us next

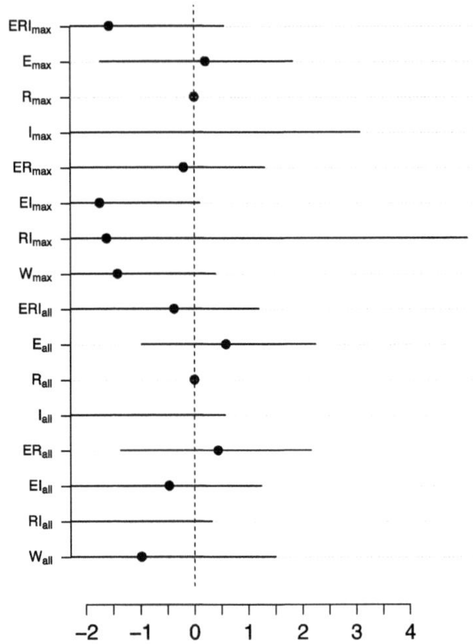

Figure 4.8.: *First difference analyses of the effect of exclusion in competitive regimes. In each case, the value of the key independent variable is increased from zero to the third quartile and the effect on the change in predicted probabilities, including 90% confidence intervals, is displayed.*

consider whether these results are robust to alternative specifications.

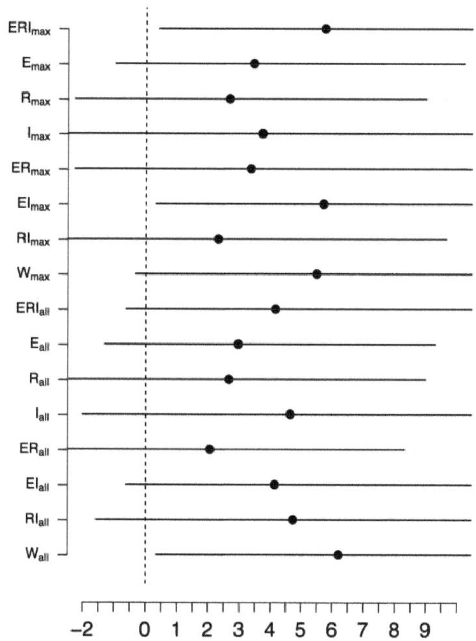

Figure 4.9.: *First difference analyses of the effect of exclusion, when comparing non-competitive and competitive regimes. The value of the key independent exclusion variable is set to zero. In each case, the value on non-competitive regimes is changed from one to zero and the effect on the change in predicted probabilities, including 90% confidence intervals, is displayed.*

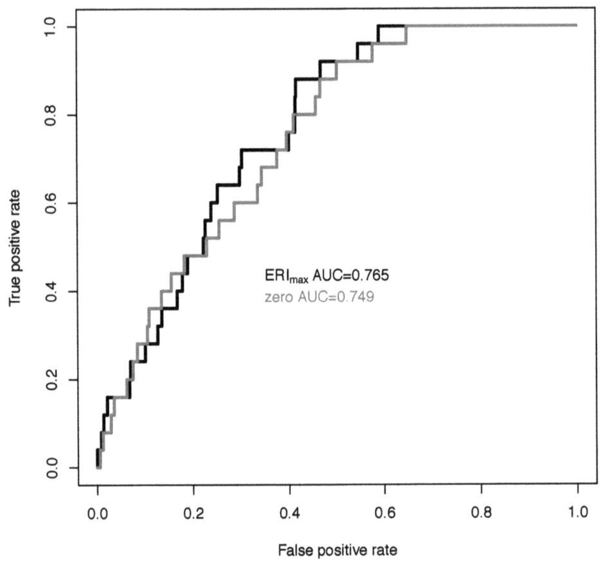

Figure 4.10.: *Receiver Operating Characteristic (ROC) curve. The ROC curve plots the true positive rate against the false positive rate at various discrimination thresholds, separately for a model that includes ERI_{max} and its interaction with regime type, and for a zero model without these variables.*

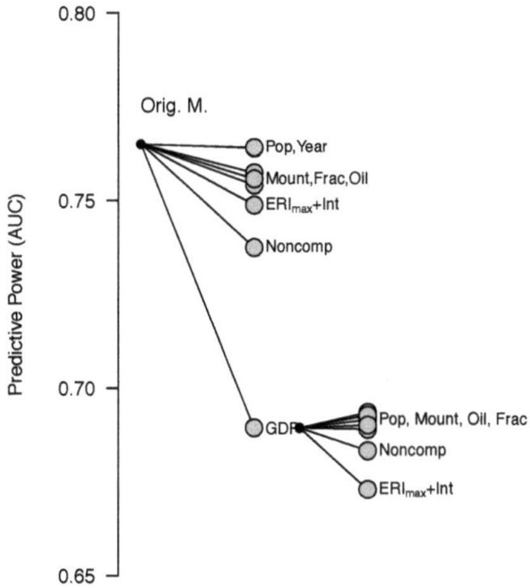

Figure 4.11.: *In-sample predictive power for a model that includes ERI_{max} and its interaction with regime type. The figure depicts the change in the AUC value, when single variables are deleted.*

Robustness Checks

Although the results do not seem to be distorted by functional form misspecification or multicollinearity, it remains possible that the results are not robust to using alternative independent or dependent variables and dropping influential observations.

The results of using a different independent variable on regime types — namely autocracy — are displayed in Table 4.8 (Model 1-3). The previously significant interaction terms on the three-dimensional (ERI_{max}) and the ethnic-ideological (EI_{max}) variable remain significant, while the interaction term including the Wimmer variable (W_{all}) becomes insignificant.[32] First difference analyses confirm these findings (see Figure 4.12). The results of using a different dependent variable are displayed in Table 4.9 (Model 1-6). In Model 1-3, I use the *onset*2 variable and in Model 4-6, I use the *onset*3 and *ongoingl* variable. The previously significant interaction terms on the largest excluded three-dimensional or ethnic-ideological subgroup remain significant if *onset*2 is used, but not if *onset*3 is used, while Wimmer's variable on the excluded ethnic population becomes insignificant in both cases. As shown in Figure 4.13, first difference analyses reveal that the substantial effects are significant for the three-dimensional (ERI_{max}) and the Wimmer (W_{all}) model for *onset*2.[33] Finally, Table 4.10 reports the results when *onset*2 or *onset*3 is combined with autocracy. First difference effects for the three-dimensional (ERI_{max}) and the ethnic-ideological (EI_{max}) variable are significant independent of whether *onset*2 or *onset*3 is used, while first difference effects for the Wimmer model are only significant if *onset*2 is used (Figure 4.14).[34] Overall, these results provide substantial backing for the size of the largest excluded three-dimensional subgroup as the key independent variable.

Finally, it might be the case that the results are only based upon a few influential observations. In order to assess this possibility, Table 4.11 (Model 1-3) reports the regression results when excluding all cases with a Pregibon leverage value above 0.05 for each of the three models. The

[32] Note in Appendix A that the systematic conflict-increasing risk of the oil variable vanishes.

[33] Of the control variables, GDP per capita and peace years significantly reduce the risk of civil conflict onset, while population size and oil significantly increase the risk of civil conflict onset (see Appendix A).

[34] Last but not least, one can show that the three-dimensional excluded population does get significant in some of these alternative specifications. Moreover, surprisingly, GDP per capita proves to be an insignificant predictor in these models (see Appendix A).

Table 4.8.: Robustness Checks: Autocracy

	Dependent variable:		
	onset1		
	(1)	(2)	(3)
autocl	−1.098	−1.106	−0.866
	(0.707)	(0.707)	(0.802)
ERI_{max}	−1.551		
	(2.834)		
EI_{max}		−1.781	
		(1.718)	
W_{all}			0.320
			(1.255)
autocl:ERI_{max}	9.548*		
	(5.116)		
autocl:EI_{max}		6.168**	
		(3.065)	
autocl:W_{all}			0.890
			(2.014)
Observations	1,235	1,235	1,235
Log Likelihood	-106.360	-106.253	-107.472
Akaike Inf. Crit.	240.720	240.506	242.944
Note:			*p<0.1; **p<0.05; ***p<0.01
			robust standard errors in parentheses

table shows that the interaction terms of the two key independent variables — three-dimensional exclusion (ERI_{max}) and ethnic-ideological exclusion (EI_{max}) — remain significant, while the Wimmer variable (W_{all}) becomes insignificant. However, first difference analyses reveal that the substantial effect of exclusion on civil conflict is insignificant for all three models. This suggests that the results are not robust to the exclusion of cases. On the other hand, these findings might have been expected given the rare events in the *onset*1 variable. Therefore, it is more appropriate to assess the robustness of the three models with an alternative, more plausible dependent variable, *onset*2, which exhibits more positive outcomes. Table 4.12 reports the regression results, and Figure 4.15 displays first difference effects. The figure clearly shows that first difference effects are significant for the three-dimensional (ERI_{max}) exclusion variable but not for the ethnic-ideological (EI_{max}) or Wimmer's (W_{all}) variable. Overall, these findings provide support for the superiority of a three-dimensional perspective.

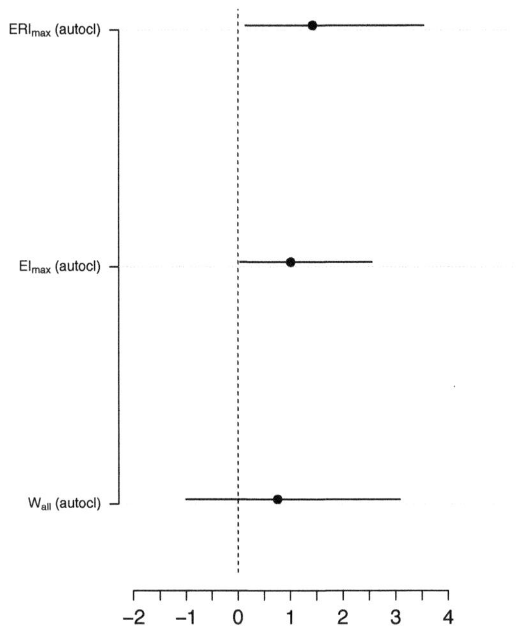

Figure 4.12.: *Robustness check: First difference analyses of the effect of exclusion in autocratic regimes. In each case, the value of the key independent variable is increased from zero to the third quartile and the effect on the change in predicted probabilities, including 90% confidence intervals, is displayed.*

Table 4.9.: Robustness Checks: Onset2, Onset3

	Dependent variable:					
	onset2			onset3		
	(1)	(2)	(3)	(4)	(5)	(6)
noncl	−0.788*	−0.783*	−1.011*	−0.619	−0.618	−0.686
	(0.439)	(0.432)	(0.567)	(0.490)	(0.464)	(0.596)
ERI_{max}	−1.118			−1.392		
	(2.187)			(2.499)		
noncl:ERI_{max}	5.725*			5.131		
	(3.360)			(3.759)		
EI_{max}		−1.785			−1.877	
		(1.637)			(1.845)	
noncl:EI_{max}		3.887*			3.614	
		(2.189)			(2.267)	
W_{all}			0.575			0.065
			(0.885)			(0.937)
noncl:W_{all}			1.665			1.198
			(1.331)			(1.413)
Observations	1,277	1,277	1,277	1,549	1,549	1,549
Log Likelihood	-168.694	-168.678	-167.776	-205.597	-205.442	-205.720
Akaike Inf. Crit.	365.388	365.357	363.553	441.194	440.885	441.440

Note: *p<0.1; **p<0.05; ***p<0.01
robust standard errors in parentheses

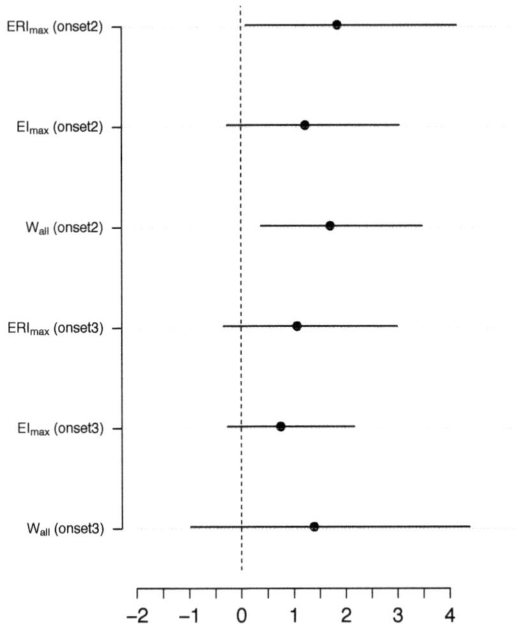

Figure 4.13.: *Robustness check: First difference analyses of the effect of exclusion in non-competitive regimes, when onset2 or onset3 is used as a dependent variable. In each case, the value of the key independent variable is increased from zero to the third quartile and the effect on the change in predicted probabilities, including 90% confidence intervals, is displayed.*

Table 4.10.: Robustness Checks: Onset2, Onset3, Autocracy

	Dependent variable:					
	onset2			onset3		
	(1)	(2)	(3)	(4)	(5)	(6)
autocl	−0.494	−0.436	−0.534	−0.464	−0.390	−0.342
	(0.486)	(0.463)	(0.580)	(0.493)	(0.466)	(0.595)
ERI_{max}	−3.279			−4.716		
	(2.790)			(3.360)		
EI_{max}		−3.026*			−3.570*	
		(1.609)			(1.933)	
W_{all}			−0.207			−0.812
			(1.111)			(1.131)
autocl:ERI_{max}	10.444**			10.244**		
	(4.086)			(4.486)		
autocl:EI_{max}		7.395***			7.031**	
		(2.501)			(2.781)	
autocl:W_{all}			2.313			2.025
			(1.425)			(1.495)
Observations	1,290	1,290	1,290	1,553	1,553	1,553
Log Likelihood	-162.029	-161.721	-162.417	-196.104	-195.937	-197.395
Akaike Inf. Crit.	352.058	351.442	352.835	422.208	421.875	424.789

Note: *$p<0.1$; **$p<0.05$; ***$p<0.01$
robust standard errors in parentheses

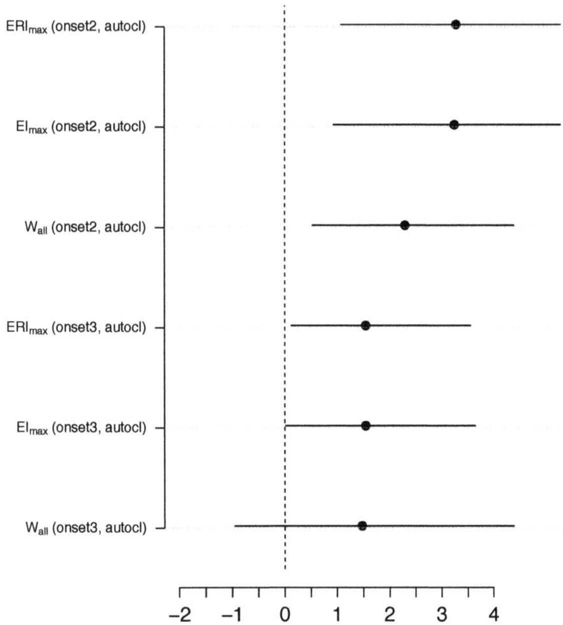

Figure 4.14.: *Robustness check: First difference analyses of the effect of exclusion in autocratic regimes, when onset2 or onset3 is used as a dependent variable. In each case, the value of the key independent variable is increased from zero to the third quartile and the effect on the change in predicted probabilities, including 90% confidence intervals, is displayed.*

Table 4.11.: Influential Obs., Onset1

	Dependent variable:		
	onset1		
	(1)	(2)	(3)
noncl	−1.207	−1.059	−1.110
	(0.753)	(0.652)	(0.807)
ERI_{max}	−2.836		
	(3.080)		
noncl:ERI_{max}	15.740*		
	(8.442)		
EI_{max}		−2.734	
		(2.023)	
noncl:EI_{max}		7.887**	
		(3.987)	
W_{all}			−0.439
			(1.216)
noncl:W_{all}			2.193
			(2.558)
Observations	1,233	1,233	1,230
Log Likelihood	-103.365	-103.702	-100.607
Akaike Inf. Crit.	234.729	235.404	229.214
Note:	*p<0.1; **p<0.05; ***p<0.01 robust standard errors in parentheses		

Table 4.12.: Influential Obs., Onset2

	Dependent variable:		
	onset2		
	(1)	(2)	(3)
noncl	−1.389**	−1.294**	−1.616*
	(0.625)	(0.596)	(0.872)
ERI_{max}	−5.623		
	(4.233)		
noncl:ERI_{max}	16.979**		
	(7.298)		
EI_{max}		−2.491	
		(1.786)	
noncl:EI_{max}		8.158**	
		(4.138)	
W_{all}			−0.292
			(1.233)
noncl:W_{all}			3.107
			(2.579)
Observations	1,244	1,248	1,241
Log Likelihood	-148.270	-152.309	-145.852
Akaike Inf. Crit.	324.540	332.619	319.704

Note: *p<0.1; **p<0.05; ***p<0.01
robust standard errors in parentheses

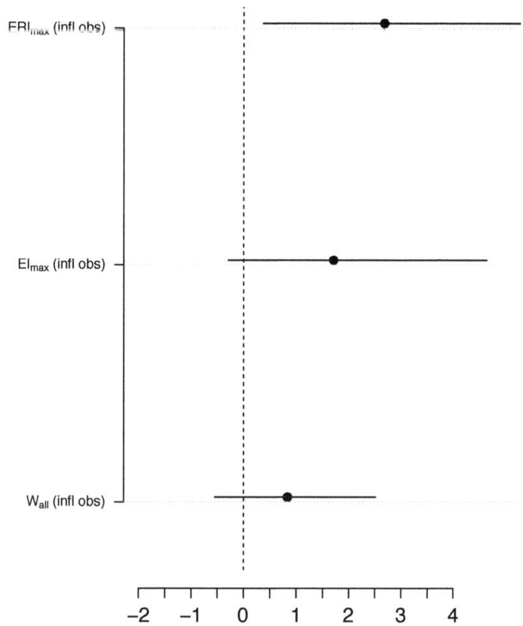

Figure 4.15.: *Robustness check: First difference analyses of the effect of exclusion in non-competitive regimes, when influential observations — cases with a Pregibon leverage value above 0.05 — are excluded. In each case, the value of the key independent variable is increased from zero to the third quartile and the effect on the change in predicted probabilities, including 90% confidence intervals, is displayed.*

Summary

The empirical analyses revealed the following results: while four models emerged with significant interaction terms, first differences were clearly significant only for the three-dimensional variable ERI_{max} and the Wimmer variable W_{all}, as well as marginally significant for the ethnic-ideological variable EI_{max}. The Clarke test established the superiority of a three-dimensional model over an ethnic-ideological model, although it was unable to distinguish between the three-dimensional model and Wimmer's model. However, Wimmer's model should be rejected for other reasons: it is not robust when interacted with autocracy — a regime type variable based upon Polity IV data — and it is not robust to the exclusion of cases with a Pregibon leverage value above 0.05.[35] Therefore, the results clearly speak in favor of a three-dimensional perspective, which performs best in terms of model fit, predictive power and alternative model specifications.

One weakness should be acknowledged. Thus far, the three-dimensional exclusion variables were not founded on a formal theoretical basis, but rather were constructed along the lines of existing ethnic exclusion variables. Accordingly, two questions emerge: is it really plausible to focus on the excluded population, thus assuming that all excluded subgroups work together rendering any self-definition irrelevant? Alternatively, is it really plausible to focus on the largest excluded three-dimensional subgroup, thus implicitly assuming that all identities are salient and completely dividing? Thus far, each of these two versions seems to be extreme. Instead, it would be much more desirable to allow for the flexible saliency of identity dimensions in a multidimensional identity setup, and allow for the possibility that only a subset of subgroups work together. Who will work together in violently challenging the government and which self-definition is chosen should preferably be determined endogenously in a formal theoretical model. The next chapter addresses this issue presenting a formal derivation of an alternative three-dimensional exclusion variable, which, ultimately, highly correlates with the variable on the largest excluded three-dimensional subgroup.

[35]Further note that the variables by Wimmer et al. (2009) stem from a data collection process that was particularly designed to collect data on excluded ethnic groups, whereas the WVS tackles multiple issues, with information on an individual's ethnicity, religion or ideology just being one issue. Given that — in a sense — the variables by Wimmer et al. (2009) are more elaborate than the WVS variables, it is difficult for the latter to perform better than the former. Thus, it seems more appropriate and fair to compare only variables from the WVS among themselves, whereby the variable on the largest excluded three-dimensional subgroup performs very well.

Chapter 5.

A Model of Violent Political Competition

While Section 2.2 established that ethnicity, religion and class-based ideology are the three latent dimensions underlying violent political competition, it also showed that neither governments nor rebel groups necessarily refer to all three dimensions when defining themselves. Why do rebel groups in some countries refer to their ethnic identity, while in other countries they stick to their religious or class-based ideological identity, and in further countries rebels even use a combination of categories from one or more dimensions? The main argument of the present chapter is that the optimal self-definition of a rebel group can be derived from the three-dimensional demographic setup of a society and the government's patterns of inclusion/exclusion. Thus, knowing these two quantities of interest for a country at a certain time point allows one to make predictions based upon expected utility calculations about the expected size of the rebel movement, which can then be used as a predictor for the onset of civil conflict.

5.1. Model Assumptions and The Game

The present section develops a formal theoretical model that allows for the flexible working together of subgroups, thus determining the rebels' self-definition and the resulting *salient* identity dimensions in a society endogenously. The key idea is that political entrepreneurs in a non-competitive society try to convince individuals in the population to support them in a violent contest over governmental control by promising individual gains, which depend on the chosen self-definition of the political entrepreneurs. While for the government the self-definition is given for a certain time period (or one round of the game), the oppositional entrepreneur can choose a definition freely. Individuals then decide whether to support the government, the opposition or neither. With all choices set, salient societal cleavages realize automatically.

Model Assumptions

This subsection introduces the most important background assumptions of the model concerning the three-dimensional identity setup of a country, the self-definition of entrepreneurs within this setup, the mode of resource distribution and the mode of competition. Regarding the conceptualization of the three-dimensional identity setup and the self-definition of the entrepreneurs, the reasoning is the same as in the informal part (Chapter 3), with the only difference being that the setup is now formalized. The other aspects extend beyond what has been said previously.

Dimensions and Categories

I assume that there are three latent identity dimensions in a society: ethnicity, religion and class-based ideology. Each dimension has a certain number of groups that are characterized by their name and their size (i.e. the number of individuals within a group proportional to all individuals in a society). The names and sizes of the groups per dimension are country-specific.

Generally, imagine a population with j identity dimensions and n_i discrete categories on dimension D_i. The list of those categories can be represented in the following way:
$D_1 : \{d_{1,1}, d_{1,2}, ..., d_{1,n_1}\}$
$D_2 : \{d_{2,1}, d_{2,2}, ..., d_{2,n_2}\}$
$D_j : \{d_{j,1}, d_{j,2}, ..., d_{j,n_j}\}$

An Individual Repertoire of Identity Attributes

The three dimensions of ethnicity, religion and class-based ideology are not isolated from one another, but rather are nested inside one another (cp. Posner 2005, 116). The reason is that each individual in a country belongs to exactly one ethnic, exactly one religious and exactly one left-right category. An individual is thus characterized by a three-dimensional repertoire of identity attributes (cp. Posner 2005, 17; Chandra 2012, 184ff.).

An individual repertoire of identity attributes comprises one category from each dimension. The background assumption is that categories on a dimension are exhaustive (everyone belongs to one category per dimension) and mutually exclusive (everyone belongs to only one category per dimension). This implies that in a population with j dimensions, an individual repertoire can be depicted by a vector with j elements. For $j = 3$, an individual *repertoire might look as follows:*

$$\begin{pmatrix} d_{1,1} \\ d_{2,1} \\ d_{3,1} \end{pmatrix}, \text{or} \begin{pmatrix} d_{1,1} \\ d_{2,1} \\ d_{3,2} \end{pmatrix}, \text{or} \begin{pmatrix} d_{1,1} \\ d_{2,2} \\ d_{3,2} \end{pmatrix} \text{etc.}$$

This implies that the share of individuals in all categories per dimension sums up to 1:

$Ds_1 : \{s_{1,1}, s_{1,2}, ..., s_{1,n_1}\}$, with $\sum_{l=1}^{n_1} s_{1,l} = 1$

$Ds_2 : \{s_{2,1}, s_{2,2}, ..., s_{2,n_2}\}$, with $\sum_{l=1}^{n_2} s_{2,l} = 1$

$Ds_j : \{s_{j,1}, s_{j,2}, ..., s_{j,n_j}\}$, with $\sum_{l=1}^{n_j} s_{j,l} = 1$

The Multidimensional Identity Setup

All individuals with the same repertoire of identity attributes form a homogeneous three-dimensional **subgroup**. The size of these subgroups cannot be deduced from the marginal distributions, but rather it has to be known ex ante. Together, the dimensions, categories and the distribution of the population over the implied subgroups — all summarized in a multidimensional table — form the so-called multidimensional identity setup of a society.[1]

As there are n_i choices on the ith dimension, the total number of distinct individual repertoires or subgroups (SG) in a population is $n = n_1 \cdot n_2 \cdot ... \cdot n_j$. The distribution of the population over the distinct subgroups can be shown in a multidimensional table with $sg : \{sg_1, sg_2, ..., sg_n\}$ indicating the relative share of people in the n different subgroups. With $j = 3$ and two categories per dimension, the multidimensional table looks as follows:

$d_{3,1}$	$d_{2,1}$	$d_{2,2}$
$d_{1,1}$	sg_1	sg_3
$d_{1,2}$	sg_5	sg_7

$d_{3,2}$	$d_{2,1}$	$d_{2,2}$
$d_{1,1}$	sg_2	sg_4
$d_{1,2}$	sg_6	sg_8

[1]Note that Chandra (2012) also formalized her ideas about a multidimensional ethnic setup of a society, albeit with a few important differences.

Possible Self-Definitions of Political Entrepreneurs

Political entrepreneurs define themselves within the multidimensional identity setup according to certain 'groups' or 'categories' (e.g. Black, White, Catholic, Protestant, Leftist, Rightist), whereby this self-definition comes along with a "representation" of the respective groups. There are no restrictions for a self-definition. Entrepreneurs can refer to one category only, to several categories from one dimension or to several categories from different dimensions. If an entrepreneur refers to several categories, I assume that these categories are connected via an 'or'-operator, implying that individuals fall under the entrepreneur's self-definition as long as they accord with at least one category.

The list of possible self-definitions can be depicted as follows:

$$SD : \{(d_{1,1}), (d_{1,2}), ..., (d_{1,1} \vee d_{1,2}), ..., (d_{1,1} \vee d_{2,1}), ..., (d_{1,n_1} \vee d_{2,n_2} \vee d_{3,n_3}), ...\}$$

The total number of an entrepreneur's possible self-definitions (SD) in a population with $z = n_1 + n_2 + ... + n_j$ *categories is* 2^z *(including the empty set and the full set of all categories), as each category can be part of an entrepreneur's self-definition or not.*

Mode of Resource Distribution and Degree of Congruence

Entrepreneurs — if they come to power — provide benefits to the groups that they represent. In democracies, the government typically makes preference-based policies and provides a large number of public or club goods, although private goods or "pork-barrel politics" also play a role (Persson and Tabellini 2000, 8). Voters are usually characterized by single-peaked preferences and the voters' utility functions take the distance of their preferred policy to the actual policy into account (Downs 1957). In non-competitive regimes, which are the primary focus here, private goods or clientelistic policies play a much more important role than preference-based policies or public goods (Deacon 2009, 242). These private goods may take different forms: politicians may coopt people of their confidence and provide them with prestigious and well-paid jobs, or they may pay them on a personal basis (Bueno de Mesquita et al. 2003, 51). Alternatively, in order to reach a broader audience, politicians may invest in infrastructure or other "regional" projects that favor exactly those groups that they seek to represent (Fearon 1999; Posner 2005; Chandra 2012). In order to formalize this idea of private goods, it is typically assumed that the fix budget available to a government is simply distributed by the number of the people who fall under a politician's definition (Posner 2005, 132).

The issue of private goods becomes a little more complicated in a multi-dimensional setting, as described above. Individuals might be part of none, one or more than one of the categories of a government's self-definition. Thus, the question naturally arises whether individuals only gain if they fulfill all criteria, or whether they also gain to a certain extent if they fulfill some criteria. As the focus lies on private goods, I assume that a government gives money to all the groups it seeks to represent, so that the money is divided by the sum of the individuals from all governmental groups. For instance, if a government is White-Protestant, the amount of money available to the government is divided by the number of people being White *plus* the number of people being Protestant. As the categories overlap, this implies that if someone is White *and* Protestant, this person gains twice, while if someone is White but *Catholic* or Protestant but *Black*, the person only gains once, and if it is *neither* White *nor* Protestant, the person does not gain at all.[2]

A political entrepreneur E in power distributes a fix government budget to all people who fall under the categories of a government's self-definition. Money is distributed according to the relative share of people that these categories represent. Thus, with an entrepreneur's self-definition of $(d_{1,1})$, a fix government budget of 1 is divided by a share of $s_{1,1}$ people, implying a so-called base promise B_E of $\frac{1}{s_{1,1}}$ for each individual, while with a self-definition of $(d_{1,1} \vee d_{2,1})$, a fix government budget of 1 is divided by a share

[2]Other formal studies sometimes determine the government budget endogenously within the model (Romer 1975; Persson and Tabellini 2000). They typically assume that a government cannot only decide to whom to provide the money, but also from whom to take or tax the money. To keep matters simple, I here assume that the government budget is exogenously given and fix. Regardless which group comes to power, the amount of money that can be distributed is always the same. This assumption is especially reasonable for countries that are characterized by a high amount of income from natural resources rather than tax revenues, as many non-democratic countries are (cp. Ross 2004). Moreover, case study evidence from rebel groups indicates that the rebels' motivation for violently challenging the government lies very often in a perception of non-representation and exclusion from the distribution of government spoils, and not in an unduly high tax rate ("Minorities at Risk Dataset", 2009, College Park, MD: Center for International Development and Conflict Management. Retrieved from `http://www.cidcm.umd.edu/mar/data.aspx` on: [2014/1/1]). Thus, the distribution of the government budget, and not the origin of the government's income, should be the main focus in a model of violent political competition.

of $(s_{1,1} + s_{2,1})$ *people implying a base promise* B_E *of* $\frac{1}{s_{1,1}+s_{2,1}}$ *for each individual. More generally, it holds that if an entrepreneur in government defines itself with respect to* x *categories* k_i*, the fix government budget of* 1 *is divided by all people who fall under these categories* $(\frac{1}{\sum_{i=1}^{x} k_i})$*.*

Further note that, if an entrepreneur refers to x *categories in its self-definition, an individual from a subgroup can accord with* 0 *to* x *categories. I call this 'the degree of congruence'* c_{Ei} *between the individual from subgroup* i *and the entrepreneur* E*.*[3] *Individuals gain for each criterion that accords with the government's self-definition, i.e. those individuals who fulfill two or more of the government's criteria gain twice or more times the amount of the base promise. This implies that, to calculate the gain* Π_{Ei} *for an individual from a certain subgroup* i *under an entrepreneur* E*, the base promise* B_E *by an entrepreneur* E *has to be multiplied with the degree of congruence* c_{Ei} *between the entrepreneur* E *and the individual* i*.*

Mode of Competition

This book focuses on political competition in the form of violent contests for political power, whereby the probability of winning and losing is determined by the relative share of people supporting one or the other entrepreneur. It assumes that the probability of winning a contest is determined via the well-established ratio form of the contest success function (Hirshleifer 1989; Garfinkel and Skaperdas 2007), which reads as follows: $p_O = s_O^m/(s_G^m + s_O^m)$ for the probability of the opposition winning the contest, and $p_G = 1 - p_O = s_G^m/(s_G^m + s_O^m)$ for the probability of the government winning the contest. Variables s_G and s_O comprise the share of people who support the respective groups, government or opposition. The "mass effect parameter"

[3] Of all 2^z possible self-definitions for an entrepreneur E, an individual from subgroup i accords with at least one category in the following number of cases:

$$\sum_{c_{Ei}=1}^{j} \binom{j}{c_{Ei}} (2^{z-c_{Ei}} - \sum_{k=c_{Ei}+1}^{j} 2^{z-k}),$$

where j is the number of dimensions, c_{Ei} represents the degree of congruence between an individual from subgroup i and the political entrepreneur E, and z is the total number of categories. The j different parts of this sum represent the number of possible self-definitions of an entrepreneur E, for which an individual from a subgroup i accords with $c_{Ei} : \{1, 2, ...j\}$ categories of an entrepreneur's self-definition. Thus, with $j = 3$ and two categories per dimension ($z = 6$), an individual accords with at least one category of all possible $2^6 = 64$ self-definitions in $\binom{3}{1}(2^5 - 2^4 - 2^3) + \binom{3}{2}(2^4 - 2^3) + \binom{3}{3}(2^3) = 24 + 24 + 8 = 56$ cases, whereby it agrees with one category in 24 cases, with two categories in 24 cases, and with three categories in eight cases.

m determines the shape of the function, and implies that, "for $m > 1$, an initial range of increasing returns exists"(Hirshleifer 1989, 102).

The Game

The Game Form

The players are the oppositional entrepreneur O and all n subgroups ($SG : \{SG_1, ..., SG_n\}$), who interact. The behavior of the government G is not modeled, as the government's self-definition for one round of the play is given.

A round starts with Nature choosing an oppositional entrepreneur from one of the subgroups, whereby the probabilities accord with the population shares of the different subgroups ($sg : \{sg_1, sg_2, ..., sg_n\}$). This implies that each individual has the same chance of becoming an oppositional entrepreneur. After Nature's move, the oppositional entrepreneur chooses one of the 2^z possible self-definitions. With the government's and the opposition's self-definition given, all individuals within all subgroups decide simultaneously whether to support the government, the opposition or neither.

Preferences

The expected utility function is the same for all actors (the oppositional entrepreneur and the subgroups), thereby implying that the oppositional entrepreneur is simply a partisan of its own subgroup.[4] The expected utility function reads as follows, when assuming that the government defines itself with respect to x categories $(g_1, ..., g_x)$ and the opposition defines itself with respect to y categories $(o_1, ..., o_y)$:

$$EU_{GOi} = p_G \cdot \Pi_{Gi} + p_O \cdot \Pi_{Oi} = p_G \cdot B_G \cdot c_{Gi} + p_O \cdot B_O \cdot c_{Oi}$$

$$\text{with } p_G = \frac{s_G^m}{s_G^m + s_O^m} \text{ and } p_O = \frac{s_O^m}{s_G^m + s_O^m},$$

[4]If the oppositional entrepreneur had the only goal of getting into office, it would simply try to divide the current government and keep the remnants in the government as small as possible. There would be no attachment to a specific identity group. While this maximizes the prospects of getting into office, a non-attachment to the group is likely to imply a quick disposal of the political entrepreneur.

$$B_G = \frac{1}{g_1 + ... + g_x} \text{ and } B_O = \frac{1}{o_1 + ... + o_y}.$$

The expected utility EU_{GOi} for an individual from subgroup i under a certain government G and an opposition O is the probability p_G of the government winning the contest multiplied with the gains Π_{Gi} for the individual under the government (a product of the base promise B_G and the degree of congruence c_{Gi} between the individual and the government) plus the probability p_O of the opposition winning the contest multiplied with the gains Π_{Oi} under the opposition (a product of the base promise B_O and the degree of congruence c_{Oi} between the individual and the opposition).[5] The expected utility for one subgroup depends on the decision of all other subgroups for supporting the government or the opposition, as these choices determine the probability of one or the other actor winning the contest. The promised gains by the government or the opposition differ for each of the subgroups to the extent that the degree of congruence between the subgroups and the government or the opposition differs.

Equilibrium Results

The model describes a sequential game that includes a strategic game with pure strategies. With the government's self-definition and Nature's draw given, the oppositional entrepreneur makes its choice for a self-definition first, whereupon all subgroups decide simultaneously whether to support the government, the opposition or neither.[6] The game is solved via backward induction. In a first step, I solve the strategic game between all subgroups for each of the oppositional entrepreneur's strategies and show that it always yields a unique pure-strategy Nash Equilibrium as long as the government and the opposition promise different gains to each subgroup. In a second step, I determine the oppositional entrepreneur's optimal choice.

Proposition 1. Individuals from subgroup i support the government G if $\Pi_{Gi} > \Pi_{Oi}$, and vice-versa for the opposition. Thus, the individuals' choice is purely based upon a comparison of the promised gains by the government and the opposition, and not on the probabilities of winning or losing the contest.

[5] Note that an individual gains from both entrepreneurs if it falls under the respective definitions, independent on whether it supported the respective entrepreneur or not.

[6] All individuals within a subgroup are technically the same and can be treated as one single actor.

Proof. Individuals from subgroup i support the government if the expected utility of doing so is higher than the expected utility from supporting the opposition. This trade-off is depicted in the following inequation with g and o being the share of people supporting the government and the opposition respectively, and x being the share of people from subgroup i. Let us further assume that $\Pi_{Gi} \geq 0$ and $\Pi_{Oi} \geq 0$ and $\Pi_{Gi} \neq \Pi_{Oi}$:

$$\frac{(g+x)^m}{(g+x)^m + o^m} \cdot \Pi_{Gi} + \frac{o^m}{(g+x)^m + o^m} \cdot \Pi_{Oi} >$$

$$\frac{g^m}{g^m + (o+x)^m} \cdot \Pi_{Gi} + \frac{(o+x)^m}{g^m + (o+x)^m} \cdot \Pi_{Oi}$$

This inequation can be simplified to deduce the condition for supporting the government:

$$\Leftrightarrow \left(\frac{(g+x)^m}{(g+x)^m + o^m} - \frac{g^m}{g^m + (o+x)^m} \right) \cdot \Pi_{Gi} >$$

$$\left(\frac{(o+x)^m}{g^m + (o+x)^m} - \frac{o^m}{(g+x)^m + o^m} \right) \cdot \Pi_{Oi}$$

$$\Leftrightarrow \frac{(g+x)^m \cdot (g^m + (o+x)^m) - g^m \cdot ((g+x)^m + o^m)}{((g+x)^m + o^m) \cdot (g^m + (o+x)^m)} \cdot \Pi_{Gi} >$$

$$\frac{(o+x)^m \cdot ((g+x)^m + o^m) - o^m \cdot (g^m + (o+x)^m)}{(g^m + (o+x)^m) \cdot ((g+x)^m + o^m)} \cdot \Pi_{Oi}$$

$$\Leftrightarrow \frac{(g+x)^m \cdot (g^m + (o+x)^m) - g^m \cdot ((g+x)^m + o^m)}{(o+x)^m \cdot ((g+x)^m + o^m) - o^m \cdot (g^m + (o+x)^m)} \cdot \Pi_{Gi} > \Pi_{Oi}$$

$$\Leftrightarrow \frac{(g+x)^m \cdot g^m + (g+x)^m \cdot (o+x)^m - (g^m \cdot (g+x)^m + g^m \cdot o^m)}{(o+x)^m \cdot (g+x)^m + (o+x)^m \cdot o^m - (o^m \cdot g^m + o^m \cdot (o+x)^m)} \cdot \Pi_{Gi}$$
$$> \Pi_{Oi}$$

$$\Leftrightarrow \frac{(g+x)^m \cdot (o+x)^m - g^m \cdot o^m}{(o+x)^m \cdot (g+x)^m - o^m \cdot g^m} \cdot \Pi_{Gi} > \Pi_{Oi}$$

$$\Leftrightarrow \Pi_{Gi} > \Pi_{Oi}(qed).$$

Proposition 2. If $\Pi_{Gi}! = \Pi_{Oi}$, it is better for an individual to support the entrepreneur with the higher promised gains than supporting neither entrepreneur.

Let us start with the premise that $\Pi_{Gi} > \Pi_{Oi}$ so that subgroup i would choose to support the government. Should it rather refrain from doing so? The trade-off is depicted in the following inequation:

$$\frac{(g+x)^m}{(g+x)^m + o^m} \cdot \Pi_{Gi} + \frac{o^m}{(g+x)^m + o^m} \cdot \Pi_{Oi} >$$

$$\frac{g^m}{g^m + o^m} \cdot \Pi_{Gi} + \frac{o^m}{g^m + o^m} \cdot \Pi_{Oi}$$

This inequation can be simplified to deduce the condition for supporting the government:

$$\Leftrightarrow \left(\frac{(g+x)^m}{(g+x)^m + o^m} - \frac{g^m}{g^m + o^m}\right) \cdot \Pi_{Gi} >$$

$$\left(\frac{o^m}{g^m + o^m} - \frac{o^m}{(g+x)^m + o^m}\right) \cdot \Pi_{Oi}$$

$$\Leftrightarrow \frac{(g+x)^m \cdot (g^m + o^m) - g^m \cdot ((g+x)^m + o^m)}{((g+x)^m + o^m) \cdot (g^m + o^m)} \cdot \Pi_{Gi} >$$

$$\frac{o^m \cdot ((g+x)^m + o^m) - o^m \cdot (g^m + o^m)}{((g+x)^m + o^m) \cdot (g^m + o^m)} \cdot \Pi_{Oi}$$

$$\Leftrightarrow \frac{(g+x)^m \cdot o^m - g^m \cdot o^m}{o^m \cdot (g+x)^m - o^m \cdot g^m} \cdot \Pi_{Gi} > \Pi_{Oi}$$

$$\Leftrightarrow \Pi_{Gi} > \Pi_{Oi}(qed).$$

The result shows that it is more beneficial to support the government rather than supporting neither the government nor the opposition if the promised gains by the government are higher than the promised gains by the opposition, which is an assumption with which we started in the first place.

To sum up, Proposition 1 and Proposition 2 show that the subgroups make their choice for supporting the government, the opposition or neither entrepreneur based upon the promised gains by both entrepreneurs, whereby this choice is independent of the choices of all other subgroups. The probability for one or the other entrepreneur winning or losing the contest — which *is* influenced by the choices of all other subgroups — plays no role in the subgroups' calculation for whom to support. Individuals from a subgroup support the entrepreneur with the higher promised gains for this subgroup. If the promised gains differ, the subgame's Nash Equilibrium is unique. However, if both entrepreneurs promise the same positive amount of gains to an individual, it is equally rational for this individual to support either entrepreneur, and if both entrepreneurs promise nothing to the individual, it is equally rational to support either entrepreneur or neither. Only in these latter cases does more than one Nash Equilibrium in the subgame exist.

Next, the oppositional entrepreneur decides how to define itself in anticipation of the pure-strategy Nash Equilibrium between the subgroups that will realize. For each of the oppositional entrepreneur's 2^z possible options of self-definition, the entrepreneur knows the probabilities for winning and losing the contest, which is implied by the subgroups' choices, as well as the promised gains. This allows the entrepreneur to calculate the expected utility for each of the 2^z options and choose the option with the highest expected utility. Theoretically, two options could provide the same expected utility for the oppositional entrepreneur, thereby yielding more than one Nash Equilibrium for the entire game. However, as empirically the subgroups' population shares usually differ, the oppositional entrepreneur's choice should be clear in most cases.

Classification of the Violent Political Struggle

In the model thus far I have assumed that Nature draws an oppositional entrepreneur from one of the subgroups and — after the entrepreneur's self-definition — that a contest between the supporters of the government and the supporters of the opposition ensues. This section asks whether all contests started by the different oppositional entrepreneurs should classify as civil conflicts — the main interest of this book — or whether some of them should rather be counted as coups d'état.

How can we distinguish civil conflicts from coups d'état? A civil conflict is a contested incompatibility between a government and an internal opposition group that is carried out with violent means, whereby the opposition has a certain strength to differentiate it from genocide. Typically, both parties fight about the control of governmental resources, whether it is complete control in the form of a run on the capital (governmental conflicts) or partial control in the form of a fight for more territorial autonomy (territorial conflicts). Moreover, the opposition's supporters are typically motivated by their impression that they do not gain (sufficiently) from the current government's distribution of spoils. At the same time, they do not perceive that they will be represented any time soon. An oppositional entrepreneur — usually from outside the government — then takes up the task of defining the opposition and typically chooses a definition that at least partially differs from the government's self-definition.

While civil conflicts have an "outside-the-government" element, coups d'état are characterized by an "inside-the-government" element. Like civil conflicts, coups d'état concern the definition of the government that comes along with a certain distribution of governmental resources. However, coups d'état are typically started by political entrepreneurs who are included in the current government in a very narrow sense of having important governmental or military posts (cp. Powell and Thyne 2011). These entrepreneurs usually convince important parts of the military that the government should be toppled violently. Societal support plays a less important role in winning the contest, although it is certainly important for the new government to consolidate its power status.

In order to distinguish civil conflicts from coups d'état, this book applies a conservative — yet save — criterion, namely the oppositional entrepreneur's identity. The key question is whether the entrepreneur already profited from the current government or not. If it did profit, the entrepreneur will more likely choose an "internal mode" of contestation like a coup d'état, while if it did not profit, it will more likely choose an "external mode" like a civil conflict. Therefore, violent contests from entrepreneurs within the government will be classified as coups d'état, while violent contests from entrepreneurs outside the government will be classified as civil conflicts. This criterion is conservative, as it might falsely exclude some civil conflicts that were started by entrepreneurs from inside. It is a save criterion, however, as outside entrepreneurs by definition almost never start a coup d'état.

Summary and Quantification

The formal theoretical model assumed that the oppositional political entrepreneur starting a civil conflict comes from one of the subgroups outside the government (not falling under the government's self-definition), with the most likely oppositional entrepreneur being the one from the largest excluded (three-/two-/one-dimensional) subgroup. Thus, the probability of this entrepreneur emerging is simply the relative share of the largest excluded subgroup (with three dimensions, it is the largest excluded three-dimensional subgroup; with two dimensions, it is the largest excluded two-dimensional subgroup; and with one dimension, it is the largest excluded one-dimensional subgroup). Thus, if one is only interested in the probability of the most likely entrepreneur emerging at all, one would simply look at the country- and time-specific size of the largest excluded subgroup. While this variable has already been used in the informal part, it now gains a more theoretically founded underpinning and seems less arbitrarily chosen.

However, the formal analysis did not stop at this point, but rather added a second step. This step concerned the relative number of people supporting the oppositional entrepreneur versus the government. The theory assumed that the individuals' choices for one or the other entrepreneur are based upon the promised gains that follow from the self-definition of the respective actors. With the government's self-definition given for a certain country and time point, the optimal choice of the oppositional entrepreneur's self-definition as well as the choices of all individuals could subsequently be determined from the theoretical model based upon expected utility calculations. These expected utility calculations crucially depend on the number of people falling under the actors' self-definition, while the exact size is determined by the underlying three-dimensional demographic identity setup.

Once the opposition's optimal self-definition and the support patterns are set, it is possible to combine the probability of an entrepreneur emerging in the first place with the relative number of people supporting this entrepreneur. This book opts for building a product term as the two quantities of interest are assumed to be independent of each other.

Thus, the seven key steps for deriving the quantities of interest are as follows:

1. Derive the three-dimensional identity setup for each country year (based upon the WVS, see page 65).

2. Obtain the definition of the government in a specific country year (see

page 69).

3. Derive the size of the largest excluded subgroup for each country year based upon 1. and 2. (see page 69).

4. Formulate all possible self-definitions of the oppositional entrepreneur coming from the largest excluded subgroup.

5. Determine the gains for each subgroup that accrue under the government and the oppositional entrepreneur for all possible self-definitions of the oppositional entrepreneur. Based upon these gains, derive the decision of the separate subgroups for one or the other entrepreneur, thereby determining the relative number of supporters.

6. Derive the expected utility (gains multiplied with the relative number of supporters) for all possible self-definitions of the oppositional entrepreneur and choose the option with the highest expected utility as the optimal choice for the oppositional entrepreneur.

7. With the optimal choice set, extract and multiply two quantities of interest: the size of the largest excluded subgroup and the size of the population supporting the oppositional entrepreneur (product term).

Note that I construct the product term for a three-dimensional world ($ERI*$), the three possible one-dimensional worlds ($E*$, $R*$, $I*$) and the three possible two-dimensional worlds ($EI*$, $ER*$, $RI*$), thereby allowing for an assessment of the superiority of a three-dimensional over a one-dimensional or a two-dimensional perspective. Again, this results in a total of seven key independent variables.

I believe that these seven key independent variables have a thorough theoretical underpinning. Recall that upon ending the informal theoretical part, I questioned the ad-hoc formulation of the key independent variables, focusing on the excluded population and the largest excluded subgroup. Concerning the excluded population, I implicitly assumed that all excluded subgroups would be acting together, although arguably this assumption is not very plausible. Concerning the largest excluded subgroup, I implicitly assumed that all latent identity cleavages are actually dividing, but this assumption is also not very plausible. The value of the formal theoretical derivation of the key independent variables is as follows: when determining which of the excluded subgroups are working together and under what kind of definition, I am able to derive both the size of the rebel group and the saliency of identity categories *endogenously*. However, despite this merit it remains to be noted that the informal and the formal variables are ultimately very highly correlated (by a correlation coefficient of 0.97). Hence, I do not expect very different results in the empirical analyses. The great value is that the previously used informal variable on the largest excluded three-dimensional subgroup now gains a formal underpinning. Based upon three case studies on Morocco, Guatemala and Thailand, let me next illustrate both the construction of the formal exclusion variable and its plausibility, before systematically examining the effect of this variable on the risk of civil conflict onset in quantitative analyses.

5.2. Case Studies

While the previous section developed the theoretical base line model, this section uses real-world data from Morocco, Guatemala and Thailand to illustrate the construction of the formal variables and conduct a plausibility check of the model.[7] For the countries in question, I provide a summary on the conflict history and the identity of the rebel group, as well as the demographic setup of the country and the government's identity. With these data set, I use the theoretical model to predict the self-definition of the most likely rebel group and compare the predictions with the facts.

Morocco

According to the Uppsala Armed Conflict Database, the only internal armed conflict in Morocco since 1975 was the conflict between the government and the oppositional group of Polisario in Western Sahara. In 1975, Spain gave administrative control over Western Sahara to both Morocco and Mauritania. However, Polisario claimed independence of the territory and proclaimed the Sahrawi Arab Democratic Republic. This led to a conflict between Polisario and Morocco/Mauritania over the control of the territory, from which Mauritania withdrew in 1979. The armed conflict between

[7] In order to select the countries, I restricted the sample to all countries with non-competitive/non-democratic periods, considering only countries with internal armed conflicts from different world regions. As the focus in the present section lies on an illustration and informal checking of the model rather than a systematic model test, a random selection of countries is not required. The following section tests the model systematically with quantitative data.

Morocco and Polisario has continued until 1989 and further, with Morocco gaining the upper hand. In 1989, a ceasefire process was initiated. Although the violent conflict has been simmering until today, it is currently (since the 1990s) too low to classify as an armed conflict according to the Uppsala Armed Conflict Database (Cunningham et al. 2009).

Sahrawis, the people from Western Sahara, are ethnically different from the rest of the Moroccan population (Cunningham et al. 2009). They are a fusion of Sanhaja Berbers, Bedouin Arabs and black African slaves (Minorities at Risk 2009) and they generally tend to be more black than the rest of the Moroccan population, which is 66% Arab and 34% Berber.[8] Moreover, Sahrawis speak a dialect of Arabic that is known as Hassaniya, while the rest of the Moroccan population speaks Moroccan-Arabic or Amazigh, a Berber language. Religiously, Sahrawis mainly pertain to Sunni Islam, like the majority of the Moroccan population. Ideologically, Polisario — the main representative of the Sahrawi population — originally adhered to Sahrawi Nationalism and Democratic Socialism, which implies a leftist ideology. Over the years, however, it changed from being leftist in the 1970s, to non-political in the 1980s and being open to free markets in the 1990s (see the Sahrawi Republic's Constitution). To sum up, in the 1970s, Polisario mainly pointed in its self-definition to both the distinct ethnic identity and the leftist ideology, whereas in the 1980s and 1990s the leftist element vanished for a more centrist self-definition, while the ethnic element remained.

According to this book's data, which are derived from the World Values Survey (WVS), the demographic setup of Morocco looks as follows: Morocco has three ethnic groups — White/Caucasian White ("White") (92.5%), Black-other/Black ("Black") (6.7%), and Asian (0.8%); three religious groups — Muslim (99.4%), Hindu (0.4%) and Jew (0.2%); and two ideological groups — Leftists (59.9%) and Rightists (40.1%). It seems that while the category of ideological Centrists was not relevant in the first years after 1975, it subsequently became relevant over time. If we also take this Centrist category into account, the distribution over the ideological groups would be 12.5% Leftist, 61.1% Centrist and 26.5% Rightist. Concerning the ethnic groups, the following relationship can be established: the category White/Caucasian White comprises Arabs and some Berbers, while the category of Black-other/Black in the WVS comprises Sahrawis and the rest of Berbers.[9]

[8] `http://www.afrik-news.com/article18043.html` on: [2013/5/27].

[9] According to the CIA World Factbook, the Moroccan population is ethnically made

Table 5.1.: Morocco's Identity Setup (in %): Left and Right

Left	Muslim	Hindu	Jew
White	54.7	0.2	
Black	4.2		
Asian	0.8		

Right	Muslim	Hindu	Jew
White	37.4	0.2	
Black	2.4		0.2
Asian			

Table 5.2.: Morocco's Identity Setup (in %): Adding a Centrist Category

Left	Muslim	Hindu	Jew
White	11.5	0.2	
Black	0.8		
Asian	0.2		

Right	Muslim	Hindu	Jew
White	24.3	0.2	
Black	2.0		
Asian			

Centrist	Muslim	Hindu	Jew
White	56.3	0.2	
Black	3.8		0.2
Asian	0.6		

The distribution over the respective three-dimensional subgroups — again based upon the WVS — is provided in Table 5.1 when considering Leftist and Rightist as the only two ideological categories, and in Table 5.2 when additionally taking the Centrist category into account. In the former case, the largest subgroup is formed by White-Muslim-Leftist people (54.7%), the second largest by White-Muslim-Rightist people (37.4%), the third and fourth largest subgroups are Black-Muslim-Leftist (4.2%) and Black-Muslim-Rightist people (2.4%). The other subgroups are not occupied or their population shares are below 1%. With the Centrist category added, according to Table 5.2, the largest subgroups are White-Muslim-Centrists (56.3%), White-Muslim-Rightists (24.3%), White-Muslim-Leftists (11.5%), Black-Muslim-Centrists (3.8%) and Black-Muslim-Rightists (2%).

According to Wimmer et al. (2009) and the Database on Political Institutions (DPI), which are these study's two main sources for determining the identity of a country's government, the government of Morocco can be characterized as follows for the non-democratic years between 1975 to 2005: in 1975 and 1976, the government was White, in 1982 and 1983 it was White, Leftist and Rightist, and from 1989 to 1992 it was White,

up of 99% Arab/Berber, and 1% of other.

Centrist and Rightist.[10] Let us assume that the Centrist category was not politically relevant under the first government, meaning that Table 5.1 is the relevant one, whereas under the second and third government, the Centrist category was politically relevant, whereby Table 5.2 holds. Let us next consider how the population was affected by the three different governments. When considering the first, White government, it is clear that all White people equally gained from it. By contrast, Asian and Black people were excluded, independent of their religion or ideology. With the second government, White people still gained, as did Leftist and Rightist people, whereas Centrist-Non-White people did not gain. Finally, with the third government only Leftist-Non-White people were excluded. This prompts the question of how the oppositional entrepreneur would define itself under these three governments, as well as which subgroups would likely be attracted by such a definition. Here, this book's formal model provides an answer.

Starting with the first, White, government (1975, 1976), the formal model gives the following answer to the question of who the opposition most likely was going to be, the result of which is summarized in Table 5.3. In sum, an oppositional entrepreneur most likely comes from the Black-Muslim-Leftist subgroup (4.2%) and chooses a self-definition of Black-other/Black-Leftist, from which all Black or Leftist people are attracted. In fact, this self-definition is exactly what we could observe in Morocco, when assuming that people from Western Sahara can be classified as Black people, and when considering that Polisario — the main representative of these people — labeled itself as Leftist. Interestingly, according to the formal model it was better for an entrepreneur of the Black-Muslim-Leftist subgroup to refer to both categories of Black *and* Leftist than to simply choose one of these two categories, or additionally combine them with a reference to the Muslim identity.

When considering the second, White plus Leftist and Rightist, government (1982, 1983), the formal model makes the following predictions summarized in Table 5.4. An oppositional entrepreneur most likely comes from the Black-Muslim-Centrist subgroup (3.8%) and chooses a self-definition of

[10] In Wimmer, the only ethnic group listed are Berber people, and they are powerless. I think it is fair to deduce from this that Arabs (or Whites/Caucasian White) — the other important ethnic category next to Berbers — were in power in Morocco. Note also that no party in government defined itself in religious terms. Ideologically, the government in 1975, 1976 was independent; and in 1982 and 1983, the Leftist Istiqlal and the Rightist MP were in power, whereas, from 1989 to 1992, the Rightist RNI and MP and the Centrist UC were in power.

Table 5.3.: Morocco's Opposition to a White Government

Entrepreneur	Prob.	Self-Definition	Attr.
Asian-Muslim-Leftist	0.8 %	Asian-Leftist	62 %
Black-Jew-Rightist	0.2 %	Black-Jew-Rightist	47 %
Black-Muslim-Leftist	4.2 %	Black-Leftist	63 %
Black-Muslim-Rightist	2.4 %	Black-Rightist	47 %

Table 5.4.: Morocco's Opposition to a White, Leftist, Rightist Government

Entrepreneur	Prob.	Self-Definition	Attr.
Asian-Muslim-Centrist	0.6 %	Asian-Centrist	61 %
Black-Jew-Centrist	0.2 %	Black-Jew-Centrist	64 %
Black-Muslim-Centrist	3.8 %	Black-Centrist	64 %

Black-other/Black-Centrist, which attracts all Black or Centrist people. Again, this is what we could observe in Morocco: the Sahrawi (Black) opposition was still very active in the 1980s, although the reference to the leftist ideology became less important and Polisario rather tended to address Centrist elements.

Finally, the third, White plus Centrist and Rightist, government (1989–1992) significantly changed matters of inclusion and exclusion. By its self-definition, the Black-Muslim-Centrist subgroup — which was the most likely challenger in the previous model — was included in government through the Centrist element. Therefore, this subgroup vanished as a possible major civil conflict contestant (see Table 5.5). Instead, only entrepreneurs from the Asian-Muslim-Leftist subgroup or the Black-Muslim-Leftist subgroup could start a civil conflict, although the likelihood of this was negligibly small. Therefore, the model correctly predicts that the probability for a civil conflict should have significantly decreased by the beginning of the 1990s.

Table 5.5.: Morocco's Opposition to a White, Centrist, Rightist Government

Entrepreneur	Prob.	Self-Definition	Attr.
Asian-Muslim-Leftist	0.2 %	Asian-Jew-Left-Rightist	39.7 %
Black-Muslim-Leftist	0.8 %	Black-Hindu-Leftist	18.8 %

Guatemala

According to the Uppsala Armed Conflict Database, Guatemala experienced an internal armed conflict from 1963 until 1995 (apart from 1964). In a first phase (1963–1982), the government of Guatemala stood against several different rebel groups (FAR I: 1963–1974, 1981; FAR II: 1970–1974; OPRA: 1979–1980; and EGP: 1975–1991), which ultimately joined in 1982 to create the URNG and together fought against the government until 1995 (1982–1995). Negotiations between the rebels and the government began in the late-1980s and the Guatemalan civil war ended in 1996, with a peace agreement between the conflicting parties.

Following this book's data from the World Values Survey (WVS), Guatemala has the following demographic setup: Guatemala has two ethnic groups — Ladinos (72%) and Indigenous people (28%); six religious groups — Catholics (63.4%), Evangelicals (30.9%), Protestants (1.9%), Buddhists (0.1%), Muslims (0.3%), and Others (3.3%); and two ideological groups — Leftists (41%) and Rightists (59%). The ethnic data strongly correspond with other sources, like the CIA World Factbook and the data by Wimmer et al. (2009), who also identify two major ethnic groups — Ladinos and Indigenous people — albeit with a slightly higher share of the latter.[11] The religious data also combine with the CIA World Factbook, which lists Roman Catholics, Protestants and people with indigenous Mayan beliefs as the three main religious groups. The distribution among the respective three-dimensional subgroups is provided in Table 5.6. The largest subgroups are formed by Ladino-Catholic-Rightists (27%), Ladino-Catholic-Leftists (19%), Indigenous-Catholic-Rightists (9%) and Indigenous-Catholic-Leftists (8%).

According to Wimmer et al. (2009) and the Database on Political Institutions (DPI), the government of Guatemala can be characterized as follows for the non-democratic years between 1975 to 2005: From 1975 until 1982, the government was Ladino-Rightist, from 1982 until 1985 it was only Ladino[12],

[11] According to the CIA World Factbook, the Guatemalan population in 2001 ethnically comprised Mestizos (Ladinos) and Europeans (59.4%), as well as several indigenous groups like the K'iche 9.1%, Kaqchikel 8.4%, Mam 7.9%, Q'eqchi 6.3%, other Mayan 8.6%, indigenous non-Mayan 0.2% and other groups 0.1%. Similarly, Wimmer et al. (2009) hold that Guatemala comprises 60% Mestizos (Ladinos) and 40% Indigenous people (Garifunas, Xinca, Mayas). If these latter figures are correct, the WVS gets the two main ethnic groups right, although it slightly underestimates the percentage of indigenous people.

[12] Guatemala had military governments under General Rios Montt (coup 1982) and Oscar Humberto Mejia (coup 1983).

Table 5.6.: Guatemala's Identity Setup (in %)

Left	Cath.	Evang.	Prot.	Buddhist	Muslim	Other
Ladino	19.0	7.7	0.4			0.8
Indigenous	8.0	4.7	0.3		0.1	0.3

Right	Cath.	Evang.	Prot.	Buddhist	Muslim	Other
Ladino	27.0	13.7	1.0	0.1		1.7
Indigenous	9.0	4.8	0.3		0.1	0.6

and from 1986 until 1996 it was again Ladino-Rightist. Thus, apart from the brief period of a military dictatorship from 1982 until 1985, both Ladino and Rightist people gained from the government. Consequently, the largest excluded subgroup was the Indigenous-Catholic-Leftist subgroup with 8%. Thus, the question emerges concerning how the oppositional entrepreneur in such a situation would ideally define itself, as well as which subgroups would be attracted by such a definition. The formal model provides an answer.

The formal model shows that from 1975 to 1982 and from 1986 to 1996, an oppositional entrepreneur would most likely come from the Indigenous-Catholic-Leftist subgroup (8%) and choose a self-definition of Indigenous/ Leftist, which would attract all indigenous or leftist people (about 56% of the population). This is exactly what we could observe in Guatemala, as the rebel movement was clearly indigenous and leftist. In the short period between 1982 and 1985, the formal model predicts that an oppositional entrepreneur would most likely come from the Indigenous-Catholic-Rightist subgroup (9%) and attract rightist people. Interestingly, there is evidence that there was "suspect right-wing violence" in Guatemala in 1983, although the extent to which that violence was directed by the government is unclear.[13]

Thailand

According to the Uppsala Armed Conflict Database, Thailand experienced an internal armed conflict from 1974 until 1982, in which the government stood against leftist rebels united in the Communist Party of Thailand (CPT). The CPT operated in Thailand's North and South and recruited

[13]see `http://www2.gwu.edu/~nsarchiv/NSAEBB/NSAEBB11/docs/` on: [2014/08/23].

from ethnic minorities.[14] Since 2003, there has been another violent conflict in the Patani region in Southern Thailand, where Malay-Muslim rebels demand independence from Thailand.

Based upon the WVS, Thailand has the following ethnic groups: Other (80.7%), Black (8.9%), White (8.1%), Asian-East (1.7%), Asian-Central (0.5%) and Asian-South (0.07%). Thus, the large majority of the people in Thailand do not define itself in terms of the specific ethnic categories provided by the WVS, but rather opt for a self-designation as 'Others', which should be read as the ethnic category of Thai people.[15] In religious terms, the WVS holds that the population largely comprises Buddhists (97%) and Muslims (2.6%), as well as diminishingly small groups of Jews (0.07%), Protestants (0.1%), and Others (0.1%). These numbers largely correspond with those from the CIA World Factbook. Finally, according to the WVS, Thailand comprises 36.1% Leftist and 64% Rightist people. The distribution among the respective three-dimensional subgroups is depicted in Table 5.7. As can be clearly seen, the largest subgroups in Thailand are Thai-Buddhist-Rightists (50.23%), Thai-Buddhist-Leftists (29.52%), Black-Buddhist-Rightists (5.5%), White-Buddhist-Rightists (4.1%) and Black-Buddhist-Leftists (2.9%).

According to Wimmer et al. (2009) and the Database on Political Institutions (DPI), the government of Thailand can be characterized as follows for the non-democratic years between 1975 and 2005: for most of the time between 1975 and 2005, the government was Thai in ethnic terms (in 1976 and 1977, it was also Chinese) and Rightist in ideological terms (apart from 1975 and 1992).[16] From 1993 until 1996, the government was additionally Buddhist. Thus, for most of the time, both Thai and Rightist people gained from the government. Consequently, the largest excluded subgroup from 1977 until 2005 was the group of Black-Buddhist-Leftists (2.9%).[17]

When applying the formal model, the optimal self-definition of the largest excluded subgroup in Thailand between 1977 and 2005 (apart from 1992–1996) would have been "Leftist or 'Other religious groups' or Asian-South or

[14] `http://www.ucdp.uu.se/gpdatabase/gpcountry.php?id=154&value=` on: [2014/09/02].

[15] According to the CIA World Factbook, 95.9% of the people in Thailand are Thai, 2% are Burmese, and 2.2% are other or unspecified. According to Wimmer, the population in Thailand comprises Thai (74%), Shan (0.5%) and Malay-Muslims (3.5%).

[16] In 1975, the government was Thai/Chinese, but not Rightist; in 1992, it was just Thai.

[17] From 1993 until 1996, the largest excluded subgroup was the group of Asian East-Protestant-Leftists with almost 1%.

Table 5.7.: Thailand's Identity Setup (in %)

Left	Buddhist	Muslim	Jewish	Protestant	Other
Other/Thai	29.52	0.2		0.1	
Black	2.9				
White	2.6				
Asian-East	0.6			0.1	
Asian-Central	0.2				
Asian-South					
Right	**Buddhist**	**Muslim**	**Jewish**	**Protestant**	**Other**
Other/Thai	50.23	0.6			0.1
Black	5.5	0.5	0.1		
White	4.1	1.3			0.1
Asian-East	1.1				
Asian-Central	0.3				
Asian-South	0.1				

Black", which would have attracted the support of 42% of the population, including the group of Thai-Buddhist-Leftists. Thus, the leftist uprising in Thailand can well be explained (although it is unclear, why it ended in 1988). It is more difficult to explain the armed conflict in the Patani region between the government and the Malay-Muslim rebel group, as the vast majority of Muslims were officially included through the rightist definition of the government.

Short Summary

The brief case study examples illustrate the working of the formal model and show that the model fits well in all three cases. Of course, there are other cases in the dataset that fit less well. Sometimes, the relevant groups do not appear in the World Values Survey, while sometimes the government's self-definition according to the Database of Political Institutions is not fine-grained enough. However, these misfits do not question the working of the formal model in general, but are rather due to inappropriate data, a problem that can be addressed once data of better quality are available. Nonetheless, the quantitative analysis provides support for the formally derived variables as the following section shows.

5.3. Empirical Results

I conduct the empirical analyses based upon the key independent variables from the formal part analogically to the analyses from the informal part. I present regression results, discuss misspecification problems, analyze substantial effects, conduct in-sample-prediction, undertake model comparison and robustness checks, always trying to relate back to previous results. The two key questions to answer are: first, whether a three-dimensional perspective is superior to a one- or two-dimensional perspective (like in Section 4.3, but this time, the variables are based upon the formal theoretical model); and second, whether the formally constructed three-dimensional variable ($ERI*$) outperforms the informal variable on the largest excluded three-dimensional subgroup (ERI_{max}).

Table 5.8 displays the results when regressing the dependent variable armed conflict onset ($onset1$) on the seven formal key independent variables, while Table 5.9 includes interaction terms for the seven key independent variables interacted with non-competitive regimes. The two models with the religious variable (without and with interaction) are again problematic and should not be further considered. For the rest of the models, the heat map statistic points to an unproblematic model specification (zero percent), although the heat map plots again reveal that the models do not fit the 45-degree line equally well (very similar to the results in the informal part): without an interaction term, all heat map plots deviate from the 45 degree line (worst for ideological and religious-ideological exclusion), including the one for the three-dimensional variable (see Figure 5.1), especially for high values of predicted probabilities. Once an interaction term is included, the three-dimensional and the other models ameliorate, whereby for high predicted probabilities the heat map line approximates the 45 degree line, although there remains no perfect fit (Figure 5.2). Multicollinearity is never an issue.

With a formal foundation for the key independent variables, only the three-dimensional variable (ERI*) emerges as significant, as the first difference analyses in Figure 5.3 show. Increasing the level of exclusion for non-competitive regimes from zero to the third quartile (0.032) statistically increases the risk of armed conflict onset from 4.7% to 5.8% (by about 1 percentage point, 90-percent-CI: [0.2; 3.0]). Figure 5.4 displays the effect of exclusion on the predicted probability of armed conflict onset graphically for the formal three-dimensional variable, for both non-competitive and competitive regimes. When focusing on the substantial effect, the picture

Table 5.8.: Logit Estimations: Effect of Formally Derived Variables Without Interaction on Conflict Onset

	Dependent variable:						
	onset1						
	(1)	(2)	(3)	(4)	(5)	(6)	(7)
noncl	−0.495	−0.650	−0.484	−0.526	−0.501	−0.490	−0.518
	(0.497)	(0.552)	(0.509)	(0.500)	(0.508)	(0.502)	(0.498)
ERI*	1.776						
	(4.116)						
E*		−0.002					
		(0.001)					
R*			–				
			–				
I*				−1.878*			
				(1.070)			
ER*					−2.584		
					(6.074)		
EI*						0.780	
						(2.345)	
RI*							−2.613*
							(1.536)
Observations	1,247	1,247	1,247	1,247	1,247	1,247	1,247
Log Likelihood	-111.183	-110.333	-111.066	-110.043	-111.129	-111.214	-110.036
Akaike Inf. Crit.	248.365	246.667	248.132	246.087	248.258	248.428	246.072

Note: *p<0.1; **p<0.05; ***p<0.01
robust standard errors in parentheses

Table 5.9.: Logit Estimations: Effect of Formally Derived Variables With Interaction on Conflict Onset

	Dependent variable:						
	onset1						
	(1)	(2)	(3)	(4)	(5)	(6)	(7)
noncl	−1.009*	−0.635	−0.484	−0.585	−0.740	−0.765	−0.454
	(0.563)	(0.548)	(0.509)	(0.533)	(0.554)	(0.523)	(0.527)
ERI*	−7.319						
	(5.989)						
E*		0.718					
		(3.200)					
R*			–				
			–				
I*				−2.027			
				(1.371)			
ER*					−5.039		
					(6.638)		
EI*						−3.703	
						(3.883)	
RI*							−2.416
							(1.837)
noncl:ERI*	16.378**						
	(7.308)						
noncl:E*		−0.720					
		(3.200)					
noncl:R*			–				
			–				
noncl:I*				0.478			
				(1.990)			
noncl:ER*					10.021		
					(12.096)		
noncl:EI*						6.825	
						(4.246)	
noncl:RI*							−0.769
							(2.733)
Observations	1,247	1,247	1,247	1,247	1,247	1,247	1,247
Log Likelihood	-109.734	-110.300	-111.066	-110.028	-110.723	-110.472	-110.018
Akaike Inf. Crit.	247.467	248.600	250.132	248.056	249.445	248.944	248.035
Note:							*p<0.1; **p<0.05; ***p<0.01 robust standard errors in parentheses

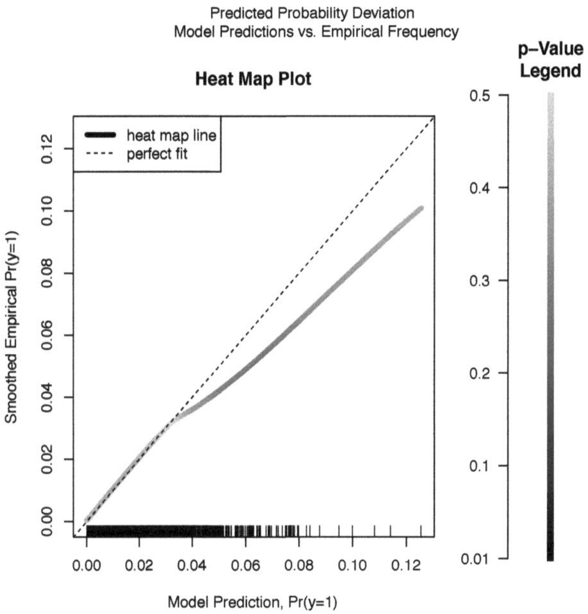

Figure 5.1.: *Fitted heat map line for Model 1 in Table 5.8. This model includes ERI∗ as the key independent variable not interacted with regime type.*

resembles the one from before: while the risk of armed conflict increases with higher levels of exclusion for non-competitive regimes, the effect is contrary for competitive regimes and the risk of armed conflict reduces with higher levels of exclusion. Moreover, with zero or minimal exclusion, competitive regimes seem to have a higher risk of armed conflict onset than non-competitive regimes. However, like in the informal case, these differences never reach clear statistical significance, although they are marginally significant for the three-dimensional exclusion variable.

Further supporting the relevance of the formal three-dimensional exclusion variable, an ROC curve shows that the three-dimensional variable interacted with non-competitive regimes indeed makes an important contribution in terms of predicting outcomes (Figure 5.5). While the AUC statistic itself with a value of 0.766 is moderate, but still not overwhelming, the contri-

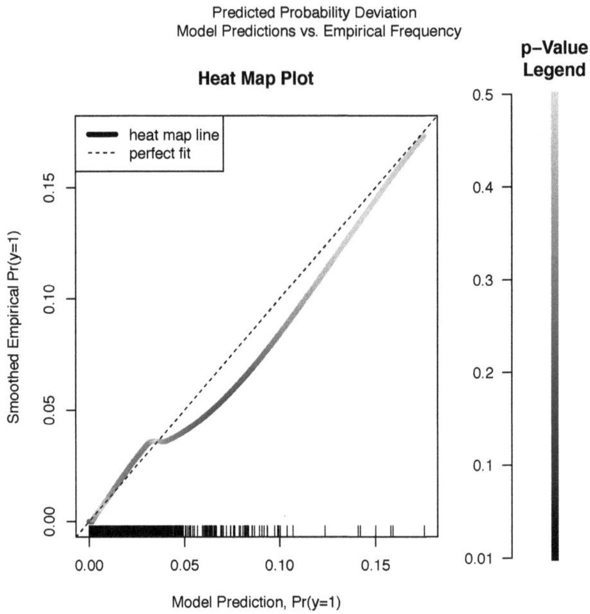

Figure 5.2.: *Fitted heat map line for Model 1 in Table 5.9. This model includes ERI∗ as the key independent variable interacted wit regime type.*

bution of the formal three-dimensional variable to the ROC curve seems similarly important as the contribution of the informal three-dimensional variable: although GDP remains the strongest predictor for being excluded first, it is followed by the formal three-dimensional exclusion variable (see Figure 5.6).

Directly proceeding to the comparison of the formal three-dimensional variable to the informal variable, the distribution of the individual log-likelihood ratios again clearly speaks in favor of the Clarke test rather than the Vuong test. The Clarke test is indifferent between a *formal* three-dimensional variable and an *informal* three-dimensional variable, which was to be expected given the extremely high correlation between these two variables.

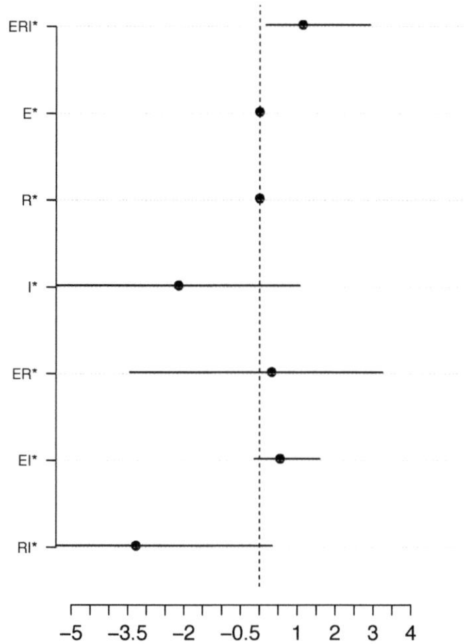

Figure 5.3.: *First difference analyses of the effect of exclusion in non-competitive regimes for the formally derived exclusion variables. In each case, the value of the key independent variable is increased from zero to the third quartile and the effect on the change in predicted probabilities, including 90% confidence intervals, is displayed.*

Robustness Checks

Let us first look at the robustness of the results with respect to different independent and dependent variables. The regression results are reported in Table 5.10 and the first difference effects are displayed in Figure 5.7. When interacted with autocracy rather than non-competitive regimes (Model 1), the formal three-dimensional interaction term ($ERI*$) remains positive and significant, although the first difference effect is insignificant. When using different dependent variables, *onset*2 and *onset*3 (Models 2, 3) and when combining them with autocracy (Models 4, 5), the interaction term remains

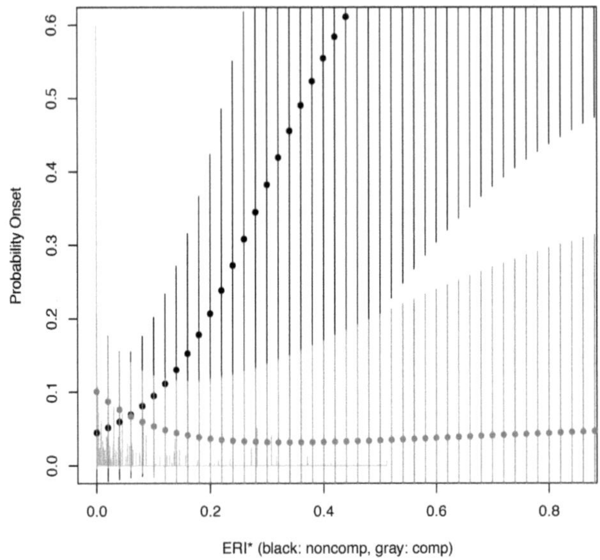

Figure 5.4.: *Predicted probability of armed conflict onset and 90% confidence interval for varying values of the variable ERI∗, separately for non-competitive and competitive regimes. (Relative frequencies of the values of the independent variable are displayed along the x-axis in gray.)*

significant, although the first difference effects becomes insignificant, apart from one case, namely when *onset*2 is combined with autocracy. Finally, let us assess the robustness of the results, when influential observations (Pregibon leverage value above 0.05) are excluded for both *onset*1 (Model 6) and *onset*2 (Model 7). While the three-dimensional interaction terms remain significant, the first difference effects are only significant for Model 7, when *onset*2 is used. Recall that the significant effect of Wimmer's variable (excluded ethnic population) was not robust to the exclusion of cases with Pregibon leverage values above 0.05.

To conclude, the results of the formal part still provide strong support for the superiority of a three-dimensional versus a one- or two-dimensional

Table 5.10.: Robustness Checks: Formal Part

	Dependent variable:						
	onset1	onset2	onset3	onset2	onset3	onset1	onset2
	(1)	(2)	(3)	(4)	(5)	(6)	(7)
autocl	−1.088			−0.426	−0.406		
	(0.724)			(0.472)	(0.475)		
noncl		−0.842**	−0.669			−1.210	−1.418**
		(0.417)	(0.454)			(0.749)	(0.564)
ERI*	−2.769	−8.855	−8.825	−9.401	−11.547	−5.848	−12.622**
	(4.604)	(5.397)	(5.753)	(6.100)	(7.120)	(5.347)	(6.392)
autocl:ERI*	16.168*			21.360**	21.778**		
	(9.532)			(8.519)	(9.536)		
noncl:ERI*		13.854**	12.958*			25.321*	25.858***
		(6.512)	(6.944)			(13.921)	(9.951)
Observations	1,235	1,277	1,549	1,290	1,553	1,234	1,249
Log Likelihood	-106.573	-168.219	-205.006	-162.157	-195.991	-103.472	-150.567
Akaike Inf. Crit.	241.146	364.438	440.011	352.315	421.981	234.943	329.133

Note: *p<0.1; **p<0.05; ***p<0.01
robust standard errors in parentheses

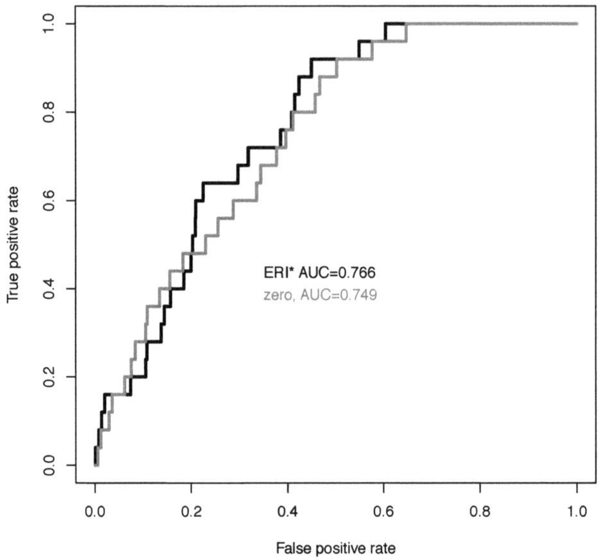

Figure 5.5.: *Receiver Operating Characteristic (ROC) curve. The ROC curve plots the true positive rate against the false positive rate at various discrimination thresholds, separately for a model that includes ERI∗ and its interaction with regime type, and for a zero model without these variables.*

perspective. However, the formal consideration of the three-dimensional perspective does not seem to yield an additional benefit vis-à-vis an informal consideration, at least in statistical terms. Theoretically, however, the formal model provides a strong underpinning for the informal exclusion variable on the largest excluded three-dimensional subgroup, which performed very well statistically.

Summary

Let me summarize the key claims that I have made thus far in the first part. I have argued that when looking at the demographic characteristics of a

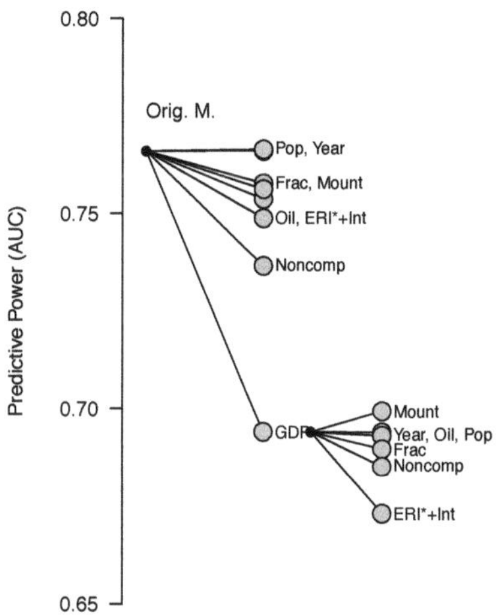

Figure 5.6.: *In-sample predictive power for a model that includes ERI∗ and its interaction with regime type. The figure depicts the change in the AUC value, when single variables are deleted.*

country, it is insufficient to consider the country's ethnic, religious or class-based ideological groups in isolation or in parallel. Given that individuals in a country belong to one group from each dimension and that all the divisions may become salient, the demographic identity setup has to be conceptualized in three dimensions, with the three-dimensional subgroups becoming the smallest unit of analysis. A government defines itself within the three-dimensional identity setup including certain parts of the population under its definition and excluding others. In countries without functioning elections, excluded subgroups generally have an incentive to violently topple the government given their goal of accessing governmental resources. The largest excluded subgroup is the one from which the challenger most likely emanates. With the challenger choosing a self-definition, individuals in the population decide whether to support the government or the opposition,

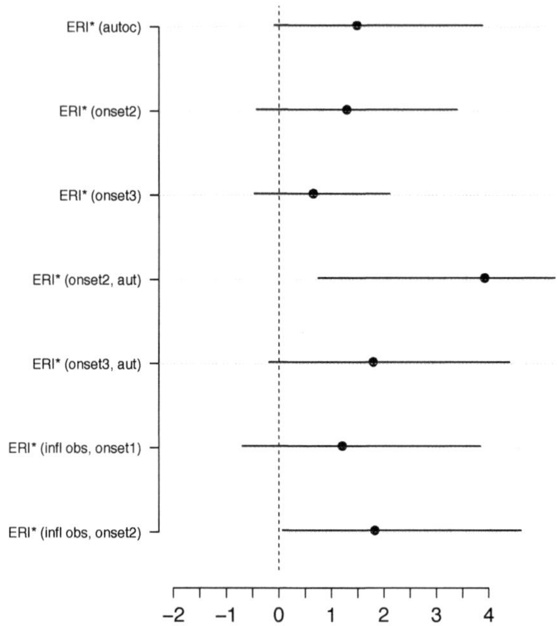

Figure 5.7.: *Robustness check: First difference analyses of the effect of exclusion for the formally derived exclusion variable $ERI*$ for different scenarios. In each case, the value of the key independent variable is increased from zero to the third quartile and the effect on the change in predicted probabilities, including 90% confidence intervals, is displayed.*

whereby the size of the rebel movement is endogenously determined.

In the empirical analyses, the size of the largest excluded three-dimensional subgroup has emerged as a powerful quantity of interest. The implicit assumption thus far is that "power is in the numbers", whereby movements with a larger support base are more threatening to the government than those with a smaller support base. While the rebels' backing in the population is certainly important, other factors influence the power of the rebel movement vis-à-vis the government. Most importantly, rebels require weapons to pose a substantial threat to the government, and the acquisition of these weapons most often requires the help of third parties. Therefore, the second part of this book extends beyond the mere consideration of numerical support from identity groups within the population and considers external states as potential providers of fighting material for rebel groups. Nonetheless, I argue that identity still plays a crucial role as it requires transnational ethnic, religious or class-based ideological linkages between the supporter and the rebel group for the support to realize.

Part II.

Transnational Support of Rebel Groups

Chapter 6.

Ethnic, Religious and Class-Based Rebel Support

This second part is interested in the transnational dimension of civil conflicts. The question is whether the exclusion of ethnic, religious or class-based ideological groups in one country in combination with the existence of co-ethnic, co-religious or co-ideological groups in neighboring countries' governments increases the likelihood that the former country will experience a civil conflict onset. The idea is that excluded identity groups are in need of and can realistically hope to receive external backing from co-identity neighboring governments. I develop a strategic theoretical underpinning consistent with the first part's theoretical reasoning concerning why and under what conditions such support should occur, whereby I test the theory with new data. The contribution in comparison to existing studies on transnational linkages in civil conflicts lies in a consideration of religious and ideological linkages in addition to ethnic ones.

It was already recognized that many civil conflicts have a transnational dimension during the Cold War (cp. Werner (2000, 347) citing Luard (1986, 69)). In various conflicts, the United States and the Soviet Union intermingled in so-called proxy wars to prevent states with the same capitalist or communist ideology from falling or helping rebels with the same ideology to enter into power (cp. Kalyvas and Balcells 2010, 420). The main goal was to secure and extend spheres of influence. Interventions by the United States occurred prominently in Afghanistan, Nicaragua, Tibet, Angola, Albania and Laos, while the United States' rivals Soviet Union and China intervened in conflicts in Angola, Greece, South Africa, Vietnam, Nicaragua, El Salvador, Somalia and Ethiopia, among others (see Findley and Teo 2006; Byman et al. 2001, 39; Balch-Lindsay and Enterline 2000; Koga 2011; Kalyvas and Balcells 2010, 418). Notably, interventions crucially changed the balance of power between the actors in the conflict (Salehyan et al. 2011, 709).

With the demise of the Soviet Union and rising attention to ethnic civil conflicts in the 1990s and religious conflicts in the 2000s, it became visible that not only class-based ideological but also ethnic and religious civil conflicts have a transnational dimension, and not only since the 1990s. In terms of the ethnic dimension, rebels have often appealed to co-ethnics in governments elsewhere, and those governments have often responded with support. Thus, Albania supported Albanian rebels in Serbia (Kosovo), Russia supported Russian rebels in Moldova, Tajikistan and recently in Ukraine, Vietnam supported Vietnamese rebels in Cambodia, Iraq supported Arabs in Iran, Uzbekistan supported Uzbeks in Afghanistan, and Armenia supported Armenians in Azerbaijan, just to mention a few examples (see Cederman et al. 2009; Woodwell 2004; Byman et al. 2001). As for the religious dimension, Iran backed Shia groups in Iraq, Lebanon, Bahrain, Kuwait, Saudi Arabia and Bosnia, Pakistan supported rebel groups in Afghanistan and Kashmir, and Saudi Arabia backed rebels in Afghanistan and Ethiopia (cp. Byman et al. 2001; Salehyan et al. 2011). By providing weapons, shelter and other means of concrete support, external governments effectively help even small excluded groups to pose a substantial threat to their governments.

Despite the overwhelming case study evidence, the quantitative literature has long largely neglected transnational factors when predicting the onset of civil conflict. Instead, domestic factors like a country's GDP, population size, fractionalization, mountainous terrain etc. have prevailed as explanatory determinants. Recently, transnational factors have come to the attention of quantitative academic scholars, albeit only in terms of ethnic linkages, while religious and ideological linkages have been neglected to date. However, given that transnational support apparently not only runs along ethnic lines, the question arises concerning whether an additional consideration of religious and ideological linkages provides a more complete picture and valuable insights.

6.1. The Literature

This section sketches the development of the quantitative literature on the transnational dimension of civil conflicts. It shows that the academic focus has shifted from the analysis of actual interventions in ongoing civil conflicts to anticipated interventions as a factor influencing the onset of civil conflicts. It also shows that assumptions about the third party's motivation for intervention have changed from disinterested reasons of humanitarian concern to more self-interested reasons concerning the question of which actor should win the conflict based upon affinity reasons, including a shared identity. However, the focus thus far has only been on ethnic linkages, while religious and ideological linkages have not been at the center of attention.

For long, the quantitative literature was primarily interested in explicit military interventions by foreign governments in ongoing civil conflicts. One strand examined whether interventions influence the severity, duration and outcome of civil conflict (Colaresi 2014, 67). Another strand tried to predict whether an intervention was going to occur, who was most likely to intervene, and on what side (Findley and Teo 2006, 828). First, it was simply assumed that the intervenor had the goal of ending the violence (Regan 1996, 340), largely for humanitarian reasons (cp. Regan 1998; Findley and Marineau 2014, 2). However, rather than hastening a conflict, it was found that interventions often tend to prolong the fighting, making it even more severe and less apt for resolution (Salehyan et al. 2011, 710). Thus, the focus turned to more narrow strategic motivations of the intervenors. It was recognized that states "carefully weigh a host of costs and benefits, including the conflict's intensity, duration, success prospected, potential spillover and electoral consequences that accrue from international, national and subnational sources in deciding to intervene" (Findley and Marineau 2014, 3). Different self-interested reasons were discussed, including the prevention of regional destabilization (Kathman 2011), opportunities for looting — most prominently exemplified by Uganda and Rwanda in the DRC (Koga 2011, 1150; Findley and Marineau 2014; Aydin 2008) — and the distraction from domestic problems (Weeks 2012; Goemans 2008; Pickering and Kisangani 2010, 2005), with mixed empirical evidence (Weeks 2012, 378).[1]

However, strategic interests not only concern the termination or continuation of the conflict per se, but they also extend to the question of who should win the conflict (Findley and Teo 2006; Salehyan et al. 2011). Often, intervenors seem to have connections to one of the parties in a conflict and want their own side to win (Cederman et al. 2009, 415; cp. Cetinyan 2002). Empirical evidence shows that an intervention on one side indeed shortens the time to this side's victory (Balch-Lindsay et al. 2008; Gent 2008). Different kinds of connections emerge as potential candidates. One first strand of the literature focuses on autocracies versus democracies,

[1]Note that there also may be several incentives not to intervene, like the incentive not to invite own people to revolt (see Coggins 2011; Cederman et al. 2009, 415). This vulnerability argument, however, has not received much support (see Belanger et al. 2005, 436). Others discuss the goal of intervenors to promote democracy, although empirical studies show that intervention is not particularly helpful in this regard (De Mesquita and Downs 2006).

finding that democratic dyads reduce the likelihood of external support in secessionist movements (Belanger et al. 2005, challenged by Saideman 2007). A second strand takes rivalries into account, based upon the idea that a state intervenes in a civil conflict involving a rival state to weaken the rival (Findley and Marineau 2014, 3; Maoz and San-Akca 2012, 723; Findley and Teo 2006, 831; Akcinaroglu and Radziszewski 2005, 352). Indeed, there seems to be some support for this perspective, with studies showing that rivalries increase the likelihood of interventions on behalf of the non-state actor (Findley and Teo 2006, 835f.; Maoz and San-Akca 2012, 730), as well as prolonging civil wars (Akcinaroglu and Radziszewski 2005). However, the results should be treated with caution due to a likely endogeneity problem: as rivalries are accumulated interstate disputes, which are often a result of interventions in civil conflicts, it might rather be the case that civil wars are followed by interventions giving rise to rivalries, in lieu of rivalries giving rise to interventions in civil wars (cp. Schultz 2010; Gleditsch et al. 2008; Woodwell 2004). That said, it is desirable to choose more exogenous predictors, like in the final strand, which takes the common identity between the intervenor and the target into account, most prominently the ethnic identity (see Forsberg 2014, 194). There is evidence that when ethnic affinities exist between the intervenor and the rebel group in the target state, intervention or support of the rebels becomes much more likely (Saideman 2007; Nome 2013; Salehyan et al. 2011). One explanation for this pattern is that like-minded governments ease communication and enhance cooperative and mutually beneficial relationships (Salehyan et al. 2011, 720). Another explanation is that ethnic groups in a country typically suffer with their co-ethnics elsewhere, wherefore they pressure their governments to intervene, otherwise threatening to withdraw their political support (Nome 2013, 751f.).

As the review thus far shows, it has been recognized in the quantitative literature that transnational ethnic linkages can influence the course of a conflict and the decision to intervene. However, transnational factors have long received much less attention when predicting the onset of civil conflict (Collier and Sambanis 2005; see Henne 2012, 757).[2] This is surprising as

[2]Thyne (2006) is exceptional in asking theoretically how transnational factors might influence the onset of internal conflict. He argues that *costly* transnational signals like military alliances, trade ties, troop mobilizations and sanctions should have no effect on internal conflict as they can well be anticipated, whereas *cheap* signals like day-to-day communications — which are somewhat unpredictable — can increase the risk of internal conflict onset if they occur on part of the opposition. If identity ties from the opposition to external governments are conceptualized as cheap signals,

the prospect of rebel groups receiving external backing might well influence their willingness to start a civil conflict in the first place (cp. Gleditsch 2007, 296).[3] Earlier studies on civil conflict onset used "very crude proxies of external ties that lack face validity" (Cederman et al. 2009, 409), such as "the size of immigrant communities from a given country in the United States as a measure of opportunities for support from diasporas" (Collier and Hoeffler 2004). However, given that case studies often point to the importance of transnational factors in civil conflict onsets, recent approaches use more specific transnational predictors; for example, they examine whether the existence of transnational ethnic ties increases the risk that an ethnic group will become involved in a civil conflict, although surprisingly there is not much support for this allegation (Cederman et al. 2009, 2013). To solve the puzzling non-finding, studies have turned to interaction effects, examining — for example — how the effect of transnational ties might possibly depend on the ethnic group's size in the host or the intervening country. One study finds that an interaction of large excluded ethnic groups and transnational ethnic kin jointly predicts the onset of civil conflict (Cederman et al. 2009[4]), while another — more up-to-date — study finds that an excluded ethnic group is only more likely to be involved in a civil conflict with the incumbent group in its country if its transnational ethnic kin group is of medium size (set relative to the incumbent group). By contrast, large transnational ethnic kin groups in power even reduce the risk of conflict (Cederman et al. 2013). What has not been considered is the effect of the host country's regime type in mediating the influence of linkages, as well as the role that other than ethnic transnational linkages play, namely religious and ideological linkages. This book tries to fill the gap and considers all three possible linkages simultaneously, in interaction with both the amount of exclusion *and* the host country's regime type. The analyses show that such a consideration yields more parsimonious and intuitive results. In order to motivate the merit of considering religious and ideological linkages on top of ethnic linkages, the following section sketches two cases, focusing on Ethiopia and Uganda.

they may influence the onset and course of an internal armed conflict.

[3]Akcinaroglu and Radziszewski (2005, 350) argue that "enduring and intense rivalries send a credible signal to the rebels that intervention is possible, thereby increasing fighting morale and prolonging the war's duration." The same argument can easily be extended for the onset of civil conflict.

[4]Note that the respective study relies on a reduced sample of countries from Eurasia and Northern Africa.

6.2. Episodes of Transnational Support

Before getting to the theoretical section on why transnational ethnic, religious or ideological linkages matter at all, let me briefly exemplify with two episodes of internal violence involving transnational support that a consideration of religious and ideological ties on top of ethnic ties provides valuable insights. These two episodes are taken from Ethiopia and Uganda, where Sudan and Tanzania emerged as key providers of external assistance to the respective rebel movements. As these cases are located in Africa, one would initially suspect that ethnic linkages were the key factor determining patterns of external support; however, upon further inspection, it becomes clear that only ideological or religious linkages can explain the specific kinds of support patterns.

When Ethiopia experienced an internal armed conflict from 1974 until 1991, the Derg government stood against several rebel groups, most prominently the Eritrean independence movement (ELF, EPLF) and the ethnic group of Tigreans (TPLF).[5] With the conclusion of the conflict and the ousting of the Derg regime, an independent Eritrea was established and Tigreans came to power in the remaining parts of Ethiopia.[6] With an exclusively ethnic perspective, one finds that Ethiopia in 1974 comprised five ethnic groups, Afar, Amhara, Oroma, Somali and Tigre, of which the Amhara were in power (Cederman et al. 2013). Among the excluded ethnic groups, Afar and Somali had external ethnic ties to three of six potential neighboring countries — namely to Djibouti, Kenya and Somalia — while there were no ethnic ties to Sudan, Saudi Arabia and South Yemen (cp. Cederman et al. 2013). However, apart from the link to Somalia, the ethnic links were never activated. The Somali link was quite short-lived and only supported the Somali people in the Ogaden region of Ethiopia. Indeed, the Somali link can certainly not explain any outside support for Tigreans and

[5] Note that the Ethiopian civil war was one of the bloodiest conflicts since World War II (see Themnér and Wallensteen 2013, 510; Themnér and Wallensteen 2014, 542).

[6] Note that Tigreans live in Northern Ethiopia, to the North of which is Eritrea. Eritrea had long been independent, but was annexed to Ethiopia in the aftermath of 1947. While the Tigray region is relatively homogeneous in ethnic terms in harboring mainly Tigreans, Eritrea is ethnically more diverse being home to about nine ethnic groups, the largest of which are the Tigrinya/Tigreans. The Eritrean independence movement was prior to and initially stronger than the Tigrean movement, but the two groups benefited from each other and Tigreans grew in strength over time (up to 1985). While both groups had partially different tactics and ideologies and were alienated from 1985 to 1988, they again got together in 1988, accepted their different goals and acted in unity in order to oust the Derg regime (cp. Young 1996).

Eritreans.[7]

However, as the UCDP External Support data (Högbladh et al. 2011) reveal, Eritrean and Tigrean rebels *did* receive massive external backing from neighboring countries, namely the Eritrean rebels from Saudi Arabia, South Yemen and Sudan (plus some non-neighboring Middle Eastern countries like Libya, Iraq, Kuwait, Syria and the United Arab Emirates) and the Tigrean rebels from Sudan (cp. Young 1996, 119). From a purely ethnic perspective, these lines of support present a puzzle given the lack of ethnic linkages to these countries. However, the view changes when taking religious and ideological linkages into account. Thus, the present data reveals that the excluded Muslim/Christian-Leftist population in *Eritrea* (Smock 1982, 452) had religious Muslim links to Saudi Arabia from 1975 to 1989[8], ideological leftist links to South Yemen from 1975 to 1989, and religious and ideological links to Sudan from 1975 to 2005 (from 1975 to 1986: leftist; from 1987 to 1989: rightist; from 1990 to 2005: Muslim).[9] Indeed, all three countries emerged as supporters for the Eritrean struggle — Saudi Arabia form 1975 to 1978, South Yemen in 1975 and Sudan from 1976 to 1978, 1982 to 1985, and 1987 to 1991. Christian-Leftist rebels in the *Tigray* region had no *religious* links to any of the neighboring countries (cp. Young 1996, 119), although — like the Eritreans — they had ideological *leftist* links to South Yemen and Sudan, whereby the latter supported the TPLF from 1976 to 1988. Of all the transnational links, the most pronounced and long-lasting transnational support to Eritreans and Tigreans certainly came from Sudan, thereby generating the question of Sudan's motivation for this support. The literature argues that Sudan wanted to use the rebels as a bargaining chip against Ethiopia because Ethiopia sponsored the rebellion in Southern Sudan (Kibreab 2000, 259ff.). However, Sudan's support for the rebels in Ethiopia came long before Ethiopia's support for the rebels in Sudan.[10] Apart from that, it is mentioned that Sudan received Eritrean rebels with great hospitality, possibly due to the fact that most of these rebels (92%) were Muslims, thus akin to the favored Muslim population in Northern

[7]According to the UCDP External Support Data (Högbladh et al. 2011), Somalia provided support to SALF from 1977 to 1980, to WSLF from 1976 to 1983, and to OLF in 1980.

[8]Note that the period under consideration is 1975–2005.

[9]Although formally all leftist groups were included in the Derg regime due to its officially leftist orientation, they de facto did not feel represented given the regime's terrorist and exclusive nature.

[10]Sudan's support started in the 1960s, whereas Ethiopia's support is documented from 1983 to 2005.

Sudan (Smock 1982, 455).[11] While Sudan's motives remain slightly in the dark, it is clear that religious and ideological links explain which countries provided transnational support to Eritrean and Tigrean rebels better than ethnic links in the Ethiopian case.

The superior explanatory power of ideological rather than ethnic linkages also becomes apparent in the second case, concerning Uganda. When Uganda experienced an internal armed conflict from 1971 until 1979, the government of Idi Amin stood against two major rebel groups: first, the rebel movement Kikoosi Malum led by Milton Obote; and second, Fronasa, led by Yoweri Museveni. These two groups together formed the UNLA/UNLF. With an exclusively ethnic perspective, one finds that the regime of Idi Amin defined itself in very narrow ethnic terms (Kakwa-Nubian), implying that other major ethnic groups like the ethnic Baganda (16%), Basoga (8%), North-West Nilers (4.9%), Karamojong (2%), Langi/Acholi (1%), South-Westerners (20%) and Teso (8%) were politically excluded or powerless (cp. Cederman et al. 2010, 2013). Obote mobilized the ethnic groups of Langi/Acholi, which had previously been in power; and Museveni mobilized the ethnic groups of Baganda and South-Westerners (Banyankole, Banyarwanda) (see Weinstein 2005, 610). Of the excluded ethnic groups, only the Banyarwanda — belonging to the group of South-Westerners — had external ethnic links, namely to Rwanda (and only at a later time period), although these links apparently only existed due to an overaggregation of the ethnic category of Banyarwanda comprising all people from Rwanda. In fact, however, the government in Rwanda was ethnically Hutu, whereas the Banyarwanda in Uganda were ethnically Tutsi and had even fled the Rwandan regime. Thus, Rwanda would definitely not emerge as a supporter for the Banyarwanda in Uganda. No external ethnic links existed with the other six neighboring countries, Tanzania, the Central African Republic, the Democratic Republic of Congo, Kenya, Burundi and Sudan.

However, as amply documented, the UNLA/UNLF received massive external support, namely from Tanzania, thereby eventually helping the rebels to oust the regime of Idi Amin and re-install the government of Obote. Given the lack of ethnic ties, ideological ties to Tanzania emerge as the critical explanatory factor. Ideologically, after having ousted leftist Obote in 1971, Idi Amin took a rather rightist stance (Acheson-Brown 2001, 3).[12] On the other hand, the government in Tanzania under Nyerere was

[11] Neither religious nor ideological links existed with the other three neighboring, but non-intervening countries, Somalia, Kenya and Djibouti.

[12] In the DPI, the government under Amin is not listed as rightist, which is why rightists

still clearly leftist and thus had explicit ideological ties to the excluded rebelling leftist population in Uganda. Moreover, Tanzania had a motive for supporting the rebels as it feared that rightist Amin might undermine the Tanzanian regime by supporting rightist rebel groups; indeed, there was some evidence supporting this allegation (Acheson-Brown 2001, 3f.). Upon first consideration, one could thus conclude that the motivating factor for Tanzania's intervention in Uganda was a rivalry between Tanzania and Uganda. However, upon further inspection, it becomes clear that the rivalry only emerged in response to the intervention in each other's internal affairs. There were plans by Tanzania to oust Amin from 1972 onwards, but Tanzania had no backing from China and feared that Britain and Israel would counter-intervene (Acheson-Brown 2001, 3ff.; Prunier 2004). Thus, the intervention gave rise to the rivalry, and not vice-versa.[13]

To conclude, religious or ideological linkages from the rebels to external governments can explain why Eritreans and Tigreans in Ethiopia received backing from Sudan and other countries, as well as why anti-Amin forces in Uganda were supported by Tanzania. Despite the prevalence of ethnicity in Africa, ethnic linkages cannot explain the respective support patterns. Let us next proceed to the question of why transnational support is based upon identity criteria at all, before examining in a subsequent chapter whether the respective linkages have systematic explanatory power.

appear among the excluded population and a transnational rightist link to the Central African Republic is documented.

[13]Of the other surrounding countries, only Sudan had transnational leftist links to the excluded population in Uganda, although these links do not seem to have been activated at that time.

Chapter 7.

Transnational Support Along Identity Lines

This chapter develops a theoretical account for why and under what conditions transnational identity linkages should matter for the onset of civil conflict, before the resulting expectations are tested in the subsequent chapter.

7.1. The Argument

The existing literature usefully distinguishes between the demand and supply sides of external support (cp. Salehyan et al. 2011, 711), positing that transnational linkages only have an effect on the risk of civil conflict onset if the demand and supply sides of transnational support converge. The present section follows this argumentation and delineates the reasons for why rebels ask for and external states provide support. These reasons should be reconcilable with the theoretical strategic-instrumentalist perspective adopted in the first part of this book (cp. Figure 3.1 on page 42), whereby politicians above everything else want to remain in office and the population seeks as many resources as possible, leading to a mutual exchange relationship of "private goods for political support". Following this line of argumentation, the effect of transnational linkages on civil conflict onset should depend on the regime type and the size of the excluded population, as developed in the following sections.

The Demand for External Support

Let us first look at the demand side, the rebels, with their goals and capacities. Suffering from political exclusion, rebels typically follow one of two goals, concerning either the control of the government or the control of more narrowly defined territory (cp. Buhaug 2006). Following the first goal, rebels typically intend to dispose the government or at least become included in the governmental coalition; with the second goal, they seek to receive territorial autonomy or secession.[1] These two forms of conflict — governmental or territorial — are closely related. Ideally and shortsightedly, all rebels would probably want to control the government and have access to the entire amount of state resources. However, considering that they might not have the power to achieve this aim, or recognizing that once in power they are likely to be challenged and disposed by other groups, rebels might opt for the second goal of achieving the control of only parts of the country, whether in the form of autonomy or secession (Buhaug 2006, 694). Concerning the frequency of these two types of conflict, about two-thirds of all civil conflicts are governmental conflicts, while about one-third are territorial conflicts (cp. page 74).[2]

Speaking of "rebels", the assumption is that a conflict between the politically excluded population and the groups in government has already turned violent. However, violence by politically excluded groups is by no means necessary or automatic. Although all politically excluded groups want to access governmental or territorial resources, so the assumption goes, whether or not this demand turns violent depends on the regime type and the group's size.

In functioning democracies, large politically excluded groups might realistically hope to win the next election (cp. page 51). Thus, they have little incentive to start a violent conflict against the government to shorten the time to power, as this only proves costly and counter-productive in the long term. In contrast to large excluded groups, small excluded groups in democracies with a lower chance of being included in the next round might sometimes have an incentive to resort to violent tactics (cp. Buhaug 2006; Cederman et al. 2013, 406). Exemplary are the small excluded ethnic groups of Bodo and Tripura in India (Cunningham 2013, 294). Nonetheless, even small groups can often hope to become a coalition partner or attain rights of self-determination after resorting to peaceful protest in the form of demonstrations, boycotts or strikes (cp. Cunningham 2013, 292, 294; Schock 2013, 285). Thus, in democracies, only small excluded groups — if any at all — should have an incentive to violently challenge the government.

In non-democracies, things are different with respect to conventional politics. Neither large nor small excluded groups can realistically hope

[1]see "UCDP," `http://www.pcr.uu.se/research/ucdp/definitions/` on: [2014/07/17].

[2]When using the conflict year, the relative frequency of the two kinds of conflicts is relatively even: according to the Uppsala Armed Conflict Database, of all 1896 internal armed conflict years from 1946–2013, 51% were governmental and 49% were territorial (cp. the data underlying Themnér and Wallensteen 2014).

to get to power any time soon via elections (cp. Celestino and Gleditsch 2013, 389, citing Tilly 2007), and the government is unlikely to make concessions voluntarily. The question remains whether excluded groups in non-democracies should resort to extra-legal *non-violent* tactics like protests, demonstrations, strikes or boycotts, or rather to extra-legal *violent* tactics like rebellion (cp. Cunningham 2010; Chenoweth and Cunningham 2013), as well as how this choice depends on the groups' size. A typical expectation in the literature is that large excluded groups more likely resort to peaceful and small excluded groups more likely to violent means (Cunningham 2013). The argument is that "power is in the numbers" (DeNardo 1985; Cunningham et al. 2009), whereby a high number of people should be able to sufficiently threaten the government, even peacefully. This argument is supposedly supported with quantitative evidence showing that peaceful movements are more successful in terms of leading to democracy than violent movements (Celestino and Gleditsch 2013), and with anecdotic case study evidence from the 1989 revolutions in Eastern Europe, the Colour Revolutions at the beginning of the 2000s (Georgia, Yugoslavia, Ukraine) or the Arab Spring in 2011 (Egypt, Tunisia) (cp. Celestino and Gleditsch 2013, 397), when large masses successfully challenged the government without resorting to violence.

However, one should be careful with hasty conclusions, as there might be a selection effect. It seems that in the few cases of successful peaceful revolutions, a very narrow personalist regime stood against almost the entire alienated population, which acted unitedly beyond identity lines as a "decentralized, loose coalitions of diverse actors" (Celestino and Gleditsch 2013, 391; Svensson and Lindgren 2011) to peacefully dispose the government and install a democracy. However, this kind of setting is not the focus of this book, which instead looks at group-based favoritism and mobilization along identity lines. As soon as we look at clearly defined identity groups, it seems more reasonable to assume that even large groups most likely resort to violent tactics, given that these seem to hurt the government more than non-violent tactics (Celestino and Gleditsch 2013, 388). Quantitative evidence supports this allegation; for example, Cunningham (2013) shows that the choice for non-violent tactics is quite rare compared to violent tactics and that — if any at all — only small movements tend to use non-violent campaigns, while large movements resort to civil war, contrary to her theoretical expectations.[3] Moreover, one can show that if campaigns

[3] Note that Cunningham (2013) constrains her research to movements with territorial rather than governmental ambitions (self-determination movements). Moreover, she

are homogeneous in ethnic, religious or class-based ideological terms, they turn violent in 86 percent of the cases, while if campaigns are diverse in ethnic, religious and class-based ideological terms, they only turn violent in 68 percent of the cases (using the Navco 2.0 data[4]). This suggests that group-based, homogeneous campaigns more likely choose violent tactics than diverse campaigns, which cross identity lines, thereby supporting the above argument.

When confronted with a violent movement, the government typically feels threatened and mobilizes its military forces to fight its opponent (Cunningham 2013, 292). Independent of whether the rebel movement comprises a large or small number of people, the conflict between the government and the rebels typically is highly asymmetric, with the government having a preponderance of military power (Sullivan and Karreth 2014, 4; Kalyvas and Balcells 2010, 415). Although the rebels can often mobilize a substantial number of people, they usually lack the weapons and military capabilities to effectively fight the government on the battlefield one-by-one. Thus, rebels without a substantial amount of military resources often turn to hit-and-run attacks using mountains and rough terrain as safe havens (Fearon and Laitin 2003), thereby sometimes attaining control of small parts of the country (cp. Kalyvas and Balcells 2010, 418). However, in order to pose a substantial threat to the government and make the territorial control more sustainable or even challenge the government at its center, rebels require concrete fighting material, ideally supplemented by financial funding, military training and shelter (cp. Salehyan et al. 2011, 716). This fighting material most likely comes from external actors with an interest in the conflict. Thus, this book holds the view that a high number of fighters generally cannot compensate for the lack of weapons. Ideally, it needs both fighters and weapons, wherefore these two entities should be conceptualized as being complementary and not substitutive.[5]

conceptualizes conventional politics as the residual category for movements with only words, no deeds.

[4] "Navco," http://www.du.edu/korbel/sie/research/chenow_navco_data.html on: [2015/05/16].

[5] Divergent are Salehyan et al. (2011, 717), who assume that more fighters can compensate for a lack of weapons, wherefore moderately strong rebels are most likely to receive support. However, empirical studies show that third parties are more likely to intervene when rebels are stronger (Akcinaroglu and Radziszewski 2005, 357, 359).

The Supply of External Support

Different sources may generate support for rebels. Most obviously, one option is direct support in the form of funding, weapons, training and shelter from external governments. This kind of support was the most common form during the Cold War, when superpowers and neighboring countries supported their ideological friends (Kalyvas and Balcells 2010, 420). After the Cold War, governmental support persisted, albeit it was more constrained to neighboring states with ethnic, religious or ideological ties to rebel movements (Byman et al. 2001, xiv). Additionally, alternative channels have been activated. Nowadays, in many cases, rebels receive funding from diaspora communities, wealthy individuals or ethnic, religious and ideological organizations (cp. Collier and Hoeffler 2004; Byman et al. 2001). In other cases, rebels have access to natural resources like oil, diamonds or coca, which in turn can be transformed into concrete fighting material (cp. Humphreys 2005, 512; Lujala 2010). However, both alternative channels — whether non-state actors or natural resources — are less independent of external state support than one might think upon first consideration. After all, the provision of money, the selling of natural resources and its turning into weapons requires at least tacit support by external governments (cp. Malet 2009, 46). Although external governments may be hesitant to provide direct rebel support due to the fear of international condemnation, the tacit acceptance of such activities allows them to support rebels indirectly. Nonetheless, why would external states want to provide rebel support at all? Moreover, why should this support run along identity lines?

Some of the typically advanced reasons for why external states provide support to rebel groups in neighboring states can be ruled out quite easily. One reason — namely that states intervene in order to prevent regional instability — is implausible because if that was the main reason, external states should rather support the government side, given that support for the rebels only prolongs the fighting. Other reasons like the goal of exploiting opportunities for looting or distracting from vanishing domestic support are implausible because in these cases, external states should intervene directly rather than having rebels fighting for them. Finally, if external states wanted to weaken their rivals by supporting violent oppositional movements, they should support any movement, rather than simply the one with the same identity that they have. That said — and assuming that the external states in supporting the rebels follow the same goals like the rebels, namely that the rebels either acquire national power or receive territorial autonomy or secession — the question emerges concerning what additional value it has for a government if a group of the same ethnic, religious or ideological identity comes into power in a neighboring state. Put differently, why do external states want co-ethnic, co-religious or co-ideological groups in government elsewhere?

From a strategic-instrumentalist perspective, the argument for why external states support rebels along identity lines might look as follows. Let me try to recapitulate and extend the original argument (see Chapter 3 and Figure 3.1 on page 42): a government favors a certain ethnic, religious or ideological group domestically because it expects to receive support from this group to remain in government. To a certain extent, the government can decide which group to support (constrained by the leader's own identity), although the government is certainly constrained by the population share of the respective group, which cannot be changed in the short term. It may well be the case that a government would ideally like to have its supporting constituency a little larger than it currently is to have a larger support base. On the other hand, the respective group should not be too large, because otherwise the resources per person would diminish and the support would likely erode. However, the government can do little internally to change the group's size. By contrast, co-identity people in neighboring states represent an opportunity to extend the share of one's own support base and thus enhance the chances of staying in office. One such mechanism is via irredentism (forceful annexation). Alternatively, the supporting country might hope that the supported rebel group will come into power and secede or decide for (re-)unification (cp. Woodwell 2004, 201).[6]

Case study examples support the alleged mechanism. In the Bosnian conflict, Serbia and Croatia supported Serbs and Croats, respectively, with the goal of partitioning Bosnia and creating a "Greater Serbia" and a "Greater Croatia" (Hayden 1993, 2, 13). Similarly, Somalia supported Somalis in the Ogaden conflict in Ethiopia to achieve a secession of the Somali Ogaden region and a unification with Somalia, which would create a "Greater Somalia" (Carment and James 1995, 87f.). Finally, in the Moldovan conflict, Russia supported the Russian-speaking population in Transnistria so that Russia would maintain its access to the region and

---

[6]This mechanism should likewise hold for co-ethnic and co-religious rebels. It holds probably less so for rebels with the same ideology. As ideological groups are typically quite large, one would receive huge additional numbers, the consequences of which are probably not in the neighboring state's interest given an optimal support group of medium size.

the possibility of future annexation (Kaufman 1996, 132). Quantitative empirical evidence shows that while outright forceful annexation is rare nowadays (cp. Cederman et al. 2009, 403), rebellions often aim at secession — often successfully — and are generally characterized by a distinct identity. After all, there are about 50 independence movements per year, and out of 256 independence movements between 1931 and 2000, 101 were successful and 41 were violent (Coggins 2011, 438, 443).[7] Moreover, of the 256 independence movements, 141 differed in their language and 203 differed in their religion from the majority in the country, almost always representing groups at risk (cp. Coggins 2011, 440).

Last but not least, having co-ethnic, co-religious or co-ideological governments around might have a positive effect, even it does not amount to an increase of the favored population at home via unification. With ideological rightist transnational ties, there is an immediate gain, whereby governments with a rightist market ideology intend to increase their welfare via privatization, specialization and international free trade, thereby profiting from like-minded rightist governments in their region (cp. Etkes and Zimring 2014; Golub and Hsieh 2000). Similarly, governments with a leftist, socialist or communist stance often believe that the capitalist system can only be overcome if the class struggle extends to the global level and like-minded leftist governments are established.[8] Additionally, a more indirect effect applies for ethnic, religious and ideological ties: if a government helps co-ethnic, co-religious or co-ideological people to come into power, it can hope to acquire a position of regional leadership, which will possibly increase its own national resources and its reputation, thus prolonging the leader's time in office. Last but not least, co-identity ties to external governments reduce the possibility that foreign governments support a violent opposition within one's own country, thereby likewise contributing to the leader's primary goal of staying in office.

[7]During the 20th century, 150 new states entered the system, most of them — over 100 — after an internal conflict in the form of anticolonialism or secession (Coggins 2011, 437).

[8]In an extreme version, communism even aims at the abolishment of the state, thus having an innate international agenda. However, it is unlikely that a government seeks to abolish itself. Likewise with capitalism, if an extremely liberalist view is advocated, the role of the state becomes diminishingly small.

7.2. Hypotheses

When combining the demand side with the supply side of external support, the following typology emerges: in non-democracies, with unconditional demand for support and the supply of support via ethnic, religious or ideological lines, all three kinds of linkages should increase the risk of civil conflict onset, especially for high levels of exclusion. In democracies, with demand for support at most in small groups and the supply of support via ethnic, religious or ideological lines, all three linkages should increase the risk of conflict, albeit only for low levels of exclusion. By contrast, for high levels of exclusion, all three kinds of identity linkages should have no effect.

Hypothesis 3: In non-democracies, the first difference effect of transnational linkages on the risk of civil conflict onset is positive and increasing in the level of exclusion.

Hypothesis 4: In democracies, the first difference effect of transnational linkages on the risk of civil conflict onset is positive when exclusion is small and zero when exclusion is large.

Finally, consider that once we formulate expectations about interactions, symmetry is implied, which means that the predictions can in principle be turned around. Following Berry et al. (2012), if the theory allows one to make predictions about these reversed relationships, one should make and test them, given that this ultimately provides additional tests for the original theory. In the concrete case, one should thus formulate expectations about the marginal effect of exclusion for a different number of links. Following the above reasoning, one would expect the following:

Hypothesis 3a: In non-democracies, the first difference effect of exclusion on the risk of civil conflict onset is positive and increasing for all number of transnational links.

Hypothesis 4a: In democracies, the first difference effect of exclusion on the risk of civil conflict onset is negative for all number of transnational links.[9]

After having derived the hypotheses on transnational linkages and civil conflict onset, the subsequent chapter proceeds to the quantitative tests.

[9]This expectation is not as straightforward as it may seem upon first consideration. The first difference effect of exclusion on the risk of civil conflict very likely depends on the starting value of exclusion and the increase in exclusion.

Chapter 8.

Testing the Argument on Links and Conflict

This chapter introduces data and variables and presents the key empirical results on the relationship between transnational linkages and civil conflict onset.

8.1. Data and Variables

I have discussed the identity characteristics of the excluded population for each of the 57 countries between 1975 and 2005 in the first part. Here, I determine how many ethnic, religious or ideological links the excluded population in three dimensions (ERI_{all}) has to external governments in neighboring states.[1] In this book's conceptualization, neighboring states are all those states within 500 km distance (cp. Cederman et al. 2013). The number of ethnic ties are derived from Cederman et al. (2013), who list for each ethnic group in their dataset all the countries within 500 km reach in which the group also resides. I match these data on the ethnic groups' ties with the ethnic data underlying this book, namely Cederman et al. (2010) and the World Values Survey[2], and I disregard all cases with ties to marginal - rather than governmental — groups. In order to determine the religious and ideological ties of the excluded population to external governments within 500 km reach, I use the Database of Political Institutions (DPI). I simply count all the cases of neighboring states where a co-religious or co-ideological group is currently in government. The resulting three key variables for each country year are the sum of all ethnic links (*ethlinksl*), the sum of all religious links (*rellinksl*), the sum of all ethnic or religious links (*ethrellinksl*)[3] and the sum of all ideological links (*ideolinksl*) from

[1]While in the first part, the largest excluded subgroup played a key role, this entity is less interesting when focusing on external ties, as external support may even make smaller excluded subgroups relatively strong.

[2]The ethnic groups per country diverge between Cederman et al. (2010), Cederman et al. (2013), and the World Values Survey.

[3]This variable is created, as ethnic and religious links exert the same directional influence in the quantitative analyses, and can thus be pooled together to increase the number

the excluded population to neighboring governments. I also determine the sum of all potential links, which is simply the sum of all neighboring states within 500 km reach (*potlinksl*). This variable is an important control as the number of actual ties is clearly constrained by the number of potential ties. Finally, I generate a total count of all ethnic, religious and ideological links (*totlinksl*).[4] Descriptive statistics show that the number of potential links ranges from 1 to 30. The number of ethnic links only reaches a maximum of four links, the number of religious links a maximum of eight links, the number of ethnic/religious links a maximum of ten links and the number of ideological links a maximum of 28 links. These differences were to be expected as the number of all different ethnic groups in the dataset by far exceeds the number of all different religious groups, which exceeds the number of all different ideological groups (page 66); and the more different groups there are, the lower the chance for co-identity linkages.

I interact the variables on linkages with exclusion and condition the effect of linkages and exclusion on the type of the political regime. I distinguish between democracies and non-democracies according to the Polity IV dataset, whereby regimes with a Polity score equal to or above 6 are classified as democracies, while those with a Polity score below 6 are classified as non-democracies. Finally, I use the dependent variable civil conflict onset (*onset2*), as explicated in Part I (see page 73), and I control for all the variables that were introduced in Part I (see page 75), namely GDP per capita, population size, oil production per capita, mountainous terrain, fractionalization and peace years (with splines).

8.2. Empirical Results

I first regress the dependent variable civil conflict onset on the key independent variables on transnational linkages (ethnic, religious, ethnic/religious, ideological) and all the controls without including any interaction terms. As shown in Table 8.1, I include these variables separately (Model 1-4), jointly (Model 5-6), and I include the total sum of all links (Model 7).[5] The table

of observations for a high number of links.

[4]Here, it may happen that a link to an external government is counted twice or even more times, if the link exists for separate groups or dimensions; however, this seems to be reasonable. The implicit assumption is that the more ties there are between an external government and the excluded population, the more reasons an external government has to intervene.

[5]The results on the control variables are not displayed here due to space constraints, although they are shown in Appendix A.

reveals that ethnic, religious and ethnic/religious links significantly increase the risk of conflict onset (Model 1-3), even when controlling for ideological links (Model 5-6). Ideological links have no significant effect (Model 4), apart from one model (Model 5), where they significantly reduce the risk of conflict onset when ethnic and religious links are added. The countervailing influence of ethnic/religious versus ideological links results in the sum of all links being insignificant (Model 7). These results suggest that ethnic, religious and ideological links do not necessarily take the same directional influence, wherefore they should be analyzed separately, as the influence of their sum might appear null. When comparing Model 1 with purely ethnic links to Model 5, which additionally includes religious and ideological links, the Likelihood Ratio (LR) Test prefers the more fully specified model with linkages from all three dimensions, rather than one dimension. More precisely, the LR test statistic shows that religious and ideological links are jointly significant at the 0.5% level, thus pointing to the superiority of a more-dimensional model. Of the control variables, population size and oil systematically increase the risk of civil conflict onset — as expected — whereas GDP is surprisingly insignificant in half of the models. According to the heat map (HM) statistic, Model 6 (ethnic/religious and ideological links) seems to be the most appropriate model.[6] Other models are more problematic, although the HM statistic partly ameliorates once I include interaction terms.

In a next step, I thus examine how the effect of transnational linkages varies for different regime types (democracies, non-democracies) and different levels of exclusion (0 to 1). As shown in Table 8.2, I interact the different types of transnational links with democracy (*democl*) and the size of the excluded population (ERI_{all}), while controlling for the same variables as previously. Model 1-4 focus separately on ethnic, religious, ethnic/religious and ideological linkages and their interactions, while Model 5 looks at ethnic/religious links and their interactions when controlling for ideological links, and Model 6 looks at ideological links and their interactions when controlling for ethnic/religious links.[7] The HM statistic indicates that Model 2, 4 and 6 are problematic, while Model 1, 3 and 5 are fine.[8] Table 8.2

[6]HM statistic without interaction terms: Model 1: 40.16%, Model 2: 14.5%, Model 3: 14.6%, Model 4: 10.7%, Model 5: 38.7%, Model 6: 1.47%, Model 7: 26.1%.

[7]Note that including the interactions for all identity linkages jointly results in an unduly high HM statistic.

[8]The HM statistic is as follows: Model 1: 0.85%, Model 2: 22.56%, Model 3: 3.57%, Model 4: 39.61%, Model 5: 1.47%, Model 6: 25.43%. Overall, the HM statistic suggests that, when focusing on ideological linkages, a model without interactions

Table 8.1.: Transnational Links Without Interaction

	Dependent variable:						
	onset2						
	(1)	(2)	(3)	(4)	(5)	(6)	(7)
exclpopSCEl	0.484	0.590	0.448	0.819	0.683	0.847	0.606
	(0.748)	(0.707)	(0.750)	(0.737)	(0.892)	(0.839)	(0.725)
ethlinksl	0.535**				0.902***		
	(0.247)				(0.308)		
rellinksl		0.223**			0.392***		
		(0.110)			(0.141)		
ethrellinksl			0.334***			0.455***	
			(0.116)			(0.133)	
ideolinksl				−0.047	−0.188*	−0.151	
				(0.061)	(0.098)	(0.094)	
totlinksl							0.014
							(0.043)
Observations	1,290	1,290	1,290	1,290	1,290	1,290	1,290
Log Likelihood	-161.351	-162.710	-160.358	-163.829	-156.112	-158.020	-164.123
Akaike Inf. Crit.	352.702	355.419	350.716	357.657	346.223	348.040	358.245

Note: *p<0.1; **p<0.05; ***p<0.01
robust standard errors in parentheses

reveals that the variable on ethnic/religious links (*ethrellinksl*) exerts a statistically significant, positive influence on conflict onset in Model 5 and Model 6.[9]

Let us now look at substantial effects. Figure 8.1 to Figure 8.4 display the predicted probabilities of conflict onset for a differing number of transnational ethnic/religious and ideological linkages separately for non-democracies and democracies when exclusion is held constant at the third quartile (0.115). Figure 8.1 and Figure 8.2 clearly show that the predicted probability of conflict onset rises with an increase in *ethnic or religious* linkages, for non-democratic and democratic regimes alike. The change in predicted probability is significant when increasing linkages from 0 to 1 or beyond. However, as the figures show, the effect is much more pronounced for non-democracies compared with democracies. By contrast, Figures 8.3 and 8.4 reveal that the predicted probability of conflict onset falls with an increase in *ideological* linkages for either regime type, although the change is not statistically significant.

In order to test the hypotheses from the theoretical part (page 164), I focus on the first difference effect of transnational ties for varying values of exclusion (ERI_{all}) separately for non-democracies and democracies. I increase transnational ethnic, religious, ethnic/religious and ideological ties from 0 to 1, when holding the excluded population constant at different values between 0 and 1, and I do this separately for non-democracies and democracies. The key results are displayed in Figure 8.5 to Figure 8.10. Let us first discuss the findings for non-democracies. Figure 8.5 shows that, in non-democracies, an increase of ethnic links from 0 to 1 increases the risk of civil conflict onset for all levels of exclusion. This increase is significant for exclusion levels up to 0.3, and it gets insignificant for exclusion levels above 0.3 due to the scarcity of observations. Similar results hold true for the religious link variable, as Figure 8.6 reveals. When combining the ethnic and the religious link variable into one of ethnic/religious links, thus increasing the number of observations for high exclusion levels, Figure 8.7 shows that having one rather than no external ethnic/religious link significantly increases the risk of civil conflict onset for all levels of exclusion. The effect is quite substantial: for instance, with an exclusion level of 20%, having one rather than no transnational ethnic/religious link increases the risk of conflict onset from 11.7% to 21.5%, namely by almost 10 percentage points

should be preferred.

[9]Of the control variables, only population size and peace years significantly influence the risk of civil conflict onset in a systematic manner.

Table 8.2.: Logit Estimations: Effect of Transnational Links With Interaction on Conflict Onset

	Dependent variable:					
	onset2					
	(1)	(2)	(3)	(4)	(5)	(6)
ERI_{all}	1.291	1.376	0.870	3.074**	1.140	2.490*
	(1.000)	(0.964)	(1.118)	(1.402)	(1.124)	(1.462)
democl	0.438	0.652	0.984*	0.758	0.816	0.899
	(0.569)	(0.505)	(0.563)	(0.582)	(0.601)	(0.624)
ethlinksl	0.454					
	(0.399)					
rellinksl		0.199				
		(0.218)				
ethrellinksl			0.263		0.370*	0.447***
			(0.173)		(0.199)	(0.134)
ideolinksl				0.065	−0.125	−0.058
				(0.063)	(0.098)	(0.092)
ERI_{all}:ethlinksl	2.210					
	(2.774)					
democl:ethlinksl	−0.011					
	(0.459)					
ERI_{all}:rellinksl		1.494				
		(1.523)				
democl:rellinksl		−0.126				
		(0.259)				
ERI_{all}:ethrellinksl			2.172		1.966	
			(1.365)		(1.421)	
democl:ethrellinksl			−0.078		−0.080	
			(0.190)		(0.200)	
ERI_{all}:ideolinksl				−0.369		−0.186
				(0.310)		(0.367)
democl:ideolinksl				−0.169		−0.146
				(0.108)		(0.134)
ERI_{all}:democl	−6.035	−4.130*	−5.856	−4.830	−5.057	−5.498
	(3.698)	(2.472)	(3.653)	(3.151)	(3.332)	(3.572)
ERI_{all}:democl:ethlinksl	−1.058					
	(3.170)					
ERI_{all}:democl:rellinksl		−1.495				
		(1.657)				
ERI_{all}:democl:ethrellinksl			−1.445		−1.250	
			(1.542)		(1.621)	
ERI_{all}:democl:ideolinksl				0.402		0.349
				(0.414)		(0.461)
Observations	1,290	1,290	1,290	1,290	1,290	1,290
Log Likelihood	-158.970	-160.246	-156.721	-161.492	-155.221	-156.089
Akaike Inf. Crit.	355.941	358.491	351.442	360.985	350.442	352.178

Note: $^{*}p<0.1$; $^{**}p<0.05$; $^{***}p<0.01$
robust standard errors in parentheses

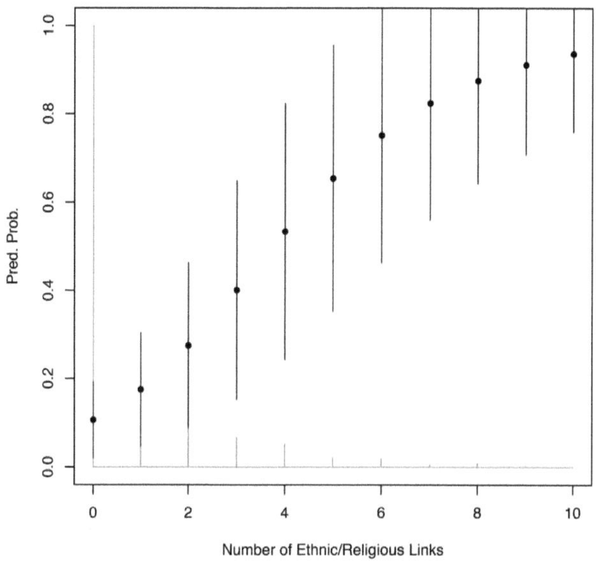

Figure 8.1.: *Predicted probability of armed conflict onset and 90% confidence interval for varying values of ethnic/religious links, when exclusion is held constant and non-democratic regimes are considered. (Relative frequencies of the values of the independent variable are displayed along the x-axis in gray.)*

(CI: [3.6; 18.1]). Moreover, Figure 8.7 shows that the effect is stronger for high levels of exclusion, pointing to an interaction effect between exclusion and ethnic/religious transnational links, in the sense that these two factors mutually reinforce each other. This is exactly what I expected in the theoretical section, where it was argued that it requires power both in the numbers, approximated by the size of the excluded population, and in fighting material — most likely supplied by external states — for an excluded group to pose a substantial threat to the government.[10] Hypothesis

[10] An alternative interpretation may be that there are many small excluded groups behind a high amount of exclusion, so that with an increasing number of small excluded groups, the likelihood that at least one of them will rebel increases.

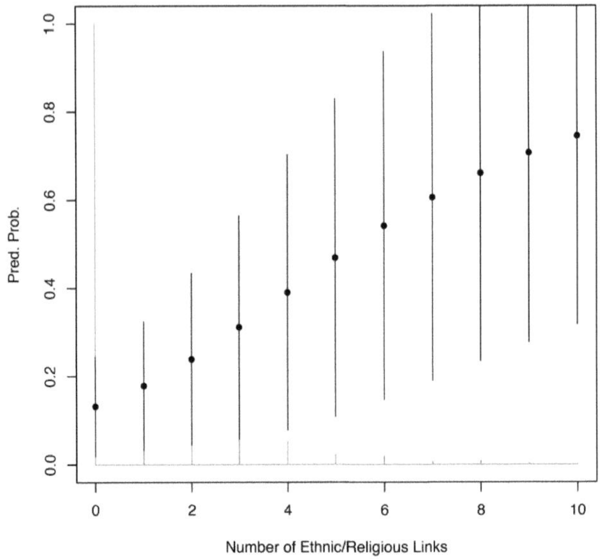

Figure 8.2.: *Predicted probability of armed conflict onset and 90% confidence interval for varying values of ethnic/religious links, when exclusion is held constant and democratic regimes are considered. (Relative frequencies of the values of the independent variable are displayed along the x-axis in gray.)*

3 is thereby confirmed, at least for ethnic and religious links.

As Figure 8.8 reveals, the positive effect of transnational ties on civil conflict onset in non-democracies does not hold when focusing on ideological rather than ethnic or religious links. An increase of ideological links from 0 to 1 does not change the risk of civil conflict onset — if at all, it seems to reduce the risk, but as the confidence intervals always include zero, this effect is not statistically significant. While the case studies on Ethiopia and Uganda pointed to the crucial role of ideological links in facilitating the conflicts, ideological links do not seem to increase the risk of civil conflict onset systematically; rather, their effect probably hinges on certain

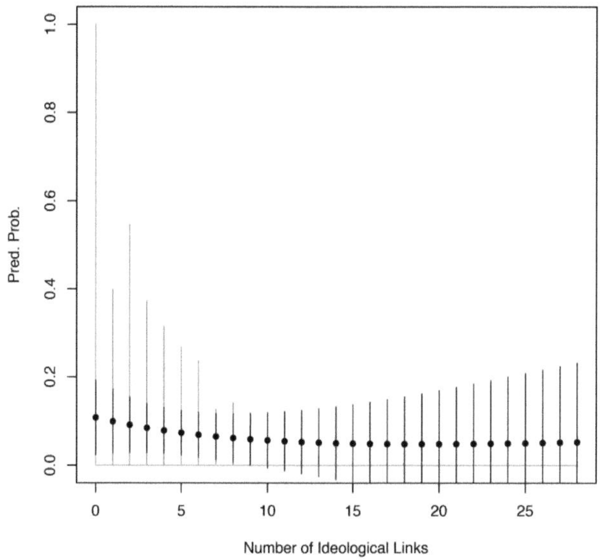

Figure 8.3.: *Predicted probability of armed conflict onset and 90% confidence interval for varying values of ideological links, when exclusion is held constant and non-democratic regimes are considered. (Relative frequencies of the values of the independent variable are displayed along the x-axis in gray.)*

additional conditions that have to be fulfilled.[11]

Next, let us shift to a consideration of democracies. In the theoretical section, I argued that in democracies, ethnic, religious and ideological links should — if at all — only increase the risk of conflict onset for low levels of exclusion, given the moderate prospects for small groups of getting into office via elections. By contrast, for high levels of exclusion, I expected that the respective transnational links should exert no effect given the good chances for large groups of getting into office via elections. Figure 8.9 clearly reveals that an increase in ethnic/religious links from 0 to 1 increases the risk

[11]Another reason for the non-finding might be that we try to predict all kinds of onsets — ethnic, religious and ideological ones — with ideological linkages.

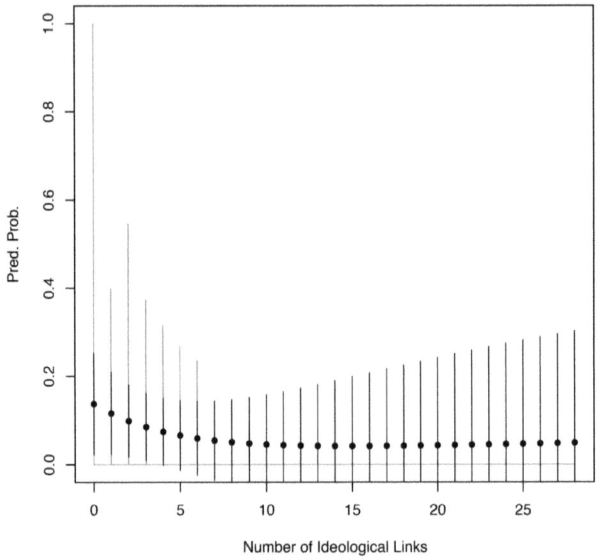

Figure 8.4.: *Predicted probability of armed conflict onset and 90% confidence interval for varying values of ideological links, when exclusion is held constant and democratic regimes are considered. (Relative frequencies of the values of the independent variable are displayed along the x-axis in gray.)*

of conflict onset in democracies, and that the effect is statistically significant for low levels of exclusion, thus fulfilling the expectation from Hypothesis 4. The effect is not as substantial as in the case of non-democracies: For an exclusion level of 20%, an increase of ethnic/religious links from 0 to 1 increases the risk of conflict onset from 10.7% to 14.9% by about four percentage points (CI: [0.5; 10.2]). Like in the case of non-democracies, the expected relationship does not hold, when focusing on ideological linkages. As Figure 8.10 reveals, an increase in ideological linkages from 0 to 1 exerts a negative, statistically insignificant influence on the risk of conflict onset, for low and high exclusion levels alike.

Finally, when including interaction terms, one can and should turn the

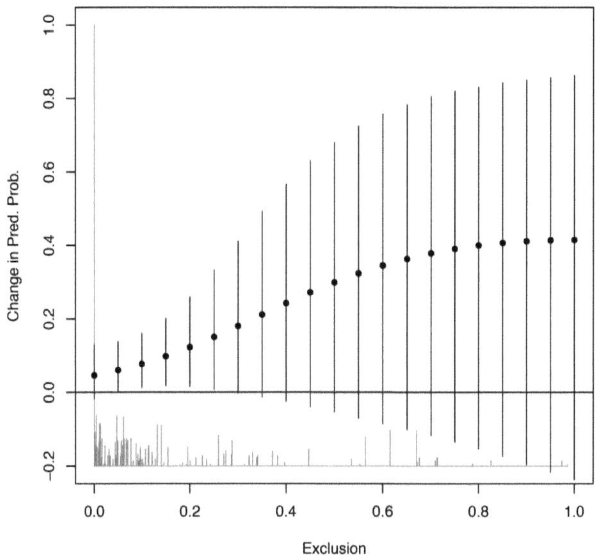

Figure 8.5.: *First difference analyses of the effect of ethnic links in non-democratic regimes for varying values of exclusion (ERI_{all}). The value of ethnic links is increased from 0 to 1, while exclusion is held constant at a certain value, and the effect on the change in predicted probabilities, including 90% confidence intervals, is displayed. (Relative frequencies of the values of the independent variable are displayed along the x-axis in gray.)*

predictions around, thus focusing in the present case on the first difference effect of exclusion when holding transnational links constant at different values, separately for non-democracies and democracies. The results are displayed in Figure 8.11 to Figure 8.14. When focusing on non-democracies and ethnic/religious links (Figure 8.11), an increase in exclusion from zero to the third quartile heightens the risk of civil conflict onset independent of the number of ethnic/religious links, whereby the effect becomes stronger for more links, thus confirming Hypothesis 3a. By contrast, for ideological links (Figure 8.12), the positive, statistically significant first difference effect

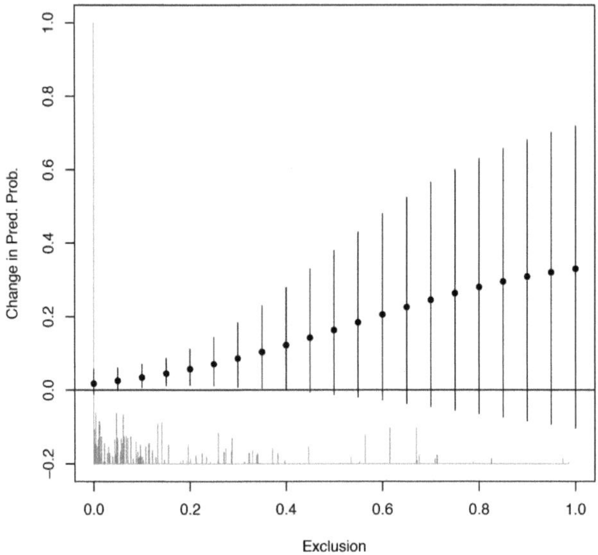

Figure 8.6.: *First difference analyses of the effect of religious links in non-democratic regimes for varying values of exclusion (ERI_{all}). The value of religious links is increased from 0 to 1, while exclusion is held constant at a certain value, and the effect on the change in predicted probabilities, including 90% confidence intervals, is displayed. (Relative frequencies of the values of the independent variable are displayed along the x-axis in gray.)*

of exclusion only holds for a low number of ideological links, thus standing only partly in line with Hypothesis 3a. When focusing on democracies (Figure 8.13, Figure 8.14), an increase in exclusion slightly reduces the risk of civil conflict onset for a low number of transnational links — whether ethnic/religious (Figure 8.13) or ideological (Figure 8.14) — and the effect vanishes for a higher number of ethnic/religious or ideological linkages, although this effect is never statistically significant. Thus, the latter finding provides no direct support for Hypothesis 4a, which expected a significant, negative first difference effect of exclusion for all number of linkages.

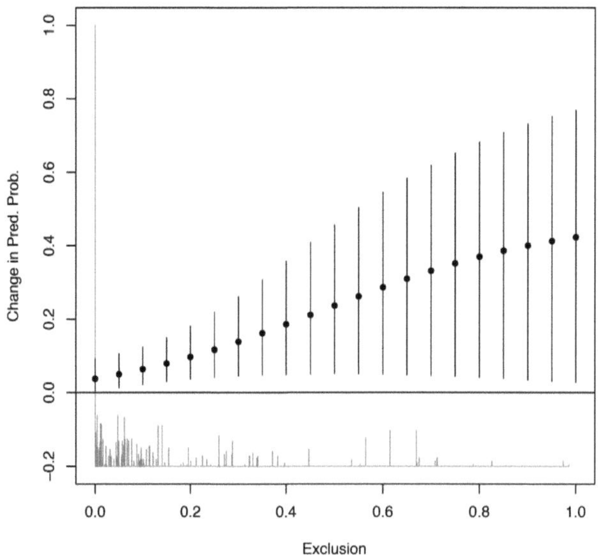

Figure 8.7.: *First difference analyses of the effect of ethnic/religious links in non-democratic regimes for varying values of exclusion (ERI_{all}). The value of ethnic/religious links is increased from 0 to 1, while exclusion is held constant at a certain value, and the effect on the change in predicted probabilities, including 90% confidence intervals, is displayed. (Relative frequencies of the values of the independent variable are displayed along the x-axis in gray.)*

When looking at the ROC curve/AUC statistic, we see that a model including the variable on ethnic/religious links and its interaction terms fits well with an AUC value of 0.84 compared to an AUC value of 0.82 for a zero model without the ethnic/religious components (see Figure 8.15). The AUC value for the ideological transnational model with interaction terms is 0.84 compared to an AUC value of 0.83 for a model without the ideological transnational components. The contribution of the transnational components is visually depicted in Figure 8.16 and Figure 8.17. Figure 8.16 shows that ethnic/religious links and their interaction terms make of all

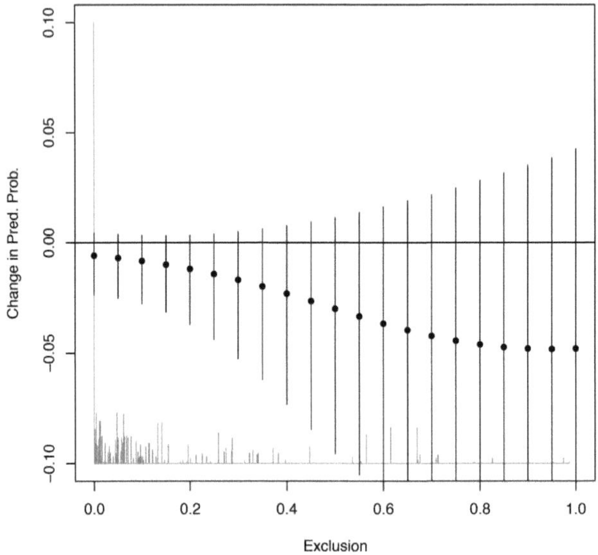

Figure 8.8.: *First difference analyses of the effect of ideological links in non-democratic regimes for varying values of exclusion (ERI_{all}). The value of ideological links is increased from 0 to 1, while exclusion is held constant at a certain value, and the effect on the change in predicted probabilities, including 90% confidence intervals, is displayed. (Relative frequencies of the values of the independent variable are displayed along the x-axis in gray.)*

independent variables the strongest contribution to the AUC, while Figure 8.17 shows that ideological links and their interaction terms make of all independent variables the third strongest contribution to the AUC, thereby pointing to the particular relevance of ethnic or religious transnational linkages.

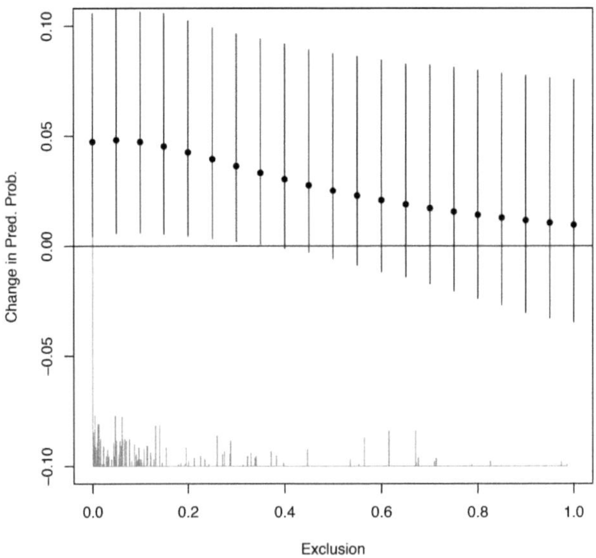

Figure 8.9.: *First difference analyses of the effect of ethnic/religious links in democratic regimes for varying values of exclusion (ERI_{all}). The value of ethnic/religious links is increased from 0 to 1, while exclusion is held constant at a certain value, and the effect on the change in predicted probabilities, including 90% confidence intervals, is displayed. (Relative frequencies of the values of the independent variable are displayed along the x-axis in gray.)*

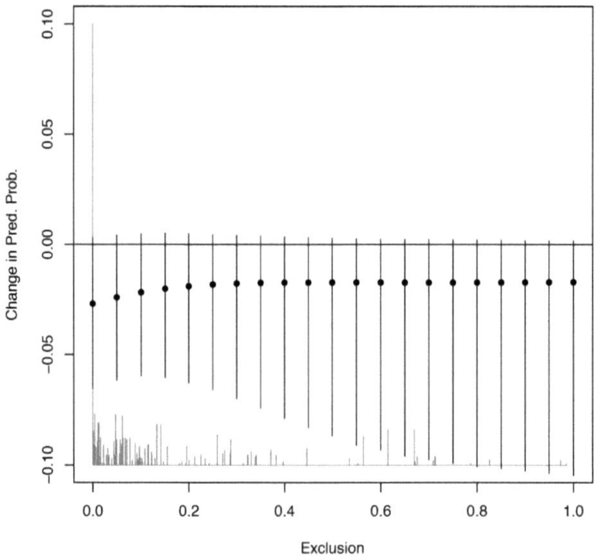

Figure 8.10.: *First difference analyses of the effect of ideological links in democratic regimes for varying values of exclusion (ERI_{all}). The value of ideological links is increased from 0 to 1, while exclusion is held constant at a certain value, and the effect on the change in predicted probabilities, including 90% confidence intervals, is displayed. (Relative frequencies of the values of the independent variable are displayed along the x-axis in gray.)*

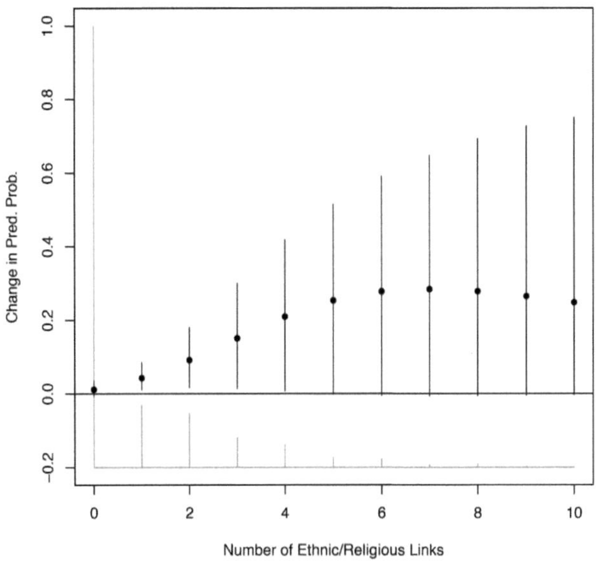

Figure 8.11.: *First difference analyses of the effect of exclusion in non-democratic regimes for varying values of ethnic/religious links. The value of exclusion is increased from zero to the third quartile (0.115), while the number of links is held constant at a certain value, and the effect on the change in predicted probabilities, including 90% confidence intervals, is displayed. (Relative frequencies of the values of the independent variable are displayed along the x-axis in gray.)*

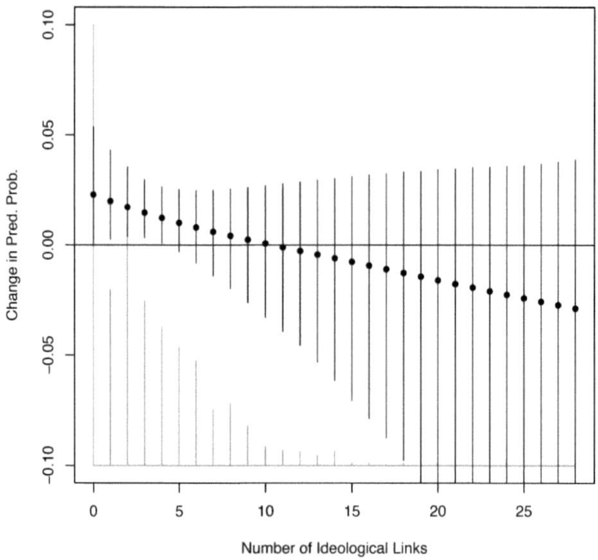

Figure 8.12.: *First difference analyses of the effect of exclusion in non-democratic regimes for varying values of ideological links. The value of exclusion is increased from zero to the third quartile (0.115), while the number of links is held constant at a certain value, and the effect on the change in predicted probabilities, including 90% confidence intervals, is displayed. (Relative frequencies of the values of the independent variable are displayed along the x-axis in gray.)*

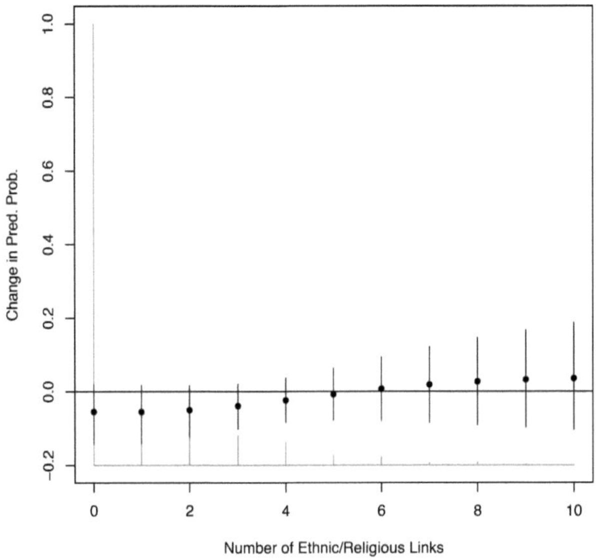

Figure 8.13.: *First difference analyses of the effect of exclusion in democratic regimes for varying values of ethnic/religious links. The value of exclusion is increased from zero to the third quartile (0.115), while the number of links is held constant at a certain value, and the effect on the change in predicted probabilities, including 90% confidence intervals, is displayed. (Relative frequencies of the values of the independent variable are displayed along the x-axis in gray.)*

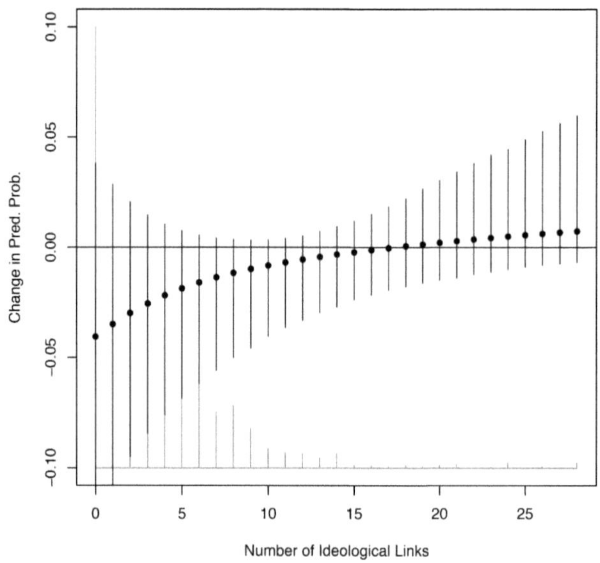

Figure 8.14.: *First difference analyses of the effect of exclusion in democratic regimes for varying values of ideological links. The value of exclusion is increased from zero to the third quartile (0.115), while the number of links is held constant at a certain value, and the effect on the change in predicted probabilities, including 90% confidence intervals, is displayed. (Relative frequencies of the values of the independent variable are displayed along the x-axis in gray.)*

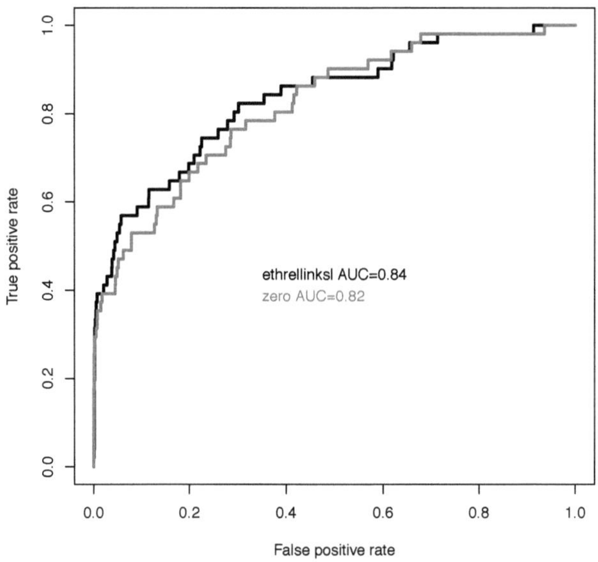

Figure 8.15.: *Receiver Operating Characteristic (ROC) curve. The ROC curve plots the true positive rate against the false positive rate at various discrimination thresholds, separately for a model that includes ethnic/religious links and the respective interaction terms, and for a zero model without these variables.*

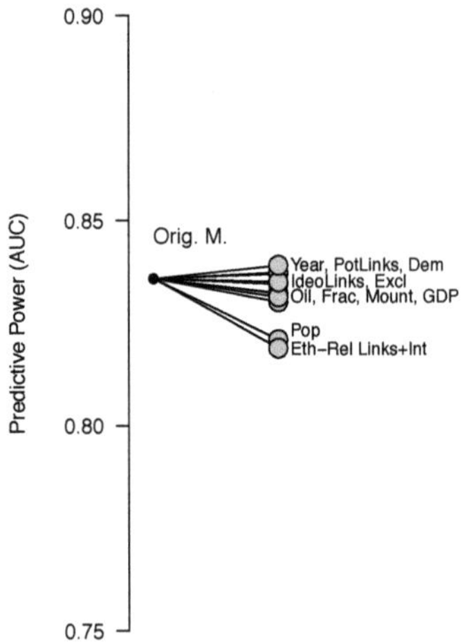

Figure 8.16.: *In-sample predictive power for a model that includes ethnic/religious links and their interaction with regime type and exclusion. The figure depicts the change in the AUC value, when single variables are deleted.*

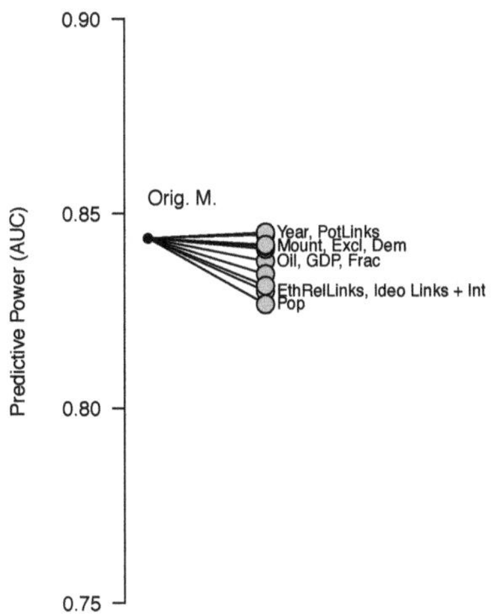

Figure 8.17.: *In-sample predictive power for a model that includes ideological links and their interaction with regime type and exclusion. The figure depicts the change in the AUC value, when single variables are deleted.*

Summary

The empirical findings on transnational linkages make an important contribution to the literature. Previous studies have found that the effect of transnational ethnic linkages is highly context-sensitive depending on the size of the ethnic group potentially challenging a government (Cederman et al. 2009), or even the size of the transnational ethnic kin group (Cederman et al. 2013). This book adds to this existing work by considering religious and ideological links in addition to ethnic links, as well as by differentiating between regime types. In doing so, the study establishes a conflict-increasing effect of ethnic/religious transnational links that — in non-democratic regimes — is independent of the size of the excluded population and independent of the size of the transnational group. The analysis also shows that a large size of the excluded population and transnational ethnic/religious linkages mutually reinforce each other, whereby the risk of conflict substantially increases when both factors are present. These findings confirm the theoretical expectations and can be used to better predict the onset of civil conflict. Surprisingly, ideological ties have no conflict-enhancing effect, either in non-democratic or democratic regimes. The case narratives in the previous section on Ethiopia and Uganda pointed to a different conclusion, suggesting that ideological ties do matter, albeit their effect probably depends on additional factors.

Chapter 9.

Conclusion

In concluding this book, this last chapter first relates the study's main insights to the very recent uprisings in the Middle East and North Africa. Unfortunately, there is not yet any systematic up-to-date data on the identity setup and the government's self-definition for most of these countries. Nevertheless, it is possible to acquire sufficient information on these countries from alternative sources, whereby it becomes possible to shed a light on these conflicts from this book's perspective and informally cross-check its findings. This endeavor yields informative insights, concerning the key sources giving rise to the violence in the context of the Arab Spring, as well as the merits and limitations of this book. Last but not least, I summarize my key results.

9.1. The Arab Spring — How Does It Relate?

The following sections review the recent cases from the Arab Spring in the Middle East/North Africa (MENA) region and discuss how these cases fit with the theory and empirics proposed in this book. The sections separately focus on patterns of political exclusion and patterns of transnational support along identity lines. I find that the theory and empirics of this book generally fit well, as in most cases *excluded religious and ideological groups* turned against their governments.[1] What these cases show and what is not accounted for in the theory thus far is that: first, even splits between non-Islamist and Islamist religious elements might give rise to tension and rebellion; and second, some factors — most notably huge governmental wealth — seem to moderate the extent to which excluded identity groups turn against their governments. Like exclusion and violence, transnational support in the recent Middle Eastern/North African cases generally runs along religious lines, with the quest for regional influence of Shia, non-

[1] Interestingly, ideological leftist groups tended to opt for peaceful means, while religious groups opted for violent means.

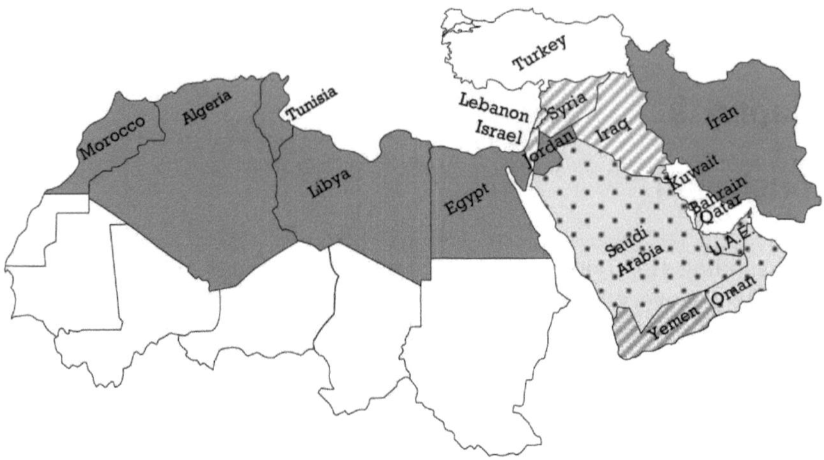

Figure 9.1.: *Map of the MENA region. Countries highlighted with stripes belong to one group of countries, which are clearly divided along religious lines and not oil-rich. Countries highlighted in gray belong to another group of countries, which are relatively homogeneous in ethnic and religious terms and not oil-rich, either. Countries highlighted with dots belong to a third group of countries, which are homogeneous or heterogeneous and oil-rich. Countries highlighted in white either belong to the MENA region, but are not discussed (North Africa), or they do not belong to the MENA region, but are discussed (Turkey).*

Islamist Sunni and Islamist Sunni forces being a major motivating factor for the third countries' provision of support.

National Exclusion and Support Patterns

Given the huge number of countries in the MENA region that were affected by the Arab Spring, it is helpful to divide these countries into three different groups according to their demographic composition and their individual wealth, as these two factors seem to have critically influenced the trajectory that the respective countries have taken in the past few years since the inception of the Arab Spring in 2010 (see Figure 9.1).

In the first group of countries — most prominently encompassing Iraq,

Syria, Lebanon, Yemen, Bahrain and Israel — the countries are clearly divided along religious lines, often between a majority Sunni population and a minority Shia population. The respective governments with their often long-term rulers do not use their governmental budget to appease all groups, but have rather opted to support one or the other group according to their own denomination. These countries already experienced political violence by the excluded groups before the Arab Spring, although the Arab Spring often worked as an extra catalyst, turning these conflicts into some of the most deadly internal uprisings since the 1950s (Themnér and Wallensteen 2012, 2013, 2014). In Iraq, a Shiite majority, which had long been politically excluded under long-term ruler Saddam Hussein, came to power in 2003 and in the first couple of years tended to systematically exclude the once-privileged Sunni minority.[2] Two subsequent rebel groups emerged, both of which addressed the excluded Sunni population.[3] The first group was Al-Quaeda in Iraq (AQI), which was displaced in 2006 by the second group, the much more efficient Islamic State in Iraq (ISIS). In 2014, ISIS succeeded in capturing large parts of Northern Iraq, even stretching its wings to Syria and aggravating the present conflict there.

In Syria, the Alawite minority (which is a Shiite branch) has long been favored under long-term ruler Assad in opposition to a huge excluded Sunni majority. With the Arab Spring, a Sunni rebellion revived with much greater rigor than before, setting moderate Sunni elements like the Free Syrian Army (FSA) and more radical Sunni Islamist forces in the form of al-Nusra or — recently — ISIS, which has spread from Iraq to Syria, against the Alawite government. Currently, some people fear that the conflict might further spread to Lebanon, a country that is divided into three major religious groups: Christians, Sunnis and Shiites (also Alawites). Although Lebanon has always sought to integrate all three groups into its government, changing demographics have left Sunnis and Shiites unsatisfied with their relative share of political power, giving rise to a protracted civil war from 1975 until 1990. The current influx of Sunni people from Syria might similarly offset the power-balance and give rise to a new violent uprising. The Syrian conflict might also revive the violent ethnic conflict between

[2]Ali Khederi, "Iraq's Last Chance," *The New York Times*, August 15, 2014, `http://www.nytimes.com/2014/08/17/opinion/sunday/iraqs-last-chance.html` on: [2014/11/25].

[3]Neil Patrick, "Analysis: Saudi Arabia faces complex regional challenges," *BBC News Middle East*, October 15, 2014, `http://www.bbc.co.uk/news/world-middle-east-29628653` on: [2014/11/25]; Khederi, "Iraq's Last Chance."

Turks and Kurds in Turkey, as Turkey currently hesitates to support Kurds in Syria against ISIS, thereby undermining — from the Kurds' perspective — the recent peace initiative.[4]

As yet another example, Yemen is characterized by a Sunni majority and a Shia minority. Until 1990, it had been divided into capitalist Northern Yemen and communist Southern Yemen, whereby the Shia majority tended to dominate the North and the Sunni minority the South. Upon re-unification, both groups were represented in government, although they felt that their share of political power was significantly reduced compared to the previous situation. Thus, Shia elements mobilized in the form of the Houthi rebellion, while Islamist Sunni elements mobilized — most prominently under the heading of Al-Qaeda in the Arabian Peninsula (AQAP) — to demand a larger or exclusive share of the national pie. In September 2014, Houthi rebels even succeeded in capturing the capital, thus establishing a fourth Shiite regime in the region, along with Iraq, Syria and Iran.[5] Similarly, Bahrain experienced civil unrest in the context of the Arab Spring and before, largely setting the rebelling Shia majority against the minority Sunni rulers. Last but not least, in Israel, Jewish Israelis have excluded Sunni Palestinians from political power since the inception of the Israeli state. For decades, Sunni Palestinians have protested and fought for independence through both moderate and radical movements. Overall, these examples show that there are numerous instances of political exclusion and violent mobilization along religious lines in the Middle Eastern region, with the largest excluded religious group becoming the primary challengers. These cases perfectly correspond to the theoretical expectations advanced in this book.

[4]Mustafa Akyol, "Turkey's New Kurdish Problem," *The New York Times*, October 22, 2014, `http://www.nytimes.com/2014/10/23/opinion/mustafa-akyol-turkeys-new-kurdish-problem.html` on: [2014/11/27]; Soner Cagaptay, "After Erdogan, Turkey's Future Will Be Liberal," *The New York Times*, August 14, 2014, `http://www.nytimes.com/2014/08/15/opinion/after-erdogan-turkeys-future-will-be-liberal.html` on: [2014/11/27]; "Turkey won't change position on joining anti-ISIL coalition unless its conditions are met: President," *Hurriyet Daily News*, November 19, 2014, `http://www.hurriyetdailynews.com/.aspx?pageID=238&nID=74527&NewsCatID=338` on: [2014/11/27].

[5]Bruce Riedel, "Houthi Victories in Yemen Make Saudi Arabia Nervous," *Al Monitor*, October 15, 2014, `http://www.al-monitor.com/pulse/originals/2014/10/houthi-yemen-victory-saudi-arabia-nightmare-iran.html` on: [2014/11/27]; "Houthis Take Over,", *The Economist*, September 27th, 2014, `http://www.economist.com/news/middle-east-and-africa/21620284-are-they-ansar-houthis-take-over` on: [2014/11/28].

The second group of countries — most prominently encompassing Tunisia, Libya, Egypt, Jordan, Morocco and Algeria — is characterized by a rather homogeneous composition in ethnic and religious terms, generally comprising a huge majority of Sunni Arabs. However, given their moderate availability of financial resources, the long-term authoritarian leaders of these countries have not appeased the entire population, but rather opted for the privileging of a narrow elite. Their strong Western alignments — most prominently to the United States — gave them international backing, although these states alienated huge parts of the population over the years: on the one hand large unemployed, young masses of people with a leftist stance; and on the other hand Sunni Islamist groups, who were dissatisfied with the secular pro-Western orientation of their governments. During the Arab Spring, which started at the end of 2010, Leftists and Islamists began to protest, partly peacefully (Egypt, Tunisia, Jordan, Morocco), and partly violently (Libya). Indeed, in three of the countries (Tunisia, Libya, Egypt), they succeeded in deposing their long-term rulers, namely Ben Ali in the case of Tunisia, Gaddafi in Libya, and Mubarak in Egypt. With the successful revolutions, Islamist elements in a first round tended to dominate the newly formed governments, such as in Tunisia (Enhada), as well as Libya (General National Congress, GNC) and Egypt (Muslim Brotherhoods under Morsi), or were integrated into the existing system, such as in Jordan and Morocco. However, different forces led to a weakening of the Islamist forces during the last three years. The population itself was dissatisfied with the policies of the Islamic governments and feared that Islamic governments would derail their freedom and liberties in a similar way like the previous authoritarian governments did. Moreover, the weakening of the Islamic movements was evident due to the strong anti-Islamist attitudes in the global arena, both in the Western communities and in some oil-rich countries of the Middle East (Saudi Arabia, United Arab Emirates). Thus, in Libya, Islamist forces in the GNC were sidelined in new elections in 2014. In Egypt, a military coup toppled the Islamist government under Morsi and brought General el-Sisi to power, who was confirmed in a rigged election in 2014.[6] Last but not least, in the October 2014 elections in Tunisia, the non-Islamist group Nidaa Tounis (with links to the former elite) won most of the seats, thereby sidelining Islamist forces. With the explicit exclusion of Islamists, Islamist elements have retreated and resorted to more violent tactics. Thus, in both

[6]The Editorial Board, "Reining in Egypt's Military Aid," *The New York Times*, October 4, 2014, `http://www.nytimes.com/2014/10/05/opinion/sunday/reining-in-egypts-military-aid.html?_r=0` on: [2014/11/28].

Libya and Egypt, Islamists are currently fighting the government: in Libya, in the form of the Shura Council of Benghazi Revolutionaries; and in Egypt, in the form of the Ansar Beit al-Maqdis movement. In Tunisia, the Islamist reaction remains to be awaited.[7]

Finally, Algeria seems to be an exception upon first consideration. While Algeria likewise experienced protests and demonstrations in the context of the Arab Spring, the uprisings have not led to a disposal of the government nor to major violent actions. However, Algeria is a special case, as it already underwent a similar trajectory to many current Middle Eastern/North African states twenty years ago. Back then, Algeria saw an opening of the political system following large-scale protests, leading to multi-party elections, which yielded Islamists as the winners. However, the military annulled the elections and sidelined the Islamists, which led to a long-lasting and brutal civil conflict between the government and Islamist forces in the form of the FIS. The conflict ended in 2002 with an amnesty for most of the rebels, while a radical Islamist splinter group has remained active. Thus, Algeria already experienced a similar development to current Egypt twenty years ago.

To sum up, in all of these countries in the MENA region — which are homogeneous in ethnic and religious terms but favored a narrow Western-oriented elite amidst economic dire conditions — leftist and radical religious elements felt excluded and challenged the governments. Facing huge masses of protesters beyond identity lines, many leaders felt threatened and the opposition sometimes achieved its short-term goal of government disposal with peaceful means. Once the conflicts polarized and a struggle over power between non-Islamist and Islamist forces ensued — to the disadvantage of the latter in the recent Arab spring — the conflicts haven often turned violent. Thus, while the logic of politically excluded identity groups challenging the government also applies to the second group of countries, it is remarkable that leftist elements thus far have used only peaceful means, and that a split between Islamist and non-Islamist forces — thus far not accounted for in the theory — was decisive.

A third group of countries — most prominently encompassing Saudi Arabia, Kuwait, the United Arab Emirates, Qatar and Oman — is characterized by enormous wealth due to huge stocks of oil. Each of these countries has a

[7]David D. Kirkpatrick, "Militant Group in Egypt Vows Loyalty to ISIS," *The New York Times*, November 10, 2014, `http://www.nytimes.com/2014/11/11/world/middleeast/egyptian-militant-group-pledges-loyalty-to-isis.html?mabReward=RI%3A14` on: [2014/11/28].

large heterogeneous proportion of foreign workers among its inhabitants, often encompassing half the population or more. Indigenously, however, only Saudi Arabia and Kuwait are internally divided in ethnic or religious terms, whereas the United Arab Emirates, Qatar and Oman are ethnically and religiously homogeneous. In Saudi Arabia, the majoritarian Sunni population (80%) discriminates against the Shia minority (20%)[8], and in Kuwait, although both Sunni (65%) and Shia (35%) elements are included in power, the ethnic group of Bedouns (estim. 120,000) is politically excluded. By contrast, the United Arab Emirates, Qatar and Oman almost completely comprise Sunni or Ibadhi Arabs, whereby these groups are completely included in power and generously financed through the distribution of money and social benefits. Immigrants are generally treated much worse than the indigenous population. However, due to their status as foreigners and their heterogeneous composition, there is not a high chance of them seriously protesting and challenging the governments.

In the more heterogeneous Saudi Arabia and Kuwait, the excluded group of Shiites in Eastern Saudi Arabia and the group of Bedouns in Kuwait have resorted to extended protests and attacks during the Arab Spring, which could not easily be contained. However, in neither of the two cases has the excluded population seriously challenged the government to a similar extent like in Iraq, Syria or Yemen.[9] Moreover, in Saudi Arabia, Kuwait, the United Arab Emirates and Oman, Leftists and Islamists went to the streets (or intended to do so), although the protests could either be nipped in the bud (UAE), appeased with money (Saudi Arabia, Oman) or acquiesced through partial political concessions (Kuwait).[10] Thus, these protests have

---

[8] "Violence erupts in Saudi Arabia after verdict," *Deutsche Welle*, October 21, 2014, `http://www.dw.de/violence-erupts-in-saudi-arabia-after-verdict/a-18009148` on: [2014/11/28].

[9] "The sword unsheated," *The Economist*, October 18, 2014, `http://www.economist.com/news/middle-east-and-africa/21625868-protests-break-out-after-shia-cleric-sentenced-death-sword-unsheathed` on: [2014/11/28].

[10] Guido Steinberg, "Leading the Counter-Revolution," *SWP*, June, 2014, `www.swp-berlin.org/fileadmin/contents/products/research_papers/2014_RP07_sbg.pdf` on: [2014/11/28]; Forstenlechner et al. 2012; Worrall 2012; Debasish Mitra, "A captivating saga of reforms and amazing transformation in Oman," *Times of Oman*, July 22, 2014, `http://www.timesofoman.com/News/37021/Article-A-captivating-saga-of-reforms-and-amazing-transformation-in-Oman` on: [2014/11/28]; Sara Hamdan, "Oman Offers Some Lessons to a Region Embroiled in Protest," *The New York Times*, April 6, 2011, `http://www.nytimes.com/2011/04/07/world/middleeast/07iht-m07-oman.html?ref=world` on: [2014/11/28]. Qatar even saw concessions, in the form of elections, despite the absence of protests, see Shadi Hamid, "There Aren't Protests in Qatar—So Why

never taken a similar form like in Egypt or Libya, and they were never a serious threat to the governments in place. Nonetheless, it seems that Saudi Arabia and the United Arab Emirates feel threatened by Islamist forces, having led them in recent months to designate Islamist groups as terrorists.[11] Other countries — especially Qatar — have engaged in more cordial relationship with Islamists, even incorporating them into the government.[12] Thus, while the Arab oil countries saw similar opposition movements like the other MENA countries during the Arab Spring, the uprisings took a much more limited scale.[13] The likely reason lies in the Arab oil countries being much more wealthy than the other countries[14], a factor that has not been highlighted as a central theme in this book's theory thus far. However, it is to be expected that once the oil wells run dry, these countries will likely see more pronounced and violent uprisings, probably even severely threatening their rulers in place. The recent fall of the oil

Did The Emir Just Announce Elections?," *The Atlantic*, November 1, 2011, http://www.theatlantic.com/international/archive/2011/11/there-arent-protests-in-qatar-so-why-did-the-emir-just-announce-elections/247661/ on: [2014/11/28].

[11] "Islamist group rejects UAE terrorism designation," *Reuters*, November 17, 2014, http://www.reuters.com/article/2014/11/17/us-qatar-emirates-qaradawi-idUSKCN0J10RX20141117 on: [2014/11/28]; Stéphane Lacroix, "Saudi Arabia's Muslim Brotherhood predicament", *The Washington Post*, March 20, 2014, http://www.washingtonpost.com/blogs/monkey-cage/wp/2014/03/20/saudi-arabias-muslim-brotherhood-predicament/ on: [2014/11/28]; The Editorial Board, "Reining In Egypt's Military Aid". The question emerges whether this is a diversionary tactic — mere window-dressing — to appease their Western backers.

[12] Bernard Haykel, "Qatar and Islamism," Norwegian Peacebuilding Research Center, February 2013, www.peacebuilding.no/var/ezflow_site/storage/original/application/ac81941df1be874ccbda35e747218abf.pdf on: [2014/11/28].

[13] Oman seems to be exceptional in certain respects. While it also experienced protests in the context of the Arab Spring — mainly over missing jobs and low payments — the authority of its very popular long-term ruler, Sultan Qaboos, has never been questioned. The Sultan strongly differs in its foreign policy from the other oil-rich states. He exerts a consequent foreign policy of non-alignment and peaceful co-existence and is internationally accepted as a wise and impartial broker. Worrall 2012; Debasish Mitra, "A captivating saga of reforms and amazing transformation in Oman"; Sara Hamdan, "Oman Offers Some Lessons to a Region Embroiled in Protest."

[14] Angela Shah, "Why the Arab Spring Never Came to the U.A.E.," *Time*, July 18, 2011, http://content.time.com/time/world/article/0,8599,2083768,00.html on: [2014/11/28]; Colin Freeman, "Qatar 'playing with fire' as it funds Syrian Islamists in quest for global influence," *The Telegraph*, April 27, 2013, http://www.telegraph.co.uk/news/worldnews/middleeast/qatar/10022759/Qatar-playing-with-fire-as-it-funds-Syrian-Islamists-in-quest-for-global-influence.html on: [2014/11/28].

price might work in the same direction.

Last but not least, let me briefly discuss Iran, which first seems to be a special case but upon further consideration its most prominent uprising — the Iranian revolution in 1979 — resembles countries like Egypt in 2010 and beyond. In 1979, Shiite Islamists and Leftists successfully stood up against the Iranian monarchy and its close ties to the United States, with the result of deposing Shah Reeza Palahvi. Islamist and Leftist forces came into power, whereby Islamists and their head Grand Ayatollah Khomeini had the greatest say in the government sidelining and overriding Leftist forces. Thus, an Islamic autocracy was established and has been maintained against a Leftist uprising (MEK) for over 35 years.[15] In the 1980s, Islamist Iran hoped to encourage similar Sunni or Shia Islamist uprisings in other countries in the Muslim world against their monarchic Western-oriented rulers, primarily targeting Saudi Arabia, which was seen as un-Islamic despite its officially Islamic orientation, as well as Iraq, which had a majority of Shiites like Iran.[16] However, the Iranian model found little direct emulation among its neighbors in the next thirty years. Nonetheless, countries like Saudi Arabia and the United Arab Emirates did fear internal uprisings following the Iranian revolution, first by Shiite forces and later — from the 1990s onwards — also by Sunni Islamist forces. Consequently, the Saudi government first portrayed Shiites and later Sunni Islamists as a national threat, probably to unite the rest of the population behind the Saudi government. Thus, the Iranian revolution severely worsened the relationship between Iran and Saudi Arabia in particular, as well as between Sunni and Shia groups more generally giving rise to a rivalry that has lasted until today.

Overall, this brief review clearly demonstrates that political exclusion and the resulting violent uprisings in the MENA region have most prominently run along religious lines in the last few years. The political exclusion of class-based ideological groups has also played a role, although this kind of exclusion has led to violent uprisings with much less frequency. As the following section shows, the patterns of transnational support strongly resonate with the patterns of political exclusion.

[15] At some times, Iran has taken a more radical stance (under Khomeini, Khamenei, Achmadinejad), at other times a more moderate stance (under Rafsanjani, Khatami, Rohani).

[16] Already in 1980, neighboring Iraq responded to the Iranian revolutionary threat with an invasion of Iran, although this only brought Iranian Islamists closer together.

Transnational Support Patterns

Generally, one can observe that transnational support for rebel groups has been quite frequent in the context of the Arab Spring. Moreover, like the exclusion patterns themselves, transnational support in recent years has mainly tended to run along religious lines. The background for this tendency is a major and enduring struggle over the regional hegemony of Sunni versus Shia groups in the Middle East, as well as another, more recent struggle between different Sunni forces. On the one hand, Shiite Iran and Syria have been the major supporters of Shiite rebels, and whether newly Shiite Iraq and Yemen are going to follow that lead remains to be seen in the coming years. On the other hand, the oil-rich Sunni Arab countries emerge as a very potent force for outside rebel support of Sunni groups. However, these countries are currently split between anti- and pro-Islamist forces, with Saudi Arabia and the United Arab Emirates very recently taking a strong anti-Islamist stance, and Qatar, Kuwait and Turkey a pro-Islamist stance.[17] That said, let us have a look at actual support patterns, before disentangling the different kinds of Islamism and their international ties, which explain, why transnational support has taken one or the other form.

In the Syrian conflict, the Alawite (Shiite) regime — as expected — currently receives support from Shiite Iran, Hezbollah and Iraq, whereas the Sunni rebel groups receive support from an alliance of Sunni Muslim countries, most notably Saudi Arabia, Qatar and Turkey.[18] The Sunni elements, however, are split over the question of who is the most desirable Syrian rebel group to support: moderate FSA (Saudi Arabia) or Islamist

[17]Robert Mendick, "Al-Qaeda terror financier worked for Qatari government,", *The Telegraph*, October 12, 2014, http://www.telegraph.co.uk/news/11156327/Al-Qaeda-terror-financier-worked-for-Qatari-government.html on: [2014/11/28]; Bernard Haykel, "Qatar and Islamism."

[18]Rod Nordland, "Iraq May Turn to Iran for Help, Maliki Aide Says," *The New York Times*, June 13, 2014, http://www.nytimes.com/2014/06/14/world/middleeast/iraq-may-turn-to-iran-for-help-maliki-aide-says.html on: [2014/11/29]; Michael S. Schmidt, "Iraqi Leader Backs Syria, With a Nudge From Iran," *The New York Times*, August 12, 2011, http://www.nytimes.com/2011/08/13/world/middleeast/13iraq.html on: [2014/11/29]; Joby Warrick, "Iraq, siding with Iran, sends 'lifeline to Assad'," *The Washington Post*, October 8, 2011, http://www.washingtonpost.com/world/national-security/iraq-siding-with-iran-sends-lifeline-to-assad/2011/10/06/gIQAFEAIWL_story.html on: [2014/11/29]; Bryan Bender, "US shouldering brunt of ISIS air campaign," *The Boston Globe*, November 10, 2014, https://www.bostonglobe.com/news/nation/2014/11/09/despite-growing-coalition-against-islamic-state-shouldering-most-air-campaign/WYj1UiefBpL7OsxMu1xCXL/story.html on: [2014/11/29].

al-Nusra (Qatar, Turkey).[19] The recent strong rise of ISIS additionally poses the question of who is behind this third group. Given the current harsh international condemnation of ISIS, each state — even Qatar — denies its support for this group, and while ISIS might indeed be self-sustaining at present, without any doubt private financiers from Saudi Arabia and Qatar with the tacit backing of their governments have contributed to ISIS's rise at the beginning and up to 2013.[20] In Lebanon, the Christian government has been supported by Israel, the United States and France in the past, while the Shiite group received support from Shiite Syria and allegedly Iran and the Sunni factions were backed by Sunni Libya and Iraq. Similarly, in Yemen, the opposing Shiite group of Houthis was supported by Shiite Iran, while the Sunni government was supported by its Sunni allies from the Gulf Cooperation Council, and the Islamist Sunni opposition group AQAP by Sunni Qatar.[21] Comparable support patterns can be found in Bahrain.

---

[19] Miriam Karouny, "Saudi edges Qatar to control Syrian rebel support," *Reuters*, May 31, 2013, `http://www.reuters.com/article/2013/05/31/us-syria-crisis-saudi-insight-idUSBRE94U0ZV20130531` on: [2014/11/29]; David D. Kirkpatrick, "Qatar's Support of Extremists Alienates Allies Near and Far," *The New York Times*, September 7, 2014; `http://www.nytimes.com/2014/09/08/world/middleeast/qatars-support-of-extremists-alienates-allies-near-and-far.html` on: [2014/11/29]; David Andrew Weinberg, "Saudi Arabia, Qatar may be playing dangerous game over Syria rebels", *CNN*, October 25, 2013, `http://globalpublicsquare.blogs.cnn.com/2013/10/25/saudi-arabia-qatar-may-be-playing-dangerous-game-over-syria-rebels/` on: [2014/11/29].

[20] "Emir tells Merkel Qatar does not fund ISIL," *Aljazeera*, September 17, 2014, `http://www.aljazeera.com/news/middleeast/2014/09/emir-tells-merkel-qatar-does-not-fund-isil-201491717515759557.html` on: [2014/11/29]; "The United States' biggest 'allies' are funding ISIL," *PressTV*, August 8, 2014, `http://www.presstv.com/detail/2014/08/08/374537/americas-biggest-allies-funding-isis/` on: [2014/11/29]; Eric Lichtblau/Eric Schmitt, "Cash Flow to Terrorists Evades U.S. Efforts," *The New York Times*, December 10, 2010, `http://www.nytimes.com/2010/12/06/world/middleeast/06wikileaks-financing.html` on: [2014/11/29]; Patrick Cockburn, "Islamic State: 'US failure to look into Saudi role in 9/11 has helped Isis'," *The Independent*, September 14, 2014, `http://www.independent.co.uk/news/world/politics/islamic-state-us-failure-to-look-into-saudi-role-in-911-has-helped-isis-9731563.html` on: [2014/11/29]; Nawaf Obaid/Saud Al-Sarhan, "The Saudis Can Crush ISIS," *The New York Times*, September 8, 2014, `http://www.nytimes.com/2014/09/09/opinion/the-saudis-can-crush-isis.html?_r=0` on: [2014/11/30]; similarly see the report by J'org Armbruster in the Christuskirche, Stuttgart, on: [2014/11/24].

[21] David D. Kirkpatrick, "Qatar's Support of Extremists Alienates Allies Near and Far;" Alessandria Marsi, "Yemen Crisis: Yemeni Islah Party Leader Mansour al-Haidary Assassinated In Car Bombing," *International Business Times*, November 18, 2014, `http://www.ibtimes.com/yemen-crisis-yemeni-islah-party-leader-`

While the opposing Shiite group allegedly receives support from Shiite Iran, the Sunni minority government is backed by its Sunni allies from the Gulf Cooperation Council.[22] Likewise, in Saudi Arabia, the separatist Shiite elements in the Eastern province are currently allegedly seeking contacts to Iran.[23] Finally, in Israel, the Jewish government counts the United States as its most important ally, whereas the Sunni Palestinian opposition in its more moderate form — Fatah/PLO — has received support from Sunni Iraq, Egypt and the Arab League, while its radical wing — Hamas — has long been supported by Syria and Iran. While Hamas, Syria and Iran were united in their common goal of eradicating Israel, they differed in their religious orientation, being Sunni in the case of Hamas and Shiite in the case of Syria and Iran. Unsurprisingly, Hamas has recently opted to shift its financier to Sunni Qatar and Turkey.[24] Finally, in Libya, Qatar has taken a pivotal role in toppling the regime by Gaddafi, steadily seeking to support Islamist Sunni rather than moderate Sunni elements. Meanwhile, a proxy war has developed, with Qatar still supporting radical Islamist Sunni groups and the United Arab Emirates, Saudi Arabia and Egypt supporting moderate, secular Sunni forces.[25] Similarly, in Egypt, Qatar and Turkey supported Islamist Morsi, whereas Saudi Arabia and the United Arab Emirates have welcomed the toppling of Morsi through non-Islamist el-Sisi.[26]

---

mansour-al-haidary-assassinated-car-bombing-1725655 on: [2014/11/30].

[22] Shabnam Nourian, "Iran's support for Bahrain protesters fuels regional tensions," *Deutsche Welle*, April 15, 2011, http://www.dw.de/irans-support-for-bahrain-protesters-fuels-regional-tensions/a-6504403-1 on: [2014/11/30]; "No satisfaction," *The Economist*, February 1, 2014, http://www.economist.com/news/middle-east-and-africa/21595480-despite-their-immense-wealth-saudis-are-not-happy-no-satisfaction on: [2014/11/30].

[23] "Violence erupts in Saudi Arabia after verdict," *Deutsche Welle*, October 21, 2014, http://www.dw.de/violence-erupts-in-saudi-arabia-after-verdict/a-18009148 on: [2014/11/30].

[24] Bernard Haykel, "Qatar and Islamism;" Colin Freeman, "Qatar 'playing with fire' as it funds Syrian Islamists in quest for global influence."

[25] Lisa Watanabe, "Qatar and the UAE in a Changing Middle East," *ISN ETH Zurich*, November 3, 2014, http://www.isn.ethz.ch/Digital-Library/Articles/Detail/?id=184991 on: [2014/11/30]; Dirk Vanewalle, "Saving Libya, Again," *The New York Times*, November 11, 2014, http://www.nytimes.com/2014/11/12/opinion/saving-libya-again.html on: [2014/11/30]; Suliman Ali Zway/David D. Kirkpatrick, "General Escalates Libya Attack," October 15, 2014, http://www.nytimes.com/2014/10/16/world/middleeast/general-escalates-libya-attack-.html on: [2014/11/30].

[26] Bernard Haykel, "Qatar and Islamism."; Laurent Bonnefoy, "Yemen's new player," *Le Monde diplomatique*, November 10, 2014, http://mondediplo.com/2014/11/10yemen on: [2014/11/30]. Note that Morsi's first visit did go to Saudi Arerabia, but in the end, Saudi Arabia was happy not to have him as an

To summarize, Shiite Iran has emerged as the key supporter for Shiite Islamist movements, Sunni Saudi Arabia and some of its Gulf allies have backed secular Sunni movements, and Sunni Qatar and Turkey have become the key backers of so-called Islamist Sunni movements, whether in the form of the peaceful Muslim Brotherhood or the violent Al-Qaeda-affiliated movements. This book can well account for the Shia-Sunni divide, whereby two major powers — Iran and Saudi Arabia, as well as their respective allies — are fighting out a struggle over regional leadership. Each state fears that the other one might undermine its own domestic power via the support of oppositional groups, thus prompting the countries to take preemptive action. The Sunni-Sunni split is less straightforward and becomes all the more puzzling once we recognize that governments that are officially themselves conservative Sunni Islamist, most prominently Saudi Arabia (but also the UAE), have *refrained* from supporting Sunni Islamist groups, whereas governments that are not officially Sunni Islamist but instead belong to the most liberal and open political systems in the Middle East — most prominently Qatar and Turkey — *did* support Sunni Islamist groups. This puzzle can only be solved if we drop the typically Western oversimplification of lumping together all Sunni Islamist movements under one banner of Sunni Islamism. Instead, it is advisable to distinguish between the different kinds of Sunni Islamism that exist in the Muslim world, which helps us understand why transnational support in the MENA region looks the way that it does. Let us revisit the three most important Sunni Islamist strands in turn to make sense of the puzzling support patterns.

Among the three most important Sunni Islamist strands lies political Islamism, missionary Islamism and jihadi Islamism (ICG 2005).[27] While all three kinds of Islamism hold that Islam should guide political life, major differences arise about the movements' exclusiveness and degree of radicalism. First, political Islamism advocates democratic politics and tries to gain access to political power via constitutional, peaceful means, favorably

---

Egyptian leader, see David D. Kirkpatrick, "In Simply Meeting, Egyptian and Saudi Leaders Open New Era," *The New York Times*, July 12, 2012, `http://www.nytimes.com/2012/07/13/world/middleeast/in-simply-meeting-egyptian-and-saudi-leaders-open-new-era.html?_r=1&ref=world` on: [2014/11/30].

[27] In the labeling of Sunni Islamist strands, I follow the International Crisis Group (2005); see ICG, "Understanding Islamism," March 2, 2005, `http://www.crisisgroup.org/en/regions/middle-east-north-africa/north-africa/037-understanding-islamism.aspx` on: [2014/11/30]. My own suggestion is to call them liberal Islamism, conservative Islamism and neo-conservative Islamism.

through electoral and party politics, generally in accommodation with other non-Islamist parties and with Western powers. The most prominent proponent of political Islamism is the Muslim Brotherhood, which primarily arose in Egypt but also exists in several countries in the MENA region. In Turkey, an officially secular country, the Muslim Brotherhood affiliate — the Justice and Development Party (AKP) under Erdogan — already came to power about twenty years ago and strongly dominates politics until today. The second strand — missionary Islamism — rejects elections and party politics and is characterized by its conservative, exclusive and strongly anti-Shiite character. Its most prominent representative can be found in Saudi Arabia, where the Saud family entered into a close alliance with the indigenous religious Wahabi clergy, a puritanical, ultra-conservative Sunni strand.[28] In contradiction to its original orientation, missionary Islamist Saudi Arabia maintains an extremely close relationship to Western countries, most prominently the United States. Third, and finally, jihadi Islamists strongly reject accommodation with non-Islamists and Westerners and conclude that political change can only be achieved through violent means against Western-oriented establishments. This strand became most prominent through Al-Qaeda and its affiliated movements, which turned against non-Islamist or missionary Islamist governments in the region and beyond, like in Afghanistan during the Cold War, in Saudi Arabia proper following the Iraqi invasion of Kuwait, in the United States (09/11), and many more Middle Eastern countries since 2001.

Against this background, it becomes easier to understand why the support patterns have materialized in their current form. Given its own Islamist orientation, Saudi Arabia had strongly supported Sunni Islamist groups of any kind abroad until the 1990s, like the Muslim Brotherhood in Egypt and Al-Qaeda in Afghanistan, with the goal of containing pan-Arabism, Nasserism, the Soviet Union and leftist movements in general.[29] However, Saudi Arabia's strong pro-US stance — which culminated in the stationing of US troops on Saudi soil during the Iraqi invasion of Kuwait in 1990 — alienated jihadi Islamist forces within the Saudi population who saw this move as irreconcilable with the Saudi Islamist orientation. Thus, a rift

[28]Sunni Wahabis in Saudi Arabia make up about 20 percent of the Saudi population, other Sunnis about 60 percent, and Shiites about 20 percent.

[29]Saudi Arabia even became the home for many Egyptian supporters of the Muslim Brotherhood, who were often used as teachers in Saudi Arabia, and some of the most prominent Al-Qaeda figures, most prominently Osama Bin Laden, emerged from Saudi Arabia proper.

emerged mainly between missionary elements in the Saud family and jihadi forces like Al-Qaeda. Al-Qaeda consequently turned against the royal Saud family, even trying to topple it in the years following 1990. Since then, Saudi Arabia has become wary about the support of jihadi Sunni Islamist forces abroad. The recent rise of political Islamist groups in the context of the Arab Spring has additionally made it wary about the own political Islamist opposition, even leading it to label the Muslim Brothers as terrorists in 2014. Thus, the internal 'threatening' political and jihadi Islamist opposition in Saudi Arabia explains why Saudi Arabia during the Arab Spring opted for the support of secular, conservative Sunni forces rather than the support of political or jihadi Islamist movements.

In contrast to Saudi Arabia, neighboring minuscule but extremely wealthy Qatar — which is also strongly influenced by the conservative Wahabi Sunni strand (about 50% of the population are Wahabi) — has taken a much more liberal and outward-looking interpretation of Islamism, which ultimately much more closely resembles the case of Turkey. Qatar has accommodated the Muslim Brothers, collaborates with Al-Qaeda and thus far has seen no forceful attack on its own government by Islamist forces, despite its extremely strong Western alignments. Similarly, despite its relatively open political character and its strong orientation towards the West, Turkey has seen no serious jihadi Islamist opposition. For both Qatar and Turkey, the Arab Spring presented a great opportunity to gain regional influence and take the lead in what they perceived to be an Islamist rise. Thus, Qatar and Turkey did not hesitate to support jihadi alongside political Islamist groups because they thought that once these groups came into power, they would be able to influence and accommodate them. Meanwhile, however, given the generally strong anti-Islamist orientation in Western countries and the recent setback of Islamist forces in the MENA region generally, the odds is against Islamist support, with countries like Qatar, Kuwait and Turkey facing major pressure and opposition to cut their support for the respective groups.[30]

Summary

Overall, this brief sketch shows that political exclusion and transnational support in the MENA region during the Arab Spring and beyond tends

[30] "Egypt pull out of Qatar's world event," *Aljazeera*, November 12, 204, `http://www.aljazeera.com/sport/olympicsports/2014/11/egypt-pull-out-qatar-swimming-event-201411121712912432.html` on: [2014/11/30].

to run along clearly defined *religious* lines of identity, thereby supporting this book's allegation that exclusion and support patterns typically run along clearly defined identity cleavages. While political exclusion along class-based *ideological* lines has also played a role in some of these conflicts — having brought huge masses of people to the streets — ideological exclusion seems to have rarely if ever led to major violent uprisings in the form of civil conflicts. While the reason for the peacefulness of ideological groups has to be assessed in detail elsewhere, this book plausibly suggests that a major factor is the absence of co-ideological groups in neighboring governments that could have provided key transnational backing. Instead, diverging religious orientations within the different governments of the region have given rise to transnational support patterns along religious lines. While this book can well account for the Shia-Sunni split, it has greater difficulty in explaining the Sunni-Sunni split, although this becomes explainable once different Islamist Sunni strands are taken into account. In any case, given the strong international condemnation of Islamist support, the Sunni-Sunni divide will probably not last too long and it is unlikely to have any major international repercussions. Finally, concerning the incentive for the respective exclusion and support patterns, the brief overview suggests that political elites in Iran, Saudi Arabia, Qatar, Turkey and elsewhere are motivated by a primary interest of staying in office. Favoritism of certain religious groups at home and abroad secures their staying in office: a goal that resonates well with the theoretical mechanisms proposed in this book.

9.2. Exclusion and Support in Three Dimensions

This book is interested in the prediction of civil conflict onset based upon patterns of political exclusion and transnational support along identity lines. Through the numerous case study examples, this book shows that political exclusion and transnational support typically run along three lines of identity: ethnicity, religion and class-based ideology. Previous studies have found that ethnic exclusion and ethnic transnational linkages can increase the risk of conflict onset, although they have neglected the two additional dimensions religion and class-based ideology.

Recognizing that it is necessary to consider ethnicity, religion and class-based ideology as the three key dimensions of political contestation, the question arises concerning what follows from this allegation for the empirical analyses. Clearly, not all three dimensions are politically *salient* in every country at every time point: governments do not necessarily define themselves with respect to all three dimensions, nor do all three cleavages necessarily divide the excluded population, making any collaboration beyond identity lines impossible. On the other hand, it is clear that the governments and the rebel groups in their self-definition often refer to more than one dimension at a time, while the kinds of politically salient dimensions within a country can and do change over time. However, there seems to be no systematic pattern that allows us to constrain our view in certain countries or time periods to only one or two dimensions ex ante.[31] Thus, this book argues that it is necessary to assume that all three identity dimensions are *latent* in all countries all the time.[32]

What does a latent demographic setup in three dimensions look like? Crucially, it is not sufficient to consider the three dimensions of ethnicity, religion and class-based ideology — including the respective groups per dimensions and their relative shares — separately or in parallel. The reason is that the three dimensions strongly overlap, whereby each individual is part of exactly one ethnic, one religious and one ideological group. Thus, if a government defines itself in more than one dimension, exclusion patterns cannot be deduced from the marginal distributions over the categories per dimension. Instead, it is crucial to know the country-specific *three-dimensional identity setup* (the population distribution over the three-dimensional subgroups): a quantity that this book develops and operationalizes for the first time, to the best of my knowledge.

In order to determine the three-dimensional identity setup, this book uses survey data. Surveys often ask questions about an individual's ethnicity, religion and ideology, and individuals generally choose their own denomination from a set of pre-specified options of the relevant groups in

[31] Note that deducing the relevant dimensions from the ones that actually became salient through the government's and the rebels' self-definition, introduces an endogeneity problem.

[32] Note that in a very recent study, Potter (2014) has taken a different approach, which already reduces the multidimensionality of the identity setup in the first step, when determining the latent identity setup, by sorting individuals into groups based upon their similarity in attributes. More precisely, Potter uses "a Bayesian generative — or Latent Dirichlet Allocation [LDA] — model [... which] can reduce (potentially) large permutations of demographic attributes into the subset of permutations that comes closest to an error-free approximation of latent group structure" (Potter 2014, 4,22). As Potter considers six dimensions, the combinatorics quickly become too comprehensive, whereby Potter is forced to reduce the combinations ex ante. While this approach is certainly appealing, it is by no means clear that each empirically observed self-definition of political entrepreneurs can actually be accounted for in the latent setup. By considering all three dimensions as latent dimensions, this book circumvents this problem.

the country. With a representative sample, it is subsequently possible to deduce the population distribution over the respective three-dimensional subgroups. In the present case, I use the World Values Survey to extract the respective data, as this is currently the best source available to my knowledge. However, the WVS in particular and survey data in general are associated with certain weaknesses; for instance, data is only available for a non-random sample of countries, the categories per identity dimension are chosen ex ante by researchers, and additional or new data collection attempts are time-consuming, cost-intensive and often fall short of being perfect in terms of representativity. Thus, it might be worthwhile for future endeavors to seek alternative sources to obtain information about the population distribution across identity categories.

With the three-dimensional identity setup derived for each country, I subsequently develop theoretical expectations about the most likely challenger and its size. I assume that the government's self-definition is exogenously given and that it can be used as an indicator for who is favored by the respective government and who is not. Valuable clues for this favoritism provide the identity of the directly included members within the government, as well as the self-definition of the government in general. For the ethnic identity of a government, I use data from Wimmer et al. (2009) on cabinet compositions, whereas for the religious and ideological identity of a government, I resort to the Database of Political Institutions (DPI), which lists the parties and factions included in a government, as well as their religious and ideological orientation. With the latent three-dimensional identity setup and the government's self-definition set, it is then possible to deduce two key quantities of interest: the size of the excluded population and the size of the largest excluded three-dimensional subgroup. These two quantities of interest are subsequently used to predict the onset of civil conflict in logistic regression models.

In the quantitative analyses, the size of the largest excluded three-dimensional subgroup emerges as a potent predictor for the onset of civil conflict in non-competitive regimes. This variable has not only a significant but also a substantial influence, in the sense that an increase of the size of the largest excluded three-dimensional subgroup from zero to its third quartile significantly increases the risk of civil conflict onset from 4.1% to 5.3%. Moreover, this variable is robust to alternative model specifications, which use a different regime type variable (Polity IV), a different dependent variable on conflict onset, or which drop influential observations. Last but not least, this variable makes an important contribution to the AUC statistic, already ranked in second place after GDP. Moreover, the three-dimensional variable generally fares better than the one- or two-dimensional variables.[33]

Although the size of the largest excluded three-dimensional subgroup is a potent predictor, it lacks a theoretical underpinning in its informal derivation. While a focus on the *largest* subgroup can be justified based upon the argument that "power is in the numbers", the focus on *three-dimensional* subgroups is more difficult to justify. This focus namely presupposes that all three identity lines of ethnicity, religion and ideology are completely dividing. In practice, however, not all cleavages are necessarily salient all the time, meaning that cooperation may in fact occur beyond identity lines. In order to account for this fact, I model the underlying mechanism of political competition more formally and derive a quantity of interest that is ultimately highly correlated with the variable on the largest excluded three-dimensional subgroup. The high correlation implies that the formally derived variable does not perform better in the quantitative analysis than the informal variable, although it at least provides a thorough underpinning for the largest excluded three-dimensional subgroup as an important predictor.

Up to this point, I assume that the relative strength of a rebel group completely emerges from the number of its supporters. However, it is well known that rebels need weapons to effectively counter the overwhelming force of the government, while external states often help rebel groups to fill this need. Thus, man power and military power should be seen as complementary and mutually reinforcing, rather than substitutive. Interestingly, external support often runs along the same three identity lines as political exclusion with external governments very often supporting their co-ethnic, co-religious or co-ideological excluded brethren elsewhere. Thus, this book uses the number of ethnic, religious and ideological ties from the excluded population to external governments as an exogenous proxy for anticipated support. This anticipated support is subsequently expected to increase the risk of civil conflict onset in non-democratic regimes, where excluded groups cannot hope to be represented via constitutional means any time soon, as well as in democratic regimes, when the excluded population is too small to seriously challenge the government in the next election. The empirical analyses confirms most of these expectations: ethnic and religious ties significantly and substantially increase the risk of civil conflict onset in non-democratic regimes independent of the amount of exclusion and have a conflict-increasing effect in democratic regimes for low levels of exclusion.

[33]However, it fared not substantially better than an ethnic-ideological exclusion variable due to religious exclusion being relatively rare in my data.

Surprisingly, ideological linkages have no conflict-enhancing effect in non-democratic or democratic regimes, probably, because other conditions have to be present for ideological links to display the expected effect.

To conclude, this book determines the amount of political exclusion and transnational support as the two key factors assumed to critically influence the onset of civil conflict, not only based upon ethnic demographic characteristics, ethnic favoritism and ethnic linkages (as previous studies have done), but it also considers two additional dimensions, namely religion and class-based ideology. This broadening of the perspective to three dimensions turns the focus to the three-dimensional identity setup of a society, as well as favoritism and transnational linkages in three dimensions. Additionally, this book crucially distinguishes between different regime types — namely non-competitive or non-democratic regimes on the one hand and competitive or democratic regimes on the other — and posits that the effect of political exclusion and transnational support should differ in the two kinds of regimes. Ultimately, this book shows that a consideration of all three dimensions yields two important insights: first, a three-dimensional exclusion variable emerges as a potent predictor for the onset of civil conflict in non-competitive regimes, outperforming the one- or two-dimensional exclusion variables; and second, the sum of ethnic and religious transnational linkages are a significant predictor for civil conflict onset in non-democratic regimes, independent of the level of political exclusion.

Appendix A.

All Models with Control Variables Displayed

Table A.1.: Logit Estimations: Effect of Excluded Population Without Interaction on Conflict Onset

	Dependent variable:							
	onset1							
	(1)	(2)	(3)	(4)	(5)	(6)	(7)	(8)
gdpcapl	−0.202***	−0.218***	−0.187***	−0.185***	−0.208***	−0.203***	−0.189***	−0.188***
	(0.062)	(0.070)	(0.061)	(0.055)	(0.063)	(0.062)	(0.052)	(0.059)
lpopl	0.053	0.082	0.051	0.047	0.058	0.052	0.043	0.051
	(0.169)	(0.169)	(0.170)	(0.171)	(0.170)	(0.169)	(0.171)	(0.167)
oilpcl	0.198**	0.201**	0.180*	0.180*	0.192**	0.198**	0.189*	0.179*
	(0.099)	(0.099)	(0.100)	(0.100)	(0.097)	(0.099)	(0.100)	(0.105)
lmtnest	0.227	0.202	0.213	0.228	0.220	0.227	0.228	0.203
	(0.154)	(0.142)	(0.150)	(0.156)	(0.150)	(0.154)	(0.156)	(0.148)
fracl	1.954	1.124	2.160	2.096	1.798	1.983	2.119	1.989
	(2.066)	(2.072)	(2.072)	(2.035)	(2.064)	(2.055)	(2.033)	(2.020)
noncl	−0.489	−0.545	−0.485	−0.533	−0.470	−0.489	−0.536	−0.513
	(0.502)	(0.510)	(0.509)	(0.510)	(0.510)	(0.502)	(0.511)	(0.501)
ERI_{all}	0.789							
	(1.079)							
E_{all}		1.555						
		(1.048)						
R_{all}			–					
			–					
I_{all}				−0.893				
				(0.638)				
ER_{all}					0.791			
					(1.252)			
EI_{all}						0.751		
						(1.088)		
RI_{all}							−0.923	
							(0.618)	
W_{all}								0.570
								(0.910)
peaceyrs	0.005	0.041	−0.007	−0.006	−0.003	0.004	−0.010	0.010
	(0.267)	(0.282)	(0.263)	(0.264)	(0.264)	(0.267)	(0.267)	(0.270)
spline1	0.002	0.003	0.002	0.002	0.002	0.002	0.002	0.002
	(0.008)	(0.008)	(0.008)	(0.008)	(0.008)	(0.008)	(0.008)	(0.008)
spline2	−0.001	−0.001	−0.001	−0.001	−0.001	−0.001	−0.001	−0.001
	(0.002)	(0.002)	(0.002)	(0.002)	(0.002)	(0.002)	(0.002)	(0.002)
spline3	0.0003	0.0003	0.0003	0.0004	0.0003	0.0003	0.0004	0.0003
	(0.0004)	(0.0004)	(0.0004)	(0.0004)	(0.0004)	(0.0004)	(0.0004)	(0.0004)
year	−0.002	−0.006	−0.003	−0.004	−0.003	−0.002	−0.004	−0.004
	(0.028)	(0.028)	(0.027)	(0.027)	(0.028)	(0.028)	(0.027)	(0.028)
Constant	−1.863	6.159	0.938	3.740	1.111	−1.742	3.640	3.702
	(56.575)	(55.626)	(54.423)	(53.340)	(55.253)	(56.563)	(53.557)	(55.454)
Observations	1,247	1,247	1,247	1,247	1,247	1,247	1,247	1,247
Log Likelihood	-111.077	-110.225	-111.001	-110.484	-111.071	-111.093	-110.413	-111.084
Akaike Inf. Crit.	248.154	246.450	248.002	246.969	248.142	248.187	246.825	248.167
Note:								*p<0.1; **p<0.05; ***p<0.01 robust standard errors in parentheses

Table A.2.: Logit Estimations: Effect of Largest Excluded Subgroup Without Interaction on Conflict Onset

	Dependent variable:							
	onset1							
	(1)	(2)	(3)	(4)	(5)	(6)	(7)	(8)
gdpcapl	−0.201***	−0.206***	−0.187***	−0.190***	−0.199***	−0.199***	−0.191***	−0.198***
	(0.061)	(0.065)	(0.061)	(0.057)	(0.059)	(0.061)	(0.055)	(0.059)
lpopl	0.056	0.079	0.051	0.052	0.052	0.051	0.051	0.042
	(0.168)	(0.168)	(0.170)	(0.171)	(0.168)	(0.168)	(0.169)	(0.168)
oilpcl	0.195*	0.195**	0.180*	0.187*	0.189*	0.191*	0.192*	0.189*
	(0.100)	(0.099)	(0.100)	(0.099)	(0.098)	(0.100)	(0.099)	(0.102)
lmtnest	0.225	0.182	0.213	0.222	0.209	0.224	0.232	0.226
	(0.153)	(0.137)	(0.150)	(0.155)	(0.145)	(0.155)	(0.153)	(0.146)
fracl	2.093	1.217	2.160	2.020	2.018	2.144	1.914	2.367
	(2.002)	(2.044)	(2.072)	(2.111)	(2.045)	(2.015)	(2.163)	(2.063)
noncl	−0.500	−0.557	−0.485	−0.514	−0.475	−0.492	−0.515	−0.483
	(0.493)	(0.511)	(0.509)	(0.510)	(0.514)	(0.499)	(0.509)	(0.509)
ERI_{max}	1.704							
	(2.625)							
E_{max}		1.674						
		(1.274)						
R_{max}								
I_{max}				−0.747				
				(0.796)				
ER_{max}					0.828			
					(2.488)			
EI_{max}						0.648		
						(1.687)		
RI_{max}							−0.896	
							(1.094)	
W_{max}								−0.261
								(1.123)
peaceyrs	0.009	0.052	−0.007	−0.011	−0.002	0.005	−0.013	−0.010
	(0.270)	(0.289)	(0.263)	(0.265)	(0.263)	(0.270)	(0.268)	(0.264)
spline1	0.002	0.003	0.002	0.002	0.002	0.002	0.002	0.002
	(0.008)	(0.008)	(0.008)	(0.008)	(0.008)	(0.008)	(0.008)	(0.008)
spline2	−0.001	−0.001	−0.001	−0.001	−0.001	−0.001	−0.001	−0.001
	(0.002)	(0.002)	(0.002)	(0.002)	(0.002)	(0.002)	(0.002)	(0.002)
spline3	0.0003	0.0003	0.0003	0.0004	0.0003	0.0003	0.0003	0.0003
	(0.0004)	(0.0004)	(0.0004)	(0.0004)	(0.0004)	(0.0004)	(0.0004)	(0.0004)
year	−0.003	−0.006	−0.003	−0.004	−0.004	−0.002	−0.004	−0.003
	(0.028)	(0.028)	(0.027)	(0.027)	(0.027)	(0.028)	(0.027)	(0.028)
Constant	0.205	7.223	0.938	3.063	2.137	−0.228	3.138	0.302
	(55.043)	(55.417)	(54.423)	(53.941)	(54.044)	(55.792)	(54.130)	(55.126)
Observations	1,247	1,247	1,247	1,247	1,247	1,247	1,247	1,247
Log Likelihood	-111.087	-110.364	-111.001	-110.854	-111.197	-111.185	-110.929	-111.226
Akaike Inf. Crit.	248.174	246.728	248.002	247.707	248.394	248.371	247.857	248.453

Note: *p<0.1; **p<0.05; ***p<0.01
robust standard errors in parentheses

Table A.3.: Logit Estimations: Effect of Excluded Population With Interaction on Conflict Onset

	Dependent variable:							
	onset1							
	(1)	(2)	(3)	(4)	(5)	(6)	(7)	(8)
gdpcapl	−0.197***	−0.207***	−0.187***	−0.183***	−0.208***	−0.197***	−0.187***	−0.190***
	(0.059)	(0.063)	(0.061)	(0.055)	(0.063)	(0.059)	(0.052)	(0.055)
lpopl	0.045	0.081	0.051	0.051	0.058	0.045	0.045	0.042
	(0.171)	(0.171)	(0.170)	(0.171)	(0.172)	(0.171)	(0.171)	(0.167)
oilpcl	0.194**	0.198**	0.180*	0.178*	0.192**	0.193**	0.187*	0.184*
	(0.097)	(0.097)	(0.100)	(0.100)	(0.097)	(0.098)	(0.100)	(0.101)
lmtnest	0.216	0.182	0.213	0.218	0.221	0.216	0.217	0.202
	(0.152)	(0.140)	(0.150)	(0.156)	(0.148)	(0.152)	(0.156)	(0.150)
fracl	2.101	1.317	2.160	2.188	1.796	2.116	2.238	1.947
	(2.077)	(2.056)	(2.072)	(2.074)	(2.069)	(2.067)	(2.088)	(2.068)
noncl	−0.830	−0.724	−0.485	−0.752	−0.467	−0.836	−0.776	−1.325*
	(0.572)	(0.592)	(0.509)	(0.581)	(0.548)	(0.573)	(0.581)	(0.755)
ERI_{all}	−0.279							
	(1.168)							
noncl:ERI_{all}	2.639							
	(1.814)							
E_{all}		1.032						
		(1.251)						
noncl:E_{all}		1.155						
		(1.741)						
R_{all}			–					
			–					
noncl:R_{all}			–					
			–					
I_{all}				−1.112				
				(0.763)				
noncl:I_{all}				0.789				
				(1.354)				
ER_{all}					0.797			
					(1.295)			
noncl:ER_{all}					−0.040			
					(3.480)			
EI_{all}						−0.339		
						(1.171)		
noncl:EI_{all}						2.693		
						(1.817)		
RI_{all}							−1.158	
							(0.733)	
noncl:RI_{all}							0.877	
							(1.357)	
W_{all}								−0.677
								(1.199)
noncl:W_{all}								3.283*
								(1.780)
peaceyrs	0.045	0.080	−0.007	−0.005	−0.003	0.045	−0.009	0.086
	(0.284)	(0.314)	(0.263)	(0.265)	(0.269)	(0.284)	(0.269)	(0.292)
spline1	0.003	0.004	0.002	0.003	0.002	0.003	0.003	0.004
	(0.008)	(0.009)	(0.008)	(0.008)	(0.008)	(0.008)	(0.008)	(0.008)
spline2	−0.001	−0.001	−0.001	−0.001	−0.001	−0.001	−0.001	−0.001
	(0.002)	(0.002)	(0.002)	(0.002)	(0.002)	(0.002)	(0.002)	(0.002)
spline3	0.0003	0.0003	0.0003	0.0004	0.0003	0.0003	0.0004	0.0003
	(0.0004)	(0.0004)	(0.0004)	(0.0004)	(0.0004)	(0.0004)	(0.0004)	(0.0004)
year	−0.004	−0.007	−0.003	−0.002	−0.003	−0.004	−0.002	−0.009
	(0.028)	(0.027)	(0.027)	(0.029)	(0.028)	(0.028)	(0.029)	(0.027)
Constant	2.974	8.558	0.938	0.064	1.131	3.204	−0.348	13.076
	(55.811)	(54.693)	(54.423)	(58.090)	(55.851)	(55.777)	(58.235)	(54.097)
Observations	1,247	1,247	1,247	1,247	1,247	1,247	1,247	1,247
Log Likelihood	-110.506	-110.030	-111.001	-110.357	-111.071	-110.502	-110.256	-109.566
Akaike Inf. Crit.	249.012	248.059	250.002	248.714	250.141	249.005	248.513	247.132

Note: *p<0.1; **p<0.05; ***p<0.01
robust standard errors in parentheses

Table A.4.: Logit Estimations: Effect of Largest Excluded Subgroup With Interaction on Conflict Onset

	Dependent variable:							
	onset1							
	(1)	(2)	(3)	(4)	(5)	(6)	(7)	(8)
gdpcapl	−0.189***	−0.196***	−0.187***	−0.188***	−0.200***	−0.184***	−0.192***	−0.198***
	(0.054)	(0.058)	(0.061)	(0.057)	(0.058)	(0.053)	(0.055)	(0.055)
lpopl	0.049	0.077	0.051	0.056	0.051	0.051	0.049	0.050
	(0.173)	(0.171)	(0.170)	(0.171)	(0.171)	(0.172)	(0.166)	(0.170)
oilpcl	0.189*	0.194**	0.180*	0.186*	0.192**	0.187*	0.192*	0.196**
	(0.098)	(0.097)	(0.100)	(0.100)	(0.097)	(0.098)	(0.099)	(0.100)
lmtnest	0.199	0.170	0.213	0.215	0.201	0.202	0.235	0.211
	(0.148)	(0.137)	(0.150)	(0.157)	(0.146)	(0.150)	(0.152)	(0.147)
fracl	2.337	1.578	2.160	2.077	2.113	2.527	1.884	2.439
	(2.042)	(2.019)	(2.072)	(2.128)	(2.040)	(2.024)	(2.165)	(2.121)
noncl	−1.087*	−0.764	−0.485	−0.668	−0.730	−1.013*	−0.416	−0.963
	(0.615)	(0.579)	(0.509)	(0.599)	(0.629)	(0.582)	(0.579)	(0.631)
ERI_{max}	−3.631							
	(3.351)							
noncl:ERI_{max}	10.456**							
	(4.785)							
E_{max}		0.684						
		(1.795)						
noncl:E_{max}		1.645						
		(2.070)						
R_{max}			–					
			–					
noncl:R_{max}			–					
			–					
I_{max}				−0.933				
				(0.975)				
noncl:I_{max}				0.612				
				(1.507)				
ER_{max}					−0.036			
					(2.087)			
noncl:ER_{max}					4.438			
					(6.352)			
EI_{max}						−3.067		
						(2.113)		
noncl:EI_{max}						6.449**		
						(2.788)		
RI_{max}							−0.751	
							(1.296)	
noncl:RI_{max}							−0.592	
							(2.016)	
W_{max}								−1.650
								(1.328)

[continued on next page]

Table A.4.: [continued]

	(1)	(2)	(3)	(4)	(5)	(6)	(7)	(8)
noncl:W_{max}								3.319*
								(1.931)
peaceyrs	0.072	0.095	−0.007	−0.010	0.009	0.086	−0.014	0.046
	(0.298)	(0.322)	(0.263)	(0.266)	(0.265)	(0.310)	(0.267)	(0.280)
spline1	0.004	0.004	0.002	0.002	0.002	0.004	0.002	0.003
	(0.008)	(0.009)	(0.008)	(0.008)	(0.008)	(0.009)	(0.008)	(0.008)
spline2	−0.001	−0.001	−0.001	−0.001	−0.001	−0.001	−0.001	−0.001
	(0.002)	(0.002)	(0.002)	(0.002)	(0.002)	(0.002)	(0.002)	(0.002)
spline3	0.0003	0.0003	0.0003	0.0004	0.0003	0.0004	0.0003	0.0003
	(0.0004)	(0.0004)	(0.0004)	(0.0004)	(0.0004)	(0.0004)	(0.0004)	(0.0004)
year	−0.008	−0.007	−0.003	−0.003	−0.004	−0.007	−0.005	−0.006
	(0.027)	(0.027)	(0.027)	(0.029)	(0.026)	(0.027)	(0.028)	(0.027)
Constant	10.796	9.546	0.938	0.698	2.350	8.918	4.701	5.888
	(54.991)	(54.151)	(54.423)	(57.829)	(52.889)	(54.527)	(56.325)	(54.543)
Observations	1,247	1,247	1,247	1,247	1,247	1,247	1,247	1,247
Log Likelihood	-109.519	-110.063	-111.001	-110.792	-110.850	-109.593	-110.900	-110.162
Akaike Inf. Crit.	247.038	248.126	250.002	249.584	249.699	247.185	249.800	248.324

Note: *p<0.1; **p<0.05; ***p<0.01
robust standard errors in parentheses

Table A.5.: Robustness Checks: Autocracy

	Dependent variable:		
	onset1		
	(1)	(2)	(3)
gdpcapl	-0.195^{***}	-0.190^{***}	-0.191^{***}
	(0.054)	(0.053)	(0.056)
lpopl	0.019	0.008	0.012
	(0.181)	(0.179)	(0.172)
oilpcl	0.155	0.151	0.147
	(0.102)	(0.103)	(0.107)
lmtnest	0.256^{*}	0.250	0.232
	(0.152)	(0.154)	(0.159)
fracl	1.530	1.575	1.377
	(1.931)	(1.934)	(2.027)
autocl	-1.098	-1.106	-0.866
	(0.707)	(0.707)	(0.802)
ERI_{max}	-1.551		
	(2.834)		
EI_{max}		-1.781	
		(1.718)	
W_{all}			0.320
			(1.255)
peaceyrs	-0.030	-0.030	-0.037
	(0.277)	(0.277)	(0.258)
spline1	0.001	0.002	0.001
	(0.008)	(0.008)	(0.007)
spline2	-0.001	-0.001	-0.001
	(0.002)	(0.002)	(0.002)
spline3	0.0003	0.0003	0.0003
	(0.0004)	(0.0004)	(0.0004)
year	-0.014	-0.016	-0.017
	(0.031)	(0.032)	(0.032)
autocl:ERI_{max}	9.548^{*}		
	(5.116)		
autocl:EI_{max}		6.168^{**}	
		(3.065)	
autocl:W_{all}			0.890
			(2.014)
Constant	24.405	27.187	28.863
	(62.891)	(64.065)	(64.717)
Observations	1,235	1,235	1,235
Log Likelihood	-106.360	-106.253	-107.472
Akaike Inf. Crit.	240.720	240.506	242.944
Note:	$^{*}p<0.1$; $^{**}p<0.05$; $^{***}p<0.01$		
	robust standard errors in parentheses		

Table A.6.: Robustness Checks: Onset2, Onset3

	Dependent variable:					
	onset2			onset3		
	(1)	(2)	(3)	(4)	(5)	(6)
ongoingl				0.626	0.623	0.588
				(0.510)	(0.511)	(0.518)
gdpcapl	−0.069*	−0.069*	−0.064*	−0.053*	−0.052*	−0.050
	(0.038)	(0.038)	(0.039)	(0.032)	(0.032)	(0.033)
lpopl	0.487***	0.475***	0.505***	0.416***	0.404***	0.428***
	(0.117)	(0.119)	(0.120)	(0.118)	(0.120)	(0.124)
oilpcl	0.167*	0.161*	0.159*	0.161**	0.159**	0.140*
	(0.088)	(0.089)	(0.092)	(0.069)	(0.069)	(0.077)
lmtnest	0.152	0.156	0.156	0.134	0.138	0.138
	(0.130)	(0.130)	(0.134)	(0.120)	(0.121)	(0.123)
fracl	1.794	2.003	1.214	1.291	1.434	1.117
	(1.363)	(1.377)	(1.520)	(1.283)	(1.293)	(1.372)
noncl	−0.788*	−0.783*	−1.011*	−0.619	−0.618	−0.686
	(0.439)	(0.432)	(0.567)	(0.490)	(0.464)	(0.596)
ERI_{max}	−1.118			−1.392		
	(2.187)			(2.499)		
noncl:ERI_{max}	5.725*			5.131		
	(3.360)			(3.759)		
EI_{max}		−1.785			−1.877	
		(1.637)			(1.845)	
noncl:EI_{max}		3.887*			3.614	
		(2.189)			(2.267)	
W_{all}			0.575			0.065
			(0.885)			(0.937)
noncl:W_{all}			1.665			1.198
			(1.331)			(1.413)
peaceyrs	−0.434***	−0.433***	−0.406***	0.066	0.063	0.082
	(0.113)	(0.114)	(0.115)	(0.122)	(0.122)	(0.121)
spline1	−0.005***	−0.005***	−0.004**	0.001	0.001	0.001
	(0.002)	(0.002)	(0.002)	(0.002)	(0.002)	(0.002)
spline2	0.003**	0.003**	0.002**	−0.0003	−0.0003	−0.0005
	(0.001)	(0.001)	(0.001)	(0.001)	(0.001)	(0.001)
spline3	−0.0005	−0.0005	−0.0004	0.0001	0.0001	0.0001
	(0.0003)	(0.0003)	(0.0003)	(0.0004)	(0.0004)	(0.0004)
year	−0.0002	0.0001	−0.002	0.022	0.022	0.023
	(0.020)	(0.020)	(0.020)	(0.018)	(0.018)	(0.018)
Constant	−7.190	−7.872	−3.245	−52.501	−52.559	−53.987
	(40.157)	(40.281)	(39.966)	(36.553)	(36.467)	(36.161)
Observations	1,277	1,277	1,277	1,549	1,549	1,549
Log Likelihood	-168.694	-168.678	-167.776	-205.597	-205.442	-205.720
Akaike Inf. Crit.	365.388	365.357	363.553	441.194	440.885	441.440

Note: *p<0.1; **p<0.05; ***p<0.01
robust standard errors in parentheses

Table A.7.: Robustness Checks: Onset2, Onset3, Autocracy

	Dependent variable:					
	onset2			onset3		
	(1)	(2)	(3)	(4)	(5)	(6)
ongoingl				0.777	0.757	0.678
				(0.540)	(0.533)	(0.540)
gdpcapl	−0.057*	−0.051	−0.051	−0.044	−0.038	−0.041
	(0.035)	(0.034)	(0.034)	(0.030)	(0.029)	(0.030)
lpopl	0.428***	0.439***	0.479***	0.370***	0.383***	0.401***
	(0.123)	(0.125)	(0.130)	(0.123)	(0.123)	(0.135)
oilpcl	0.148*	0.141	0.103	0.139**	0.133*	0.093
	(0.089)	(0.092)	(0.102)	(0.069)	(0.070)	(0.084)
lmtnest	0.157	0.139	0.139	0.148	0.128	0.141
	(0.136)	(0.135)	(0.139)	(0.131)	(0.127)	(0.129)
fracl	1.834	1.940	1.427	1.463	1.483	1.470
	(1.426)	(1.399)	(1.602)	(1.351)	(1.310)	(1.425)
autocl	−0.494	−0.436	−0.534	−0.464	−0.390	−0.342
	(0.486)	(0.463)	(0.580)	(0.493)	(0.466)	(0.595)
ERI_{max}	−3.279			−4.716		
	(2.790)			(3.360)		
EI_{max}		−3.026*			−3.570*	
		(1.609)			(1.933)	
W_{all}			−0.207			−0.812
			(1.111)			(1.131)
peaceyrs	−0.435***	−0.435***	−0.420***	0.078	0.079	0.071
	(0.120)	(0.119)	(0.116)	(0.131)	(0.130)	(0.125)
spline1	−0.005***	−0.005***	−0.004**	0.001	0.001	0.001
	(0.002)	(0.002)	(0.002)	(0.002)	(0.002)	(0.002)
spline2	0.003**	0.003**	0.002**	−0.0003	−0.0004	−0.0004
	(0.001)	(0.001)	(0.001)	(0.001)	(0.001)	(0.001)
spline3	−0.001	−0.001	−0.0004	0.0001	0.0001	0.0001
	(0.0004)	(0.0004)	(0.0003)	(0.0004)	(0.0004)	(0.0004)
year	−0.001	−0.002	−0.008	0.028	0.025	0.023
	(0.021)	(0.022)	(0.022)	(0.020)	(0.020)	(0.020)
autocl:ERI_{max}	10.444**			10.244**		
	(4.086)			(4.486)		
autocl:EI_{max}		7.395***			7.031**	
		(2.501)			(2.781)	
autocl:W_{all}			2.313			2.025
			(1.425)			(1.495)
Constant	−4.322	−3.812	8.277	−63.473	−58.612	−54.457
	(42.537)	(42.998)	(44.308)	(40.493)	(40.154)	(40.839)
Observations	1,290	1,290	1,290	1,553	1,553	1,553
Log Likelihood	-162.029	-161.721	-162.417	-196.104	-195.937	-197.395
Akaike Inf. Crit.	352.058	351.442	352.835	422.208	421.875	424.789

Note: *p<0.1; **p<0.05; ***p<0.01
robust standard errors in parentheses

Table A.8.: Influential Obs., Onset1

	Dependent variable:		
	onset1		
	(1)	(2)	(3)
gdpcapl	−0.182***	−0.177***	−0.176***
	(0.055)	(0.053)	(0.053)
lpopl	−0.014	−0.005	0.012
	(0.175)	(0.174)	(0.171)
oilpcl	0.200**	0.199**	0.219**
	(0.100)	(0.099)	(0.106)
lmtnest	0.199	0.179	0.180
	(0.152)	(0.156)	(0.157)
fracl	1.885	2.167	1.438
	(2.151)	(2.113)	(2.159)
noncl	−1.207	−1.059	−1.110
	(0.753)	(0.652)	(0.807)
ERI_{max}	−2.836		
	(3.080)		
noncl:ERI_{max}	15.740*		
	(8.442)		
EI_{max}		−2.734	
		(2.023)	
noncl:EI_{max}		7.887**	
		(3.987)	
W_{all}			−0.439
			(1.216)
noncl:W_{all}			2.193
			(2.558)
peaceyrs	−0.116	−0.120	−0.236
	(0.290)	(0.298)	(0.285)
spline1	−0.002	−0.001	−0.005
	(0.008)	(0.008)	(0.008)
spline2	−0.00000	−0.0001	0.001
	(0.002)	(0.002)	(0.002)
spline3	0.0002	0.0002	0.0001
	(0.0004)	(0.0004)	(0.0004)
year	0.003	−0.0002	0.012
	(0.032)	(0.032)	(0.031)
Constant	−9.281	−3.908	−26.926
	(63.707)	(63.636)	(61.238)
Observations	1,233	1,233	1,230
Log Likelihood	-103.365	-103.702	-100.607
Akaike Inf. Crit.	234.729	235.404	229.214
Note:			*p<0.1; **p<0.05; ***p<0.01 robust standard errors in parentheses

Table A.9.: Influential Obs., Onset2

	Dependent variable:		
	onset2		
	(1)	(2)	(3)
gdpcapl	−0.045	−0.047	−0.052
	(0.040)	(0.039)	(0.042)
lpopl	0.411***	0.454***	0.468***
	(0.130)	(0.126)	(0.132)
oilpcl	0.155	0.164	0.191*
	(0.100)	(0.101)	(0.106)
lmtnest	0.105	0.077	0.107
	(0.145)	(0.143)	(0.146)
fracl	1.652	1.459	0.568
	(1.535)	(1.461)	(1.687)
noncl	−1.389**	−1.294**	−1.616*
	(0.625)	(0.596)	(0.872)
ERI_{max}	−5.623		
	(4.233)		
noncl:ERI_{max}	16.979**		
	(7.298)		
EI_{max}		−2.491	
		(1.786)	
noncl:EI_{max}		8.158**	
		(4.138)	
W_{all}			−0.292
			(1.233)
noncl:W_{all}			3.107
			(2.579)
peaceyrs	−0.397***	−0.437***	−0.371***
	(0.129)	(0.130)	(0.134)
spline1	−0.004**	−0.005**	−0.004**
	(0.002)	(0.002)	(0.002)
spline2	0.002*	0.003**	0.002*
	(0.001)	(0.001)	(0.001)
spline3	−0.0004	−0.0004	−0.0003
	(0.0004)	(0.0004)	(0.0003)
year	0.013	0.011	0.021
	(0.024)	(0.023)	(0.024)
Constant	−32.821	−28.409	−48.406
	(47.356)	(46.584)	(48.776)
Observations	1,244	1,248	1,241
Log Likelihood	-148.270	-152.309	-145.852
Akaike Inf. Crit.	324.540	332.619	319.704
Note:			*p<0.1; **p<0.05; ***p<0.01 robust standard errors in parentheses

Table A.10.: Logit Estimations: Effect of Formally Derived Variables Without Interaction on Conflict Onset

	Dependent variable:						
	onset1						
	(1)	(2)	(3)	(4)	(5)	(6)	(7)
gdpcapl	−0.198***	−0.188***	−0.188***	−0.194***	−0.193***	−0.198***	−0.193***
	(0.060)	(0.053)	(0.061)	(0.057)	(0.056)	(0.060)	(0.054)
lpopl	0.051	0.070	0.050	0.065	0.034	0.050	0.063
	(0.168)	(0.170)	(0.170)	(0.175)	(0.168)	(0.168)	(0.173)
oilpcl	0.190*	0.188*	0.181*	0.191*	0.181*	0.190*	0.195**
	(0.099)	(0.098)	(0.100)	(0.100)	(0.098)	(0.099)	(0.100)
lmtnest	0.225	0.178	0.214	0.225	0.231	0.224	0.231
	(0.155)	(0.149)	(0.151)	(0.158)	(0.153)	(0.157)	(0.158)
fracl	2.177	2.018	2.184	1.672	2.718	2.169	1.512
	(2.004)	(2.058)	(2.072)	(2.071)	(2.019)	(2.000)	(2.113)
noncl	−0.495	−0.650	−0.484	−0.526	−0.501	−0.490	−0.518
	(0.497)	(0.552)	(0.509)	(0.500)	(0.508)	(0.502)	(0.498)
ERI*	1.776						
	(4.116)						
E*		−0.002					
		(0.001)					
R*			−				
			−				
I*				−1.878*			
				(1.070)			
ER*					−2.584		
					(6.074)		
EI*						0.780	
						(2.345)	
RI*							−2.613*
							(1.536)
peaceyrs	0.003	0.074	−0.006	−0.014	−0.006	0.002	−0.011
	(0.268)	(0.311)	(0.263)	(0.264)	(0.266)	(0.269)	(0.266)
spline1	0.002	0.004	0.002	0.002	0.002	0.002	0.002
	(0.008)	(0.009)	(0.008)	(0.008)	(0.008)	(0.008)	(0.008)
spline2	−0.001	−0.001	−0.001	−0.001	−0.001	−0.001	−0.001
	(0.002)	(0.002)	(0.002)	(0.002)	(0.002)	(0.002)	(0.002)
spline3	0.0003	0.0003	0.0003	0.0004	0.0003	0.0003	0.0003
	(0.0004)	(0.0004)	(0.0004)	(0.0004)	(0.0004)	(0.0004)	(0.0004)
year	−0.003	−0.008	−0.003	−0.005	−0.003	−0.003	−0.005
	(0.028)	(0.028)	(0.027)	(0.027)	(0.027)	(0.028)	(0.027)
Constant	0.373	10.299	1.049	4.329	−0.287	0.028	6.344
	(55.192)	(55.317)	(54.486)	(53.466)	(53.513)	(55.733)	(53.621)
Observations	1,247	1,247	1,247	1,247	1,247	1,247	1,247
Log Likelihood	-111.183	-110.333	-111.066	-110.043	-111.129	-111.214	-110.036
Akaike Inf. Crit.	248.365	246.667	248.132	246.087	248.258	248.428	246.072
Note:							*p<0.1; **p<0.05; ***p<0.01 robust standard errors in parentheses

Table A.11.: Logit Estimations: Effect of Formally Derived Variables With Interaction on Conflict Onset

	Dependent variable:						
	onset1						
	(1)	(2)	(3)	(4)	(5)	(6)	(7)
gdpcapl	−0.193***	−0.191***	−0.188***	−0.194***	−0.194***	−0.188***	−0.193***
	(0.056)	(0.056)	(0.061)	(0.057)	(0.055)	(0.056)	(0.054)
lpopl	0.041	0.076	0.050	0.067	0.027	0.042	0.061
	(0.174)	(0.175)	(0.170)	(0.174)	(0.172)	(0.172)	(0.170)
oilpcl	0.191*	0.190**	0.181*	0.191*	0.184*	0.187*	0.196**
	(0.098)	(0.096)	(0.100)	(0.100)	(0.097)	(0.098)	(0.100)
lmtnest	0.215	0.181	0.214	0.222	0.235	0.208	0.234
	(0.154)	(0.151)	(0.151)	(0.159)	(0.156)	(0.156)	(0.157)
fracl	2.507	1.832	2.184	1.694	2.897	2.535	1.495
	(2.024)	(2.081)	(2.072)	(2.079)	(1.998)	(1.971)	(2.110)
noncl	−1.009*	−0.635	−0.484	−0.585	−0.740	−0.765	−0.454
	(0.563)	(0.548)	(0.509)	(0.533)	(0.554)	(0.523)	(0.527)
ERI*	−7.319						
	(5.989)						
E*		0.718					
		(3.200)					
R*			–				
			–				
I*				−2.027			
				(1.371)			
ER*					−5.039		
					(6.638)		
EI*						−3.703	
						(3.883)	
RI*							−2.416
							(1.837)
peaceyrs	0.047	0.072	−0.006	−0.014	0.003	0.049	−0.011
	(0.284)	(0.311)	(0.263)	(0.264)	(0.269)	(0.291)	(0.265)
spline1	0.003	0.004	0.002	0.002	0.003	0.004	0.002
	(0.008)	(0.009)	(0.008)	(0.008)	(0.008)	(0.008)	(0.008)
spline2	−0.001	−0.001	−0.001	−0.001	−0.001	−0.001	−0.001
	(0.002)	(0.002)	(0.002)	(0.002)	(0.002)	(0.002)	(0.002)
spline3	0.0003	0.0003	0.0003	0.0004	0.0003	0.0004	0.0003
	(0.0004)	(0.0004)	(0.0004)	(0.0004)	(0.0004)	(0.0004)	(0.0004)
year	−0.006	−0.008	−0.003	−0.004	−0.001	−0.005	−0.006
	(0.027)	(0.028)	(0.027)	(0.028)	(0.027)	(0.027)	(0.028)
noncl:ERI*	16.378**						
	(7.308)						
noncl:E*		−0.720					
		(3.200)					
noncl:R*			–				
			–				
noncl:I*				0.478			
				(1.990)			
noncl:ER*					10.021		
					(12.096)		
noncl:EI*						6.825	
						(4.246)	
noncl:RI*							−0.769
							(2.733)
Constant	6.994	10.227	1.049	3.275	−3.223	4.702	7.482
	(54.596)	(55.631)	(54.486)	(56.309)	(54.902)	(54.789)	(55.389)
Observations	1,247	1,247	1,247	1,247	1,247	1,247	1,247
Log Likelihood	-109.734	-110.300	-111.066	-110.028	-110.723	-110.472	-110.018
Akaike Inf. Crit.	247.467	248.600	250.132	248.056	249.445	248.944	248.035

Note: *p<0.1; **p<0.05; ***p<0.01
robust standard errors in parentheses

Table A.12.: Transnational Links Without Interaction

	Dependent variable:						
	onset2						
	(1)	(2)	(3)	(4)	(5)	(6)	(7)
gdpcapl	−0.049	−0.078*	−0.086**	−0.051	−0.062	−0.078**	−0.061
	(0.038)	(0.040)	(0.038)	(0.040)	(0.038)	(0.039)	(0.039)
lpopl	0.560***	0.491***	0.547***	0.461***	0.580***	0.513***	0.483***
	(0.136)	(0.139)	(0.137)	(0.133)	(0.146)	(0.136)	(0.132)
oilpcl	0.214**	0.148	0.157*	0.190**	0.233**	0.179*	0.174*
	(0.092)	(0.096)	(0.094)	(0.096)	(0.100)	(0.098)	(0.095)
lmtnest	0.224	0.180	0.214	0.167	0.252*	0.216	0.173
	(0.141)	(0.143)	(0.141)	(0.142)	(0.141)	(0.141)	(0.141)
fracl	2.277	1.979	2.447	1.594	2.438	2.090	1.829
	(1.610)	(1.533)	(1.570)	(1.548)	(1.606)	(1.588)	(1.556)
democ2l	−0.095	0.128	0.180	−0.101	−0.086	0.084	−0.012
	(0.428)	(0.447)	(0.433)	(0.445)	(0.481)	(0.458)	(0.437)
exclpopSCEl	0.484	0.590	0.448	0.819	0.683	0.847	0.606
	(0.748)	(0.707)	(0.750)	(0.737)	(0.892)	(0.839)	(0.725)
ethlinksl	0.535**				0.902***		
	(0.247)				(0.308)		
rellinksl		0.223**			0.392***		
		(0.110)			(0.141)		
ethrellinksl			0.334***			0.455***	
			(0.116)			(0.133)	
ideolinksl				−0.047	−0.188*	−0.151	
				(0.061)	(0.098)	(0.094)	
totlinksl							0.014
							(0.043)
numberpotlinksl	−0.001	−0.004	−0.037	0.036	−0.024	−0.017	0.018
	(0.031)	(0.032)	(0.040)	(0.029)	(0.042)	(0.040)	(0.033)
peaceyrsacrec	−0.432***	−0.425***	−0.420***	−0.431***	−0.390***	−0.387***	−0.442***
	(0.117)	(0.117)	(0.116)	(0.117)	(0.115)	(0.116)	(0.117)
spline1acrec	−0.005***	−0.005***	−0.005***	−0.005***	−0.005***	−0.005***	−0.005***
	(0.002)	(0.002)	(0.002)	(0.002)	(0.002)	(0.002)	(0.002)
spline2acrec	0.003**	0.003**	0.003**	0.003**	0.003**	0.003**	0.003**
	(0.001)	(0.001)	(0.001)	(0.001)	(0.001)	(0.001)	(0.001)
spline3acrec	−0.001*	−0.001	−0.001*	−0.001	−0.001*	−0.001*	−0.001
	(0.0003)	(0.0003)	(0.0003)	(0.0003)	(0.0004)	(0.0003)	(0.0003)
year	−0.004	−0.007	−0.010	0.001	−0.005	−0.007	−0.003
	(0.022)	(0.022)	(0.022)	(0.022)	(0.023)	(0.022)	(0.022)
Constant	−0.634	5.176	11.418	−9.132	1.080	5.272	−2.303
	(43.901)	(43.293)	(43.927)	(43.245)	(46.420)	(44.619)	(43.655)
Observations	1,290	1,290	1,290	1,290	1,290	1,290	1,290
Log Likelihood	-161.351	-162.710	-160.358	-163.829	-156.112	-158.020	-164.123
Akaike Inf. Crit.	352.702	355.419	350.716	357.657	346.223	348.040	358.245

Note: *p<0.1; **p<0.05; ***p<0.01
robust standard errors in parentheses

Table A.13.: Logit Estimations: Effect of Transnational Links With Interaction on Conflict Onset

	Dependent variable:					
	onset2					
	(1)	(2)	(3)	(4)	(5)	(6)
gdpcapl	−0.044	−0.056	−0.068*	−0.042	−0.063*	−0.068*
	(0.043)	(0.038)	(0.037)	(0.039)	(0.038)	(0.039)
lpopl	0.464***	0.438***	0.415***	0.432***	0.399***	0.460***
	(0.157)	(0.147)	(0.147)	(0.143)	(0.148)	(0.145)
oilpcl	0.196**	0.084	0.066	0.185*	0.094	0.164*
	(0.093)	(0.110)	(0.106)	(0.098)	(0.113)	(0.098)
lmtnest	0.205	0.150	0.186	0.135	0.187	0.189
	(0.146)	(0.149)	(0.149)	(0.147)	(0.147)	(0.144)
fracl	2.949*	2.051	2.899*	1.594	2.409	2.237
	(1.726)	(1.515)	(1.592)	(1.607)	(1.612)	(1.636)
potlinksl	0.003	−0.008	−0.041	0.030	−0.027	−0.027
	(0.032)	(0.033)	(0.039)	(0.030)	(0.039)	(0.044)
ERI_{all}	1.291	1.376	0.870	3.074**	1.140	2.490*
	(1.000)	(0.964)	(1.118)	(1.402)	(1.124)	(1.462)
democl	0.438	0.652	0.984*	0.758	0.816	0.899
	(0.569)	(0.505)	(0.563)	(0.582)	(0.601)	(0.624)
ethlinksl	0.454					
	(0.399)					
rellinksl		0.199				
		(0.218)				
ethrellinksl			0.263		0.370*	0.447***
			(0.173)		(0.199)	(0.134)
ideolinksl				0.065	−0.125	−0.058
				(0.063)	(0.098)	(0.092)
peaceyrs	−0.413***	−0.406***	−0.385***	−0.422***	−0.364***	−0.378***
	(0.121)	(0.121)	(0.121)	(0.120)	(0.120)	(0.121)
spline1	−0.005***	−0.005***	−0.005**	−0.005***	−0.004**	−0.005**
	(0.002)	(0.002)	(0.002)	(0.002)	(0.002)	(0.002)
spline2	0.003**	0.003**	0.003**	0.003**	0.003**	0.003**
	(0.001)	(0.001)	(0.001)	(0.001)	(0.001)	(0.001)
spline3	−0.001	−0.001	−0.001	−0.001	−0.001	−0.001
	(0.0004)	(0.0004)	(0.0004)	(0.0004)	(0.0004)	(0.0004)
year	−0.003	−0.006	−0.012	0.002	−0.009	−0.005
	(0.024)	(0.023)	(0.024)	(0.022)	(0.024)	(0.023)
ERI_{all}:ethlinksl	2.210					
	(2.774)					
democl:ethlinksl	−0.011					
	(0.459)					
ERI_{all}:rellinksl		1.494				
		(1.523)				
democl:rellinksl		−0.126				

[continued on next page]

Table A.13.: [continued]

	(1)	(2)	(3)	(4)	(5)	(6)
		(0.259)				
ERI_{all}:ethrellinksl			2.172		1.966	
			(1.365)		(1.421)	
democl:ethrellinksl			−0.078		−0.080	
			(0.190)		(0.200)	
ERI_{all}:ideolinksl				−0.369		−0.186
				(0.310)		(0.367)
democl:ideolinksl				−0.169		−0.146
				(0.108)		(0.134)
ERI_{all}:democl	−6.035	−4.130*	−5.856	−4.830	−5.057	−5.498
	(3.698)	(2.472)	(3.653)	(3.151)	(3.332)	(3.572)
ERI_{all}:democl:ethlinksl	−1.058					
	(3.170)					
ERI_{all}:democl:rellinksl		−1.495				
		(1.657)				
ERI_{all}:democl:ethrellinksl			−1.445		−1.250	
			(1.542)		(1.621)	
ERI_{all}:democl:ideolinksl				0.402		0.349
				(0.414)		(0.461)
Constant	−3.125	4.166	14.268	−12.111	9.472	0.733
	(47.320)	(44.858)	(47.070)	(43.833)	(47.514)	(45.636)
Observations	1,290	1,290	1,290	1,290	1,290	1,290
Log Likelihood	-158.970	-160.246	-156.721	-161.492	-155.221	-156.089
Akaike Inf. Crit.	355.941	358.491	351.442	360.985	350.442	352.178

Note: *p<0.1; **p<0.05; ***p<0.01
robust standard errors in parentheses

References

Abrahamian, E. (2008). *A History of Modern Iran*. Cambridge University Press.

Acemoglu, D. and J. A. Robinson (2001). A Theory of Political Transitions. *American Economic Review 91*(4), 938–963.

Acemoglu, D. and J. A. Robinson (2005). *Economic Origins of Dictatorship and Democracy*. Cambridge University Press.

Acheson-Brown, D. (2001). The Tanzanian Invasion of Uganda: A Just War? *International Third World Studies Journal and Review 12*, 1–11.

Akaike, H. (1973). Information Theory and an Extension of the Maximum Likelihood Principle. In *Selected Papers of Hirotugu Akaike*, pp. 199–213. Springer.

Akbaba, Y. (2009). Who Discriminates More? Comparing Religious Discrimination in Western Democracies, Asia and the Middle East. *Civil Wars 11*(3), 321–358.

Akcinaroglu, S. (2012). Rebel Interdependencies and Civil War Outcomes. *Journal of Conflict Resolution 56*(5), 879–903.

Akcinaroglu, S. and E. Radziszewski (2005). Expectations, Rivalries, and Civil War Duration. *International Interactions 31*(4), 349–374.

Akdede, S. H. (2010). Do more Ethnically and Religiously Diverse Countries Have Lower Democratization? *Economics Letters 106*(2), 101–104.

Aldrich, J. H. (1993). Rational Choice and Turnout. *American Journal of Political Science 37*(1), 246–278.

Alesina, A., A. Devleeschauwer, W. Easterly, S. Kurlat, and R. Wacziarg (2003). Fractionalization. *Journal of Economic Growth 8*(2), 155–194.

Alesina, A. and E. L. Ferrara (2005). Ethnic Diversity and Economic Performance. *Journal of Economic Literature 43*(3), 762–800.

Alubo, O. (2008). Identity Construction and Citizenship Conflicts in Central Nigeria. In N. R. Slocum-Bradley (Ed.), *Promoting Conflict or Peace through Identity*, pp. 41–60. Ashgate.

Arena, P. and N. P. Nicoletti (2014). Selectorate Theory, the Democratic Peace, and Public Goods Provision. *International Theory 6*(03), 391–416.

Arriola, L. R. (2009). Patronage and Political Stability in Africa. *Comparative Political Studies 42*(10), 1339–1362.

Asal, V., M. Brown, and A. Dalton (2012). Why Split? Organizational Splits among Ethnopolitical Organizations in the Middle East. *Journal of Conflict Resolution 56*(1), 94–117.

Aydin, A. (2008). Choosing Sides: Economic Interdependence and Interstate Disputes. *The Journal of Politics 70*(04), 1098–1108.

Balch-Lindsay, D. and A. J. Enterline (2000). Killing Time: The World Politics of Civil War Duration, 1820–1992. *International Studies Quarterly 44*(4), 615–642.

Balch-Lindsay, D., A. J. Enterline, and K. A. Joyce (2008). Third-Party Intervention and the Civil War Process. *Journal of Peace Research 45*(3), 345–363.

Baldwin, K. and J. D. Huber (2010). Economic versus Cultural Differences: Forms of Ethnic Diversity and Public Goods Provision. *American Political Science Review 104*(04), 644–662.

Bapat, N. A. and K. D. Bond (2012). Alliances between Militant Groups. *British Journal of Political Science 42*(04), 793–824.

Bartusevičius, H. (2014). The Inequality–Conflict Nexus Re-examined. Income, Education and Popular Rebellions. *Journal of Peace Research 51*(1), 35–50.

Basedau, M., G. Strüver, J. Vüllers, and T. Wegenast (2011). Do Religious Factors Impact Armed Conflict? Empirical Evidence from Sub-Saharan Africa. *Terrorism and Political Violence 23*(5), 752–779.

Bates, R. H. (1981). *Markets and States in Tropical Africa. The Political Basis of Agricultural Policies.* University of California Press.

Bates, R. H. (1983). Modernization, Ethnic Competition, and the Rationality of Politics in Contemporary Africa. In D. Rothchild and V. A. Olunsorola (Eds.), *State versus Ethnic Claims: African Policy Dilemmas.* Boulder, CO: Westview Press.

Bauer, G. and S. D. Taylor (2011). *Politics in Southern Africa: Transition and Transformation.* Lynne Rienner Publishers.

Baylies, C. L. and M. Szeftel (1982). The Rise of a Zambian Capitalist Class in the 1970s. *Journal of Southern African Studies 8*(2), 187–213.

Belanger, L., É. Duchesne, and J. Paquin (2005). Foreign Interventions and Secessionist Movements: The Democratic Factor. *Canadian Journal of Political Science 38*(02), 435–462.

Benaabdelaali, W., S. Hanchane, and A. Kamal (2012). Educational Inequality in the World, 1950–2010: Estimates from a New Dataset. In J. A. Bishop and R. Salas (Eds.), *Inequality, Mobility and Segregation: Essays in Honor of Jacques Silber (Research on Economic Inequality)*, Volume 20, pp. 337–366. Bingley: Emerald.

Benoit, K., M. Laver, et al. (2006). *Party Policy in Modern Democracies.* Routledge.

Berry, W. D., M. Golder, and D. Milton (2012). Improving Tests of Theories Positing Interaction. *The Journal of Politics 74*(03), 653–671.

Besançon, M. L. (2005). Relative Resources: Inequality in Ethnic Wars, Revolutions, and Genocides. *Journal of Peace Research 42*(4), 393–415.

Blaydes, L. and D. A. Linzer (2012). Elite Competition, Religiosity, and Anti-Americanism in the Islamic World. *American Political Science Review 106*(02), 225–243.

Booth, J. A. (1991). Socioeconomic and Political Roots of National Revolts in Central America. *Latin American Research Review 26*(01), 33–73.

Brambor, T., W. R. Clark, and M. Golder (2006). Understanding Interaction Models: Improving Empirical Analyses. *Political Analysis 14*(1), 63–82.

Brubaker, R. and D. D. Laitin (1998). Ethnic and Nationalist Violence. *Annual Review of Sociology 24*, 423–452.

Bueno de Mesquita, B., A. Smith, R. M. Siverson, and J. D. Morrow (2003). *The Logic of Political Survival.* Cambridge, MA: MIT Press.

Buhaug, H. (2006). Relative Capability and Rebel Objective in Civil War. *Journal of Peace Research 43*(6), 691–708.

Burdick, J. (2005). Why is the Black Evangelical Movement Growing in Brazil? *Journal of Latin American Studies 37*(02), 311–332.

Burgess, R., R. Jedwab, E. Miguel, A. Morjaria, and G. P. i Miquel (2011). Ethnic Favoritism. *Unpublished manuscript.*

Byman, D., P. Chalk, B. Hoffman, W. Rosenau, and D. Brannan (2001). *Trends in Outside Support for Insurgent Movements.* Rand Corporation.

Calvo, E. and M. V. Murillo (2004). Who Delivers? Partisan Clients in the Argentine Electoral Market. *American Journal of Political Science 48*(4), 742–757.

Campante, F. R. and D. Chor (2012). Why was the Arab World Poised for Revolution? Schooling, Economic Opportunities, and the Arab Spring. *The Journal of Economic Perspectives 26*(02), 167–187.

Caprioli, M. (2005). Primed for Violence: The Role of Gender Inequality in Predicting Internal Conflict. *International Studies Quarterly 49*(2), 161–178.

Carment, D. and P. James (1995). Internal Constraints and Interstate Ethnic Conflict. Toward a Crisis-Based Assessment of Irredentism. *Journal of Conflict Resolution 39*(1), 82–109.

Caselli, F. and W. J. Coleman II (2006). On the Theory of Ethnic Conflict. Technical report, National Bureau of Economic Research.

Casey, G. P. and A. L. Owen (2014). Inequality and Fractionalization. *World Development 56*, 32–50.

Cederman, L.-E. and L. Girardin (2007). Beyond Fractionalization: Mapping Ethnicity onto Nationalist Insurgencies. *American Political Science Review 101*(01), 173–185.

Cederman, L.-E., L. Girardin, and K. S. Gleditsch (2009). Ethnonationalist Triads: Assessing the Influence of Kin Groups on Civil Wars. *World Politics 61*(03), 403–437.

Cederman, L.-E. and K. S. Gleditsch (2009). Introduction to Special Issue on "Disaggregating Civil War". *Journal of Conflict Resolution 53*(04), 487–495.

Cederman, L.-E., K. S. Gleditsch, and S. Hug (2013). Elections and Ethnic Civil War. *Comparative Political Studies 46*(3), 387–417.

Cederman, L.-E., K. S. Gleditsch, I. Salehyan, and J. Wucherpfennig (2013). Transborder Ethnic Kin and Civil War. *International Organization 67*(02), 389–410.

Cederman, L.-E., N. B. Weidmann, and K. S. Gleditsch (2011). Horizontal Inequalities and Ethnonationalist Civil War: A Global Comparison. *American Political Science Review 105*(03), 478–495.

Cederman, L.-E., A. Wimmer, and B. Min (2010). Why do Ethnic Groups Rebel? New Data and Analysis. *World Politics 62*(01), 87–119.

Celestino, M. R. and K. S. Gleditsch (2013). Fresh Carnations or all Thorn, no Rose? Nonviolent Campaigns and Transitions in Autocracies. *Journal of Peace Research 50*(3), 385–400.

Cetinyan, R. (2002). Ethnic Bargaining in the Shadow of Third-Party Intervention. *International Organization 56*(03), 645–677.

Chandra, K. (2005). Ethnic Parties and Democratic Stability. *Perspectives on Politics 3*(02), 235–252.

Chandra, K. (2006). What is Ethnic Identity and Does it Matter? *Annual Review of Political Science 9*, 397–424.

Chandra, K. (2007). *Why Ethnic Parties Succeed: Patronage and Ethnic Head Counts in India.* Cambridge University Press.

Chandra, K. (2012). *Constructivist Theories of Ethnic Politics.* Oxford University Press.

Cheibub, J. A., J. Gandhi, and J. R. Vreeland (2010). Democracy and Dictatorship Revisited. *Public Choice 143*(1-2), 67–101.

Chenoweth, E. and K. G. Cunningham (2013). Understanding Nonviolent Resistance. An Introduction. *Journal of Peace Research 50*(3), 271–276.

Chhibber, P. and J. S. Sekhon (2013). The Asymmetric Role of Religious Appeals in India. *Unpublished manuscript.*

Clarke, K. A. (2001). Testing Nonnested Models of International Relations: Reevaluating Realism. *American Journal of Political Science 45*(03), 724–744.

Clarke, K. A. (2003). Nonparametric Model Discrimination in International Relations. *Journal of Conflict Resolution 47*(1), 72–93.

Clarke, K. A. (2007). A Simple Distribution-Free Test for Nonnested Model Selection. *Political Analysis 15*(3), 347–363.

Clarke, K. A. (2011). A Nonparametric Approach to Testing Multiple Competing Models. *Unpublished manuscript*.

Coggins, B. (2011). Friends in High Places: International Politics and the Emergence of States from Secessionism. *International Organization 65*(03), 433–467.

Colaresi, M. (2014). With Friends Like These, Who Needs Democracy? The Effect of Transnational Support from Rivals on Post-Conflict Democratization. *Journal of Peace Research 51*(1), 65–79.

Collier, P. and A. Hoeffler (2004). Greed and Grievance in Civil War. *Oxford economic papers 56*(4), 563–595.

Collier, P. and N. Sambanis (2005). *Understanding Civil War: Africa*, Volume 1–2. World Bank Publications.

Cunningham, D. E. (2010). Blocking Resolution: How External States can Prolong Civil Wars. *Journal of Peace Research 47*(2), 115–127.

Cunningham, D. E., K. S. Gleditsch, and I. Salehyan (2009). It Takes Two: A Dyadic Analysis of Civil War Duration and Outcome. *Journal of Conflict Resolution 53*(4), 570–597.

Cunningham, K. G. (2011). Divide and Conquer or Divide and Concede: How do States Respond to Internally Divided Separatists? *American Political Science Review 105*(02), 275–297.

Cunningham, K. G. (2013). Understanding Strategic Choice. The Determinants of Civil War and Nonviolent Campaign in Self-Determination Disputes. *Journal of Peace Research 50*(3), 291–304.

Cusack, T. R. (1997). Partisan Politics and Public Finance: Changes in Public Spending in the Industrialized Democracies, 1955–1989. *Public Choice 91*(3-4), 375–395.

Davidson, R. and J. G. MacKinnon (1981). Several Tests for Model Specification in the Presence of Alternative Hypotheses. *Econometrica: Journal of the Econometric Society 49*(3), 781–793.

De Mesquita, B. B. and G. W. Downs (2006). Intervention and Democracy. *International Organization 60*(03), 627–649.

Deacon, R. T. (2009). Public Good Provision under Dictatorship and Democracy. *Public Choice 139*(1-2), 241–262.

DeNardo, J. (1985). *Power In Numbers*. Princeton, NJ: Princeton University Press.

Desmet, K., S. Weber, and I. Ortuño-Ortín (2009). Linguistic Diversity and Redistribution. *Journal of the European Economic Association 7*(6), 1291–1318.

Dincer, O. C. (2008). Ethnic and Religious Diversity and Corruption. *Economics Letters 99*(1), 98–102.

Dixit, A. and J. Londregan (1996). The Determinants of Success of Special Interests in Redistributive Politics. *Journal of Politics 58*(4), 1132–1155.

do Valle Silva, N. (2000). A Research Note on the Cost of Not Being White in Brazil. *Studies in Comparative International Development 35*(2), 18–27.

Downs, A. (1957). *An Economic Theory of Democracy.* New York: Harper.

Easterly, W. (2007). Inequality Does Cause Underdevelopment: Insights from a New Instrument. *Journal of Development Economics 84*(2), 755–776.

Easterly, W. and R. Levine (1997). Africa's Growth Tragedy: Policies and Ethnic Divisions. *The Quarterly Journal of Economics November*, 1203–1250.

Eifert, B., E. Miguel, and D. N. Posner (2010). Political Competition and Ethnic Identification in Africa. *American Journal of Political Science 54*(2), 494–510.

Elkins, Z. and J. Sides (2007). Can Institutions Build Unity in Multiethnic States? *American Political Science Review 101*(04), 693–708.

Esarey, J. and A. Pierce (2012). Assessing Fit Quality and Testing for Misspecification in Binary-Dependent Variable Models. *Political Analysis 20*(4), 480–500.

Esteban, J., L. Mayoral, and D. Ray (2012). Ethnicity and Conflict: An Empirical Study. *The American Economic Review 102*(4), 1310–1342.

Esteban, J. and D. Ray (2011). Linking Conflict to Inequality and Polarization. *The American Economic Review 101*(4), 1345–1374.

Esteban, J. and G. Schneider (2008). Polarization and Conflict: Theoretical and Empirical Issues. *Journal of Peace Research 45*(2), 131–141.

Esteban, J.-M. and D. Ray (1994). On the Measurement of Polarization. *Econometrica: Journal of the Econometric Society 62*(4), 819–851.

Etkes, H. and A. Zimring (2014). When Trade Stops: Lessons from the Gaza Blockade 2007–2010. *Journal of International Economics 95*, 16–27.

Faksh, M. A. (1984). The Alawi Community of Syria: a New Dominant Political Force. *Middle Eastern Studies 20*(2), 133–153.

Fatton, R. (1988). Bringing the Ruling Class Back in: Class, State, and Hegemony in Africa. *Comparative Politics 20*(3), 253–264.

Fearon, J. D. (1999). Why Ethnic Politics and "Pork" Tend to Go Together. In *SSRC-MacArthur sponsored conference on "Ethnic Politics and Democratic Stability," University of Chicago.*

Fearon, J. D. (2003). Ethnic and Cultural Diversity by Country. *Journal of Economic Growth 8*(2), 195–222.

Fearon, J. D. (2005). Primary Commodity Exports and Civil War. *Journal of Conflict Resolution 49*(4), 483–507.

Fearon, J. D., K. Kasara, and D. D. Laitin (2007). Ethnic Minority Rule and Civil War Onset. *American Political Science Review 101*(01), 187–193.

Fearon, J. D. and D. D. Laitin (1996). Explaining Interethnic Cooperation. *American Political Science Review 90*(04), 715–735.

Fearon, J. D. and D. D. Laitin (2003). Ethnicity, Insurgency, and Civil War. *American Political Science Review 97*(01), 75–90.

Fedderke, J., J. Luiz, and R. De Kadt (2008). Using Fractionalization Indexes: Deriving Methodological Principles for Growth Studies from Time Series Evidence. *Social Indicators Research 85*(2), 257–278.

Findley, M. G. and J. F. Marineau (2014). Lootable Resources and Third-Party Intervention into Civil Wars. *Conflict Management and Peace Science*, 1–22.

Findley, M. G. and T. K. Teo (2006). Rethinking Third-Party Interventions into Civil Wars: An Actor-Centric Approach. *Journal of Politics 68*(4), 828–837.

Finke, R. and R. R. Martin (2012). Religious Freedom and Conflict: A Review of the Evidence. *A report prepared for the USAID Conflict Management and Mitigation Office 65.*

Fjelde, H. and D. Nilsson (2012). Rebels Against Rebels. Explaining Violence Between Rebel Groups. *Journal of Conflict Resolution 56*(4), 604–628.

Fletcher, E. and M. Iyigun (2010). The Clash of Civilizations: A Cliometric Investigation. *Institute for the Study of Labor, University of Colorado*.

Forsberg, E. (2014). Diffusion in the Study of Civil Wars: A Cautionary Tale. *International Studies Review 16*(2), 188–198.

Forstenlechner, I., E. Rutledge, and R. S. Alnuaimi (2012). The UAE, the "Arab Spring" and Different Types of Dissent. *Middle East Policy 19*(4), 54–67.

Fox, J. (2004). The Rise of Religious Nationalism and Conflict: Ethnic Conflict and Revolutionary Wars, 1945-2001. *Journal of Peace Research 41*(6), 715–731.

Fox, J. (2013). Religious Armed Conflict and Discrimination in the Middle East and North Africa: An Introduction. *Civil Wars 15*(4), 407–410.

Franck, R. and I. Rainer (2012). Does the Leader's Ethnicity Matter? Ethnic Favoritism, Education, and Health in Sub-Saharan Africa. *American Political Science Review 106*(02), 294–325.

Francois, P., I. Rainer, and F. Trebbi (2012). How Is Power Shared in Africa? *National Bureau of Economic Research (NBER) Working Paper No. 18425*.

Freston, P. (2004). Evangelical Protestantism and Democratization in Contemporary Latin America and Asia. *Democratization 11*(4), 21–41.

Gandhi, J. and A. Przeworski (2007). Authoritarian Institutions and the Survival of Autocrats. *Comparative Political Studies 40*(11), 1279–1301.

Garfinkel, M. R. and S. Skaperdas (2007). Economics of Conflict: An Overview. *Handbook of Defense Economics 2*, 649–709.

Gartzke, E. and K. S. Gleditsch (2006). Identity and Conflict: Ties that Bind and Differences that Divide. *European Journal of International Relations 12*(1), 53–87.

Gelman, A., J. B. Carlin, H. S. Stern, and D. B. Rubin (2004). *Bayesian Data Analysis. Texts in Statistical Science Series*. Boca Raton, FL: Chapman and Hill/CRC.

Gelman, A., G. King, and W. J. Boscardin (1998). Estimating the Probability of Events That Have Never Occurred: When is Your Vote Decisive? *Journal of the American Statistical Association 93*(441), 1–9.

Gent, S. E. (2008). Going in When it Counts: Military Intervention and the Outcome of Civil Conflicts. *International Studies Quarterly 52*(4), 713–735.

Gerber, A. S., G. A. Huber, D. Doherty, C. M. Dowling, and S. E. Ha (2010). Personality and Political Attitudes: Relationships Across Issue Domains and Political Contexts. *American Political Science Review 104*(01), 111–133.

Gill, A. J. (1994). Rendering unto Caesar? Religious Competition and Catholic Political Strategy in Latin America, 1962-79. *American Journal of Political Science 38*(2), 403–425.

Gleditsch, K. S. (2007). Transnational Dimensions of Civil War. *Journal of Peace Research 44*(3), 293–309.

Gleditsch, K. S., I. Salehyan, and K. Schultz (2008). Fighting at Home, Fighting Abroad: How Civil Wars Lead to International Disputes. *Journal of Conflict Resolution 52*(4), 479–506.

Gleditsch, N. P., P. Wallensteen, M. Eriksson, M. Sollenberg, and H. Strand (2002). Armed Conflict 1946-2001: A New Dataset. *Journal of Peace Research 39*(5), 615–637.

Goemans, H. E. (2008). Which Way Out? The Manner and Consequences of Losing Office. *Journal of Conflict Resolution 52*(6), 771–794.

Golub, S. S. and C.-T. Hsieh (2000). Classical Ricardian Theory of Comparative Advantage Revisited. *Review of International Economics 8*(2), 221–234.

Goodwin, J. and T. Skocpol (1989). Explaining Revolutions in the Contemporary Third World. *Politics & Society 17*(4), 489–509.

Gordon, A. (1995). Gender, Ethnicity, and Class in Kenya: "Burying Otieno" Revisited. *Signs 20*(4), 883–912.

Grim, B. and R. Finke (2011). *The Price of Freedom Denied: Religious Persecution and Violence.* Cambridge, United Kingdom: Cambridge University Press.

Grim, B. J. and R. Finke (2006). International Religion Indexes: Government Regulation, Government Favoritism, and Social Regulation of Religion. *Interdisciplinary Journal of Research on Religion 2*(1), 1–40.

Gubler, J. R. and J. S. Selway (2012). Horizontal Inequality, Crosscutting Cleavages, and Civil War. *Journal of Conflict Resolution 56*(2), 206–232.

Gurr, T. R. (1993). Why Minorities Rebel: A Global Analysis of Communal Mobilization and Conflict Since 1945. *International Political Science Review 14*(2), 161–201.

Gurr, T. R. (2000). *Peoples versus States: Minorities at Risk in the New Century*. US Institute of Peace Press.

Ha, E. (2012). Globalization, Government Ideology, and Income Inequality in Developing Countries. *The Journal of Politics 74*(02), 541–557.

Habyarimana, J., M. Humphreys, D. N. Posner, and J. M. Weinstein (2007). Why Does Ethnic Diversity Undermine Public Goods Provision? *American Political Science Review 101*(04), 709–725.

Harris, A. S. and M. G. Findley (2014). Is Ethnicity Identifiable? Lessons from an Experiment in South Africa. *Journal of Conflict Resolution 58*(1), 4–33.

Hayden, R. M. (1993). *The Partition of Bosnia and Herzegovina, 1990-93*. National Council for Soviet and East European Research, University of Pittsburgh.

Hegre, H. (2014). Democracy and Armed Conflict. *Journal of Peace Research*, 1–14.

Hegre, H., T. Ellingsen, N. P. Gleditsch, and S. Gates (2001). Towards a Democratic Civil Peace? Opportunity, Grievance, and Civil War 1816–1992. *American Political Science Review 95*(1), 33–48.

Hegre, H. and N. Sambanis (2006). Sensitivity Analysis of Empirical Results on Civil War Onset. *Journal of Conflict Resolution 50*(4), 508–535.

Henne, P. S. (2012). The Two Swords Religion–State Connections and Interstate Disputes. *Journal of Peace Research 49*(6), 753–768.

Hicken, A. (2011). Clientelism. *Annual Review of Political Science 14*, 289–310.

Hirshleifer, J. (1989). Conflict and Rent-Seeking Success Functions: Ratio vs. Difference Models of Relative Success. *Public Choice 63*(2), 101–112.

Högbladh, S., T. Pettersson, and L. Themnér (2011). External Support in Armed Conflict 1975–2009: Presenting New Data. In *52nd Annual International Studies Association Convention, Montreal, Canada*, pp. 16–19.

Holden, W. N. (2009). Ashes from the Phoenix: State Terrorism and the Party-List Groups in the Philippines. *Contemporary Politics 15*(4), 377–393.

Hooker, J. (2005). Indigenous Inclusion/Black Exclusion: Race, Ethnicity and Multicultural Citizenship in Latin America. *Journal of Latin American Studies 37*(02), 285–310.

Horowitz, D. L. (1985). *Ethnic Groups in Conflict.* University of California Press.

Hosmer, D. W. and S. Lemeshow (1980). Goodness of Fit Tests for the Multiple Logistic Regression Model. *Communications in Statistics-Theory and Methods 9*(10), 1043–1069.

Huber, J. D. and L. Mayoral (2013). Inequality, Ethnicity and Civil Conflict. *Unpublished manuscript, Instituto de Análisis Económico, Barcelona.*.

Hug, S. (2003). Selection Bias in Comparative Research: The Case of Incomplete Data Sets. *Political Analysis 11*(3), 255–274.

Humphreys, M. (2005). Natural Resources, Conflict, and Conflict Resolution Uncovering the Mechanisms. *Journal of Conflict Resolution 49*(4), 508–537.

Humphreys, M. and J. M. Weinstein (2006). Handling and Manhandling Civilians in Civil War. *American Political Science Review 100*(03), 429–447.

Humphreys, M. and J. M. Weinstein (2008). Who Fights? The Determinants of Participation in Civil War. *American Journal of Political Science 52*(2), 436–455.

Huntington, S. P. (1993). The Clash of Civilizations? *Foreign Affairs 72*(3), 22–49.

Hyde, S. D. and N. Marinov (2011). Which Elections Can Be Lost? *Political Analysis 20*, 191–210.

Imai, K. and D. Tingley (2012). A Statistical Method for Empirical Testing of Competing Theories. *American Journal of Political Science 56*(1), 218–236.

Jackman, R. W. (1987). Political Institutions and Voter Turnout in the Industrial Democracies. *American Political Science Review 81*(02), 405–423.

Joshi, M. and T. D. Mason (2011). Peasants, Patrons, and Parties: The Tension Between Clientelism and Democracy in Nepal. *International Studies Quarterly 55*(1), 151–175.

Kalyvas, S. N. and L. Balcells (2010). International System and Technologies of Rebellion: How the End of the Cold War Shaped Internal Conflict. *American Political Science Review 104*(03), 415–429.

Kalyvas, S. N. and M. A. Kocher (2007). How "Free" is Free Riding in Civil Wars?: Violence, Insurgency, and the Collective Action Problem. *World Politics 59*(02), 177–216.

Kalyvas, S. N., P. Lange, R. H. Bates, E. Comisso, P. Hall, J. Migdal, and H. Milner (2006). *The Logic of Violence in Civil War*. Cambridge University Press.

Kandil, H. (2012). Why did the Egyptian Middle Class March to Tahrir Square? *Mediterranean Politics 17*(2), 197–215.

Kanet, R. E. (2006). The Superpower Quest for Empire: The Cold War and Soviet Support for "Wars of National Liberation". *Cold War History 6*(3), 331–352.

Kasara, K. (2007). Tax Me If You Can: Ethnic Geography, Democracy, and the Taxation of Agriculture in Africa. *American Political Science Review 101*(01), 159–172.

Kathman, J. D. (2011). Civil War Diffusion and Regional Motivations for Intervention. *Journal of Conflict Resolution 55*(6), 847–876.

Kaufman, S. J. (1996). Spiraling to Ethnic War: Elites, Masses, and Moscow in Moldova's Civil War. *International Security 21*(2), 108–138.

Keefer, P. and R. Vlaicu (2008). Democracy, Credibility, and Clientelism. *Journal of Law, Economics, and Organization 24*(2), 371–406.

Kibreab, G. (2000). Resistance, Displacement, and Identity: The Case of Eritrean Refugees in Sudan. *Canadian Journal of African Studies/La Revue canadienne des études africaines 34*(2), 249–296.

Kieh, G. K. and P. O. Agbese (1993). From Politics Back to the Barracks in Nigeria: A Theoretical Exploration. *Journal of Peace Research 30*(4), 409–426.

King, G. and M. E. Roberts (2014). How Robust Standard Errors Expose Methodological Problems They Do Not Fix, and What to Do About It. *Political Analysis*, 1–21.

King, S. J. (2007). Sustaining Authoritarianism in the Middle East and North Africa. *Political Science Quarterly 122*(3), 433–459.

Koga, J. (2011). Where Do Third Parties Intervene? Third Parties' Domestic Institutions and Military Interventions in Civil Conflicts. *International Studies Quarterly 55*(4), 1143–1166.

Kramon, E. and D. N. Posner (2012). Ethnic Favoritism in Primary Education in Kenya. *Unpublished manuscript.*

Kramon, E. and D. N. Posner (2013). Who Benefits from Distributive Politics? How the Outcome one Studies Affects the Answer one Gets. *Perspectives on Politics 11*(02), 461–474.

Kudamatsu, M. (2009). Ethnic Favoritism: Micro Evidence from Guinea. *Unpublished manuscript.*

Kuhn, P. M. and N. B. Weidmann (2013). Unequal we Fight: The Impact of Economic Inequality within Ethnic Groups on Conflict Initiation. *Unpublished manuscript.*

La Porta, R., F. Lopez-de Silanes, A. Shleifer, and R. Vishny (1999). The Quality of Government. *Journal of Law, Economics, and Organization 15*(1), 222–279.

Lake, D. A. and M. A. Baum (2001). The Invisible Hand of Democracy Political Control and the Provision of Public Services. *Comparative Political Studies 34*(6), 587–621.

Lichbach, M. I. (1989). An Evaluation of "Does Economic Inequality Breed Political Conflict?" Studies. *World Politics 41*(04), 431–470.

Lilja, J. and L. Hultman (2011). Intraethnic Dominance and Control: Violence Against Co-Ethnics in the Early Sri Lankan Civil War. *Security Studies 20*(2), 171–197.

Lindberg, J.-E. (2008). Running on Faith? A Quantitative Analysis of the Effect of Religious Cleavages on the Intensity and Duration of Internal Conflicts. Master's thesis, University of Oslo.

Luard, E. (1986). *War in International Society: A Study in International Sociology.* I.B.Tauris.

Lujala, P. (2010). The Spoils of Nature: Armed Civil Conflict and Rebel Access to Natural Resources. *Journal of Peace Research 47*(1), 15–28.

Madrid, R. L. (2005). Indigenous Parties and Democracy in Latin America. *Latin American Politics and Society 47*(4), 161–179.

Magaloni, B., A. Diaz-Cayeros, and F. Estévez (2007). Clientelism and Portfolio Diversification: a Model of Electoral Investment with Applications to Mexico. In H. Kitschelt and S. I. Wilkinson (Eds.), *Patrons, Clients, and Policies*, pp. 182–205. Cambridge University Press.

Malet, D. S. (2009). *Foreign Fighters: Transnational Identity in Civil Conflicts*. Ph. D. thesis, The George Washington University.

Maoz, Z. and B. San-Akca (2012). Rivalry and State Support of Non-State Armed Groups (NAGs), 1946–20011. *International Studies Quarterly 56*(4), 720–734.

Markussen, T. and F. Tarp (2014). Political Connections and Land-Related Investment in Rural Vietnam. *Journal of Development Economics 110*, 291–302.

Marshall, M. G., K. Jaggers, and T. R. Gurr (2002). *Polity IV project*. Center for International Development and Conflict Management at the University of Maryland College Park.

Melander, E. (2005). Gender Equality and Intrastate Armed Conflict. *International Studies Quarterly 49*(4), 695–714.

Miguel, E., S. Satyanath, and E. Sergenti (2004). Economic Shocks and Civil Conflict: An Instrumental Variables Approach. *Journal of Political Economy 112*(4), 725–753.

Misra, A. (2002). Subaltern and the Civil War: An Assessment of Left-Wing Insurgency in South Asia. *Civil Wars 5*(4), 56–76.

Montalvo, J. G. and M. Reynal-Querol (2003). Religious Polarization and Economic Development. *Economics Letters 80*(2), 201–210.

Montalvo, J. G. and M. Reynal-Querol (2005). Ethnic Diversity and Economic Development. *Journal of Development Economics 76*(2), 293–323.

Morton, R., J.-R. Tyran, and E. Wengström (2011). Income and Ideology: How Personality Traits, Cognitive Abilities, and Education Shape Political Attitudes. *Univ. of Copenhagen Dept. of Economics Discussion Paper* (11-08).

Muller, E. N. (1985). Income Inequality, Regime Repressiveness, and Political Violence. *American Sociological Review*, 47–61.

Nome, M. A. (2013). Transnational Ethnic Ties and Military Intervention: Taking Sides in Civil Conflicts in Europe, Asia and North Africa, 1944–99. *European Journal of International Relations 19*(4), 747–771.

Ntsebeza, L. (2011). The Land Question: Exploring Obstacles to Land Redistribution in South Africa. In I. Shapiro and K. Tebeau (Eds.), *After Apartheid: Reinventing South Africa?* University of Virginia Press.

O'Brien, R. M. (2007). A Caution Regarding Rules of Thumb for Variance Inflation Factors. *Quality & Quantity 41*(5), 673–690.

Oliver, P. E. and G. Marwell (1988). The Paradox of Group Size in Collective Action: A Theory of the Critical Mass. II. *American Sociological Review*, 1–8.

Olson, M. (1965). *The Logic of Collective Action: Public Goods and the Theory of Group*. Harvard University Press Cambridge.

Olsson, O. and H. C. Fors (2004). Congo: The Prize of Predation. *Journal of Peace Research 41*(3), 321–336.

Ortiz, I. and M. Cummins (2011). Global Inequality: Beyond the Bottom Billion–A Rapid Review of Income Distribution in 141 Countries. *Unpublished manuscript*.

Østby, G. (2008). Polarization, Horizontal Inequalities and Violent Civil Conflict. *Journal of Peace Research 45*(2), 143–162.

Padró i Miquel, G. (2007). The Control of Politicians in Divided Societies: the Politics of Fear. *The Review of Economic Studies 74*(4), 1259–1274.

Parsa, M. (2000). *States, Ideologies, and Social Revolutions: A Comparative Analysis of Iran, Nicaragua, and the Philippines*. Cambridge University Press.

Persson, T. and G. Tabellini (2000). *Political Economics: Explaining Economic Policy*. Cambridge, MA: The MIT Press.

Petersen, R. D. (2002). *Understanding Ethnic Violence: Fear, Hatred, and Resentment in Twentieth-Century Eastern Europe*. Cambridge University Press.

Petras, J. F., M. H. Morley, and P. Dewitt (1981). *Class, State, and Power in the Third World, with Case Studies on Class Conflict in Latin America.* Allanheld, Osmun.

Philpott, D. (2007). Explaining the Political Ambivalence of Religion. *American Political Science Review 101*(03), 505–525.

Pickering, J. and E. F. Kisangani (2005). Democracy and Diversionary Military Intervention: Reassessing Regime Type and the Diversionary Hypothesis. *International Studies Quarterly 49*(1), 23–44.

Pickering, J. and E. F. Kisangani (2010). Diversionary Despots? Comparing Autocracies' Propensities to Use and to Benefit from Military Force. *American Journal of Political Science 54*(2), 477–493.

Posner, D. (2004). The Implications of Constructivism for Studying the Relationship Between Ethnic Diversity and Economic Growth. *Unpublished manuscript, University of California, Los Angeles.*

Posner, D. N. (2005). *Institutions and Ethnic Politics in Africa.* Cambridge University Press.

Potter, J. D. (2014). Demographic Diversity and District-Level Party Systems. *Comparative Political Studies 47*(13), 1801–1829.

Powell, G. B. (1986). American Voter Turnout in Comparative Perspective. *American Political Science Review 80*(01), 17–43.

Powell, J. M. and C. L. Thyne (2011). Global Instances of Coups from 1950 to 2010. A New Dataset. *Journal of Peace Research 48*(2), 249–259.

Pregibon, D. (1981). Logistic Regression Diagnostics. *The Annals of Statistics*, 705–724.

Prunier, G. (2004). Rebel Movements and Proxy Warfare: Uganda, Sudan and the Congo (1986–99). *African Affairs 103*(412), 359–383.

Quimpo, N. G. (2005). The Left, Elections, and the Political Party System in the Philippines. *Critical Asian Studies 37*(1), 3–28.

Quimpo, N. G. (2009). The Philippines: Predatory Regime, Growing Authoritarian Features. *The Pacific Review 22*(3), 335–353.

Regan, P. M. (1996). Conditions of Successful Third-Party Intervention in Intrastate Conflicts. *Journal of Conflict Resolution 40*(2), 336–359.

Regan, P. M. (1998). Choosing to Intervene: Outside Interventions in Internal Conflicts. *The Journal of Politics 60*(03), 754–779.

Reynal-Querol, M. (2002). Ethnicity, Political Systems, and Civil Wars. *Journal of Conflict Resolution 46*(1), 29–54.

Romer, T. (1975). Individual Welfare, Majority Voting, and the Properties of a Linear Income Tax. *Journal of Public Economics 4*(2), 163–185.

Ross, M. L. (2004). What Do We Know about Natural Resources and Civil War? *Journal of Peace Research 41*(3), 337–356.

Russett, B. M. (1964). Inequality and Instability: The Relation of Land Tenure to Politics. *World Politics 16*(03), 442–454.

Saideman, S. M. (2007). Ties versus Institutions: Revisiting Foreign Interventions and Secessionist Movements. *Canadian Journal of Political Science 40*(03), 733–747.

Salehyan, I., K. S. Gleditsch, and D. E. Cunningham (2011). Explaining External Support for Insurgent Groups. *International Organization 65*(04), 709–744.

Sambanis, N. (2001). Do Ethnic and Nonethnic Civil Wars Have the Same Causes? A Theoretical and Empirical Inquiry (Part 1). *Journal of Conflict Resolution 45*(3), 259–282.

Schmidt, S. W., L. Guasti, C. H. Landé, and J. C. Scott (1977). *Friends, Followers, and Factions: A Reader in Political Clientelism.* University of California Press Berkeley.

Schneider, G. and N. Wiesehomeier (2010). Diversity, Conflict and Growth: Theory and Evidence. *Diversity 2*(9), 1097–1117.

Schock, K. (2013). The Practice and Study of Civil Resistance. *Journal of Peace Research 50*(3), 277–290.

Schultz, K. A. (2010). The Enforcement Problem in Coercive Bargaining: Interstate Conflict over Rebel Support in Civil Wars. *International Organization 64*(02), 281–312.

Schwarz, G. et al. (1978). Estimating the Dimension of a Model. *The Annals of Statistics 6*(2), 461–464.

Scott, J. C. (1969). Corruption, Machine Politics, and Political Change. *American Political Science Review 63*(04), 1142–1158.

Selway, J. S. (2011). The Measurement of Cross-cutting Cleavages and Other Multidimensional Cleavage Structures. *Political Analysis*, 1–18.

Sklar, R. L. (1979). The Nature of Class Domination in Africa. *The Journal of Modern African Studies 17*(04), 531–552.

Smith, C. (1996). Correcting a Curious Neglect, or Bringing Religion Back in. *Disruptive Religion: The Force of Faith in Social Movement Activism*, 1–25.

Smock, D. R. (1982). Eritrean Refugees in the Sudan. *The Journal of Modern African Studies 20*(03), 451–465.

Solt, F. (2009). Standardizing the World Income Inequality Database. *Social Science Quarterly 90*(2), 231–242.

Stewart, F. (2009). A Global View of Horizontal Inequalities: Inequalities Experienced by Muslims Worldwide. *Unpublished manuscript.*

Stokes, S. C. (2005). Perverse Accountability: A Formal Model of Machine Politics with Evidence from Argentina. *American Political Science Review 99*(03), 315–325.

Stoll, H. (2007). Social Cleavages and the Number of Parties: How the Measures you Choose Affect the Answers you get. *Comparative Political Studies*, 1–27.

Sullivan, P. L. and J. Karreth (2014). The Conditional Impact of Military Intervention on Internal Armed Conflict Outcomes. *Conflict Management and Peace Science*, 1–20.

Svensson, I. (2013). One God, many Wars: Religious Dimensions of Armed Conflict in the Middle East and North Africa. *Civil Wars 15*(4), 411–430.

Svensson, I. and M. Lindgren (2011). Community and Consent Unarmed Insurrections in Non-Democracies. *European Journal of International Relations 17*(1), 97–120.

Tajfel, H. and J. C. Turner (1979). An Integrative Theory of Intergroup Conflict. *The Social Psychology of Intergroup Relations 33*(47), 74.

Themnér, L. and P. Wallensteen (2012). Armed Conflicts, 1946–2011. *Journal of Peace Research 49*(4), 565–575.

Themnér, L. and P. Wallensteen (2013). Armed Conflicts, 1946–2012. *Journal of Peace Research 50*(4), 509–521.

Themnér, L. and P. Wallensteen (2014). Armed Conflicts, 1946–2013. *Journal of Peace Research 51*(4), 541–554.

Thomas, S. M. (2000). Taking Religious and Cultural Pluralism Seriously: The Global Resurgence of Religion and the Transformation of International Society. *Millennium-Journal of International Studies 29*(3), 815–841.

Thyne, C. L. (2006). Cheap Signals with Costly Consequences The Effect of Interstate Relations on Civil War. *Journal of Conflict Resolution 50*(6), 937–961.

Toft, M. D. (2006). Religion, Civil War, and International Order. *Unpublished manuscript*.

Tusicisny, A. (2004). Civilizational Conflicts: More Frequent, Longer, and Bloodier? *Journal of Peace Research 41*(4), 485–498.

Urdal, H. (2006). A Clash of Generations? Youth Bulges and Political Violence. *International Studies Quarterly 50*(3), 607–629.

Vale, P. and G. Barrett (2009). The Curious Career of an African Modernizer: South Africa's Thabo Mbeki. *Contemporary Politics 15*(4), 445–460.

Van Cott, D. L. (2007). Latin America's Indigenous Peoples. *Journal of Democracy 18*(4), 127–142.

Van der Waal, J., P. Achterberg, and D. Houtman (2007). Class is Not Dead – It Has Been Buried Alive: Class Voting and Cultural Voting in Postwar Western Societies (1956–1990). *Politics & Society 35*(3), 403–426.

Vanhanen, T. (1999). Domestic Ethnic Conflict and Ethnic Nepotism: A Comparative Analysis. *Journal of Peace Research 36*(1), 55–73.

Vásquez, M. A. and P. J. Williams (2005). Introduction: The Power of Religious Identities in the Americas. *Latin American Perspectives January*, 5–26.

Vreeland, J. R. (2008). The Effect of Political Regime on Civil War Unpacking Anocracy. *Journal of Conflict Resolution 52*(3), 401–425.

Vuong, Q. H. (1989). Likelihood Ratio Tests for Model Selection and Non-Nested Hypotheses. *Econometrica: Journal of the Econometric Society 57*(2), 307–333.

Wallensteen, P. and M. Sollenberg (2001). Armed Conflict, 1989-2000. *Journal of Peace Research 38*(5), 629–644.

Wantchekon, L. (2003). Clientelism and Voting Behavior: Evidence from a Field Experiment in Benin. *World Politics 55*(03), 399–422.

Ward, M. D., B. D. Greenhill, and K. M. Bakke (2010). The Perils of Policy by P-Value: Predicting Civil Conflicts. *Journal of Peace Research 47*(4), 363–375.

Weede, E. (1986). Income Inequality and Political Violence Reconsidered. *American Sociological Review 25*(4), 438–441.

Weeks, J. L. (2012). Strongmen and Straw Men: Authoritarian Regimes and the Initiation of International Conflict. *American Political Science Review 106*(02), 326–347.

Weidmann, N. B. (2009). Geography as Motivation and Opportunity: Group Concentration and Ethnic Conflict. *Journal of Conflict Resolution 53*(4), 526–543.

Weinstein, J. M. (2005). Resources and the Information Problem in Rebel Recruitment. *Journal of Conflict Resolution 49*(4), 598–624.

Werner, S. (2000). The Effects of Political Similarity on the Onset of Militarized Disputes, 1816-1985. *Political Research Quarterly 53*(2), 343–374.

Wiesehomeier, N. and D. Doyle (2012). Attitudes, Ideological Associations and the Left–Right Divide in Latin America. *Journal of Politics in Latin America 4*(1), 3–33.

Wilkinson, S. (2002). Memo on Developing Better Indicators of Ethnic and Non Ethnic Identities. In *LICEP 5th Meeting, Stanford University.*

Wilkinson, S. I. (2008). Which Group Identities Lead to Most Violence? Evidence from India. In S. N. Kalyvas, I. Shapiro, and T. E. Masoud (Eds.), *Order, Conflict, and Violence*, pp. 271–301. Cambridge University Press.

Wimmer, A., L.-E. Cederman, and B. Min (2009). Ethnic Politics and Armed Conflict: A Configurational Analysis of a New Global Data Set. *American Sociological Review 74*(2), 316–337.

Wimmer, A. and B. Min (2006). From Empire to Nation-State: Explaining Wars in the Modern World, 1816–2001. *American Sociological Review 71*(6), 867–897.

Woodwell, D. (2004). Unwelcome Neighbors: Shared Ethnicity and International Conflict During the Cold War. *International Studies Quarterly 48*(1), 197–223.

Worrall, J. (2012). Oman: The "Forgotten" Corner of the Arab Spring. *Middle East Policy 19*(3), 98–115.

York, R. (2012). Residualization Is Not the Answer: Rethinking How to Address Multicollinearity. *Social Science Research 41*(6), 1379–1386.

Young, J. (1996). The Tigray and Eritrean Peoples Liberation Fronts: A History of Tensions and Pragmatism. *The Journal of Modern African Studies 34*(01), 105–120.

MIX
Papier aus verantwortungsvollen Quellen
Paper from responsible sources
FSC® C105338

If you have any concerns about our products,
you can contact us on
ProductSafety@springernature.com

In case Publisher is established outside the EU,
the EU authorized representative is:
Springer Nature Customer Service Center GmbH
Europaplatz 3, 69115 Heidelberg, Germany

Printed by Libri Plureos GmbH
in Hamburg, Germany